American Citizens,
British Slaves

American Citizens, British Slaves

Yankee Political Prisoners in
an Australian Penal Colony
1839–1850

*Cassandra Pybus and
Hamish Maxwell-Stewart*

MICHIGAN STATE UNIVERSITY PRESS
EAST LANSING

MICHIGAN STATE UNIVERSITY PRESS
East Lansing, Michigan 48823-5202

First published 2002
Melbourne University Press

08 07 06 05 04 03 02 1 2 3 4 5 6 7 8 9 10

CATALOGING-IN-PUBLICATION DATA

Cassandra Pybus & Hamish Maxwell-Stewart, eds.
   American citizens, British slaves: Yankee political prisoners in
   an Australian penal colony 1839–1850 / Cassandra Pybus &
   Hamish Maxwell-Stewart, eds.
   p. cm.
   Includes bibliography and index.
   ISBN 0-87013-623-2
   1. Political prisoners—Tasmania. 2. Political prisoners—
   United States. 3. Political prisoners—Canada. 4. Convicts—
   Tasmania. 5. Convicts—United States. 6. Convicts—
   Canada. 7. Canada—History—Rebellion, 1837–1838.
   I. Maxwell-Stewart, Hamish. II. Title.
994.602

Typeset in Meridien Roman 10 point by
Syarikat Seng Teik Sdn. Bhd., Malaysia
Printed in Australia by McPherson's Printing Group

Visit Michigan State University Press on the World Wide Web at:
www.msupress.msu.edu

And Cain said unto the Lord, 'My punishment is greater than I can bear.

Behold, thou hast driven me out this day from the face of the earth; and from thy face shall I be hid; and I shall be a fugitive and a vagabond in the earth; and it shall come to pass, that every one that findeth me shall slay me.'

And the Lord said unto him, 'Therefore whosoever slayeth Cain, vengeance shall be taken on him sevenfold.' And the Lord set a mark upon Cain, lest any finding him should kill him.

And Cain went out from the presence of the Lord, and dwelt in the land of Nod, on the east of Eden.

Genesis 4: 13-16

Contents

Illustrations

Figures

Plates   *(following page 80)*

Port Arthur (detail), 1854 etching by artist N. Remond. Courtesy of the Allport Library and Museum of Fine Arts, Tasmania, AUTA 001124072364.

Port Arthur, lithograph by Charles Hutchins from a sketch by Charles Hext, 184?. Courtesy of the Allport Library and Museum of Fine Arts, Tasmania, AUTA 0011240720059.

Hobart Town and Derwent River, lithograph by Charles Hutchins from a sketch by Charles Hext, 1845. Courtesy of the Allport Library and Museum of Fine Arts, Tasmania, AUTA 001124071788.

The windmill at Prescott, watercolour by Thomas Ainslie, 1838. Courtesy of the National Archives of Canada, C-130815.

Kingston from Fort Henry, etching by James Gray, 1828. Courtesy of the Toronto Reference Library, T14967.

Green Ponds, Van Diemen's Land, lithograph P. Blanchard, 1841?. Courtesy Allport Library and Museum of Fine Arts, Tasmania, AUTA 001125646760.

St Mary's Church, Green Ponds, architectural drawing. Courtesy of the Archives Office of Tasmania.

The Upper Canadian town of Prescott, a contemporary painting. Courtesy Metropolitan Toronto Reference Library.

Extract from a letter of Elijah Woodman. Courtesy of the J. J. Talman Regional Collection, University of Western Ontario, RC E26.

Petition from Woodman and Sheldon. Courtesy of the J. J. Talman Regional Collection, University of Western Ontario RC-E26.

The Eagle and the Lion. Courtesy of the National Archives of Canada, C-129228; redrawn by Simon Barnard.

Convict uniform and caps. Courtesy of the National Library of Australia.

The Windmill at Prescott, photography courtesy of Elinor Morrisby.

Treadwheel, lithograph 1840. Courtesy State Library of Tasmania.

Acknowledgements

This project was assisted by an Australian Research Council large grant and a research grant from the Canadian Department of External Affairs. Heartfelt thanks are due to Elinor Morrisby, Tom Dunning, Ian Duffield, Lyn Rainbird and Monica O'Neill for their invaluable assistance on this project. For additional research assistance, thanks to Patricia Kennedy of the National Archives of Canada; Tony Marshall and Gillian Winter of the Tasmaniana Library; Robyn Eastley and the staff of the Archives Office of Tasmania; Theresa Regnier of the Talman Collection at the University of Western Ontario; Terry Prior, curator of the Oswego Museum; Ron Ridley, curator at Fort Henry, Kingston; the staff of the Mitchell Library in the State Library of New South Wales; the staff of the Niagara Historical Society, Lockport, and the staff of the Public Records Office in England. Our gratitude for their help and encouragement to Beverley Boissery, Ramsay Cook, Colin Duquemin, Brian Petrie, Colin Read, Chris and Pat Raible, Barry Wright, Margaret Garber in Canada; Stuart Scott, Robert and Jeannie Brennan, Sheila Weinbach in the United States; Raymond Evans, Stefan Petrow, Peter Chapman, David Young, Brett Noble, Sue Hood in Australia; and our colleagues at the University of Tasmania.

Cassandra Pybus
Hamish Maxwell-Stewart

Authors' Note

In attempting to construct a single coherent narrative of the experience of the ninety-two Patriots transported to Van Diemen's Land, we have drawn primarily on the autobiographical testimony of those few who wrote accounts of their political engagements, their trials and their subsequent exile. Seven book-length accounts were published in the United States between 1843 and 1850. These narratives are: Benjamin Wait, *Letters From Van Dieman's Land Written During Four Years Imprisonment for Political Offences Committed in Upper Canada*; Caleb Lyon (ed.), *Narrative and Recollections of Van Dieman's Land During Three years Captivity of Stephen S. Wright*; Linus Miller, *Notes of an Exile in Van Dieman's Land*; Samuel Snow, *An Exiles Return*; Robert Marsh, *Seven Years of My Life*; Daniel D. Heustis, *A Narrative of the Adventures and Sufferings of Captain Daniel Heustis*; William Gates, *Recollections of Life in Van Dieman's Land*. Unless otherwise specified, the quotations within the text are taken from these narratives and the page numbers refer to the original publications. The idiosyncrasies of original text have been maintained throughout, including the consistent misspelling of Van Diemen's Land.

In addition to the published narratives, we have drawn on the unpublished letters and diaries of Elijah Woodman, held in the Woodman Papers at the University of Western Ontario; the letters of John Tyrrell, held in the Fred Landon Papers at the University of Western Ontario; the diary of Aaron Dresser Jr held in the National Archives of Canada; a letter from James Gemmell first published in the *Plebeian* newspaper and reprinted in the *Jeffersonian*; and letters from John Gilman, Elizur Stevens and Alvin Sweet held in the Mackenzie-Lindsey Papers in the Archives of Ontario. With the exception of the letter from James Gemmell, which is most probably the work of someone else, all of these sources are authentic first-person narratives, although the later narratives sometimes cannibalise earlier publications, notably William Gates, *Recollections of Life in Van Dieman's Land*, which borrows liberally from the narrative of Robert Marsh.

For the most part the Patriot narratives have a high degree of verisimilitude and historical veracity. That said, the Patriots should not be considered as entirely reliable narrators of their experience, especially in their published accounts. In the growing literature on the convict narratives a recurrent theme is the problematic nature of the convict voice, and the Patriot narratives are a case in point.[1] The proselytising purpose was often quite overt, especially in the narratives of Robert Marsh and Stephen Wright. The cruelty of the British system and the venality of imperial officials are the dominant themes of all seven books. In their political intent and their emphasis on physical brutality, the Patriot narratives echoed the highly effective slave narratives which were published at much the same time, but there was more to the Patriots' political construction of themselves than brutalised victims. While the emphasis of the slave narrative was a catalogue of horror inflicted upon the passive body of the African, this could not have the same political impact for white, often middle-class, Yankees such as the Patriots. No white American male could be positioned in the public perception as the abject victim of imperialist task-masters, cruelly enduring the indignity of being treated like a dog. As a result there is a crucial tension in the narratives between the vivid recreation of the systematic degradation and brutality of convict life and the presentation of their superior American manliness and their republican virtue.

The Patriot narratives remain the most important body of convict texts in existence. While they are to be read and interpreted with a degree of caution, they are an invaluable window into the everyday experience of many thousands of mute men and women forced to endure calculated cruelty on 'the fatal shore'.[2]

Conversions

Length

1 foot = 30.5 cm
1 yard = 0.9 m
1 rod = 5.0 m
1 mile = 1.6 km

Mass

1 ounce (oz) = 28.3 g
1 pound (lb) = 454 g
1 hundredweight (cwt) = 50.8 kg

Area

1 acre = 0.40 ha

Volume

1 pint = 568 mL
1 quart = 1.1 L

Food energy

1 calorie = 4.2 kJ

Currency

There were 12 pennies (d) in 1 shilling (s), and 20 shillings in 1 pound (£).
Sums such as 2s and 2s 6d were often written as 2/- and 2/6.

Introduction

> Still their columns continued filling up in the rear till the river banks, fields and woods, appeared alive with the red coats. Soon after, they formed in battle array, displaying their numbers to as great advantage as possible, and with what pomp and parade they were masters of, to strike dismay into the bosoms of our little band. . . . instead of being frightened from our wits, and going out upon knees and imploring their gracious clemency, we strengthened each others hearts with kind words and valiant councels, . . . it was a wonderment to her gracious majesty's hirelings, that the handful of rebels were so presumptious as to entertain the idea of resisting those who had come down like a swarm of locusts to devour us from the face of the earth. [21–2]

The battle of the windmill in November 1838, here described with heroic gusto by William Gates, was one of the most vainglorious episodes in Anglo-American relations in the nineteenth century. Code-named 'the great hunt in the north woods', the invasion of the British colony of Upper Canada (Ontario) by a few hundred deluded 'Patriots' from the United States, bent on inspiring a republican revolution, was a disaster from start to finish.[1] Only one-third of the hastily assembled invasion force that left Sackets Harbor on the night of 12 November had actually landed on the Canadian shore. Barely had they secured control of a stone windmill and unfurled the Patriot flag—an eagle and two stars on a background of blue—than they came under attack from Her Majesty's 83rd Regiment and the local militia. The ensuing battle provided a fine spectacle for the thousands of spectators who had congregated along the American shore of the St Lawrence, waving scarves and little flags and shouting encouragement to the startled Patriots.

Gates reported that he and his comrades watched the redcoats approach with 'nervous anxiety', which doubtless accelerated once the British sounded their bugles and began a barrage of heavy, uninterrupted fire. Although the Americans had not expected this ferocious response, they fought back for

1

over three hours, eventually forcing the British platoons to retreat, 'still sending their inoffensive bullets in search of patriot blood, which riddled the air or spent their force upon the inanimate objects about us', Gates boasted (24). The Patriots took the opportunity to make a break for the safety of the mill. As he ran for cover, Gates noticed that the field was 'literally covered' with the fallen British soldiers, and although he 'felt but little sympathy for them, the groans and imprecations of the wounded and dying were heart-rending to hear' (25–6). When the British commander sent out a white flag requesting hostilities to cease in order to collect the dead and wounded, Gates's anxiety dissolved into self-congratulation:

> and when we take into account the very great disparity of numbers, we may search history in vain for its parallel. At least, so small a band had never with-stood such a large force of British troops, many of whom were veterans in the service of their mistress, Queen Victoria. [27]

American losses were also high and, as Gates was only too well aware, the young Americans who huddled behind the stone walls of the mill had little reason to congratulate themselves. Poorly armed and lacking any clarity of purpose, they were greatly outnumbered and cut off by two British gun-boats patrolling the St Lawrence. Theirs was a perilous position, as fellow Patriot Daniel Heustis observed:

> Our leaders had also proved traitors and cowards. We had lost much of our ammunition. Our position was exposed to attack, both by land and water, by a force vastly larger than we could muster. Amid all these unfavorable circum-stances, foreboding almost certain defeat, there was no repining, no wavering, no flinching from the contest, on the part of the resolute and heroic band of young men at Windmill Point. [46]

Thirteen of the Patriots were killed, and another twenty-eight wounded. The despairing doctor found that all his medicines and instruments had been left on a schooner that had grounded on the American side of the St Lawrence in Ogdensburg, along with the bulk of their ammunition, five artillery pieces, 176 rifles and five hundred muskets. He had no medical supplies and nothing to ease the pain of the wounded men.[2] Stephen Wright, who was wounded in his left arm by a musket-ball, lay awake all night listening to the wind whistling shrilly through the arms of the old mill and 'the groans of the stricken and the dying, who lay shelterless in the night's wild storm' (9). He remembered it as the loneliest night of his life. The Patriot flag, so lovingly sewn by the women of Ogdensburg, was still nailed to the apex of the mill and 'flapped like the wings of a raven above our heads', appearing to Wright as an omen of doom rather than a proud standard of republican triumphalism (9). When the sun rose on the next day, he understood the situation was hopeless:

There lay the broad, beautiful St. Lawrence, and beyond it the land of the free—how we longed to see our wounded beyond its waters. The field before us was studded with the bodies of the dead. Some lay with their eyes turned to heaven, with an imploring gaze—others had a mild benignant smile upon their marble faces; the crimson coats were dyed a deeper color in blood, and the snow drifted beside their bodies, covering them as with a shroud, while their only dirge was the beating of the waves against the rock-bound shore. A mist curtained the sun—and mist gathered in the eyes of many of our comrades, as we thought of the weeping mothers, the agonized sisters, and the heart-broken wives that had been made in the short space of a single day. [9–10]

When neither medical supplies nor reinforcements appeared from across the St Lawrence, the last glimmer of hope was extinguished. Three days and nights 'passed dreamily away' in the mill, as Wright remembered, before the Patriots sent out the flag of truce and gave themselves over to the commander of the 83rd Regiment. As the regimental band played a mocking rendition of 'Yankee Doodle Dandy', the Patriots were marched to nearby Prescott, to be transferred to Fort Henry in Kingston for trial.

Even in their most desperate moments, these humiliated and disillusioned American citizens could not have conceived that their tilt at Her Majesty's loyal government in Canada would lead them into exile at the very end of the world, or that the US government would abandon them to suffer the calculated cruelties of the British penal system. In all, ninety-two prisoners known as the 'Patriot exiles' were transported from Upper Canada to Australia's Van Diemen's Land as punishment for their participation in three separate raids across the border between June and December 1838. Ninety per cent of them were citizens of the United States, while the rest were from the Canadian colonies or were recent immigrants from Ireland and Scotland. When they were loaded onto British transports to be taken away, these unhappy souls must have known that they were not the first to have been 'reserved for a punishment worse than death itself', as Heustis put it (80). Nor would they be the last.

Measured against the flow of prisoners cast into exile by the British State, the tiny trickle of Patriots transported to the antipodes in three separate vessels in the late 1830s appears insignificant. Between the early seventeenth century and the outbreak of World War II, the British transported as many as 350 000 individuals. From the reign of James I on, transportees were packed off to the West Indies, where often they were traded for sugar, while others were shipped to Carolina and to the Cheasapeake to be auctioned off.[3] Sold for the length of their sentence, many were forced to work in the plantations of the New World—a punishment which Daniel Defoe likened to the Roman practice of sending condemned slaves to work in the mines.[4] The trade expanded after the passing of the Transportation Act in

1718. At least 50 000 convicts, one in nine of British eighteenth-century transatlantic emigrants, were prisoners shipped into exile to satisfy the colonial demand for labour.[5]

After the American Revolution, Britain was forced to direct its stream of convicted labour to other sites, settling eventually on its newly acquired possession of New South Wales. In all, about 165 000 convicts were landed on Australia's shores between the arrival of the First Fleet in 1787 and the ending of transportation to Western Australia in 1868. About 45 per cent of these were sent, as the Patriots were, to the island colony of Van Diemen's Land, later renamed Tasmania.

Previous historians of Australian convict transportation have tended to see the Patriots' plight as something of an exotic exception to the general flood of British and Irish street thieves and burglars.[6] This is a distinction with which the Patriots concurred. Ever anxious to portray themselves as the victims of monarchical oppression, they distanced themselves from the run-of-the-mill British and Irish convicts. When viewed in the wider context of British transportation policy, however, the Patriots' experience hardly rates as exceptional. While the majority of British transportees were convicted in Britain and Ireland, this was not invariably the case. The flow of convicts from the presidencies of Madras, Bengal and Bombay to the penal settlements in the Straits of Malacca, Upper Burma and the Andaman Islands probably numbered in excess of 70 000.[7] Other minor trickles of exiled prisoners criss-crossed the oceans that linked Britain's overseas colonial possessions. Prisoners were landed at various times in Newfoundland, Nova Scotia, Rattan Island off the coast of Honduras, Gibraltar, Bermuda, Mauritius and Aden, as well as several locations in West Africa, including Sierra Leone, Senegal and Cape Coast Castle.[8] The ports of departure were even more diverse than points of penal disembarkation. In the eighteenth and nineteenth centuries convicts were shipped from the West Indies, Canada, the Cape Colony, New Zealand, Hong Kong, Mauritius, Burma and Ceylon.

It was not unusual for the British to transport political prisoners. Many of those dispatched from Ireland to the West Indies in the seventeenth century were defeated soldiers. After the defeat of the Irish at Drogheda, Oliver Cromwell is alleged to have ordered 'Every tenth man of the soldiers killed, and the rest shipped off for the Barbadoes'. So common was transportation from Ireland to the Caribbean in the 1650s that 'to be Barbadoes' became something of a general expression.[9] Thousands of prisoners were transported after the Civil War battles of Preston, Dunbar, Colchester and Worcester, and sent to the plantations of the New World.[10] A similar fate met many of those who participated in the Wexford and Monmouth uprisings and the Jacobite revolts of 1715 and 1745.[11] The Trelawny Maroons and the Black

Caribs were transported from Jamaica and St Vincent to Honduras and Nova Scotia in 1796.[12] Two years later, the British transported several hundred rebels from Ireland to New South Wales.[13] These were followed by a stream of Whiteboys, Ribbonmen and others who had become embroiled in the complex infighting characteristic of Ireland's nineteenth-century land war.[14]

The Andaman Islands south of Burma were re-established as a penal station for the express purpose of receiving rebels transported from India, in the wake of what the British called the 'Great Mutiny' of 1857. This initial cohort of political prisoners was followed by those involved in the Mapilah uprising and the Alipore bomb case, and by members of the Ghadr Party.[15] Slave rebels were also transported from the West Indies to Honduras, Sierra Leone and Australia. Those who were shipped to the antipodes were joined by other colonial subjects who had struck out against British rule on the Empire's frontiers, including rebellious Khoi from the Cape Colony and Maori rebels from New Zealand.[16]

Still more were shipped from closer to home. They included the Scottish Jacobins, the sailors from the Nore naval mutiny and other mutineers; the Pentrich rebels who had tried to seize Nottingham Castle in 1817; the Cato Street Conspirators who plotted to blow up the cabinet; participants in the Glasgow weavers' rebellion of 1820; Luddite, Swing and Rebecca rioters; the village followers of the self-styled 'Sir William Courtenay'; as well as Tolpuddle martyrs, Chartists, Young Irelanders and Fenians.[17] Even by the most conservative estimates, the Patriots were few in number compared with the great mass of political prisoners placed in the holds of transport vessels and sent across the oceans. They were but a small handful of republicans lost within a babble of protesting voices shackled and dispatched to the corners of the British Empire.

Nonetheless, there was a certain irony in this insignificant cohort of American citizens shipped to Van Diemen's Land. Nearly one hundred years before their departure Benjamin Franklin had called for the trade in convicts to the American colonies to be made reciprocal. He argued that for every human serpent shipped across the Atlantic, the American colonists should trap a rattlesnake as it emerged from winter hibernation in the woods and send it in the opposite direction. Franklin reasoned that this would be a justifiable arrangement since 'from the beginning of the world' all venomous reptiles had been regarded as 'felons-convict' who should be subjected to death 'by virtue of an old law, "Thou shalt bruise his head"'.[18] The old law was God's curse placed on the serpent that had inveigled Eve, but in keeping with the sentiments of a more enlightened age, Franklin reasoned that it might prove possible to work improvement in the nature of this mischievous creature through a change in climate.[19] He thus argued that the serpent's 'general sentence of death' be changed to transportation in the hope that the air of St James's Park and the gardens of the nobility and gentry of Britain would have a beneficial effect on the rattlesnake's disagreeable disposition.

The British had now obliged, and rather than bruising the heads and stretching the necks of all the quarry they had caught during 'the great hunt in the north woods', they reprieved the majority on condition of transportation for life. Now, like Benjamin Franklin's hypothetical rattlesnakes, the Patriots were to be trussed up and shipped eastwards, in the opposite direction from that taken by 80 000 or so prisoners transported to the New World colonies by the British over the course of the previous centuries. Like snakes, however, the Patriots would bite back.

Although fourteen of their number did not survive the experience of transportation, many of the Patriots managed to make their way home to the United States. By 1850 several of them had published accounts of their experiences. This makes them unique among British transportees: not because they were political offenders or were shipped from one distant British colony to another, but because they recorded the experience of their ordeal in a series of remarkable interlocking accounts that constitute the largest collection of convict narratives in existence. The purpose of the Patriot narratives was didactic and political: they aimed to instruct the reader in the naked barbarism of the British penal system. As Linus Miller demanded of his readers, 'Wilt thou look upon the dark picture of Van Dieman's Land and learn wisdom?' (253).

1

Patriot Hunters

OR AMERICANS IN THE 1830s it was no simple matter to regard the British colony beyond the Great Lakes as a separate country. Originally settled by loyalist refugees from the rebellious American colonies, Upper Canada had continued to attract many immigrants. Indeed, so many American settlers crossed over the border that during the war between the United States and Britain in 1812, a significant proportion of the populace either remained indifferent to the British cause or favoured the neighbouring republic. Had it not been for the British regular army in the colony and the Indians of the Six Nations, the province would surely have fallen to the Americans.[1] The Iroquois, who were valuable allies of the British during the revolutionary war, had been granted over half a million acres in Upper Canada and, although land transfers had eroded the original grant by 70 per cent, the people of Six Nations remained unwavering in their loyalty to the Crown.

After 1813, various attempts were made to reduce immigration from the United States, yet in the 1830s movement across the border remained fluid, especially in the western part of the province where the majority of the population were American-born or the offspring of American parents. These Americans had come to Upper Canada for the promise of land, not out of any loyalty to the British Crown. British travellers found it difficult to make any distinction between the loyalist Canadians and the republican Americans, with one Irish traveller commenting in 1835 that he found the people of Upper Canada 'the most accomplished Yankees on this side of the Atlantic'.[2] Many citizens of the United States regularly travelled or worked in Upper Canada, continually crossing and re-crossing the political frontier. Naturally, they took a keen interest in the political affairs of the province.

One such was Daniel Heustis, a fiery young commercial traveller from New York, who worked on both sides of the border purchasing pelts and selling morocco leather. Throughout his travels he listened avidly to bitter complaints against the colonial government in Upper Canada; complaints which struck a chord of deep sympathy. Canadians, Heustis believed, 'were harassed in a thousand ways, robbed of their dearest rights, plundered of their substance, and all their remonstrances no more heeded than the idle wind' (17). The main bone of contention was that they 'were taxed, most exorbitantly, to support a host of proud, overbearing, insolent, and virtually irresponsible government-officers, in whose appointment they had no voice, and over whose conduct they could exercise no control or supervision' (17). To the staunchly republican Heustis, this litany of complaint suggested that the people of Upper Canada 'were tired of British rule, and would fain throw off the yoke that was on their necks, as our fathers had done when that yoke oppressed them' (18). Certainly, many in Upper Canada did have grievances of the kind Heustis described, concerning political and administrative processes that were inherently conservative and mirrored the class-bound structures of Britain. The chief executive of the colony was a governor appointed by the Crown, with wide decision-making powers, who was supported by an executive council to frame administrative policy, and a legislative council to enact legislation. Positions on these councils were by appointment, a principle that fostered an entrenched network of interconnected conservatives known as the 'Family Compact'. While there was a democratic component in the colonial government—a legislative assembly elected by a propertied franchise—it was consistently overruled by the executive arm. A profound sense of grievance took root among many of the elected members of the Legislative Assembly, whose legislation was turned back with such regularity that it was little more than a forum for debate.[3] Equally aggrieved were those excluded from the culture of patronage. Another rich source of grievance was that in every township land had been set aside for the Church of England. These lots, known as Clergy Reserves, amounted to one-seventh of surveyed land and the revenue from them went solely to support the clergy of the Church of England, even though the established church was only the third religion in the province, lagging behind the Methodist and Presbyterian. In addition to widespread anger at this blatant ecclesiastical favouritism, these reserves were seen as a hindrance to settlement. The American-born and their offspring, as well as many other immigrants from Britain who were not of the established church, regarded the Clergy Reserves as a particular grievance and the most obvious symbol of a privileged and corrupt oligarchy.

The late 1820s saw the beginnings of a robust reform movement that sought to diminish the privilege and power of the entrenched oligarchy. During the next decade the reformers took heart from the Reform movement against the established order in Britain and the rise of Jacksonian democracy in the United States. William and Robert Baldwin, a father and son of Anglo-Irish stock, were the leaders of the moderate reform faction and exponents of the theory of government whereby the executive coun-cillors would be required to have the confidence of the elected assembly. The radical reform element was led by William Lyon Mackenzie, a lowland Scot whose fiery temper was suggested by the red wig he wore, who was first elected to the Legislative Assembly in 1828, as part of the reformist majority in the assembly, but expelled in December 1831. He was subse-quently re-elected and expelled five times. Mackenzie railed against those he had dubbed 'the Family Compact' in his newspaper, the *Colonial Advocate*, which was all but destroyed by an outraged Tory mob in 1826.[4] After the sweeping Tory victory in 1836, he sold the *Advocate* and established a new paper, the *Constitution*. In it he began to sing the praises of American-style institutional arrangements which, he argued, would offer the ordinary settler a far greater voice in government as well as improvement in the economic state of the province. For Mackenzie, republican democracy and prosperity went hand in hand. In November 1837 he published a proposed constitution for an independent Upper Canada inspired by the US model.[5]

By this time, unhappily, the neighbouring republic was in the grip of a disastrous economic depression that inevitably affected Upper Canada. Poorer than usual harvests in Upper Canada added to the severe economic distress. On both sides of the border money was in short supply, prices rose dramatically and farmers were being forced off their land. In this volatile period of economic distress the disgruntled Mackenzie began to consider more dramatic means to effect change, spurred on by the news on 23 Nov-ember of an armed rebellion of French-speaking *patriotes* in the eastern province of Lower Canada (Quebec).[6] On 4 December, Mackenzie led a haphazard insurrection of about five hundred poorly armed men in the provincial capital of Toronto; almost immediately after, a second insurrection broke out in the west of the province, led by Dr Charles Duncombe who had mobilised some two hundred men.[7]

The speed with which both these uprisings were crushed and the failure to attract the support of many of the leading reformers in Upper Canada were testament to the poor planning and execution of the rebellion, as well as the lack of a unified political movement behind it. Mackenzie himself, seeing how quickly the raggle-taggle rebel forces were dispersed, made a bolt into the woods north of Toronto and eventually made his way onto the Niagara Peninsula. On 11 December he crossed over the Niagara River into Buffalo. Two of his lieutenants, Samuel Lount and Peter Matthews, also fled, but they were apprehended before they could reach the border. In the west, Charles Duncombe and several of his key supporters managed to elude capture and escaped to the United States. In the weeks that followed, over seven hundred suspected rebels were rounded up and arrested. They were held without bail in the crowded province's gaols, and writs of habeas corpus were not returned for thirty days. In order to deal with such a large number of treason trials, special legislation was enacted which permitted prisoners to admit their guilt and petition the governor for a pardon prior to trial.[8] Of the 262 prisoners indicted for their part in the rebellion, 181 petitioned under this statute.[9] Lount and Matthews also petitioned the governor under this statute, but in their cases a pardon was denied. Both men were executed for treason.

From the moment William Lyon Mackenzie took refuge in the United States, the cry went out throughout the border communities of the United States to raise a Patriot army to help the Canadians win their independence from the Crown. The day after he arrived in Buffalo, Mackenzie addressed a rally where he spoke for an hour, pleading for arms and volunteers to assist the reformers in Upper Canada. Handbills were printed calling for Patriot volunteers to mass under the flag of liberty on Navy Island in the middle of the Niagara River, where Mackenzie proclaimed government. A few days later, a proclamation offered 300 acres of land in Canada and one hundred dollars in silver to each man who volunteered for the Patriot force before 1 May.[10] As the provisional government had no reserves of money, Mackenzie issued currency to be redeemed by the victorious Patriots at Toronto City Hall four months hence.[11] Support for the Patriot cause was said to be running high, with four-fifths of the population of cities such as Rochester and Buffalo.[12] When the small steamer engaged by the Patriots to ferry men and supplies to the island was destroyed by a British naval force in American waters, the Patriot cause briefly became a national issue. Newspapers across the country hummed with outrage about this violation of American territorial integrity. According to Heustis, this single act was 'a national insult, of the grossest kind', (48) which greatly increased the recruitment possibilities for the Patriot army. On the Michigan side of the border, a 'Patriot Army of the Northwest' was organised early in the New Year under the direction of the self-styled 'General' Henry S. Handy.[13] Among the first to respond to the call for volunteers was Robert Marsh, aged twenty-four. He was born in Detroit and resided in Niagara, but had most recently been working in Upper Canada, running bakery deliveries between St Catharines and Fort Erie. Marsh was among about five hundred volunteers who spent several weeks on Navy Island drilling and building earth fortifications, before the island was abandoned on 13 January 1838.[14]

Daniel Heustis was not looking for material reward when he found himself among thousands of men at Watertown, in upstate New York, galvanised by the appeals of the Upper Canadian refugees. Like Marsh, Heustis responded to Mackenzie's rally because he believed himself to be a courageous political activist impelled by moral duty to liberate his neighbours.

As he read the situation, intervention in Canadian affairs was necessary to sunder the chains that bound their hapless neighbours to the British throne. The Upper Canadian rebellion had failed only because the imperial government had sapped the moral will of the Canadians, Heustis believed. He was thrilled to be given the opportunity to dedicate himself to the cause of Canadian liberty and believed that no American could fail to lend support, just as they had done when news of nationalist rebellions in Greece and Poland reached America. 'The chivalry of the nation was roused, and thousands of our gallant spirits rushed to the battle-field', Heustis later wrote. 'All the means necessary to continue these contests were freely furnished. The press was pregnant with good will; thronged assemblies were convened; loud huzzas answered to eloquent appeals; and the whole people were moved as by the upheaving of the volcano' (13). If such popular enthusiasm were unleashed by rebellions in far distant parts, he reasoned, surely the struggle for republican democracy in neighbouring Canada would gain the backing of the US government. He was infuriated to find that the US government did not share this view and considered his sympathy for the Canadian rebels 'had been indulged a little too freely' (34). He was arrested for violating the neutrality laws in January 1838.

William Gates, a New York farm labourer 'of an impulsive nature', aged twenty-two, found that he was unable 'to remain an idle spectator in the midst of such stirring times' (12). He too was incensed to find the government had actually enacted laws to *prevent* Americans supporting their northern neighbours. Gates drew a bitter comparison between the Canadian experience and the much more dubious cause on their southern border, only a few years earlier. 'When Texas revolted from a sister republic, our men were permitted to organize companies and depart armed for the scene of conflict', he bitterly reminded his readers (17–18). An 'imbecilic republic' like Mexico was an easy mark, Gates allowed, especially since Texas wanted to have a slave economy and had the support of the powerful slave states of the south. By contrast, the Canadians had rebelled against the might of the British monarchy, just as Gates's heroes Washington, Lafayette, Franklin and John Adams had done, and for the very same rights that Americans now enjoyed. Gates pictured President Van Buren, who enacted legislation to prohibit intervention in Canada, 'abjectly crouched at the feet of the British lion. . . . frightened by the roar of the royal whelp, were vieing with that royalty itself to crush the rising of the oppressed for liberty's sake' (10). George Washington would turn in his grave, Gates believed. 'I felt the spirit stirring my youthful blood in sympathy for the down-trodden of England's rule', he wrote (11).

The belief that the colonists of Upper Canada were desperate to liberate themselves from imperial control was commonly held by the many thousands of Americans recruited into the various secret societies that mushroomed along the border early in 1838. The earliest was the Sons of Liberty, established in Michigan by General Handy, commander of the Patriot Army of the Northwest.[15] Handy's intention was to use his secret society in Michigan as a recruiting base, and he began to send confidential agents into Canada to recruit for the invasion of Canada. Independent of Handy another secret society, known as the Hunters' Lodge, began to proliferate along the border in May 1838 and by late June had absorbed the Sons of Liberty within its rapidly expanding network.[16] On the Detroit frontier General Handy's army engaged in a series of disastrous minor skirmishes to seize a strategic island from which to launch an attack. On 9 January, a group of Patriots invaded Bois Blanc Island on the schooner *Anne*, which then ran aground on the Canadian shore. It was captured by local militia along with twenty Patriots and a substantial quantity of ammunition and artillery. Another brief invasion across the frozen lake to Pelee Island, about 35 miles off the coast, occurred on 26 February. Again the Patriots were driven back by British regulars and Canadian militia. Eleven Patriots were killed and another eleven arrested, while one man drowned when he fell through the thin ice trying to escape.

Heustis was one of many New Yorkers convinced that the Canadians 'manifested a strong desire to be relieved from British thraldom' (18), and consequently was among the very first to be admitted to the Hunters' Lodge when it was established at Watertown. 'Very soon our lodge numbered *nineteen hundred members*', Heustis wrote, and recruiting in the neighbouring towns raised new lodges in 'nearly every town in that region' (41). Just as eagerly, Gates joined the Hunters at nearby Cape Vincent, New York, when a lodge was established there.

The Hunters' Lodges were the largest and most significant of several secret societies sworn to defend liberty and republican virtue in borderlands America. The lodges claimed a membership as high as 100 000 although official US and Canadian reports put the number of members somewhere between 25 000 and 40 000 at the height of their activity. The Hunters were better funded than the other secret societies and created their own financial institution known as the Republican Bank of Canada, in which the Hunters bought shares to be redeemed when Canada was liberated. The bank's dollar bills displayed the heads of the two Canadian martyrs Lount and Matthews and carried the motto '*Liberty, Equality, Fraternity*'.[17] The Hunters' Lodges were hierarchical and highly ritualised, and their members would communicate in rudimentary code that had its origins in the language of hunting. The lowest level, the Snowshoe, could be distinguished with several signs: the palm of the left hand placed over the back of the right with the fingers of both hands extended, or by lifting the right hand, palm out, to the ear and pressing it forward. To be identified by a compatriot a Snowshoe would be asked: 'Are you a hunter?', in which case he would give the name of the preceding day. The more senior Beaver would be asked: 'Do you know the beaver to be a dangerous animal?' and would give the answer no, but lift his hand to his mouth with a bent forefinger and gnaw on his nail to imitate a beaver at work. The most senior, the Hunter, would be required to answer the question 'Trouble?' with the word 'calm', at the same time as moving his right hand to the left side of his body with fingers extended upwards. One lodge member meeting another in public might ask: 'Do you snuff and chew?' to which the respondent would reply, 'I do', and take out a snuff box or hook thumb in waistcoat and make three scratches.[18] On initiation, the Patriot Hunters took an oath:

> To promote republican institutions throughout the world—to cherish them, to defend them and especially to devote myself to the propagation, protection and defence of these institutions in North America ... I promise, until death, that I will attack, combat and help to destroy ... every power authority of Royal origin upon this continent; and especially never to rest until all tyrants of Britain cease to have any dominion or footing whatever in North America.[19]

The members of the lodges elected military officers—majors, colonels and the like—and kept in contact with a network of lodges that stretched from Maine to Ohio. A system of spies and couriers, each with a beat of 10 miles a day, gathered intelligence and spread news of the grand plan to invade Canada. In Hunter parlance, the attack on Upper Canada planned for 4 July, was 'the great hunt in the north woods'.[20] The idea was to capture one of the key towns in Upper Canada, with arms obtained from the arsenal in Detroit where the sentries were Patriot sympathisers. This bold move was expected to galvanise disgruntled residents of Upper Canada, who were just waiting their chance to throw out the imperial overlords. Once the signal was given, these Canadians were expected to flock to the Patriot standard and carry the burden of the revolution. The spark of rebellion need only be reignited by magnanimous republican neighbours and Canadians would rise up *en masse*, just as the Americans had done in the glorious revolution of 1776. In their furtive lodge meetings, the Hunters plotted and planned 'the great hunt in the north woods', in the fervent and foolish belief that tens of thousands of their oppressed neighbours would rally to their side.[21] As Heustis explained:

> It had been represented to us that thousands in Canada were ready to flock to the patriot standard as soon as it could be planted on their soil. They were destitute of arms; and any attempt to revolt, without assistance from abroad, would but result in defeat, the consequences of which would be terrible to

themselves and their families. If we could take Fort Henry, a rallying-point would be established, where the Canadians could muster, provide themselves with arms, and prepare to meet the tyrants who were oppressing them. [33]

Heustis, Gates and Marsh were among several hundred Patriots to be bitterly disenchanted. Certainly, there were those in Upper Canada who looked longingly at the political institutions across the border; but in the main, Upper Canadians had no overwhelming enthusiasm for American republicanism, for all their political dissatisfaction with the ruling oligarchy against whom Mackenzie led his rag-tag rebellion.[22] In fact, there were many in Upper Canada who continued to view their republican neighbours with suspicion and abhorrence. The Lieutenant-Governor of Upper Canada may have overstated the case when he told the Secretary of State for the Colonies 'that hatred that exists in the breast of every loyal subject of Upper Canada toward the Americans and American institutions is incurable'.[23] But it was true that Canadians still clung to the British colonial system. Affection for the Crown and preference for the imperial system were sentiments many of the 1837 rebels had shared. The rebellion had been against the corrupt colonial officials of the Crown, many of the imprisoned rebels were at pains to point out, never against the Crown itself. This was a distinction the Patriot Hunters never could grasp.

2

Theatre in the Short Hills

A T THE BEGINNING of June 1838, a group of rogue Patriots crossed the border across Lake St Clair into Sarnia, only to be pursued back across the lake by Mohawk warriors from the nearby Six Nations Reserve. It is not clear whether these intruders were members of the Patriot Army of the Northwest, and it may be that the object of this foray was to plunder, since the men broke into the government stores and stole supplies. Equally, there could have been a strategic purpose. Among the five men taken, Horace Cooley was found to be carrying dispatches from the Patriot Army commander. Even though Cooley and six others were arraigned on the charge of treasonable practices, these cases never came to trial.[1] Cooley and one other man were subsequently tried for burglary and sentenced to death.[2] Whatever its aim, the crudely executed raid achieved nothing, except to throw the planning for the 4 July invasion into complete disarray. The Canadian authorities were put on their mettle, and the sympathetic guard at the Detroit arsenal was changed. From that point on, the Patriot cause was destined for disaster.

A second serious breach of border neutrality occurred on the Niagara Peninsula on 10 June 1838, when a group of about thirty-five men from the Patriot Army of the Northwest crossed over the Niagara River and concealed themselves in woods near the Short Hills, where they were supplied by farmers sympathetic to the Patriot cause.[3] The group was led by men commissioned as officers: Colonel James Morreau (Morrow), a man of quiet dignity, aged thirty-three, who was a tanner from Pennsylvania; Major Benjamin Wait, aged twenty-five, who had at one time operated a sawmill in the Short Hills and was married to the daughter of a prominent rebel; Major Samuel Chandler, aged forty-nine, originally from Albany in the United States, but well-established in the village of St Johns as a wagonmaker. Two years earlier, Wait had quit Canada to live in the United States

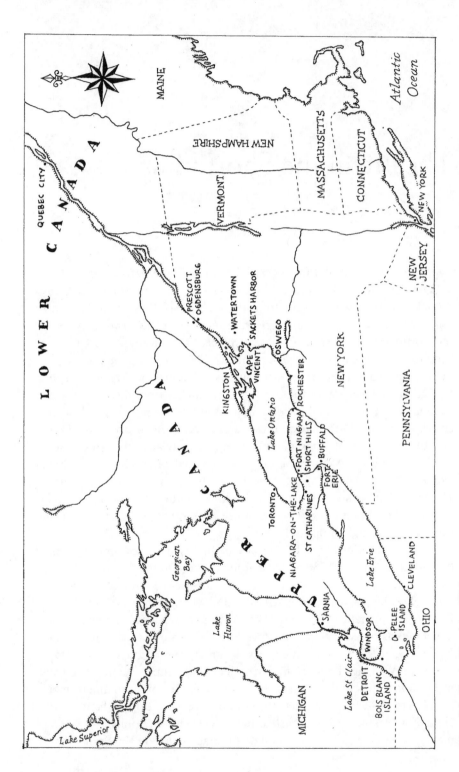

Sites of the Patriot Invasions, 1838

because of financial problems, while Chandler had escorted the fugitive William Lyon Mackenzie across the Niagara River into New York State and had taken temporary refuge there, leaving his wife and ten children in Upper Canada. When arrested, Chandler was carrying a list of 526 residents in the vicinity who had promised to aid an invasion, while Wait carried muster rolls, letters, maps, and a blue flag with two stars and the word LIBERTY. The expedition leader, Morreau, was carrying a printed proclamation that read:

> Canadians:—
> We have at last been successful in planting the standard of liberty in one part of our oppressed country—Fort George and Fort Massassauga are now in our possession. Canadians! Come to our assistance as you prize property, happiness and life, come to our assistance.
>   Canadians! This is the hour of your redemption, rally to the standard of the Free, and the tyranny of England shall cease to exist in our land.
>   We pledge the safety of property, of life and all who do not oppose us; but resistance shall be met by men who are determined to conquer or die.[4]

Of the remaining Patriot raiders, about half were Canadian refugees from the original rebellion in December 1837. One of these, James Gemmell, twenty-three, was a Scottish emigrant to Canada, who said of his engagement in the rebellion that he was 'little disposed to quarrel about forms of government—but I had witnessed an accumulation of real oppressions and acts of injustice which I could see no other way to get rid of—remonstrance to the legislature, or by it to the British power in the colony or England had long proved unavailing'.[5]

Another political refugee was Jacob Beemer. Of all the Patriots, this man was distinguished as the least worthy, by all accounts a thoroughly venal character in whom neither the Executive Council of Upper Canada nor his fellow Patriots could find a single redeeming feature. Beemer, a married carpenter of twenty-nine, had been active in the uprising led by Dr Charles Duncombe in the western provinces. He had managed to escape across the border at Niagara, but his uncle and other prominent rebels were captured and imprisoned in the grand stone house of the local militia commander, Allan MacNab, which was known as Dundern Castle, where they faced possible execution for treason.[6] Yet, according to Linus Miller, a colonel in the Patriot Army, it was Beemer who provided the Canadian authorities with the information to foil the Patriot plan to rescue the rebels. One of the biggest problems facing the Patriot cause in 1838 was the number of paid informers within their ranks supplying information to the Canadian authorities, and Beemer was almost certainly one of these.[7]

Linus Miller, a law student aged twenty from Pennsylvania, was aide-de-camp to the commander of the Patriot Army. He was sent to join the

Short Hills raid into Upper Canada on 15 June. If Miller is to be believed, his job was to urge the men to withdraw before they ruined the whole Patriot enterprise, a task for which he proved totally ineffectual. Miller was alarmed to find 'the *Prince of Traitors*, JACOB BEEMER' had induced the men across the border before the appointed time and was spoiling for a fight (17). Finding that neither he nor Morreau was able to control Beemer or to deflect his purpose, Miller decided to stay with the party to prevent trouble. Or so he claimed in his spirited account of himself facing down the villainous Beemer, who was intent on plunder, mayhem and murder.

Miller recounted that, after robbing a local tavern-keeper, Beemer ordered an attack on another tavern in the village of St Johns where a company of Lancers was stationed. When the astonished Lancers surrendered, Beemer announced his intention to hang seven of them in retaliation for the recent execution of Lount and Matthews in Toronto. As the terrified soldiers reminded Beemer that he had accepted their surrender as prisoners of war and implored him to spare their lives in consideration of their innocent wives and children, Miller took control:

> I gave the word of command to halt! The whole party obeyed, and all eyes were instantly turned upon me. Beemer turned round, and was met by my trusty pistols staring him in the face, and I noticed that the coward quailed before them: the man who was about sending seven men, unprepared, into eternity, could not look, without the greatest trepidation, into the muzzle of a cocked pistol! [27]

Having freed the prisoners from Beemer's grasp, Miller allowed them to leave, once they had sworn on the Bible that they would immediately quit Her Majesty's service and never take up arms again. Clearly, he had no concept of the employment contract of British soldiers, which held desertion to be a capital crime. Still, this kind of flourish was typical of Miller, who was given to grandiloquent exultation of American democracy and flamboyant self-dramatisation. One suspects he was drawn to the Patriot cause by his desire for heroic theatre more than his grasp of the principles of good government. In his account he rendered the whole business of the invasion and his subsequent capture as a series of heroic adventures, casting himself as a kind of republican version of the Count of Monte Cristo. His companions in arms, by contrast, found him rather fanciful, if not downright odd. In evidence given at the trial of the Short Hills raiders, various witnesses swore that it was Morreau and Chandler, not Miller, who had made the stand against Beemer and who freed the Lancers.[8]

Needless to say, those freed Lancers did not head to their homes as instructed. They went straight to the headquarters of the local militia and called out a sizeable force of enthusiastic volunteers. Together with the warriors of the nearby Six Nations Reserve, the militia made short work of rounding up the Patriots as they made their way back into the United States. By adopting a series of disguises, Miller managed to stay at large longer than most, but his theatrical ploys failed to get him safely home. He was run to ground by a cavalry officer in a field near Niagara. Confessing to 'feelings of deep mortification', Miller ruefully acknowledged that his reception in Canada was a far cry from his expectations 'of splendid victories won—of the triumph of liberty over our northern regions—and deeds of noble daring and renown', performed by his heroic self (44). Greater mortification awaited Miller when he was reunited with his Patriot comrades in the Niagara gaol. He found himself in a cell with nothing but an iron bedstead and some water. When a loaf of bread was shoved into his new abode, Miller 'kicked with my foot until it was in a thousand pieces, and then kicked over the piggin of water'. As the cell door was shut and bolted the true enormity of his situation sunk in: 'for the first time in my life, I heard the key turned upon me, and felt myself a *captive!*' (52).

Miller had good reason to be appalled at his fate. His brief period at large had been sufficient to indicate that there was scant sympathy for the Patriot action in Upper Canada. While there may have been silent Patriot sympathisers in the Niagara region, widespread community outrage at these American interlopers was immediate and vociferous, quite the reverse of the enthusiastic support the Patriots had been led to expect. Instead of being hailed as liberators, they found themselves denounced in shrill hyperbole as worse than 'the veriest savages that ever prowled the forest'.[9] In this respect the Upper Canadians proved themselves to be, in the words of one American newspaper, 'a cowardly people . . . an inert, stupid mass without a spark of the fire of seventy-six'.[10] This was a view belatedly shared by the Short Hills raiders languishing in their Spartan prison cells.

The dejected Patriots continued to harbour expectations that the invasion might still go ahead on 4 July, and that they would be liberated along with the people of Upper Canada. As Miller reported, the men all anticipated 4 July 'with feelings of deepest anxiety, hoping that a blow would be struck for Canadian liberty . . . effecting the great end for which we had so long been laboring, and the salvation of us poor prisoners' (62). They were sorely disabused of this idea. Miller ruefully recorded that the 'Glorious Fourth' came and went without incident: 'our hearts sank within us, and we mourned as those who have no hope' (62).

As half of the group were American citizens, they still entertained the hope of being repatriated to the United States. Such hope was dealt a severe blow when Lieutenant-Governor George Arthur paid them a visit in the gaol soon after their capture. They could expect no mercy from those whose sovereignty they had violated, Arthur sternly informed them; hanging would be too good for them. Miller, who had carefully scrutinised the governor as he spoke, saw no reason to think the man would not be as good as his word:

> He was, I should judge, about fifty years of age, in stature rather below medioc-
> rity, round shouldered, his head gray and somewhat bald, visage long, eyes
> small and piercing, and the general expression of his countenance perfectly
> passionless. If he had feelings, they were hidden by his exterior. No physiog-
> nomist, in studying his face and features, would accuse him of possessing a
> heart. But there was a compression about his lips, which strikingly evinced his
> great perseverance, determination, promptitude, and decision of character. [63]

George Arthur was indeed a severe man, a martinet by nature and by training. While he had shown a capacity to be merciful with the hundreds of Upper Canadians imprisoned following the original rebellion, he had no such inclinations for the Patriot raiders. In his view they should be dealt with so severely that it would terrorise any more Yankees wishing to export their abhorrent ideology to the Queen's domain.[11] He believed he had the legal apparatus to do so, since earlier that year the Upper Canada govern-ment had passed a special statute known as the Lawless Aggressions Act (Vic. 1 c. 10), which made the armed invasion of Canada a felony that could be tried by either civil court or court martial. The Act had not yet received royal assent, but it had already been used in the case of an American arrested after the abortive invasion of Pelee Island.[12] The Law Officers in London had begun to express concerns about the validity of the Act, although this was a complication that Arthur chose to overlook.[13]

The first American from the Short Hills raid tried under the Lawless Aggressions Act was George Cooley, aged nineteen, a farm labourer from New York State who had lived briefly in Upper Canada, described as 'a young man of very insignificant appearance'.[14] He was consistently described as being young but his age is given as twenty-nine in the court record. This was a mistake; he was nineteen and was said to be aged twenty-three when he arrived in Van Diemen's Land. His trial was held at the courthouse in Niagara on 20 July 1838. Cooley conducted his own defence, even though he could neither read nor write. He was found guilty on the word of a fellow prisoner turned Queen's evidence, but his sentence was held over for a week. The second trial was of much more significance. Colonel James Morreau called no witnesses and offered no defence for his actions. He was found guilty and sentenced to death, with the sentence to be carried into effect immediately.

Arthur was well aware that the Secretary of State for the Colonies, Lord Glenelg, would look askance at this execution. Glenelg had been hor-rified by the execution of Lount and Matthews after the Toronto rebellion of the previous year. In May 1838, he wrote to Arthur to express his 'earnest hope' that there would be no more capital punishments. 'Nothing would cause Her Majesty's Government more sincere regret', he wrote.[15] Defending the decision to execute another man—and this one a citizen of the United States—Arthur told Glenelg that he could find no good reason to issue a pardon. As for Morreau being tried under the as yet unapproved and highly problematic Lawless Aggressions Act, Arthur noted that the Act 'had at least been noticed by Her Majesty's Government and considered by the Law Officers to be in operation'.[16] At this point Arthur was unaware that the Law Officers had declared the Lawless Aggressions Act to be 'irregular and defective' and that Glenelg had sent a directive on 23 June saying the Act was to be disallowed 'as the most effective security against it being drawn into a precedent'.[17]

Arthur did not trouble to wait for Glenelg's reply to his letter about Morreau, who was hanged three days later. On that occasion, the public hangman, a free black man, absented himself from duty. Sheriff Alexander Hamilton had to perform the grisly act, to his supreme distaste. As it transpired, Arthur was to regret his haste in calling in the hangman. When he did receive Lord Glenelg's directive on the Lawless Aggressions Act, it was unequivocal that 'no sentence of death, under any circumstances however extreme will be carried into effect'.[18] While this dispatch arrived too late to save Morreau, the unwelcome opinion of the Law Officers contained within it made all the difference for those condemned Patriots who came after him.

At Linus Miller's trial he entered a plea of not guilty on the grounds of temporary insanity. In his defence, witnesses from the raid reported that Miller was 'curious in his manners' and 'would never give a sensible answer'. One reported having seen Miller 'demean himself in a singular way', while his brother explained that Miller had suddenly left home in New York State, without telling his family of his intentions. He had not always been in his right mind, the brother told the court, and 'often changeable in his conversation'. Miller was at that time a law clerk but his family believed he was unlikely to succeed at law, 'since his mind appeared filled with speculation and other flighty things'.[19] The defence was a ruse, Miller later protested. Had he been aware that his 'brave and generous friend' Colonel Morreau would be hoisted on the gallows, 'I should most certainly have stood my trial and yielded up my life without a struggle', he wrote (73).

His ruse did him no good. Miller was found guilty and sentenced to death, albeit with a strong plea for mercy. George Cooley received the same sentence, as did Norman Mallory and Garrett Van Camp, also labourers from New York State, aged twenty-three and twenty-eight respectively, and Williams Reynolds (also known as David Deal), a saddler from Pennsylvania, who claimed to be only eighteen. Samuel Chandler was charged as a British subject because he had owned property in Canada. He was sentenced to death, although he received a unanimous recommendation for mercy, 'in consequence of his good feeling and humanity toward his neighbour-hood'.[20] Benjamin Wait received the same treatment, even though he was described at capture as an American. He was also recommended for mercy. Alexander McLeod, a farmer from Upper Canada, aged twenty-four, was given a similar sentence.

Jacob Beemer insisted that his was a case of mistaken identity. Curiously, those witnesses who had readily identified and condemned their fellow Patriots found themselves unable to swear that the man in the dock was the same Beemer who had been with them at the Short Hills: that man was not so tall and had a scar on his face, they said. Their contradictory evidence was to no avail. Beemer was condemned to death. The jury made no recommendation of mercy as they had for the other defendants.

The remaining British subjects who were tried for treason pleaded guilty, perhaps because they had been led to expect a pardon in return for a guilty plea.[21] They were: Eurastus Warner, a farmer, aged twenty; David Taylor, a farmer, aged twenty-four; James Waggoner, a farmer, aged thirty-three; John Grant, a wheelwright, aged thirty-four; James McNulty, a carpenter, aged thirty; John Brown, a labourer, aged twenty; John Vernon, a carpenter, aged twenty; and James Gemmell, a recent emigrant from Scotland. Eventually these men did receive a pardon. So too did the five Americans.

In their case Governor Arthur's exercise of mercy was the occasion for dismay rather than joy, since the pardons did not entail banishment to the United States, as the men had been led to expect, but were conditional on transportation for life to a penal colony. As a previous governor of Van Diemen's Land, Arthur was well aware that a life sentence to a penal colony was a punishment almost equal to hanging: 'calculated to strike terror into a whole army of brigands'.[22]

On 21 August those who had received conditional pardons were sent to the more secure penitentiary at Fort Henry, in Kingston. Benjamin Wait recalled the distress with which they were separated from their still-condemned companions:

> When they were separated from us and manacled for their journey, the scene became replete with sorrow—tears rolled from the eyes of the poor fellows who supposed they were bidding us adieu for ever—the cheeks of manhood were blanched with grief, and there was more dejection in the hearts of those whose lives were to be prolonged in slavery, than amongst us for whom there was no hope. [56]

On arrival at Fort Henry, Linus Miller was rendered even more dis-traught by the conditions he encountered at the penitentiary where he and his comrades were to be kept:

Dirt and filth were the most prominent objects within the walls; but hunger was no stranger there, our daily rations being only twelve ounces of bread, and a pint of bullock's head soup. This last was so very filthy, that nothing but starvation could have enabled any Christian to eat it. Upon its surface was never seen floating anything that resembled grease; but something which looked very much like the jaw-bone of an ass, was found one day in the bottom of the soup-bucket. Alas! there was no Samson present strong enough to slaughter a thousand of the Philistines with it. [61]

It was at Fort Henry that one of the prisoners, David Taylor, died. His death was a result of neglect and mistreatment, in Miller's view, as Taylor had caught a severe cold at Niagara but was ignored by the doctor at Fort Henry, who ordered him to be shackled like the rest. 'He never left the bed for an hour after our arrival', Miller reported. 'Crushed in spirit, his soul seemed to loathe prison life and hastened to be free' (102).

The condemned men at the Niagara gaol were left to contemplate their doleful fate and the awful consequence of their impulsive action which left their families to survive destitute and alone, bereft of a breadwinner. Wait's spirited young wife Maria was not prepared to endure that fate, nor to see her newborn child lose his father. Leaving her baby to the care of a friend and taking Chandler's eldest daughter with her, Maria set out to appeal for mercy directly to the new Governor-in-Chief, Lord Durham. In making her appeal over the head of Governor Arthur, Mrs Wait put her faith in the reputation of Durham as a political radical, believing that if they 'could but get his Lordship to lend an ear to our application, we need not fear that the lives of any of the others would be sacrificed'.[23]

Lord Durham was sufficiently moved by the appeals of the two women, and his own abhorrence of capital punishment, to write a note to Arthur requesting a stay of execution. When she presented Durham's note to Arthur, Mrs Wait claimed that his lips 'quivered with rage' (76). Some would still swing, Arthur assured her, in particular 'that execrable character Beemer . . . no mercy for him' (77). Meanwhile, at Niagara the executions were scheduled for one o'clock on 25 August 1838. By midday that day no official word to the contrary had been received. Wait recalled tension and terror of that last hour waiting for the sheriff to bring a stay of execution from Arthur:

Sir George detained him until the last boat upward bound for the day, had put off, then gave him an order. Should he wait until the following day, the hour for our execution would be passed at his peril; and the execution of Morrow had made such an impression upon his mind, that he was glad of the respite, and determined to make an effort to obtain the Governor's boat; in which he was successful after considerable altercation, and succeeded in gaining the

Niagara dock at half past twelve . . . It would appear by this elusive conduct of the Governor, that he had determined to execute us at all hazards, and then lay the blame at the door of some of his officials . . . but his temerity was scarce adequate to this step. The respite extended to six days only . . . [57]

Although all the four men still shivering in the Niagara gaol were British subjects, their appeals for mercy had been given a boost by concerns about the Lawless Aggressions Act used for the trial of the Americans.[24] On this matter the Law Officers stuck firmly to their opinion, despite strenuous objections from Upper Canada. Their objection was that US citizens could not be detained on any charge other than treason, arguing that the Patriot invaders must be tried for treason as individuals owing a temporary allegiance to the Crown from the time they set foot in Canada. Strong differences of legal opinion between the Crown Law Officers and those in Upper Canada over this Act were raised in the parliament, notably by Lord Brougham, who declared the Act to be 'manifestly and grossly absurd'.[25] As the authorities in Upper Canada and those in England continued to argue the toss about whether Americans could be tried for treason, Glenelg held firm to his view that no one should be executed. Arthur's view, as expressed to Lord Durham, was that 10 per cent should be hanged and the rest ordered for transportation. He was furious when Lord Durham commuted the sentences of all four men remaining on sentence of death.[26] In an apoplectic response to Glenelg, Arthur insisted that he should at least be allowed to hang Beemer, whom the Legislative Council refused to consider for mercy.[27] 'It is far from satisfactory to me that only Morrow [*sic*] has been executed', Arthur told Glenelg, while pleading for his authority to be upheld.[28] For his part, Glenelg expressed regret that even Morreau had been hanged, and he took the occasion to impress upon Arthur that capital punishment placed Her Majesty's government in a very bad light.

Equally disturbing to Glenelg was Arthur's use of the fanatically loyal Mohawk warriors called out after the Short Hills and St Clair raids. Despite Arthur's protests that the Mohawk were 'under the guidance of humane leaders who scrupulously observed the merciful rules of civilised warfare . . . [and] would sustain a comparison with that of men laying claim to a higher degree of civilisation', Glenelg could not be mollified. He had already been subjected to a fierce attack on this matter from Joseph Hume in parliament. Nothing was more calculated to inflame the radicals in the British parliament that an attempt to loose 'the horrors of savage warfare', he warned.[29]

Deeply offended and disgruntled, Arthur was able to wring the concession that if he were to reprieve the Patriots he could transport them all to the penal colony of Van Diemen's Land. If he were not able to hang these miscreants, at least he still had this terrifying deterrent in his grasp. Unfortunately for Arthur, transportation of prisoners from Canada was beset with problems, as Lord Durham learnt at his cost. The British government jealously guarded the prerogative of transportation as belonging solely to the Crown and insisted that a colonial governor must be dependent on the officers of the Crown to put the penalty into effect. Penal transportation of prisoners was a Home Office responsibility, and a directive of 1835 insisted that those sentenced to transportation must be sent to the hulks in Britain and thence to such destinations as Her Majesty—in the person of John Capper, Superintendent of Convicts at the Home Office—should direct. Consequently, previous warrants and conditional pardons authorising penal transportation from Canada had required that the prisoner should 'suffer himself to be transported' to whatever place Her Majesty should direct. Thus, when the governor of Lower Canada sent three dozen civilians destined for the penal colonies to the hulks in England in May 1837, there had been no suggestion of illegality, although these civilians were shipped out just in time to avoid a new Home Office directive which prohibited any more convicts being transported from the North American colonies.

When Lord Durham arrived in Quebec in May 1838, he was unaware of the legal conventions and the prohibition on penal transportation. For him, the pressing issue was how to deal with eight political prisoners from the rebellion in Lower Canada still without trial. Rather than risk a jury acquitting these men, Durham hastily passed an ordinance to allow them to be transported to Bermuda for life. He did not consult the British government. Nor did he consult the governor of Bermuda, who promptly freed the prisoners when they arrived, saying that Lord Durham had 'no power to impose restrictions on prisoners with a view to their destiny in Bermuda'.[30] His view was upheld by the Law Officers of the Crown, with the Attorney-General elaborating this point in a statement to parliament. The precedent was firmly established that the powers of a colonial governor related only to legislative matters within the colony; that he could not dispose of his prisoners to another colony; that he could authorise banishment out of his jurisdiction, but not to another place. By the time Arthur was negotiating to transport his own political prisoners, in September 1838, the British government had disallowed Durham's ordinance. The Governor-in-Chief immediately resigned his post in a fit of rage and returned to England, to Arthur's barely disguised delight.

Mindful of the embarrassment to his *bête noire*, Arthur demanded assurance that there would not be a legal hitch should he send his prisoners to England to be transported to Van Diemen's Land. He was promised that, despite the Home Office prohibition on convicts from North America, there could be no legal impediment to his sending to England fourteen men from the Short Hills raid, plus another nine from the original rebellion, to the hulks.[31] This was not so, as it transpired.

3

Mr Capper's Discretion

FOURTEEN OF THE Short Hills raiders, chained together in pairs, made the trip to England on the *Captain Ross*. With them went another nine of the original Toronto political rebels, who had been sentenced under the special act (Vic. 1, c. 3) which allowed them to admit their guilt and ask for a pardon before being arraigned in court.[1] Also travelling to England on the *Captain Ross* were a number of civil prisoners from Lower Canada, all French-Canadians, whom Lieutenant-Governor Colborne had managed to slip on board in defiance of the Home Office prohibition. The Lower Canada prisoners were the source of great indignation on the part of the political prisoners, who considered it an insult that they had common felons— thieves and murderers and highwaymen—thrust among them. At the very least, Linus Miller consoled himself, they did not have to commune with these felons, since they spoke no English.

Not long out of Quebec, when the crew were debilitated with cold, the Patriots plotted to seize the ship and sail to New York, or so Linus Miller claimed. The incipient mutiny was nipped in the bud by the captain, acting on information from Jacob Beemer. Each chained pair of men was dragged on deck and interrogated. Benjamin Wait was astonished by the ludicrous supposition that a ship could be taken by a group of unarmed and manacled men. His explanation was that Beemer had manufactured the story, attempting to ingratiate himself in the hope of a pardon. This would seem to be the more likely explanation. According to Wait, Miller was too debilitated by seasickness to leave his bunk to plot any supposed mutiny.

Once in England, both groups of political prisoners set about petitioning for their release on the grounds that their transportation was illegal. Wait addressed letters to influential radical members of parliament, Joseph Hume and John Arthur Roebuck, 'liberal spirits, who had so long stood up in the British Parliament, as the unbiased champions of reform, and the undaunted opposers of an evil, iniquitous ministry' (174). Wait pleaded that the Short Hills prisoners had been tried under an Act passed just before their trial, which had not yet received the sanction of the Queen:

> I appealed on the score of fellow feeling, and earnestly solicited their aid, in bringing our cases before the eye of the government; so that, in the event of our sentences being carried fully into effect, there might be no ground upon which the *British* ministry could get rid of the onus of an illegal transportation. [174]

He also drew attention to the nine prisoners who had entered into a pre-trial compact with the governor.

Hume responded with an encouraging letter, while Roebuck engaged a solicitor to represent the Canadian political prisoners. With the notable exception of Beemer, all the men signed an agreement with Roebuck's agent. The radical parliamentarian made his appearance at the gaol not long after. In order to procure information to bring a writ of habeas corpus before the Queen's Bench, Roebuck conferred with Wait, who represented the Short Hills men, and with John Parker, representing the prisoners from Toronto. Wait felt that the visit of such an eminent parliamentarian was most encouraging, but also problematic, since Roebuck was persuaded by Parker that the Toronto prisoners had a stronger case, because the Short Hills men had received a trial, and the others had not. Roebuck quickly grasped the point that the latter nine men had sentences given under an *ex post facto* law, which was directly opposed to the spirit of the British code. The sentence of the Short Hills men 'was illegal and unjust', Roebuck admitted to Wait, but their cases were not so clear cut, 'for, by the time we were captured, Sir George Arthur had become somewhat more way-wise' (179).

Roebuck explained that the cost involved in applying for writs of habeas corpus meant that only twelve would be able to apply for a writ and be taken to London for investigation and special pleadings before the Queen's Bench. On the basis of Parker's representation all nine of the *ex post facto* prisoners were selected by Roebuck, and three others: Linus Miller, William Reynolds and John Grant. This separation of the cases gave Wait great concern—which proved well-founded—since Wait and the remaining Short Hills men were transferred to the hulks at Portsmouth on 5 January 1838. Wait understood that 'those prison ships were only regarded as receptacles for men whose cases were positively decided' and that being sent to the hulks meant they were slated for transportation:

> I felt it a duty to draw up a protest against a removal, intimating that if we yielded at all, it would be on the ground of *expediency*. This paper was presented at the Queen's bench, when the Attorney general pledged his honor, 'that, although the government views them as being *in transitu*, none should be sent away until each has his case thoroughly investigated.' [188]

Wait had every right to be anxious. His case, and that of his companions on the *York* hulk, was never investigated. Once the Patriots arrived at the hulks they quickly found that the distinction they had consistently made between themselves as 'state prisoners' and ordinary felons was not a distinction made by the Superintendent of Convicts, Mr Capper. On arrival at the *York*, their names were read out with a recommendation from the gaoler in Liverpool that they were men of 'property, respectability and family' and of very high character, 'intelligent, *praying* men'. Wait was at first amused by this palaver about character, especially on the lips of 'men who could not be supposed to possess any but the most heinous' (203, 204). He came to see that this was no mere burlesque but a crucial aspect of the hulk regime where 'every *thing* must have a character, and *that* is one great point of their system of prison discipline' (204). To be reduced to a *thing*, Wait discovered, was the purpose of the hulks. The men were stripped, shorn, clothed in the hulk dress—'every article of which was marked, remarked and marked again with the "crows foot" '—and placed in irons:

> The apparel of these hulks I viewed as a peculiar badge of disgrace, and the iron band as the stern token of unmitigated slavery. And it was not with much calmness, that I regarded the progress made ... to assimilate us, as much as possible to the condition, *character* and appearance of the 'world's most degraded wretches,' preparatory to their immersing us into [an] undistinguishable state of debasement. [205]

The Patriots protested, of course, sending letters of complaint—signed by all except Beemer—to Joseph Hume and to the Home Secretary, Lord John Russell, insisting that as prisoners of state they should not be treated as felons. Their protest bought a personal visit from Mr Capper, who made sympathetic noises, but did nothing to mitigate their debasement.

In late January the application for habeas corpus before the Queen's Bench failed, with the court maintaining that the detention of the prisoners in England was valid. The court made no distinction between the prisoners in terms of their legal proceedings in Upper Canada, nor did they make a ruling on the validity of the sentence of transportation.[2] An appeal to the Court of the Exchequer was instigated on 24 January 1839, but the hearing was delayed as the court was in recess until April. The Home Office saw no grounds for concern in this appeal. Once it was known that the habeas corpus writs had failed, the Home Office arranged on 2 February for the *Marquis of Hastings* to be chartered as a convict ship to take 240 male convicts, including the Patriots at the *York* hulk, to Van Diemen's Land.[3]

In an attempt to stop the transportation of the American citizens, the US Ambassador to the Court of St James, Andrew Stevenson, requested an interview with the Home Secretary, Lord John Russell, on 13 February.[4]

Despite this informal intervention by the United States, and the loud protest from Wait, nine prisoners from the Short Hills were put aboard the ship on 13 March 1839. Two Patriots remained behind: Gemmell, who was in the prison hospital, and Beemer, who was busily trying to secure a pardon for having informed on his comrades on the *Captain Ross*. On 16 March the Colonial Office sent the clearance that the master of the *Marquis of Hastings* need be detained no longer and was to sail for Van Diemen's Land.[5]

As the Colonial Office had anticipated, the appeal to the Exchequer failed to reverse the decision of the Queen's Bench. The new Secretary of State for the Colonies, the Marquis of Normanby, was jubilant as he reported to Governor Arthur on 19 May that all difficulties respecting detention and transportation had been removed.[6] Lord John Russell instructed Mr Capper that the order for transportation was valid and would be put into effect as soon as practicable.[7] The only exception to transportation was the young American, William Reynolds (David Deal), who was issued a pardon on 9 May on account of his youth, after representation from Ambassador Stevenson.[8] Miller thought it was a bit rich that David Deal should be released. He was three years older than Miller and had been involved in the burning of the British ship *Caroline* that had sparked a still unresolved diplomatic incident between the United States and Britain. To avoid detection Deal had judiciously changed his name and lowered his age when arrested.

On instruction from President Van Buren, Stevenson had already tried informally to persuade the Prime Minister to release Linus Miller, but Lord Palmerston was adamant that he could not, because of the effect it would produce in Canada. The release of David Deal/William Reynolds, because of his youth, was the only concession the United States could wring out of him. As Stevenson wrote to the President: 'They seem to think that if they were to interpose as you suggest it might produce the state of things we all wish to avoid e.g. more bloodshed & excitement in Canada. I endeavored to enforce your views, but I fear without effect'.[9]

For all the confidence about transportation in the Home Office and Colonial Office, there was a fly in the ointment. Maule, the solicitor to Treasury, was anxious to see that Her Majesty's government would not be exposed to law suits for wrongful imprisonment, in addition to the considerable cost of transporting these political prisoners. In January that year the Chief Justice of Upper Canada Robinson had been utterly confident that Maule would 'oppose the release of the prisoners' and that he was happy with the legality of their transportation.[10] Yet Maule was not reassured by reassurance from Lord John Russell that the order for transportation was valid and would be put into effect, nor did he agree with a legal opinion to that effect by the Attorney-General sent to Treasury on 25 May. By June the Treasury concerns had infected the Law Officers, who now raised a concern that 'no law exists in Van Diemen's Land that would justify detention and punishment of these excepting such cases as has been convicted by due course of law'.[11] The Secretary of State for the Colonies was most unhappy at having to explain to the apoplectic Governor Arthur that he was forced to set the prisoners at liberty since, as matters stood, they could not be legally held in Van Diemen's Land. The choice for the government was to try them for treason (which would inevitably fail) or let them go. Prudently, Her Majesty's government chose the latter course.[12]

The initial pardon document, dated 9 July 1839, was written in the names of all the prisoners, beginning with the Short Hills prisoners, Linus Miller and John Grant, who were described as having been convicted of a felony and treason respectively. The warrant was signed by Lord John Russell and forwarded to the Sheriff of London. At some point however, the names of Grant and Miller were crossed out. On 10 July their names had been removed from the pardon documentation.[13] Why? The most obvious answer is that they had been tried in the court at Niagara and thus arguably they could be legally restrained in Van Diemen's Land. Nevertheless, Linus Miller had been tried under the problematic Lawless Aggressions Act that the British Law Officers had consistently deemed to be improper. After lengthy disputation with the authorities in Upper Canada, the Law Officers reluctantly conceded that the colonial authorities could proceed with the Act using the option of court martial, but this concession did not apply to the Americans from the Short Hills.[14] On the strength of their opinion about the Lawless Aggressions Act, the Law Officers could well have concluded that the governor in Van Diemen's Land had no authority in law to hold the Americans convicted by a civil court under that act. They may well have expected that Governor Franklin would discharge the American prisoners. In his own hyperbolic account, Miller says that his English supporters had not made a separate case for the Short Hills prisoners, as they had full expectation that he and Grant would be pardoned, on much the same grounds as the others. He claims to have been told by his radical friends '"the government will never be mean enough to transport you, if all the others with whom you have been so long connected . . . are discharged, and you will, as a matter of course, be pardoned *free gratis*"' (218). This reasoning, however, turned out to be 'poor logic' (218).

Ambassador Stevenson tried again to get a pardon for Miller once he heard about the pardons for the nine Canadians, arguing that the pardon for David Deal/William Reynolds had 'the best effect in kindling kind feeling of the whole of the country toward Her Majesty', and he promised Lord John Russell that he personally would give 'security for his never entering the Canadian provinces'.[15] In Miller's opinion, Stevenson 'might as well have believed that his Satanic Majesty would engage in the Bible trade, as that the British government would do an act of either justice or mercy, unless compelled'. He thought the government was enraged at having to liberate the others, so was determined to punish Grant and himself 'out of mere spite' (219). Whatever his reasoning, Lord John Russell remained unmoved by Stevenson's pleas.

The real problem facing Her Majesty's government was that it had already transported the other Short Hills men to Van Diemen's Land and would certainly face suits of wrongful imprisonment if Miller and Grant were pardoned. So on 5 August 1839, these two were dispatched to the *York* hulk at Portsmouth, where they joined Gemmell, who was still in hospital, and Beemer, who was still trying to negotiate a pardon for having informed on his fellow Patriots on the *Captain Ross*. In despair Miller wrote letters to Joseph Hume and John Roebuck.

Like his compatriots before him, Miller found the forced degradation of the hulks terrifying and humiliating. With only Grant as company he could find no safety in numbers. Miller, a fastidious young man of twenty, may have been especially at risk of sexual exploitation. This was an aspect of life on the hulks which most shocked and repelled him:

> Vice and crime of the most revolting nature, such as called down the vengeance of heaven upon ancient Sodom and Gomorrah, are prevalent to an alarming extent ... the natural result of herding depraved men together in such a system—a system which ensures not only their entire ruin in this world, but, what is of far more importance, in that which is to come. [237]

Rather than present himself as cowed or victimised by the weight of the systematic dehumanisation of the hulks, Miller claimed that he and Grant hatched a plan to escape. It was foiled at the last minute when Beemer got wind of it and, true to form, informed on them to the authorities. We have only Miller's word for this escape plan; it may well have been just another case of retrospective wish fulfillment.

In Miller's account of himself he conjured this bold escape plan, foiled only by the ubiquitous villain Beemer, to confirm his status as a true American; a *man* who would never *willingly* submit to degradation and slavery.

In September, before any more petitions could be got up or any other loopholes about the legality of their transportation exploited, the remaining Short Hills men were transferred to the convict ship *Canton*, 'with about as much ceremony as would have been shown to as many swine', Miller wrote (241). At half past ten on Sunday, 22 September, the ship weighed anchor. To the customary sea shanty of the sailors, the *Canton* sailed out of Portsmouth harbour and it seemed to Miller that 'the anchor of hope, which held my soul to earth, was being torn from the rock of faith, and confidence in God' (244).

For the swashbuckling Miller, life at sea on a convict ship bought the greatest humiliation. The revolting spectre of seasickness in confined spaces was bad enough, but the real horror of this 'floating hell' was the company he was forced to keep:

> The most horrid blasphemy and disgusting obscenity, from daylight in the morning till ten o'clock at night, were, without one moment's cessation, ringing in my ears. The general conversation of these wretched men, related to the crimes of which they professed to have been guilty, and he whose life had been most iniquitous was esteemed the best man. I tried to close my ears and shut my eyes against all, but found this a difficult task . . . [246]

That he should be so lucky! those on the *Marquis of Hastings* might have said. They had endured a horror trip to Van Diemen's Land that had almost killed them. Benjamin Wait described the situation on the *Marquis of Hastings* as almost unendurable:

> The hospital incumbents were daily increasing, until the salt waves closed over thirty unhappy victims of cruelty and starvation. Vermin, the most loathed of all objects to an American, generated too, in such abundance, that our beds and clothing became literally alive with them. My dreams were always about them, and I would often awake in the act of killing them. . . . scurvy broke out among us, and continued to carry off the poor fellows long after we had landed . . . [251–2]

When the *Marquis of Hastings* arrived in July 1839, so great was the concern for the condition of the convict cargo landed in Hobart that an inquiry was instituted into the management of the ship. Predictably, the Surgeon Superintendent attributed 'this great and unusual mortality' to 'the prevalence of wet and cold weather', rather than venal ineptitude on the part of the master and the surgeon.[16] On arrival Wait, Chandler, McLeod, McNulty and Van Camp were hospitalised, near death. The first two did recover, but McLeod, McNulty and Van Camp died soon after in hospital.

Miller and his companions on the *Canton* were fortunate that the worst they had to endure was the boisterous company of felons. The ship's diet, Miller allowed, was unusually good, the prisoners were kept on deck for quite long periods and good health was maintained throughout the voyage. In praising the ship's surgeon, Miller was probably unaware that the surgeon was paid a bonus for every convict disembarked healthy in the antipodes. Still, Miller was in no way inclined to complain about the ship's officers. He reserved all his high-minded scorn for the intemperate 'herd of criminals'. They gave him plenty to write about:

> Although the quantity of wine allowed each man was small, its effects were always visible for a few succeeding hours. Loud talk, singing songs, spinning yarns, altercations, and fighting, were the order of the day the moment the

wine was served out. I have often counted a dozen men settling their little quarrels at such times. A ring around the belligerent was always formed on these occasions by the 'lookers-on,' and seconds duly appointed to see *fair play*. The practice of fighting, among the lower classes of the English and Irish, is far more common than with my countrymen. Indeed, I do not recollect having seen but three or four instances of this disgraceful practice during my life in my own country. [248]

The *Canton* arrived in Van Diemen's Land on 12 January 1840, taking three months less than the *Marquis of Hastings* to complete the journey from Portsmouth. The Patriot prisoners knew little about their destination, but had already formed very negative opinions about the place, which they believed bore the stamp of the despotic and bloodthirsty George Arthur. With characteristic flourish, Miller expressed his sense of foreboding approaching landfall:

Land! Land! Van Dieman's Land! How the word flies through the ship! What feelings of pleasure, or horror, thrill the breasts of the various inhabitants of our little floating world! The captain, the British officer, and the kind hearted surgeon pace the quarter deck with quick step, occasionally taking a look through the glass, and exchange glances of mutual satisfaction as the wind freshens on our starboard quarter. The soldiers and sailors, forgetting their usual jealousies, crowd together on the forecastle, and anxiously watch to catch a glimpse of their common mother earth, and talk of anticipated pleasures. But the poor prisoner, the convict, where is he? Does *he* strain his eyes to descry the cursed shores ... the future, its dark and cruel uncertainty, the years of hopeless misery and woe, shame, degradation and death, haunt his gloomy spirit, and he bitterly curses *'the land!'*—*'the land!'* [254]

4

Great Hunt in the North Woods

Rather than defuse Patriot agitation, the severe sentences handed down to the Short Hills men inflamed Patriot passions further. All along the border the Hunters' Lodges were spoiling for action. Daniel Heustis had been among fifty Patriots who assembled at Watertown in August 1838 with the intention of marching to Niagara to save the condemned Patriots captured in the Short Hills, only to be foiled when their comrades were moved out of danger to Fort Henry in Kingston. Pressure was exerted on the Patriot leadership for concerted action. In September there was a national convention of Hunters in Cleveland to plan for the liberation of Canada.[1] By November 1838 it was decided that the time had come to mount a real invasion. The immediate object was the town of Prescott on the Canadian side of the St Lawrence, where there was a small fort, believed to be the key to controlling Upper Canada. During November men from various Hunters' Lodges began converging on Sackets Harbor in New York State. It was understood that arms and ammunition would be brought from the south by boat and transferred to two small schooners, both named *Charlotte*. The main Patriot force was to seize control of the civilian steamer *United States* on its regular run between Sackets Harbor and Prescott on the Canadian shore. At Prescott the Patriot army planned to seize Fort Wellington and once this was accomplished, all three vessels would be used to ferry reinforcements across the St Lawrence from Ogdensburg.[2]

William Gates, foundation member of the Hunters' Lodge at Cape Vincent, was keen to translate the ideology of incarnate republicanism into virtuous action. He was aware that some among the Patriot Hunters regarded the invasion as an opportunity for adventure and plunder, but Gates insisted that 'the precarious prospects of booty' could never have induced him to leave his family (14). It was philanthropy, pure and simple, which thrust him into the action. 'I felt impelled by a sense of duty for the good of others, to assist in securing for them the same blessings which I was myself enjoying', he explained. He gave little thought for his own danger but was impelled by the thought that in the future, he could claim to have been 'one of those who aided in securing full liberty to Canada's sons and daughters' (14).

On 11 November, the captain of the *United States* was only a little surprised when about one hundred and fifty young men without luggage came aboard, nor was he alarmed when another large group boarded at Cape Vincent. These men included Daniel Heustis and William Gates, who was in charge of the action on the *United States*. A curious New York banker observed that these young men were very reserved, later reporting that they 'said little and drank nothing'.[3] Gates was the first to admit that, as the happy band of Hunters sailed past the myriad of islands in the St Lawrence on that bright moonlit evening, there was no thought that their noble cause might fail:

> We believed we were about to do our neighbors a deed of charity, such as the golden rule inculcates, when it teaches us to do to our fellows as we would they should do to us. We believed our Canadian neighbors to be struggling for that freedom which we were enjoying, and which with a little aid they would be successful in securing. Was it therefore wrong that we should stifle our feelings and refuse to *act* out our sympathy? For one, I can place no credit in that charity which does not exhibit itself by its works. [13]

The captain was so little concerned by his passengers that he agreed to tow the two *Charlottes* to Ogdensburg, but he was mightily surprised a few hours later when most of the silent young men transferred to the schooners amid much argument from those who refused to go. Heustis reported that at this point the Patriots were deserted by about half their force. Despite threats and entreaties, only about two hundred men transferred to the *Charlottes*, which were cut free from the ferry and headed for Prescott. At this point everything began to unravel. The two schooners ran aground on a mud bank at Ogdensburg and only one was re-floated the next morning.

At 10 am on 12 November, the first *Charlotte* deposited its cargo of men at Windmill Point on the opposite shore, just a mile from Prescott. Lost to them, on the second *Charlotte*, were nearly all their stores, ammunition, guns and artillery pieces. Command of the party was assumed by a supposed Polish nobleman, Nils Von Schoultz, whose military training told him that the windmill provided an almost impregnable position. He was not to know that the news of their invasion had reached Prescott where the soldiers of the 83rd Regiment were preparing for battle, but Von Schoultz wisely directed the men to fortify the mill in order to secure their position.[4]

General Birge, the commander of the force, became ill almost immediately the invasion force left; rather than proceed to Prescott, he returned to Ogdensburg, promising to come back with reinforcements. The company was made up of less than two hundred men, nearly one-third of whom were under the age of twenty-one. A British gunboat, which had been alerted to trouble, patrolled the narrow St Lawrence, harassing any further attempts to land, while the Patriots looked desperately to their fellow Hunters for reinforcements. One very angry young man in the party was Stephen Wright, a 25-year-old carpenter from Denmark in Lewis County, New York. Like most of his anxious compatriots, Wright had been assured that Upper Canada 'could be taken without the discharge of a gun, and that thousands of the people of the frontier were ready, and would join us as soon as the standard of liberty had been raised upon her shackled soil' (5). Already he was bitterly disillusioned:

> Our leaders proved themselves utterly unequal to the task of directing or guiding the men under their control, and it is a startling fact, that previous to our leaving the Harbor, they knew not where we were to land, or to what particular point we were bound. This inability on their part produced confusion; and ultimately resulted in the ruin of those . . . led to volunteer their efforts to achieve the emancipation of an oppressed people, under the guidance of men who lacked both the energy and *common sense* necessary for success. [5]

Gates also came to the cruel realisation that the Patriots he had so avidly embraced were in dire straits, with not a solitary Canadian coming to their side. Consequently he and his comrades were forced to rely on their own scant resources in hostile territory:

> Yet our hearts fainted not, though deserted by friends and left on foreign soil, with no prospect of effecting anything decisive in our then situation. . . . We had expected large companies to follow us, enough to have made a triumphant ingress, and which would have enabled us to make such a stand in the country that all who wished could have joined us. With the faint hope that some of them would remember their solemn protestations, and evading the surveillance, join our standard—we toiled that night with all our alacrity in the strengthening of our position. [19]

Confident that those who had sought American intervention would still rally to the cause, Von Schoultz decided that the Patriots must make a stand. Amid cheers from his army, as well as the watchers on the opposite shore, he unfurled the Patriot flag and prepared to make a stand in and around the mill. By the morning of 13 November the regulars of the 83rd Regiment, together with the militia now swollen to two thousand by eager volunteers, had surrounded the windmill and begun a siege. As the battle progressed, the greatly outnumbered Patriots could hear the cheers from their comrades watching on the beach across the water at Ogdensburg. According to the editor of Ogdensburg's paper, nearly every man and woman in the town had dropped the business of the day in favour of 'gossip and sightseeing'.[5] Wright found this vocal encouragement all the more galling, since those men 'whose tongues could beguile so successfully had not the moral courage to aid us in the hour of trial' (7).

On the night of 14 November, after the British and militia retreated, the Patriots made further attempts to get reinforcements and medical aid. Wright recounted how one man had swum the near-freezing river 'when the frost glassed the pebbles of the shore' and received no help, only 'rotten and faithless promises' (9). Wright was even more outraged by the exhibition of the Canadians he had come to liberate. In a break in hostilities, the militia, 'like so many harpies' (9), engaged in a looting spree among the dead bodies on the field of battle. Revolted by the spectacle, Wright reflected on the awful irony that 'these were the men that we came to fight for, and to succor from the galling yoke of the tyrant!' (10).

Gates, with two others, undertook to get medicine and surgical supplies, launching an old yawl they found half submerged in the sand. The ancient craft immediately started taking water before they reached the United States, and Gates and his companions were taken prisoners aboard a British gunboat. Gates insisted that they were actually in American territory and arrested illegally. Not that he expected this to carry any weight in his favour, since he believed the government of President Van Buren 'would permit down right murder to go unavenged' (21). An American relief party did manage to land at the windmill later the following night, but the besieged men declined the offer of escape, wishing instead to demonstrate the heroic character of American republicanism. Wright probably expressed the view of many in that 'Spartan band' (6) huddled behind the stone walls of the mill when he characterised the battle as a contest between the unmanly Canadians and manly republicans, as embodied in the form of Colonel Von Schoultz: 'brave and daring to a fault . . . with firm and graceful limbs, with a well-bred gentleness in his manners, and an eye which blazed in its own liquid light' (6).

Masculine virtue proved no match for two eighteen-pound guns firing at close range. On 16 November the Patriots surrendered, with twenty dead and many others wounded. Thirteen of the British and militia were dead, including one British officer whose body was said to have been mutilated, a charge Wright hotly disputed. The damage to the dead officer's penis was the work of wild hogs that the Patriots had been unable to fend off, Wright insisted. Since a similar thing happened at a subsequent Patriot battle—also attributed to the pigs—it is tempting to see such mutilation as the ultimate expression of manly disgust at those who would be governed by a woman.

One hundred and sixty men were taken prisoner, tied by rope in single file and marched to Fort Henry at Kingston. For the dejected Patriots this was the ultimate humiliation. Heustis was appalled at the response of the people that he had fondly thought himself to be liberating from vile tyranny. The Canadian citizenry who lined the route, some of whom were known to Heustis, displayed no admiration for his efforts. Instead they reacted with violent hostility, and he was 'subjected to the foulest abuse from the spectators, pelted with clubs, and spit upon with impunity' (61).

If popular response in Upper Canada was hostile, it was not much better across the border in the United States. The press did admire the courage (some said foolhardiness) of the Patriots, though the reports gave the sense that the Patriots got what they deserved. As the *Oswego County Whig* put it:

> we do hope it will teach our honest sympathizers to withhold their sympathies and assistance from a race of men who have proved themselves unworthy of either—who have seen these men risking their lives for their benefit, without an exertion on their part to help themselves, and have tacitly yielded up these friends to a cruel and ignominious death, without a struggle in their behalf . . . Pearls should not be cast before swine, and blessings should not be forced upon a people who cannot appreciate or retain them. They live like dogs, and if they are dogs, they should wear the collar.[6]

The Battle of the Windmill finally moved the US government to be serious about its neutrality agreement with the Canadian provinces. A proclamation of 21 November from President Van Buren made it clear that any American citizen who invaded a friendly neighbour, in violation of the country's Neutrality Act, would forfeit his claim to protection and could expect no legal interference from the United States government on his behalf.[7] And so it was. The arrested Patriots found themselves entirely on their own, tried as piratical invaders under the problematic Lawless Aggressions Act.

To serve as judge advocate, Lieutenant-Governor Arthur chose Lieutenant-Colonel William Draper, who also happened to be the colony's Attorney-General. Draper had determinedly defended the Lawless Aggressions Act against the Law Officers of the Crown, having finally worn them down to reluctantly agree that they would not disallow the Act on condition that the authorities use courts martial rather than civil trials. The choice of such a senior legal figure indicated that Arthur understood the importance of these courts martial, and the possibility that the radicals in the British parliament would scrutinise proceedings looking for any legal loophole. Also present at the courts martial was a lawyer, John Macdonald, who had been engaged to help the Patriots' defence.

Heustis had no hesitation in condemning these hastily convened courts martial as arbitrary and illegal. In his view it was little different from the reign of terror in revolutionary France and his captors were 'the Robespierres of Canada' (72). Seventeen of the prisoners agreed to turn Queen's evidence and 140 men faced court martial. They were tried in batches of four or five, occasionally more, after first being interviewed by a Queen's Counsel. Prisoners could not be represented in court. Gates's description of a perfunctory court martial is consistent with his fellow Patriots' accounts:

> Our indictment being read, we were severally asked, 'Guilty? or Not Guilty?' 'Not Guilty,' was our response. The Queen's witness was asked if he recognized us; to which he replied, 'I do not.' No other questions were asked, and we were remanded back to our prison room, wondering what the sentence of the court would be on such overwhelming testimony! In a similar manner were all our comrades tried, often a dozen or fifteen at a batch, whilst the whole time occupied, from the moment they left the room till their return to it again, would not exceed generally over one hour. [47]

The trial reports agree that all the evidence against them was given by the same handful of turncoat Patriots. However, contrary to the Patriot accounts, the records show that they were permitted to give their own defence and to cross-examine the witnesses. There are many other inconsistencies, not the least of which was that Gates pleaded guilty and said in his defence that he was an unwilling participant, forced into the fray. He claimed that he had been misled by a man named Prendagast who told him 'we were only going up to the lake and would not have to fight', he told the court:

> We were put aboard a schooner down in the hold and our lives were threatened if we offered to land I was told only after by Prendagast that we were going to Prescott. Several men myself amongst them begged hard to be let go. Prendagast said there would be no danger that he would not take us where there would be a shot fired. He said he would not ask one to set a foot in Canada's shore until he did himself.[8]

This account of his action is a far cry from the heroic tale of the moonlight voyage to liberate his benighted neighbours offered in Gates's retrospective narrative. The same was true of fiery Heustis, who pleaded not guilty, but offered the defence that he was with the Patriots by accident and had no intention of taking part in any action. His was a common defence: that he was on board the schooner as a passenger to Ogdensburg, having paid one dollar for his fare. He had been confined on board, Heustis swore, and had refused to disembark until forced to do so. At the windmill he had not taken arms and had merely 'assisted in laying stones at the mill door'.[9] None of the Patriots admitted to having carried arms or willingly engaged in battle. Most insisted they had been forced into participation, like Wright, who denied taking arms and claimed he was in a house upstairs keeping out of the way until he was wounded and captured.[10] James Inglis, a Scot, said he had not fired his gun except to drive off a hog tearing at the dead body of a British officer. John Swanberg gave vent to a common feeling of disillusion, when he closed his defence by stating that 'if the people of Canada wanted a change of government they should get it for themselves'.[11] Such protestations of innocence and mislaid trust were not accepted by the court. The men were all found guilty of piratical invasion of Canada.

A common and insistent thread in the narratives is that no sentence was ever formally passed by the courts martial. In this respect Heustis was speaking for his fellows when he reported the proceedings:

> After the farcical ceremony of examining the witnesses, the members of the court busied themselves for about two minutes and a half, apparently in a very profound exchange of opinions among themselves, and then we were remanded to our prison again, without any intimation as to what the verdict was; and never, from that day to this, has it been communicated to us, or any sentence passed upon us, though we have seen and felt some things that have induced us to believe that we were adjudged guilty. [78]

There could be some truth in this. It does appear from the trial records that sentencing was held over, and the men may not have been present when the sentences were confirmed. The narratives report that every Wednesday death warrants were sent to the High Sheriff and it was by only this means they knew they had received capital sentences. 'Not one of us', Gates wrote, 'knew but the next Wednesday was to seal his fate with a death warrant. This was a suspense that added very much to our mental sufferings' (48). The information of the number to be hanged was given to the prisoners on the Wednesday evening, but no names were given until the following morning when the sheriff would read the warrants. Those whose names were listed were taken to the condemned cells, where they usually remained four days, awaiting execution. By December 1838 eleven men had been executed and the remainder lingered in Fort Henry under sentence of death.

If Governor Arthur was nervous about the response of the US government to his strong medicine, he was firmly reassured by the British Ambassador to Washington that his 'severe and just chastisement' was well calculated 'to make the Americans understand that to wage a privateering war against Her Majesty's peaceful subjects ... is something more than a mere idle frolic'. Ambassador Fox knew that a great deal of pressure had been put on the US President to intervene, especially from the border states, which had been 'steadfastly refused'. President Van Buren's refusal to intervene had cost him 'a vast deal of annoyance and trouble and no inconsiderable loss of popularity and political influence' in an election year, Fox reported. Van Buren's personal opinion was that a show of clemency would be the best way to undermine hostility toward Canada, but here Fox vehemently disagreed. 'A man must be blind', he wrote, 'who would expect that British authorities should be able by gentle means to repress the detestable crusade against Canada'. Nor was the ambassador swayed by the argument that the men who invaded Windmill Point believed they were responding to the request of the Upper Canadians: 'If an assassin breaks into a house at night and murders his wife and family, it will hardly be accepted as a defense for the assassin that he thought the man wished his family to be murdered.' In his view every one of those raiders not hung should be sentenced to transportation for life, since this penalty above all was 'regarded with extreme terror by the Americans'.[12]

Even as the courts martial at Kingston were dispensing their rough justice, with no protest from the government of the United States, there was another farcical invasion at Windsor, just across Lake St Clair from Detroit. On 3 December, Detroit citizens were treated to a parade of Patriots, about four hundred strong, led by self-styled Patriot General L. V. Bierce, in preparation for an assault across the border. Among them was Samuel Snow, a married man with several children, from Strongsville, Ohio. Snow later claimed that he was 'responding to a call that 'Liberty—the inestimable birthright of man—was unknown on the other side of Lake Erie' (3).

At the Detroit docks General Bierce commandeered the steamer *Champlain* that had been laid up for the winter, and embarked about one hundred and fifty men. Crowds of spectators cheered as the lines were cast off, and the hometown supporters could still be seen and heard shouting encouragement when a shower of flames announced the arrival of the Patriots on the Canadian side of the narrow divide. Aboard the steamer was Elijah Woodman, a 42-year-old farmer and lumberman, who had fled from Upper Canada following reprisals for his support of the rebels in 1837. In the account he later wrote in gaol, he claimed that he had boarded the *Champlain* only because he wished to get back to his family and he was told it was going to the Black River in Canada. Taking a seat in the aft of the steamer he found himself next to Robert Marsh, a 25-year-old from Detroit who seemed to Woodman 'a fine young man who would not deceive me'. He was alarmed when the boat landed near Windsor, everyone was ordered to get aboard a smaller boat and the officers were told 'to shoot down every man that left the ranks'.[13]

Woodman's account of being forced into battle may sound like *ex post facto* defence, and was probably written for that purpose. The same story is told by a good many of the men tried after the Windsor debacle. However

Robert Marsh's retrospective account makes no mention of this. Nor do any other contemporaneous accounts. The first act of the invasion was to set fire to a small steamer, burn down the militia barracks in which two men were burnt to death, and torch two houses, as well as shoot dead an unarmed black man who expressed monarchist sympathies. This does not read like the work of an army of unwilling participants.

Having shown that the Patriots meant business, General Bierce read out a proclamation written by the son of the executed rebel, Samuel Lount, telling the Upper Canadians that the Americans had come to restore the liberty that a tyrannical oligarchy had destroyed. In a small apple orchard on the waterfront, clearly visible to the cheering throng across the river, the Patriots ran up their flag. Yet no Canadians made any moves in their direction. It was a far cry from the righteous cause in which Samuel Snow thought he had enlisted in the Patriot service, 'only wishing that our Canadian neighbors might, in the end, enjoy the same civil, religious, and political freedom, with which the citizens of the United States were blest' (3).

The invasion force was poorly armed and many had no arms at all, merely long poles with a lance on the end. Since Bierce had sent the steamer away, no provision had been made for a safe retreat. Marsh felt his republican fervour drain away when he realised the Patriot force could expect no help from the Canadians. He looked expectantly in the direction of his fellow republicans swinging their hats and cheering from the top of buildings on the Detroit shore, but was sorely disappointed. Still resolute however, he chose to remain rather than cross back into American territory. Showing their determination to act, the Patriots raised the Patriot flag, Marsh reported, just as they came under attack by the British army and militia:

> seeing their determination to surround us, after seven or eight rounds we thought it best to occupy the woods, three-fourths of a mile from our stand. We had likewise been disappointed in the approach of our rear-guard, for we had taken up our line of march in two divisions, Gen. B. was with the latter. . . . when they discovered his determination to retreat, he was addressed by men in tears as follows:—'For God sake do not leave our party who have already commenced the action, for unless we advance to their aid they will all be cut off!' But he could not be persuaded to advance. . . . Will you believe me when I say for the rising generation as well as many of this, that have been imposed upon by designing sycophants, that the cause of the failure was not because Canada did not want freedom, but because of bribery, cowardice, and a false pretension to greatness and ability, in some of the leading characters. [23–4]

Following pitched battle with the militia led by Colonel John Prince, conducted in full view of the cheering crowd across the river, the Patriots surrendered. Twenty-one Patriots died in this battle, while another five Patriot prisoners were shot by Colonel Prince when he applied his own version of running the gauntlet for the edification of the watching crowd. Prince gave the American prisoners the chance to run for their lives and if they cleared the fence before being shot they were free to go. None reached the fence.[14] Four militia men were killed, including a surgeon who was said to have been mutilated by the hogs.

Forty-four prisoners, ten of whom were under twenty years old, were manacled and taken to London in Upper Canada for court martial. Marsh was entirely unprepared for the degradation of life as a state prisoner, marching in single file with a large body of dragoons on either side. According to his account, the party was constantly forced to stop at every grog shop because he was told it 'was against the law to pass without calling'. While the guards stoked up on rum, Marsh and his companions were obliged 'to sit, (it is hard to tell how long,) shivering and some freezing for a long hour, when the orders were "ready, march!"' (33–4). After sitting repeatedly for hours in the freezing cold and bound tight together with irons, some in the group could not stand upright. Woodman was one who suffered very badly from swollen and frozen feet. That night they were accommodated in a small room on the beach of Lake Erie without heating or bedding of any kind, and manacled together by twos. Being manacled made sleeping very difficult, as Marsh recalled:

> if one should stir in the least without the knowledge of the other it would cause him to cry out, 'you are tearing my ankle or wrist off,' and perhaps one would want to get up to go to the *tub* which was sitting in one corner of the *same room*, but could not go without his mate, who was perhaps asleep, and in getting to it, obliged to pass over others, that were sleeping, causing them to cry out, 'get off! Oh God! you are killing me!' others, 'you are breaking my legs!' 'you are breaking my head!' 'Oh! get off my arms!' &c. &c.; but to the tub must go; which frequently was not emptied until the contents were all over the floor, and running under us while sleeping. You may judge our room did not send forth a very savory smell. [36]

As they had been warned, the Windsor Patriots received no legal intervention on their behalf from their government. Marsh believed that President Van Buren had abandoned them to the untender mercies of the tyrants of Upper Canada, at the very same time as his son was in England, 'kissing the Queen's hand' (41). In fact, Van Buren did send his son who was in England to make an informal request for clemency with the British Prime Minister, Lord Palmerston, but he was careful not to make any public intervention.[15] Van Buren was in real fear of a war with Britain as tensions mounted over the disputed northeastern boundary, greatly exacerbated by the antics of the Hunters along the border. He could not afford to risk further enraging the British by offering any succour to those Americans who had violated the Neutrality Act.[16]

The courts martial in London presided over by two senior British officers began on 27 December. According to Snow's account, it was the same procedure as the courts martial at Kingston. A handful of prisoners at a time were called and witnesses for the Crown gave evidence against them. Snow claimed that prisoners were not permitted to interrogate the witnesses, yet this is belied by trial records. According to the transcripts, several of the Patriots, particularly Robert Marsh, who fancied himself as a man with legal knowledge, fully exercised their right to interrogate the witnesses against them. They also called witnesses in their own defence.

For his part, Snow denied being active in the battle, but he did admit to being a member of the Hunters' Lodge, unlike many of the others on trial, who insisted that they had been taken to Windsor against their will, or that they merely happened to be asleep on board the steamer when it was commandeered. Marsh denied all the charges and refused to make any statement about his involvement. 'I was so provoked I could not utter a word', he later wrote; 'besides I knew it was of no use for me to attempt to speak at any length, so I merely remarked, that it was useless for me, or any of the prisoners to say a word, for sentence was passed before we were brought into the presence of the court' (44). Others of the defendants reported that they had been promised hundreds of acres of land and payment of eight or nine dollars a month to join the foray. There was no expectation of any fighting, they said.[17]

Marsh never wavered from the view that the entire proceedings were illegal and the members of the court martial were 'in league to please their beloved Governor' (42). He described those empowered to hear the case as a dissolute lot who were forever taking adjournments to an anteroom where the grog was stored, leaving the prisoners standing in the witness box the whole time. 'We had suffered much, and many were very unwell; one man fainted, and was obliged to be carried out', Marsh recalled, 'yet there we had to stand during the whole trial' (44). This was especially hard on the two eldest Patriots, Chauncey Sheldon and Elijah Woodman, who were last to be tried. Moreover, the prisoners were intimidated by 'the gallows ... erected at the front of the gaol, close to the wall' (43), and as one lot of Patriots was being tried, they could hear the trapdoor drop as another of their companions was hanged.

Everyone who had not turned witness for the Queen was found guilty of the capital felony of piratical invasion. Both Snow and Marsh were adamant that no sentence was ever passed at the bar. As soon as a man was tried, Marsh wrote, he was ordered back to his cell 'without knowing what was to be his fate, until the sheriff came to the door, called a name, and read the warrant, which gave some twelve, and some twenty-four hours, to prepare for death' (44). When it came time for Woodman to contemplate his turn, two of his comrades had already been hanged. In his journal he confided his deepest fear that he would be buried with no ceremony, as these men had been, and his aged parents would never know what had become of him.[18] He later wrote to his parents that he had been prepared for death and had 'selected my funeral sermon to be preached at some future date in the new meeting house I had helped to build'.[19] When the date set down for Woodman's execution passed without incident, he wrote prophetically in his journal: 'I may perhaps be reserved for a worse fate, transportation to some outlandish place'.[20]

5

The Caprice of the Mercenaries of Royalty

THE COURTS MARTIAL at Kingston and London took place at the same time as the habeas corpus application to the Queen's Bench in England. Rattled by the attacks on the colonial administrations in both Upper and Lower Canada, the British government was especially anxious to limit the political fallout which would flow from overly punitive action in either colony. For his part, Lieutenant-Governor Arthur was in no mood to be lenient. He told the Secretary of State, Lord Glenelg, in no uncertain language that at least sixteen of the Patriot raiders must be hanged. These executions may have 'exceeded the limit Your Lordship would have prescribed', he wrote, but 'every class of humane person in Upper Canada' believed that he was being merciful. Respecting His Lordship's scruples about capital punishment, Arthur proposed that he might extend clemency to most of those tried, and for the most severe cases, transportation to some penal colony 'which they dread exceedingly'.[1] Lord Glenelg was determined to limit the number of executions that might flow from courts martial in Canada, which he felt cast the British government in a barbaric light. He had already somewhat reluctantly agreed to accept the transportation of political prisoners sentenced to death by courts martial in Lower Canada as an alternative to further executions. In his letter to the Lieutenant-Governor of Lower Canada, Sir John Colborne, Glenelg referred to the 'necessity of waiting for instructions before conveying the prisoners . . . you will of course send to this country'.[2] It seemed to Glenelg only prudent to extend the same provision to the governor of Upper Canada, and he reluctantly agreed to transportation for a percentage of the Patriot prisoners, even though he knew this course of action was 'replete with difficulty'.[3]

Having wrung the concession to pardon the Patriots on condition of transportation for life, Arthur agreed that about half of them—the youngest and least culpable—could be repatriated to the United States 'as a present to the President'. The United States must be taught to appreciate that 'Canadians are not to be had on easy terms', he told Glenelg.[4] He took to heart the advice of the British Ambassador to Washington, 'The penalty of transportation is regarded with extreme terror by the Americans',[5] and was happy that sending some eighty men to a penal colony at the end of the world would teach the Americans that armed incursion into Canada would not be tolerated.[6] Despite his hard line with Glenelg, Arthur understood that the Canadian appetite for retributive justice was more than satisfied and that further execution would not be acceptable. In Kingston, the newspapers had begun to urge a policy of tolerance, arguing that as 'a generous and brave people' who enjoyed 'just and equitable laws', Upper Canadians could not want to see 'undue severity'. The editor was quick to point out he did not speak on behalf of the misguided Americans; rather, he was anxious 'for the character of a great people and a powerful nation'. To execute any more prisoners found guilty, he believed, could not possibly 'add to the dignity of the Empire'.[7]

It remained the case that penal transportation posed a real dilemma for the British government. The 'difficulty' to which Glenelg had alluded was the habeas corpus applications before the court in England. In sending prisoners to England for transportation, as legally required, the government risked their being given liberty by the courts. Arthur was well aware of this complication. 'I have accordingly been restrained from sending to England any more convicts', he explained in a confidential letter to Governor Colborne, 'until I get further instruction'.[8]

The idea of getting a ship to take the Patriot prisoners direct from Canada to the penal colonies in Australia seems to have originated in an informal discussion between the Home Secretary, Lord John Russell, and others in the government of Lord Melbourne at the time the habeas corpus applications were being heard. In private letters between December 1838 and January 1839, Russell flagged the possibility of sending troops to Canada in the event of trouble on the disputed border between Maine and New Brunswick, where a war of words and threatened military action had erupted over the lumber and navigation rights along the St John's River and in the rich Aroostook Valley.[9] These hostilities brought with them a resurgence of Hunter activity in Maine and real fears of another war with Britain, as there appeared no satisfactory ground for settling the disputes through negotiation. In February 1839 the governor of Maine had dispatched the state militia to the scene of the dispute and the US Congress passed an appropriation of $10 000 000 for the defence of Maine.[10] The timing could not have been worse for the Patriot prisoners in Upper

Canada. Fearing an outbreak of another war with Britain, the US government felt constrained not to push for any more clemency for those of its misguided citizens imprisoned in Canada.

It was during discussions about army reinforcements for the New Brunswick border that Lord John Russell hinted that the troop ship which disembarked soldiers in Quebec could then take on board those convicted by courts martial in the provinces of Upper and Lower Canada and transport them directly to Australia. Russell was particularly keen that no more Canadian prisoners came to England to provide another *cause célèbre* for the radicals such as Hume and Roebuck, who were orchestrating an attack on the prerogatives and unaccountable colonial administration in the North American colonies. In February 1839 a highly critical report on the troubles in the Canadian colonies, written by Lord Durham on his return to England, was tabled in parliament and printed in full in the *Times*. The resulting uproar forced Lord Glenelg to resign as Secretary of State for the Colonies— he was hastily replaced by the Marquis of Normanby—and exacerbated the crisis that led to the fall of the government of Lord Melbourne in May. It was during this volatile period that the besieged government connived at a solution which would remove the political prisoners from Upper and Lower Canada but would not see them released by the English courts.

On 25 January 1839 Glenelg sent a highly confidential report to Colborne concerning measures for the removal of prisoners from Lower Canada.[11] The content of this report was made clear on 27 March: 'a naval vessel under orders for Quebec with troops serving in Canada . . . will take on board and transport convicts for Australia'.[12] Soon after, the Admiralty sent requests to the governors of Lower and Upper Canada for the numbers required to be transported.[13] While Russell may have seeded the idea, officially he kept at arm's length from this unusual procedure, advising the Colonial Office that they should negotiate the matter directly with the Admiralty.[14] Significantly, there appears to have been no intervention by the Superintendent of Convicts, even though the transportation of prisoners was his responsibility.

For the imprisoned Patriots, all this high-level negotiation was a complete mystery. They had their own highly coloured theories about what was happening. In the main their thoughts were dominated by fear for their families and the appalling conditions in the gaol. Heustis wrote of Fort Henry that 'Queen Victoria's boarding-house, on the whole, afforded rather poor accommodations' (61). In Wright's opinion, it was bad enough 'to be shut out from the balmy air and confined in a vermin-infected den, with loathsome food', but it was even worse to be 'subjected to the upbraidings of the minions of England's crown' (17). The whole process at Fort Henry was calculated to degrade and humiliate them, so Gates believed:

> Our food tub when brought to us was placed in the centre of the room, around which we gathered, and with the one knife and fork allowed the whole company, divided the amount as equitably as the circumstances would permit. To each was given a small tin plate; with this in one hand we ate, squatting on the floor or standing as best we could, using our fingers as the only means of conveying the food to the mouth.—Thus were we compelled to eat what in other circumstances our stomachs would have loathed with disgust. But the insatiate gnawings of hunger will force men to eat strange food, stranger indeed than was ours. In one corner of the room was kept standing a tub for the reception of filth . . . [40]

The same tenor of complaint came from Marsh who, together with seventeen from the Windsor raid, had been lodged in the Toronto gaol, which 'was alive with vermin', with rations 'hardly sufficient to keep us alive, what there was, was more filthy' (49). He describes receiving rations that the rats had infested and concluded the intention was poison them all.

Although these accounts were written nearly a decade later, some reports of this kind leaked out to the American press and impelled President Van Buren to dispatch a retired diplomat, Aaron Vail, to Upper Canada to investigate the conditions under which the Americans were held. To Arthur's great satisfaction, Vail was able to report that the arrangements for the prisoners were quite adequate and that conditions in Canadian gaols were no worse than in the United States.[15] Perhaps the most trustworthy account is in the diary and letters of Woodman, who was Marsh's companion at Toronto. Certainly, Woodman suffered terribly from frozen feet and the tight manacles, just as Marsh suggested, but his journal reports no great discomfort in the Toronto gaol. In May, when the remaining eighteen Windsor prisoners were transferred to Fort Henry, Woodman wrote quite cheerfully to his brother that Sheriff McDonnell 'is kind and obliging and does everything to make us comfortable. We do not want for anything but tobacco'.[16] As the only contemporaneous witness, Woodman is perhaps the most reliable; especially as he was the only one not writing a political tract. On the other hand, he was very concerned about the impact of his imprisonment on his family, and his sanguine letters were almost certainly written to allay concern and underplay the extent of his suffering.

For all their loud rumble of complaints, the Patriot narratives were also determined to show that stout American spirits could not be extinguished, no matter how great the degradation, especially on 4 July. Several of the narratives recalled the *ad hoc* celebration of that day, which Heustis described as being in the best republican tradition:

> Out of several pocket handkerchiefs a flag was manufactured, as nearly resembling the 'star-spangled banner' as we could conveniently make it. This emblem of freedom and national independence we hoisted in our room, taking good care that the officers did not get a peep at it. We procured some lemons and sugar, which enabled us to pass round a refreshing bowl of lemonade. We then let off our toasts, in which the heroes of '76 were duly remembered. Their success had saved them from the gallows, and bequeathed freedom to their posterity, while our failure had procured us a dungeon, and riveted the chains which bound the hapless Canadians as vassals of the British throne. . . . we had faced the enemy, as did the heroes of Bunker Hill, if not with equal success in the final result, at least in the same spirit and for the attainment of the same object, and we saw no cause for self-reproach. [81]

When it came to the contemplation of their future, the Patriots' thoughts were fixated upon the singular character of George Arthur who, they believed, acted toward them with a calculated capriciousness in order to satisfy his inherently cruel nature. Snow volunteered that he had been told by those who knew Arthur's administration, that the 'Pharaoh of Egypt established a more moderate system of police, and governed the children of Israel with greater lenity' (12), while Gates was reminded that Arthur had previously been the Lieutenant-Governor of Van Diemen's Land, where he was said to have signed the death warrants of over 1200 people:

> He loved it as he did his meat and drink, for he was never known to pardon a man condemned to die, unless forced to do it by a power superior to his own. He was short of stature, rather corpulent, with a head whitened with the cares and crimes of sixty years, and a face and nose bearing the purple bloom of bacchanalian revels. [53]

Despite Arthur's reputation as a stern and devout moralist, the characterisation of the governor as a 'modern personification of Dionysius', to quote Snow (12), was a necessary rhetorical device for men whose only comfort in desperate circumstances was their shared sense of manly virtue and moral uprightness. They could not allow that Arthur might be moved by the same Christian moral precepts as themselves, nor that their judges and gaolers were anything other than corrupt and debauched minions of 'Victoria Coburg', unable to function without a resort to grog.

In his description of Arthur's visit to the prison in Fort Henry, Wright is at pains to portray the governor as a brutish tyrant:

> Instead of consoling us in our misfortune, he made us feel the bitterness of our captivity, calling us buccaneers, pirates and ruffians; and that if we were not hung we should be life-slaves, and that we might take his word for it, inter-

larding his conversation with horrid imprecations; and he appeared to gloat over our misery with the joy of a fiend incarnate. We all felt relieved when he departed, and we surmised that something was to be done with us besides death, for his actions seemed like those of a starving tiger, from whose mouth some precious morsel had been torn by a higher power, and his reproaches, the growlings of the infuriated animal . . . [17]

All the Patriot narratives dwell on Arthur's size—his being short and somewhat stout—while Wright also lingered on the 'dull withered color' of the governor's face, with the eyes which 'gleamed from beneath its heavy brush with the ferocity of a blood-hound breaking cover' (16–17). The sub-text was very clear: the Queen's man was not a true man, like those Patriot heroes he dispatched to the gallows, he was nothing more than a brute. Yet Governor Arthur was not an inhumane fellow. His letters to the Secretary of State for the Colonies stress the reluctance with which he undertook capital punishment, given his deep religious beliefs and the deep personal pain it caused him. The Patriots knew nothing of the struggle Arthur was having with his conscience, as well as a Legislative Council and public opinion bent on exacting the heaviest punishment. Their distaste for him was probably coloured by their painful bewilderment at the apparently arbitrary process which saw more than half their number pardoned, while they lingered under sentence of death.

At various times between December 1838 and May 1839, sixty-four of the Patriots from the windmill raid were pardoned on condition of leaving the province for the United States, as were another eighteen from the Windsor raid. Though Arthur wanted a show of determination for the Americans, he was disinclined to be as severe with the entire cohort of raiders as Ambassador Fox had urged him to be. The sorry fate of these mis-guided men haunted him. 'So many of these poor creatures were killed at Prescott—so many more at Windsor—besides those who suffered at the hands of the executioner', Arthur told Ambassador Fox, 'I must say I felt it a duty to extend mercy to the younger culprits'.[17]

Both Gates and Heustis insisted that a further lot of pardons, including their own, were written out during May 1839 but were withdrawn at the governor's fancy, which only went to show, Heustis charged, 'how com-pletely we were subject to the caprices of the unprincipled mercenaries of royalty' (80). Gates too thought the act unprincipled and unfair, but did allow that there had been a particular incident that made Arthur change his mind. 'During this time, a British officer for some unknown purpose crossed the lines to French Creek, in Jefferson County,' he explained. 'Our American friends not relishing his presence, treated him with that attention which they thought most befitting such gentlemen' (55). So angry was the incensed

Arthur that he burnt their pardons, 'thus wreaking his vengeance upon the heads of poor defenceless victims' (56).

Both Heustis and Gates were mistaken. Governor Arthur was under considerable pressure from Lord Glenelg to show clemency, but he was under even more pressure from outraged public opinion baying for retribution. He stuck to his determination that about eighty of the Patriots over the age of twenty-one would be transported to a penal colony for life. Arthur had selected those to go as early as March.[18]

It is not clear when the men in the Kingston and Toronto gaols understood that, rather than be released with their compatriots, they were reserved for a punishment many felt would be worse than death. Several claim not to have known they were going to the penal colony until they were well under sail. However, the most reliable source for this is Woodman's journal, where on 1 April he wrote: 'Orders have arrived for us to be transported to Van Demans Land'.[19]

6

Bound for the Fatal Shore

O N 22 SEPTEMBER 1839, the Patriots remaining at Fort Henry left Kingston
on board a canal-boat destined for the port city of Quebec. According
to Wright, the men were ignorant of 'whither we were going or what was
to be our fate' (17). Gates understood that they were being taken to Quebec,
'to receive free pardons from the governor general in person, who was
anxious to see us, and who would do generously by us' (56). Though woe-
fully wrong-headed, this retrospective memory has a ring of truth about it.
These men were grasping at straws. They knew that prisoners sent to
England had been freed only months earlier and had heard that Lord
Durham had written a highly critical report on the state of affairs in Canada
in which he said he could not blame the Canadians for rebelling.[1] The
report had been leaked to the *Times* and was published in instalments
during January 1839. Perhaps the Patriots did not know Durham had quit
his post of governor-in-chief in high dudgeon, and that the position was
without an incumbent.

Gates remembers the Patriots being in high spirits about escaping
the iron grip of Governor Arthur, and they were 'in high glee' at the news
when they left for Quebec (57). As Gates described it, many of the Patriots
burst into song: '"Hail Columbia," "The Star Spangled Banner," "Hunters of
Kentucky," "Yankee Doodle," &c., resounded through the prison, calling
quite a crowd about the doors and windows' (57). Others on the journey
were in a more sombre mood. What stood out in Wright's recollection was
the sight of the looming fortress of the citadel at Quebec:

> I thought of our brave countryman, Montgomery, who fell fighting with
> unparalleled courage upon the battlements of the citadel; and of Wolfe, the
> ambitious and chivalrous Briton . . . could Wolfe's bones repose beneath that

white pyramid, which rose amid the rocks and trees so pure and bright, and see his blood-bought citadel in the hands of tyrants?—the degenerate sons of once noble ancestors! [17–18]

Seventy-nine Patriots made the trip to Quebec, including Horace Cooley, the one man remaining from the raid across Lake St Clair.[2] The voyage of five days and five nights was horrendous; the prisoners suffered greatly as the boat was very cramped and they were all in irons. Robert Marsh was deeply suspicious of their additional companions in irons, four non-political prisoners who had been added to the group—three who had been convicted of murder and one army deserter—whom Marsh believed had been put among them as spies.

Whatever the Patriots may have thought was their fate, being put aboard the British warship *Buffalo* rendered the situation starkly: they were destined for a penal colony and unlikely ever to return. 'Our fate was hid in the dark future', wrote Samuel Snow, 'even hope was little inclined to flatter us, that we should ever return to our native land' (8). According to Marsh, the men were 'left to our own surmisings as to our destination' and no enlightenment was to be had from other involuntary passengers, fifty-eight political prisoners from Lower Canada, who had come on board the previous day. Marsh insisted that the Lower Canadians too 'had been tried by a corrupt court, and had received no sentence and did not know where they were bound'. At least they had enough forewarning for their friends to provision them for the trip, Marsh contended, unlike the Patriots who had 'not thirty-five minutes from the time our irons were on, before we were under way', and departed North America 'entirely destitute of the comforts of life, and literally alive with vermin' (59).

It was not until the master of the *Buffalo*, Captain Wood, arrived at Quebec that he understood that his charges from Upper Canada were destined for Van Diemen's Land and those from Lower Canada were going to New South Wales.[3] Some of the Patriot narratives insist that they did not know of their destination until they entered the Derwent River, although the memory of Wright was otherwise. 'Our captain was a kind, humane man', Wright recalled, 'when his orders were opened, we found that we were bound for Van Dieman's Land direct' (18). Marsh was adamant that shipping them out of Canada was illegal. He was not far wrong. The men aboard the *Buffalo* were being transported with warrants made out by the colonial governors.[4] As the Bermuda affair of the previous year had made indelibly clear, a colonial governor did not have the power to order the restraint of prisoners in another place, nor did he have the authority to transport prisoners out of his domain to be restrained in a penal colony elsewhere.

Uniformly the Patriot narratives warmly praise the humane behaviour of both the *Buffalo*'s captain and its surgeon, 'a man and a gentleman', Marsh allowed, even though he could not resist adding the rider that the doctor 'had a certain sum for all delivered alive, therefore, it was for his interest to keep us alive if possible' (61–2). Writing to his family, the good-hearted Elijah Woodman was full of praise for his seaboard captors:

> The commander of this ship, Capt. Wood, has treated us with every degree of generosity and is making us as comfortable as we could expect. His officers and the surgeon spare no pain in administering to our health and fare. The food is much better than we expected . . .[5]

The *Buffalo* was an aged warship mostly used to carry troops and supplies, and as such had been sent to Quebec with a regiment to reinforce the British army, in case of any further trouble over the question of the border between Maine and New Brunswick. When she left Quebec, in addition to the prisoners, the ship carried 140 soldiers, marines and crew, including a few women and children. Heustis gives a good description of the ship transformed into a floating prison:

> She had a full poop-deck, which extended before the mizenmast, and under which were the great cabin and the state-rooms for the officers. Forward there was a topgallant forecastle, divided into two galleys, or cook-houses. Before the mainmast, and abaft the foremast, there were two strong gratings or barricades, of oak, lined with iron, and about eight feet high. In the midships of this space, the long boat and spare spars were stowed, leaving about eight feet space of gangways on each side. On the quarter-deck, she mounted six nine-pounders, carriage guns, but as she was pierced with ports fore and aft, it is reasonable to suppose that she had guns below, which, if required, could easily be hoisted on deck, and mounted. Her between-decks, and the squares of her hatchways, were also gratied off, having only small doors of communication with the deck above. Forward there was a sick bay, or doctor's shop, and the other parts of the deck were fitted for accommodation of the sailors, marines, and soldiers, each class, however, occupying distinct divisions. In the hold, about seven feet below the between-decks, was a platform-deck, constructed of rough deals, laid on the ballast, and stanchioned down. In the wings were two tiers of berths, each berth designed for the reception of four persons. A grating extended fore and aft, and the squares of the hatchways were also barricaded. This place was to be the home of 140 prisoners, during a long and monotonous voyage at sea. It did not afford room for us all to stand, and some were obliged to occupy the berths, day and night, being relieved at suitable intervals. We had no air except what came down the hatchway. Abaft, the hold was stowed with stores, provisions and water. Such was the ship *Buffalo*. [86]

Heustis, in contrast to Woodman, had no kind words for the food, claiming that the usual allowance for four marines had to serve six prisoners:

Skilly, composed of oat-meal, bran, and dust, mixed with boiling water, was our breakfast; and this stuff was almost as black as the kids [tubs] in which it was served out. We had neither plates nor spoons, to eat with, but were under the necessity of dipping a piece of biscuit into the kid and licking therefrom the skilly which adhered to it. Each mess had its kid, containing six quarts, or a pint for each man, around which, at meal times, a circle was formed, to enable us all to partake of the glorious feast! We could heartily exclaim, in the language of Wackford Squeers, as he gave the well-diluted milk to one of the pupils of his celebrated school at Do-the-boys Hall [in Dickens' novel *Nicholas Nickleby*], 'here's richness!' For dinner, we had pork and pea soup one day, and beef and duff the next. The pork was not as bad as it might have been, but the beef had doubtless served an apprenticeship of seven years at Gibraltar, besides going two or three voyages around the world, before it was opened for our use. It was salt as brine, hard as Pharaoh's heart, and about as nutritious as wooden nutmegs. For supper, we had some fair cocoa. Add to the foregoing luxuries half a pound of biscuit, and a quart of water, for each man, and you have our daily bill of fare during the voyage. I cannot, however, leave the biscuit without mentioning its quality. Whether it was originally composed of rye, ground peas, oat-meal, or of all together, I cannot positively assert. It was so hard, coarse, and unpalatable, that there would have been no danger of our growing dyspeptic upon it, if it had been perfectly clean. But when we found there was a peculiar feline odor attached to it, indicating that it had been in the vicinity of cats, we felt little inclination to eat it. . . . [88]

The distribution of rations was highly regimented. The men were divided into messes of twelve, of which one was appointed to receive the rations and divide them among his fellows, a ritual Marsh describes thus:

When the cook called out from the hatchway 'dinner, O!' the sentry from the upper deck would pass the word to the sentry on the main, or 2d deck, and he to the 3d, when he would unlock the trap door, and the captain, as they were called, of each mess would ascend the narrow ladder up to the 2d deck, for the doorway was so narrow and small that but one man could pass up or down at a time, make their way to the cook's galley; each one take his kidd and return one at a time until all was below. The door was fastened at once after the last one was up, and opened again as they returned with their Kidds, and then opened again until they were passed up to the sentries or cook's mate, who carried them to the galley on the upper deck. [60]

In at least one respect the conditions on board were superior to the prison, in that the Patriots were not regarded as felons by the ship's company, and although they were guarded, the *Buffalo*'s crew were happy to engage in conversation and trade with them. Heustis recounts that several of his companions bought mess utensils from the soldiers that enabled them 'to eat our food more like men' (90). It transpired that the soldiers had stolen the articles from the ship's sailors, and the Patriots were forced to return their spoons and plates. Not disheartened by this summary proceeding, Heustis reported, 'we again opened trade with the soldiers, and soon supplied ourselves with a similar assortment of mess utensils, which we were allowed to keep' (90).

This treatment was in stark contrast to the situation of the French-Canadian prisoners, several of whom also wrote narratives unanimous in their condemnation of the degrading circumstances in which they were forced to eat. Unlike the Americans, they were not able to obtain utensils nor were they permitted to carve wooden implements, a restriction they believed was prompted by malicious prejudice against them. Without utensils they were 'compelled to tear with their teeth their meat which they held'.[6] The Patriots had next to no interaction with their counterparts from Lower Canada. The two groups were kept strictly segregated in separate compartments and had little if any communication. As devout Catholics without much English, the French-speaking *Canadiens* were happy for it to remain that way, although among them there was one American, Benjamin Mott, from Vermont. Mott, who claimed to have been inadvertently caught up in the rebel action in Lower Canada, suffered severely from alienation from his own kind.

Most of the involuntary passengers on the *Buffalo* had never been to sea before and suffered motion sickness that became chronic even before they entered the ocean. When a violent storm hit the ship in the Gulf of St Lawrence, Heustis described a hellish situation in the ship's hold:

> we could hear the rushing of the waves, as they bounded to leeward, or broke in foaming fury over the deck. The shrill screaming of the boatswain's whistle,—followed by his hoarse voice, bellowing forth, 'All hands reef topsails,' or some other order,—rose high and dismal amid the wailing of the tempest. Our situation below was extremely nauseous and suffocating. The hatches were battered down, which excluded the air, and two thirds of our number were vomiting with sea-sickness. [89]

Robert Marsh supplied further details of the disgusting circumstances:

> the sea beating against her sides, which often resembled thunder; the ship rolling and tumbling, throwing us from side to side; the tubs for use, perhaps full at the commencement of the rolling, and now going with us, and among us, from side to side; emptied of their contents, together with the effects of sea-sickness, which caused the deck to be slippery, sending forth not a very agreeable smell . . . [60]

Over the next few days, those few who remained immune to the vomiting did the best they could to clean up the revolting environment in which they were confined. Once the sea-sickness was over, Heustis explained, the men were inducted into a regime of cleanliness established by the ship's surgeon, which involved scrubbing their quarters every morning and regularly applying a coat of whitewash:

> At first, we wet-holystoned our deck, by sprinkling water and sand on the planks, and then kneeling and rubbing them with freestones, until every particle of dirt had been loosened, after which they were washed with water, and then dried up with swabs. The ship's doctor soon discovered that wet holy-stoning was injurious to our health, and he therefore substituted the dry oper-ation, which consisted in rubbing the deck as before, without using water. The dust created by this method of cleaning, was almost as bad as the dampness of wet holystoning, but cleanliness was indispensable, and the last alternative was adopted and adhered to throughout the voyage. [87–8]

No amount of scrubbing and rubbing could control the infestations of cock-roaches, fleas and lice of which all the Patriot narratives complained.

The log of the master of the *Buffalo* indicates that the Patriots were allowed on deck each day, twenty-four at a time, on alternate days, and they were required to air their bedding, wash their clothes and scrub the deck.[7] They were never left alone. There were guards at every vantage-point on the ship and they were strictly segregated.

'When we wanted to smoke', Heustis explained, 'a light was passed to us through the forward grating; upon no pretence whatever were any of us allowed outside of the barriers that separated us from the rest of the ship's company' (89).

Time passed slowly, with little hope of escape. Even though the Patriots were not in irons, as male convicts on transport ships often were, they were guarded by armed sentries. This was dramatically brought home to them one day when a guard accidentally shot off his gun as he was sitting at his post by the hatchway. The bullet lodged in the side of the ship, barely missing Robert Marsh who was seated on a bench on the deck contem-plating the wonders of the ocean.

Although Heustis complained of the monotony of the voyage, where 'the scene was unchanged; sky and water bounded the view above and around us' (89), some of the Patriots found genuine pleasure in the vistas of vast ocean and sky, even though it went against the grain. Wright con-fessed that it was 'a glorious sight to gaze upon the vast expanse of bright blue waters, reflecting heaven in their depths, and catch the soft balmy breezes . . . and watch the stormy petrel, that bird of the waters, upon our lee' (18). For others, nothing could repair the trauma of separation from family and home. On 19 October, Asa Priest, a 45-year-old New Yorker who had been captured at the windmill, died and was buried at sea. Priest had given the common defence of being in Canada by mistake, claiming he had come to Sackets Harbor to get payment for a cow and finding his debtor had boarded the schooner, had followed him; once on board, he had fallen asleep and unwittingly been carried across the border. Perhaps this was the real reason that a farmer with a dependent wife and six children would put himself in such a ludicrous and dangerous situation. At the time of his trial Priest was already ill.[8] Fellow raider Heustis thought that he understood why Priest had given up the struggle with life:

> The thought of being separated from his wife and children, and compelled to drag out a miserable existence among convicts, in a land far away from home and its endearments, was too much for him. He made no complaints, but the slow progress of the canker which was eating at his soul was plainly visible. Gradually he pined away and died. . . . [94]

Priest's body was sewed up in a hammock and carried on deck, where it was laid on a grating resting on the lee gangway covered with a Union Jack. His messmates, and the captains of the other messes, were permitted to witness the Church of England burial service. When the main-topsail was hove back and the ensign hoisted half-mast, the grating was raised, and the shroud launched into the ocean with the traditional words, *we therefore commit his body to the deep*. Woodman, who was closest to Priest in age and circumstances, was especially moved by the funeral, which he described in a letter to his own family:

> the melancholy countenances of the prisoners, the ship moving with a light breeze over the blue waves and the canopy of heaven spreading over its blue and splendid appearance . . . filled me with solemnity which I never before witnessed. Nothing could have been done in more order. And it surprised me to see so much respect paid to the remains of a fellow prisoner by the captain and his officers . . . For a number of days before his death he seemed to have no disposition to live. At one time when talking to Capt. Morin [*sic*] he inquired how far it was to the Cape of Good Hope. The Captain told him and he said, 'I shall get there first' . . .

No doubt unsettled by similarity in their cruel circumstances, Woodman reassured his family that he had no intention of giving up the spirit, as Priest had done, no matter what fate might have in store:

> although the Atlantic is now between us and I am bound to where I do not know yet I am in full faith that Divine Providence will yet sustain me and order my return to my affectionate wife and lovely children. We do not get any light on the subject of our fate. All is silent as the hour of death and veiled in

midnight darkness. I really hope when I arrive at the Cape to be enabled to finish this letter with the news to you so that you may know as well as I, be it what it will.[9]

Woodman claimed to have been unsure exactly where the *Buffalo* was headed, but according to Marsh most of the Patriots had already reached the terrible conclusion that they were bound directly for Van Diemen's Land. This knowledge made them desperate to try to turn the ship back to America:

> we had with us an old and able sea captain, that had followed the business from his youth up, and under his instructions, we would in case of emergency soon have become sailors. . . . During our short visits on deck as above described, on looking aft, near the cabin door, we discovered some 40 or fifty muskets with bayonets in a stationary rack, so fixed that rough weather could not affect them. They were spare arms, so called, that in case of necessity, the sailors could be quickly armed. It was mentioned that if we could manage to get hold of those muskets, and at the same time keep down the hatches, that none could come against us but those on deck, and at the same time let up the prisoners, the ship might be taken. As hazardous as was the prospect, I believe that nearly all were willing to attempt it rather than go to Van Dieman's Land . . . [61–2]

Whether there was a plot to take over the ship is debatable. Woodman makes no reference to an attempted mutiny in his detailed letters, nor does Aaron Dresser in his daily journal. The ship's log of Captain Wood is entirely silent on the matter. In the first of the published narratives from this group, Wright stated that 'there was a conspiracy formed to take the ship: about eight prisoners were engaged in it zealously' but, he added, 'two Judases accidentally overheard the names of those concerned in it, and reported the same to the captain' (18, 19). Where the highly politicised Wright described a fully fledged conspiracy, the milder Samuel Snow put a different spin on events, claiming that a couple of the Patriots were overheard to remark how easily the ship might be taken and were reported to the captain. When Heustis's narrative was published several years later, the plot had been given a much fuller and more heroic treatment:

> the leader of the party whose turn it was on deck, by a concerted sign, was to communicate the fact to those who followed; then, as the last man was passing through the door, an impediment to its closing was to be inserted, and while the sentinel's attention was engaged in removing it, he was to be seized, disarmed, gagged, and thrust back into the hold, which would enable those below to rush hastily on deck. In the mean time, those already up, leaving a guard of six men to protect the fore hatchway, were to rush aft, in a body, secure the small-arms racked in front of the poop, block up the main hatchway, cabin doors, and every outlet from below, except the fore hatchway, which would be

in our possession. . . . even if all the watch and officers were armed, we could not fail of clearing the decks, by a simultaneous rush fore and aft, armed with belaying-pins, heavers, boarding-pikes, or whatever small-arms we could capture. . . . Once in possession of the deck, we designed that all, excepting such of the crew as we could control, should be sent into the hold, and there guarded, while we shaped our course for New York. No violence was intended, beyond what was absolutely necessary to the success of our enterprise. We had seamen enough among our number to work and navigate the vessel. The morning was considered the most favorable time . . . [90]

The heroics so carefully rehearsed were never put on display. When the morning came, Heustis reported, the Patriots ate their 'insipid meal' in meaningful silence, although their faces were lit with the hopes of freedom, knowing as they did 'that our leaders were fully determined to carry out their designs, or perish in the attempt' (92). Yet, Heustis regretted, that was not what happened:

> Another minute and we should be mustered on deck; in fact, we could hear the sergeant's tread along the between-decks, walking forward to open our prison door. It was the sergeant; I could see him through the gratings; and now, high heaven assist us, we crave but liberty! A few moments will decide our fate!
>
> He descended,—my heart sinks while I record it,—not to open our door, but to double the sentinels, and to oversee the securing of the hatchway! Not one word did he speak to us, or we to him. . . . It was evident that our scheme had been discovered by the treachery of some of our comrades. [92]

Gates, whose narrative shows a tendency to echo (and embellish) those of Marsh and Heustis, had much the same heroic tale to tell. For these three writers, each of whom spent so much of their narrative on political posturing and attacks on an effete, imbecilic and corrupt imperial system, it was imperative that their account include heroic action aimed at a return to their glorious republic. Equally, it was essential for their proselytising purpose that the plot be not defeated by the British, but be betrayed by informers whom they considered to be the lackeys and dregs of the imperial system. Consequently, all three narrators named two non-political prisoners as the informers, even though all the earlier accounts identify the Windsor raider, John Tyrrell, as the Judas in their midst.[10]

There can be no doubt that the master of the *Buffalo* did get wind of a plot—illusory or real—since one morning in October all the prisoners suddenly found the hatches bolted down and their quarters thoroughly searched. And while Captain Wood's log did not record the incident, it was recounted in a letter from a sailor on the *Buffalo* that was published in the shipping news of the *Greenock Advertiser* in Scotland on 26 November 1839 and republished *verbatim* sometime later in Upper Canada:

The prisoners on the whole behaved remarkably well, owing, in all probably, to the very strict guard kept upon them; for the Americans came on board with a most infamous character, as a most daring and villainous set, willing to sacrifice their lives rather than be transported. We fortunately detected a conspiracy among them in time to prevent an unpleasant affair—they having had it in agitation to rise against us. They have since been very quiet . . .[11]

All these varying accounts are not entirely contradictory. Those narratives that speak of the conspiracy stress that only a few were part of the plot. Aaron Dresser, a young American arrested at the windmill, may have known about the plot, but did not write anything in his diary for fear it could be used against him. In all probability, Samuel Snow and Elijah Woodman would not have been in on the plot, since they were older men with large families. They had escaped the gallows once and were unlikely to be drawn into such foolhardy heroics a second time. The conspirators all seem to have been at the windmill, whereas Woodman and Snow were from the Windsor raid. Moreover, John Tyrrell, variously identified as the informer, was also from the Windsor escapade. More telling, perhaps, was that Tyrrell, from Upper Canada, was one of the few non-Americans among the group and was the nephew of a well-placed member of the Upper Canada Legislative Assembly.

Snow reported that the hatches were closed and everything was thoroughly searched, 'and no signs of mutiny appearing, we were again liberated, and our informer severely reprimanded' (9). Captain Wood did more than reprimand the informer, he doubled the guard and stopped the prisoners from coming on deck, something greatly resented by the *Canadiens* who had taken no part in this. Yet, Wright reported, 'not a syllable escaped the captain on the subject of the mutiny' (19). Marsh believed the captain was doubtful about the veracity of the informer and more than half suspected that he had made it up. Nevertheless, Tyrell was granted a pardon almost a year earlier than other prisoners, so he may have been rewarded for his information after all.

After the supposed mutiny, conditions for the convicts on the *Buffalo* worsened. Confined to their putrid quarters in the hold, the Patriots began to fear for their sanity, if not their lives. As Heustis complained, the increased heat encouraged 'myriads of vermin, that no cleanliness on our part could prevent from preying upon us'. The men had to share their provisions with 'cockroaches, ants, and flies . . . and, as if our bread was not bad enough before, maggots and other animalcules made it their home' (95). When the weather became boisterous, the sea rolled in over the gangways, flooding the openings that permitted the flow of fresh air. The desperate men agreed to address a letter to Captain Wood pledging good conduct if they could again be allowed to go on deck each day.[12] The surgeon also intervened on their behalf. Captain Wood agreed to allow twelve men on deck at a time, instead of twenty-four, but he took care to see that at all times they were strongly guarded. Despite being granted a turn on deck, the men found that their health began to deteriorate. As they neared the tropics they began to display all the signs of scurvy, the terror of all long sea voyages; 'Our teeth loosened in our heads, and often were so painful as to quite produce delirium', so Gates recounted (66).

If anything, the *Canadiens* fared even worse, with several coming close to death. One of the French narratives claimed that sailors supplied the ill with water laced with their daily rum ration, until they were caught and flogged, although this recollection was not confirmed by the ship's log, which records only one flogging, for a different matter.[13] Even an increase in the ration of lime juice made little difference. Scarcely a day passed, Marsh reported, 'but some one of us had one, two, three or four teeth extracted, and some were obliged to call the doctor from his berth in the middle of the night to extract teeth for them' (63). He feared they would all be toothless before they reached port. Luckily, the ship called into Rio de Janeiro to resupply with fresh provisions before the scurvy became life-threatening.

The Patriots were captivated by the sight of Rio during a big celebration, none more so than Heustis, who grew rapturous at the sight of 'this finest of nature's paintings', framed by the hills 'rising in picturesque gradation from the beach till they seem to rest against the sky', and in the foreground the beautiful city itself (96). What made the scene especially marvellous was the maritime display in the bay:

> All the vessels in the harbor—and among them almost every Christian maritime nation was represented—were ornamented with flags and streamers. The foreign ships of war wore the Brazilian flag at the fore, and were also clothed with colors from the trucks to the rails. Boats innumerable, filled with people from the shore, singing and waving flags, were continually rowing and sailing about the bay. Ashore, the batteries belched forth their thunder, which was answered by the ships of war, who manned their yards at the same time. All Rio Janeiro was boiling over with joy, excepting us poor prisoners, whose misery was increased by the contrast. [96]

The sight of an American warship, with the Stars and Stripes waving proudly from the peak, increased the misery of the American prisoners, at the same time as it stimulated a surge of dormant patriotism. Heustis thought the American ship was so long that it seemed to stretch across the bay:

> Most beautifully did she thread her way among the fleet of merchant vessels, and, when in stays, came round like a pilot-boat, darting to windward without impeding her headway. . . . she came in before the wind, with studding-sails on both sides, skimming along like a sea-gull, until she reached within a cable's length of her anchorage, when, as if by magic, at the order, 'shorten sail,' even before the echo of the words had died away, every stitch of canvas disappeared,

and once more, head to wind, she was riding at her anchors. The American merchant-men in port manned their rigging, and gave the brig three cheers. Our captain, who was himself every inch a sailor, was heard to remark that he had never witnessed an exploit of that kind which displayed better seamanship. [96–7]

Heustis was actually beginning to enjoy his time at sea. Not long after leaving Rio, he recounted with relish a severe gale that whipped up waves, 'like tottering mountains, about to roll on board and crush us in their ruins' (98). He was so exhilarated by the monstrous seas that he almost forgot about his personal misery:

> perched upon the giddy summits, the noble ship would tremble, and appear to pause for a few seconds, and then descend again into the boiling valley, with such tremendous velocity as to becalm the sails, and make the inexperienced tremble for fear that she would never rise again; but, buoyant as a bird, in the long lull between the waves she would recover herself, and again impelled onward, ascend the giddy height that foamed before her. [98]

When the gale caused the aged vessel to leak copiously, the prisoners were called upon to help work the pumps. Marsh found himself wondering whether it would not be better for the ship to sink. The soldiers and crew worked like maniacs to pump the water, Marsh reported, but the Patriots 'cared but little about her staying above water, it appeared to us a matter of little consequence; I know some may say life is sweet, but to us it appeared very bitter' (64).

The *Buffalo* did not sink, and with the assistance of gale force winds she had a quick run from Rio round Cape Horn and across the Pacific to Hobart Town. Almost before they knew it, the Patriots had arrived in Van Diemen's Land. Their first indication that they had reached their destination came when a sailor on the mast-head suddenly gave the call 'Land ho!' After a rapid succession of orders and much excitement, strong headwinds drove the ship up the Derwent River, giving the Patriots their first view of their new home. The scene was dominated by the brooding Mount Wellington, which, Wright noted, 'loomed above the waves long before the town at its base was in sight' (20). For Snow the realisation that they had reached the antipodes was something of a shock: 'to see the sun to the north of us, and the people harvesting grain'. He had poor expectation of what kind of a place they had been brought to 'on the very south-eastern outskirts of habitable creation. . . . not be likely to hold out many inducements to those who could find a home elsewhere' (10). For Snow, as for the other Patriots, mixed emotions attended at the voyage end: very pleased to escape from the putrid and suffocating floating prison, but deeply apprehensive about what to expect from a new life in this demon's land at the end of the world.

7

Mysteries of a Penal Colony

B Y THE TIME the *Buffalo* arrived in Hobart on 12 February 1840, two contingents of Patriots had already arrived from England on the *Marquis of Hastings* and the *Canton*. For all three groups, the initiation into convict life in Van Diemen's Land was the same as it was for every other convict arriving in the colony.[1]

Once the ship had been piloted to its mooring within the harbour, it was visited by health officials who removed the sick and dying. They also requested a report from the ship's surgeon that would form the basis for a report on the bonus he was to be paid by the Home Office.[2] On the next day the ship was visited by the Superintendent of the Convict Barracks, William Gunn, and his retinue of clerks to catagorise and process the convicts like goods destined for the Commissariat Store or beasts about to be sold at market. Linus Miller, who arrived on the *Canton* in January 1840, did not take kindly to this officious intrusion:

> On the following morning the work of initiation into the mysteries of a penal colony commenced. William Gunn, Esq., principal superintendent of convicts, accompanied by several subordinates, all of whom affected *importance*, took possession of the cabin. Proclamation was made that every prisoner should instantly make his appearance at the cabin door when called, under penalty of *'severe punishment.'* [255–6]

The men were summoned in alphabetical order, and in due time it was Miller's turn. He was collected by the doorkeeper, a ticket-of-leave convict, who asked him his name. When Miller replied, the response was sharp: 'Say "*sir*," when you address *me*'. Somewhat taken aback, Miller was about to step into the cabin when he was seized by the collar and ordered to '*wait*'. The doorkeeper then instructed him: 'When you go in, take off your cap, say *sir* when the clerks speak to you, and be sure and *kelp* Mr. Gunn.' Miller

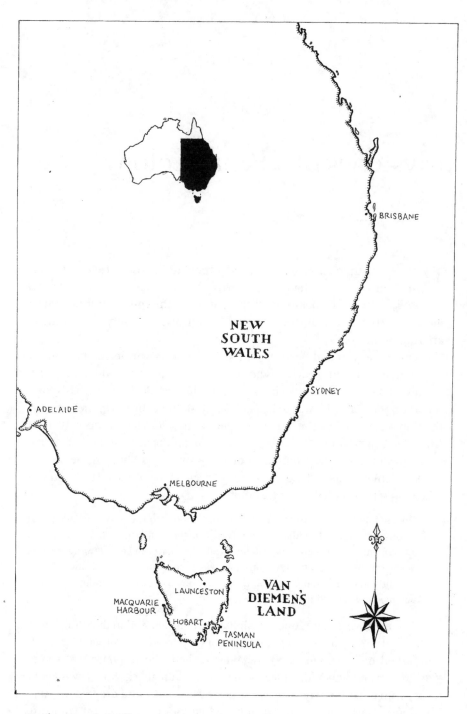

South-eastern Australia

told the doorkeeper to mind his own business but was threatened with a tanning. The run-in with the doorkeeper was interrupted by the instruction to 'Send in Miller', and the young law clerk entered the *'sanctum sanctorum'* of the *Canton*. He described the scene in front of him. Mr Gunn occupied the *'uppermost'* seat at the table, and before him was an immense register 'in which he was writing *"remarks"'*. Around him sat three clerks at work on an equally imposing set of leather-bound tomes. Miller stood before the board, an overseer at his back, while his 'predecessor was *finished off'* by four scratching quills. It was then his turn, and after he had been cautioned to 'answer promptly and truly', the barrage of questions commenced:

> 'What is your name? Have you parents living? What are their names? How old are they? Where do they live? What is their religion? Do they know of your being here? Are they wealthy or poor? Have you brothers and sisters? How old are they? Are they married? Have they any children? What is your own age? Are you married? Where were you born? What is your trade? What is your religion? What is your crime? What sentence? Can you read, write, and keep accounts?' [256]

What Miller did not know was that Gunn already knew the answers to some of these questions, having scrutinised the ship's papers. This procedure was designed to catch out those prisoners who gave misleading or false information, thus ensuring that the data collected by the Convict Department was largely accurate. Every detail was recorded in the leather-bound volumes, ordered by ship and police number to aid retrieval. If a prisoner were to escape from the colonies, the convict administration would circulate details of his next of kin. Of course in the case of Miller and his fellow Patriots, this would prove pointless. If they ever managed to get back to the bosom of their families they would be beyond the reach of the British State. The interview process, however, served a second function. Miller's induction 'into the mysteries of a penal colony' (255) was also designed to intimidate him. This became all too clear when he was subjected to the second phase of his interview:

> Answers to these questions being duly chronicled, I was ordered to pull off my shoes and stockings, which being done, the 'measuring rod' was applied. 'Stand up straight, no shrinking, no stretching.' My height was declared to be 'jest six feet.' I was then commanded to strip to the waist, and my person was closely scrutinized for any *marks* or *scars* by which I might be identified in case I became wicked and depraved enough to run away. After my head and face had been minutely described, 'that will do,' was pronounced in a condescending tone . . . [256–7]

The order to strip was resented by other Patriots. As William Gates described: 'By this method, and to which every person is forced to submit, such a minute description is obtained, that it is utterly hopeless for a prisoner to think of escaping from the infernal clutches of those petty tyrants, that hold such detestable sway in that prison land' (71). According to Stephen Wright, at the end of the questioning and physical inspection, 'this minutiae was particularly inserted and afterward read over to each, and signed with his own hand' (20)—thus forcing each prisoner to acknowledge his degraded circumstances.[3]

To make matters worse, the Patriots' clothes were removed by British convict trustees. Not only were they forced to parade before the condescending gaze of Mr Gunn who, as the tallest man in the colony, was able to look down on even the six-foot frame of Miller, but also they were disrobed by the sweepings of Britain's imperial gaols. The process was an utterly humiliating invasion of privacy, which was to have a particularly lasting impact on the young law clerk. When Miller recollected Gunn, he imbued him with encyclopaedic powers of recall:

> He has only to see a prisoner once, to be able to detect him in almost any disguise for years afterwards. It is said he can call every prisoner in Van Dieman's Land by name, when he meets them, tell the name of the ship they arrived, the year and day, their original sentences, additional sentences received in the colony &c., &c.; in short that he never forgets any thing . . . [285–6]

Governor Arthur had once described the operation of the convict system as a panopticon without walls—a reference to Jeremy Bentham's famous design for a prison, where the incarcerated would be controlled by constant surveillance.[4] For the Patriots it was almost as though they had walked through the doors of the Eastern State Penitentiary in Philadelphia, with its numbered radial cells and central observation tower.[5] Instead of being confined by prison architecture, however, they were incarcerated by William Gunn's elephantine memory, and his elaborate cross-referenced registers which contained an account of the career of every convict to step upon the shores of Van Diemen's Land. The description process complete, Gunn had merely to wait for an army of convict informers, policemen, overseers, superintendents, catechists, commandants and magistrates to provide the information which would flesh out the details of each convict's life. Every scrap of information would be squirrelled away in the appropriate register. Before any decision was made affecting the fate of a prisoner, the registers were consulted to see whether, by dint of good or bad conduct, the prisoner merited relief from suffering, or an increased measure of pain.[6]

In the case of the Patriots, however, the convict registers contained at least one significant gap—it is evident that Gunn and his associates censored their records. Miller, usually so attentive to detail, neglected to report his responses to his quick-fire interrogation—including the instruction to list the nature of his crime. The reply that convicts gave to this all-important question was written down under the heading 'stated this offence'. The question was intended to elicit an admission of guilt—yet another little step in the ritual process of humiliation which marked the introduction to Van Diemen's Land. While most convicts played along, providing routine answers such as 'burglary, prosecutor William Hunter near Stirling & stealing £15—I broke open the door',[7] others poked fun at the state, managing to hoodwink clerks into writing spurious answers. The English convict Joshua Moore, for example, informed the convict establishment that he had been transported for a 'waistcoat & small clothes I received them from a man named Bastard to pledge—he was not caught'.[8] According to Miller's convict record, however, his response was laconic 'Stated this offence: High Treason'.

Now this offence may have been true for the British subjects on the *Canton*—James Gemmell, John Grant and Jacob Beemer—but treason was neither something Miller would ever have confessed to, nor the crime for which he had been convicted. In fact when the records of the other political prisoners disembarked from the *Canton* are inspected, their replies are recorded in identical terms to Miller's—'Stated this offence: High Treason'. It seems most unlikely that men like the Scot James Gemmell would ever have admitted to treason, or that all should have provided the same terse response to their inquisitor's question. Instead, it seems more likely that the offence was copied off the warrant made out in England.

If this were the case, it is most curious that the warrant for Miller's transportation stated that he had been sentenced for treason, even though all the legal documentation in Canada and England, including the pardon warrant from which he had been removed, clearly stated him to have been sentenced for the felony of armed incursion under the Lawless Aggressions Act. Much the same thing seems to have happened to the American prisoners who arrived on the *Marquis of Hastings* and whose sentences were also recorded by the Muster Master as treason.[9]

The likely explanation is that the nervous Home Office recast the Americans' conviction as treason, regardless of their civil trial in Canada that stated them to be guilty of the felony of piratical invasion. By rewording the offences as treason, at a time when they were arguing for the disallowance of the Act under which they had been tried, the Crown may have tried to head off any further problems about the legality of the transportation raised by sympathetic reformers in England.

Robert Marsh, equally radical in his view of the British legal system, provided a further insight into the process of recording the offence and the sentence:

> We were brought in before him, one at a time, and asked . . . 'What were you tried for? Where were you tried? What was your sentence?' An answer, 'never had any sentence.' 'For what length of time were you sent?' An answer, 'cannot say.' (Turning to his clerk.) 'Put them down for life'. [68–9]

William Gates, whose narrative tends to follow that of Marsh, says much the same: 'Of course we could not tell what our sentence, or how long its duration; for of this we were entirely ignorant ourselves, whereupon the clerk was ordered to put us down for life' (71).

The convicts' records transcribed by Mr Gunn's clerks demonstrate that the statement of offence for these particular convicts was also taken directly from their warrants, rather than from their own words, much as Marsh and Gates reported. Under the section labelled 'stated this offence', all seventy-six prisoners on the *Buffalo* convicted under the Lawless Aggressions Act have an identical response inserted into their record, 'piratical invasion', while for St Clair raider Horace Cooley the offence was recorded, correctly, as burglary. In contrast to their fellow Patriots who arrived earlier, the offence of treason does not appear on the *Buffalo* transportees' records, not even for those who were British subjects. The reason is obvious: these warrants were written by the Upper Canadian authorities, who had won their argument that the Lawless Aggressions Act could be used against Americans facing courts martial at Kingston and London. George Arthur felt little need to worry about agitation on behalf of the Patriots in distant Van Diemen's Land where his old cronies still held sway, and where vast distance effectively removed the prisoners from communication with the radical members of parliament, Messrs Hume and Roebuck. Moreover, there was scant sympathy for republicans in Van Diemen's Land. Even the most radical paper, which was vehemently opposed to transportation, wrote of the American prisoners on the *Buffalo*:

> They are not . . . patriots fighting for their liberty, nor are they even Canadians. They are Borderers from the States—Bushmen, like our sawyers, splitters and fencers—who, being attracted by the troubles in Canada, took arms, not to support the cause of liberty, but to gratify their love of rapine and plunder. They will no doubt make useful men, after they have undergone a little 'probation', and got rid of their 'notions' of Lynch law and mob sovereignty.[10]

Unfortunately, this act of official censure has deprived us of the replies that the Patriots actually gave to Gunn and his attendant clerks. If the Patriots railed against British injustice then the clerks were either under instructions not to record their replies or, perhaps more likely, never entered them into the final version of the record.

The *Canadiens* on board the *Buffalo* were not subject to a similar interrogation, since their warrants were written out for New South Wales. The

Patriots were puzzled as to why the French did not disembark at Hobart as they did, and attributed the segregation to the malice of Van Diemen's Land's governor, Sir John Franklin. Marsh, echoing an earlier assertion by Linus Miller, claimed Franklin told the Patriots they would be punished more severely than those rebels from Lower Canada going on to New South Wales, who were 'poor simple Canadians ... excited to rebellion by you Americans' (72–3). Whether Franklin made such a distinction or not, history has borne it out, by accident more than design. When the *Buffalo* reached Sydney, Governor Gipps informed the captain that Sydney was no longer receiving convicts, and that he was to take his charges to the harsh penal colony on Norfolk Island. Captain Wood refused to comply, insisting that his orders were to leave the convicts in Sydney, dismantle the fittings for a convict ship, and load up with a cargo for New Zealand as soon as possible. Reluctantly, the decision was made to allow the *Canadiens* to stay in Sydney as there was no other available transport.[11] In Sydney, the prisoners from Lower Canada had a much easier time of their penal servitude than those from Upper Canada disembarked in Van Diemen's Land.

When the *Marquis of Hastings* arrived in September 1839, many of those on board were debilitated by the effects of disease, so it is unclear how many Patriots were submitted to Mr Gunn's inquisition. The report of the health officers who boarded the ship on the first day records that 'eight were so ill labouring under various diseases, as to require to be immediately removed on shore and of whom one or two will most probably die'.[12] Those removed included Alexander McLeod, James McNulty, Samuel Chandler, Garret Van Camp and Benjamin Wait. Three subsequently died in hospital: James McNulty on 19 July 1839, Alexander McLeod, 24 July 1839 and Garret Van Camp on 3 September 1839.[13]

Wait and the other sick prisoners who had been shifted to the penitentiary hospital from the *Marquis of Hastings* missed out on the interrogation presided over by William Gunn in Captain Naylor's cabin. Instead, the prison hospital served as an induction of a quite different kind. Wait was later to regard this as something of 'a providential circumstance, inasmuch as I there obtained much information that, no doubt, was a great assistance in averting blows often designed for me, by those beings whom I afterward was forced into contact with'. Many of the occupants of the hospital were 'old hands', who had been long in the colony. They whittled away the hours teaching Wait various tricks:

> [how] to raise the ready for 'lush', (drink) and to evade discovery—how they made up the deficiencies of provision, caused by penury of their masters, by 'weeding' them—while the company took turns in conveying the booty to a general receptacle, and the proceeds were thrown into a public purse— subject only to public wants, or the necessities of a 'gala' time, such as Christmas. [264]

For those on the *Canton*, who had fared so much better during the voyage, the order to disembark was greeted by a near riot. According to Miller, cheering prisoners rushed for the gangway:

> what crowding and jamming, pushing and pulling, cursing and blaspheming among the poor wretches! Little do they realize what the shore will prove to them, or they would be less hasty . . . when I once more set foot on land there was a sensation attending it delightful in the extreme, known only to those who have been long at sea. [261]

Once on land, the whole party was 'marshalled' into some kind of order and, flanked by constables, they were marched towards the Hobart Town Prisoners' Barracks, or the 'Tench' as it was known in convict parlance.[14] All new arrivals were temporarily housed in these barracks before being ordered to march to a more permanent residence. As well as fresh hands, however, the barracks also housed the town chain gangs and those sentenced to punishment on the treadwheel—an enormous revolving structure pushed by the feet of dozens of men who worked in rotation grinding flour for government use. The Tench was also home to public works mechanics who laboured for the Engineering Department, and a myriad of bakers, butchers, clerks, errand boys, boatmen, gatekeepers, watchmen and overseers. In all, the building could accommodate one and a half thousand men.[15] As Miller described it, the Tench was constructed on a rectangle enclosing a yard of about 2 acres. At one end was a church, the basement of which had been converted into cells where the wicked could be detained and locked in the dark to contemplate the error of their ways.[16] On the opposite side was the superintendent's residence. The space between these two symbols of authority was occupied by two wings, one containing the storehouse, cook and bakehouse, mess-room, treadmill, and the barracks, and the other the offices for the superintendent and his attend-ant clerks and a large hospital. The whole area was surrounded by a high wall, 'the top of which was covered with sharp bits of broken glass which would deter', Miller thought, 'any person not made of mahogany from attempts to escalade it'. The *Canton* men were herded through the gates of this building 'like so many cattle' (262). That night they were quartered in an old barn, which Miller found most uncomfortable since '*Vermin* of every description were common, and I generally passed our sleeping hours in real or imaginary battles with these enemies' (274).

The next morning at half past four the 'bell rang for *"turn out,"*' and, as Miller put it, 'there was a terrible rattling of nuisance-tubs, kids, pannakins, &c., until the breakfast hour was over' (263). The recent arrivals were then penned up in a corner under the guard of a pair of constables while 1200 men were mustered by name, ranked into their respective gangs, and marched out through the gates under the charge of public works overseers. Although no communication was permitted with other prisoners, throughout the day, small groups of public works 'idlers' came out to give the *Canton* convicts the once-over—searching for familiar faces.

While Wait had been educated in the hospital, the *Canton* Patriots received their own initiation into the trials and tribulations of a penal colony. Miller had already noted that the constables who were stationed at the gate day and night 'were fond of a *"tip,"*' and that 'trade of all kinds went on briskly' (262). It was thus with some suspicion that he and his companions complied with the order to hand over their own clothes and remaining personal items, including the small amounts of money and tobacco, penknives and watches which they had managed to hold onto until now. These were tied into bundles marked with each man's name and number and thrown into a common storehouse. Although they were assured that their belongings would be safe until such time as they could be collected, the *Canton* convicts never saw their clothes again. Miller claimed that the venal Beemer, who was rewarded for his treachery on board the *Captain Ross* by being promoted to the rank of constable, fraudulently managed to obtain their 'clothing, books, &c., from Mr. Williams, the storekeeper, sold them, and was rioting upon the money' (289). Clad in a prison uniform and stripped of the last mementoes of their distant home, the *Canton* Patriots waited to meet their new penal masters.

8

Ben Franklin's Nephew

THE MEN ON BOARD the *Buffalo* were landed at New Town and were marched through the streets of Hobart to the road station at Sandy Bay, south of the town. This departure from routine procedure spared them the delights of being warehoused in the centre of the town with other recent arrivals and the old hands who had been sentenced to hard labour in one of the Hobart road or chain gangs. In a dispatch to the Colonial Office, the Lieutenant-Governor of Van Diemen's Land, Sir John Franklin, wrote, 'I have not allowed these men to pass through the usual ordeal of the Convict Barracks, not wishing them to be thrown amongst the usual class of Thieves and Rogues who are kept in such places of punishment'.[1] It appears that the decision to separate the *Buffalo* Patriots from the general mass of the prison population was made, not by the Lieutenant-Governor of Van Diemen's Land, but by the Lieutenant-Governor of Upper Canada who, in addition to transmitting a résumé of the character of each of the Patriots for the information of the colonial authorities, also sent 'orders to keep these prisoners distinct in every respect from others'.[2] This may explain why a similar privilege had not been extended to the Patriots on the *Canton* and the *Marquis of Hastings,* as these transports had departed from England under instructions from the Home Office. In fact, when Franklin's dispatch arrived in London, a Colonial Office official wrote, 'This should not be sent to the Home Office, until it shall have been seen by Lord John Russell'.[3] At the heart of the matter was an old question—'whether political offences to which a punishment similar to other crimes is awarded should be visited with the same severity'. Grimly, Russell added the following note: 'The offence is Treason for which death is often inflicted'.[4] In the end, clarification of the issue was sought from Lord Sydenham who was the newly appointed Governor-General of Canada. This confusion was symptomatic of the process by which the *Buffalo* Patriots had been condemned to penal servitude on the other side of the globe.

Spared the horrors of the barracks, the *Buffalo* prisoners had instead to walk the gauntlet of the streets of Hobart. Finding their land legs was a problem for all convicts who had experienced long ocean voyages, and their drunken lurching and stumbling invariably gave the old hands in Hobart plenty of merriment. William Gates described the sensation:

> For two or three weeks we were more or less bothered with this phantom movement of the earth—and for the whole of this time, the ceaseless beating of the surges on the ship's side, continued to ring in our ears; whilst our 'bunks' in the 'cabins' rocked to and fro as did those on the water. We could not work the idea out of our heads, but gradually the feeling wore away. [75]

As they staggered through town, they had to pass a reception committee of field police, dressed in blue and equipped with batons. Marsh described how these convict trusties yelled out to the Americans: 'you are not quite so smart now as when you was in Canada, shooting the Queen's Loyal Subjects, with your yankee rifle's; you've got no rifle here, but you'll find plenty of carts and stone' (70). With some satisfaction he reported that a Yankee sailor amid the company of hecklers had spoken out on their behalf: 'if they had their rifles now, you would not dare talk so' (70). Others apparently came out of curiosity to see the rebels from Canada, as if Marsh and his fellow stumbling Americans were a sideshow attraction at a travelling fair.

They competed for the attention of the inhabitants, however, with the other attractions of the town. They had gone just a short distance when they passed four men standing on a scaffold about to be executed. A little further down the road they encountered a gang of two hundred convicts working in heavy irons. The Patriots regarded this as a more ominous reception, as Gates recounted:

> We had hardly our feet on the soil, when almost the first objects that greeted our vision, were gibbets, and men toiling in the most abject misery, looking more degraded even than so many dumb beasts. Such sights, and the supposition that such might be our fate, served to sink the iron still deeper in our souls. [74]

Reference to contemporary newspapers reveals that the executions actually occurred five days *after* Gates and his fellow Patriots had been marched through the streets of Hobart. The four unfortunate men who were launched into eternity, John Davis, John Riley, Edward Martin and George Petitt, did indeed go to their eternal account in front of a sizeable crowd. According to the *Colonial Times*, this interest was largely because the crowd was witnessing the first public execution to have been held in Hobart for some time. There had been no hanging at all the previous year. For Gates this was too good an opportunity to miss, however, and he appears to have conflated the Patriots' arrival and the execution in order to infuse his account with dramatic punch.[5]

Having passed through the town, the *Buffalo* men finally reached their new home. It proved to be not much to look at, as Marsh recalled, consisting 'of eight or nine huts, built of split stuff, standing upright; ten or twelve feet in length, fastened at the bottom to logs or sleepers, and thatched rough' (70). The huts were arranged in a square and surrounded by a palisade punctured by a single gate which was kept locked. It was customary for the Lieutenant-Governor of Van Diemen's Land to address newly arrived prisoners. Marsh recalled that, on the morning before the address, a clerk visited each hut and instructed the *Buffalo* prisoners to appear 'as well as possible' (71). Having adjusted their slop clothing and wiped their boots, they were ranked up in a line two deep by an overseer from Yorkshire who, according to Gates, instructed the Patriots in the 'mysteries of that etiquette which behoved men of low degree, crushed down to the earth, to observe in the presence of those who, [were] clothed with British power' (79). At ten in the morning, there was a commotion heralding the approach of the Patriots' official welcoming party. The gates of the yard were opened and Franklin rode in, according to Marsh, accompanied by a train of officials both mounted and on foot. In the presence of 'Capt. Sir John Franklin, R.N. K.T. Lieutenant-Governor of the Island of Van Dieman's Land and its dependencies, commander-in-chief of her Majesties forces therein, &c. &c.' (71), the overseer ordered the prisoners to doff their leather side caps which, although designed for army use, had become standard convict issue. Heustis was outraged to be commanded by a common British felon to bare his head 'to a servant of royalty'. For a moment he considered resisting the order, but in the end decided that, 'situated as we were, unconditional submission, however revolting to our feelings, was the best policy' (100).

At an almost identical welcoming reception held in the Hobart Prisoners' Barracks, Linus Miller had observed that Franklin surveyed the whole party before selecting a commanding position 'six paces in front of the line' (267), where he addressed the massed ranks of prisoners from the lofty elevation of his horse. Miller's account of the event was larded with sarcasm:

> Only think that I, thy humble servant, who as a matter of course could not have seen during the twenty-two years of my blissful existence, any body of more importance than a country squire, parson, or village pettifogger, should, by a single stroke of fortune, be thrown into the presence and society of this *great man*! Truly, I was born to behold wonders! [263]

After 'half-a-dozen "*a-hems*"', the governor commenced. The speech proved to be long and tedious, despite—or perhaps because of—the fact that it had been trotted out on each of the twenty-three times that convicts had been disembarked from a transport during Franklin's term of office.[6] Miller was under the impression that the entire speech was delivered to invisible beings which somehow hovered in the air above Sir John's bare-headed congregation, for Franklin's eyes seemed to be permanently fixed on the heavens. It seems likely that the address would have proved monotonously dreary to all the assembled prisoners, British and American alike. They would have already heard the same homilies from judges and gaol and hulk chaplains who preached from court benches and pulpits as each parcel of prisoners was bundled towards their final antipodean destination.[7] As Miller recalled, Franklin constantly repeated the word 'bad', which he intoned like the beat of a drum: 'men! you have been sent here by the laws of your country as bad men; unfit to go at large; dangerous to the peace of society; dangerous to the security of property; you are all *bad* men! very bad men indeed!' (267). He contrasted the wickedness of his literally captive audience with the mercy of the laws of England that, through their 'mild' nature had enabled prisoners like themselves to escape the gallows.

The *Buffalo* prisoners found Franklin's homily equally tedious. Gates thought that the speech, which lasted two hours, could have been delivered by any American schoolboy 'extemporaneously in twenty minutes' (81). To make matters worse, Franklin repeatedly paused in mid-speech, rolling his eyes and looking skywards. Miller thought that he looked like 'a person undergoing the most excruciating agony' (267), while Heustis, who had once worked as a Morocco leather salesman, thought that the governor resembled 'a dying calf, in the hands of a butcher' (101), constantly rolling his eyes to the heavens as if unwilling to look his charges in the face. In Gates's view, however, it was not Franklin who was butchered, but the Queen's English which 'suffered not a little—for his words were spoken in half finished sentences, with stammering pauses between that exceeded the sentences themselves, and his language was excessively poor and tautological' (81).

Franklin's address varied little from one convict intake to the next, and usually concluded with a dire warning, as Miller recounted:

> 'You have been sent here for various periods of time, varying from seven years to the term of natural life; and you are sent here for punishment. You will, therefore, submit to whatever treatment you may be subjected, during your respective sentences, without murmuring or complaint.' [267–8]

However, to the horror of the Patriots transported on the *Canton*, Franklin did not stop at that point. While the British convicts were dismissed at the end of his address, the Patriots were ordered to stand. Having dismounted from his horse, Franklin marched over to face the four men. On being informed that these were the state prisoners from Canada, he drew himself up to his full height and stared the Patriots full in the face for what Miller thought was at least five minutes. During the uneasy silence the young law clerk pondered his fate: 'I felt that the time had come which was in a great measure to decide our fate. The horrid past, the dreadful future, visions to make the heart ache, the pulse to stop, the blood to congeal, were sporting with my imagination' (269).

When Franklin finally spoke, however, it was merely to repeat a by now tedious refrain—'You are bad men, very bad men indeed'. Standing to attention in his prison slops, Miller was informed that the crime of rebellion under any circumstances was one of:

> the highest crime known in law, under any, even the worst of governments; but to rebel against the government of England and against her excellent laws; to attempt to overthrow the one and subvert the other, is the height of human wickedness. [269–70]

At this point the *Canton* surgeon, John Irvine, intervened, reminding the governor that Miller and his fellow Patriots were American citizens.[8] The news did little to placate Franklin; rolling his eyes to the heavens once more, he exclaimed that while the Canadians, if they thought that they had been badly governed, might have had some excuse for their actions, Miller and his fellow Yankees could have none. In invading a country at peace with their own, they had violated not only the laws of the United States, but also those of England. Franklin turned to address Miller but he did little more than bang on his favourite tin drum:

> '*You* are an *extremely* bad man. I can not conceive how any man could be so desperate, so depraved. How merciful her Majesty was to spare your life! Hanging would have been too good for you!—*Sympathiser! Bad man! Very bad man!*' [270]

Benjamin Wait had a somewhat different take on Franklin's distaste for American republicanism. He and his fellow Patriots on the *Marquis of Hastings* had likewise been singled out by Franklin, and berated:

> with high invectives, for 'offences against God, and all the ties of social government—for treason, a crime the foremost in all the *British code* . . . some of you, while in England, rendered yourselves quite notorious, for writing disrespectfully of the authorities under whose control you were placed, and even of the government. I will have you understand that you are in a *penal Colony* now, where public sympathy will be no advantage to you, and where all the inhabitants will deem it their duty to keep the strictest watch over you—where, for a slight censure of the government, your punishment will be severe'. [262–3]

Sir John Franklin was a polar explorer who had gained his fame following an expedition across the arctic tundra to the Polar Sea, where he had been forced to eat the soles of his boots to keep himself alive.[9] Hailed by the British establishment as a hero, 'the man who ate his shoes' was seen very differently by Miller:

> Clad in his official garb, adorned with his star, and covered with his cocked cap and feather, no nabob of India could affect more dignity and importance. He appeared to feel, as he strutted about, that he was the only man upon earth. His height was, I should judge, about five feet nine inches; his circumference quite out of proportion, and clearly indicating, that however starved he might have been as 'Captain Franklin', in his northern expedition, he had never been more fortunate in the south as governor of the land of Nod, and that here there was no scarcity of grease and good foraging. [266–7]

Standing in ranks in the yard of the Hobart Town Tench, Miller suspiciously eyed Franklin's boots. Not, as he explained, from the supposition that the great explorer had once more been driven to the necessity of chewing on his soles, but because there 'was no certainty what the man, who was evidently a great glutton, might do' (266). Franklin's gluttony was source of much savage glee for all the Patriots, who took their revenge on the great man by casting him as the very opposite of a hero. On another occasion Marsh described the governor as 'an enormous mass of blubber and wind' (74) and estimated his weight at 300 pounds, although he added:

> there was so much combustible matter that the great mass might fall a little short in weight, you need not laugh, for I assure you it was the largest lump of human composition that I ever beheld. I suppose it was on account of his bulkiness and knavery, that he had been allowed such great honor amongst the brother-hood; I am sure it was not on account of fluency of speech. [74]

It was Franklin's horse that Marsh felt pity for, as the animal was forced to stand in the yard for two hours supporting that great weight. When Franklin finally turned to make his leave, Marsh reported that 'The horse, although a large one, fairly reals as he moves off' (74).

There was a group of fifteen or twenty old hands ranked behind Marsh and his comrades disembarked from the *Buffalo*. These men were cooks, mechanics and other 'idlers' attached to the road party at Sandy Bay. As Franklin 'puffed and blowed like a porpoise' (74), Marsh overheard the following exchange:

> 'I think the old mutton-eater, will want as many as two sheep for his dinner today,' 'why,' says one, 'is he so fond of mutton?' 'yes,' says he, 'one sheep at ordinary times, satisfies him for a meal, but on over action, like this, it takes two.' 'I should think so,' says the other, 'to supply the vacancy in the loss of so much wind.' [73]

Gates derived much amusement from the '*great* man's appearance'. He confessed that whereas he was at a loss to know whether Franklin was great in mental qualities, 'he was truly great in all that makes the man, physically—flesh and blubber'. As Franklin preached from the back of his horse, Gates noted that he lacked a neck and that his head, rather than standing aloft from his torso, 'was chucked down between his shoulders, for the wise provision, no doubt, of shortening the esophagus'. On further examination Gates observed that Franklin's stomach 'made equal advances toward the head, thus bringing the two in such close proximity, that the sympathy which is said by physiologists to exist between these organs was extraordinarily developed'. He thought it thus all the more strange that Franklin seemed to be permanently out of breath. As he spoke, air was driven in puffs through 'his brandy bottled nose, like steam from the escape pipe of an asthmatic boat'. Gates concluded that 'the vital organs were so much encroached upon' by their neighbours 'that they found it exceedingly difficult to keep the old man in sufficient wind' (79–80). Wright was more to the point. He thought that Franklin looked 'like a *bon vivant*, without any strong marks, save obesity and imbecility' (21).

Miller could not help being struck by the irony that this pompous official, his chest adorned with the star of the Order of Bath and his head covered with a cocked hat and feathers, was 'a nephew of our immortal Benjamin Franklin'. How was it possible that a man 'so destitute of honorable feelings and principles' (274) could be related to one of the founding fathers of Yankee republican virtue? For Miller and his fellow Patriots, this must have seemed a cruel twist of fate—that their gaoler-in-chief, who strutted around on his horse as if 'he was the only man upon earth' (267), was not just the representative of monarchical oppression, but a relative of one of the founding fathers of American liberty. Worse still, this 'old woman', appointed to office by her Majesty's advisers, turned out to bear what Miller believed to be an 'inveterate malice against *Americans*' (274).

Franklin's appearance seems to have seared itself on the collective consciousness of the Patriots. Marsh, for example, thought that his half-closed eyes resembled 'two large pealed turnips' (72), while Gates remarked that, with his head thrown back and his eyes perpetually elevated skywards, 'all that could be seen of the dull orbs of a still duller soul, was a halo of dingy whiteness, emblazened with a network of scarlet' (81). Both Heustis and Miller described Franklin's features with the exactness of a phrenologist. They recorded the colour of his complexion and eyes, and the size of his forehead, mouth, chin and nose. Just as they had stood semi-naked before Gunn and the Board of Health while their physical features were described for the clerks to copy into the registers of the Convict Department, so Heustis

John Tyrrell, photographer unknown. Tyrrell was one of the few Upper Canadians transported on the Buffalo *and was suspected of being an informer. He was the first to be pardoned in Van Diemen's Land.*

Samuel Chandler, photographer unknown. Chandler was a major in the Patriot Army and a key figure in the Short Hills invasion. He escaped from Van Diemen's Land with Benjamin Wait in 1841.

Elijah Woodman, artist unknown. Woodman was the oldest of the Patriots and dogged by ill-health. This drawing was done on the Young Eagle *just before he died, during his voyage home.*

William Gunn, photographer J. W. Beattie. Gunn, the imposing Superintendent of the Prisoners' Barracks, lost his arm in a shootout with bushrangers. He was regarded with reluctant admiration by the Patriots.

Sir John Franklin, lithograph by Alfred Bock, after a portrait by L. Hage. A decidedly flattering portrait of the polar explorer in his role as Lieutenant-Governor of Van Diemen's Land. The Patriots described Franklin as a glutton and a fool, calling him 'the old granny'.

Sir George Arthur, watercolour from a painting by G. T. Berthon. Previously Lieutenant-Governor of Van Diemen's Land before becoming Lieutenant-Governor of Upper Canada, Arthur was seen as a brutal martinet, even though he did pardon the great majority of the Patriots sentenced to death for invading Canada.

John George Lambton, Earl of Durham, engraved by Charles Turner after Thomas Lawrence, 1829. Nicknamed 'radical Jack', the Earl of Durham was appointed Governor-in Chief of Canada in 1838 but quit soon after and then published a highly critical Report on the Affairs of British North America in 1839. The Patriots placed great faith in his fairmindedness.

Linus Miller, photographer unknown. Law clerk Linus Miller held a commission in the Patriot Army and was one of the youngest Patriots transported to Van Diemen's Land. He published an account of his trials and subsequent exile, Notes of an Exile in Van Dieman's Land, in 1846.

Port Arthur (detail), 1854 etching by artist N. Remond. One of the few representations of the handcarts pulled by convicts on which the Patriots were forced to work.

Port Arthur, lithograph by Charles Hutchins from a sketch by Charles Hext, 184?. Named after their nemesis, George Arthur, the penitentiary at Port Arthur was a fearsome site of secondary punishment to which six of the Patriots were sentenced for trying to escape.

Hobart Town and Derwent River, lithograph by Charles Hutchins from a sketch by Charles Hext, 1845. Hobart Town was a busy whaling port with many American whaling ships which offered the Patriots several opportunities to escape.

The windmill at Prescott, watercolour by Thomas Ainslie, 1838. This site of the invasion of Prescott shows Mile Point in the United States, across the narrow St Laurence, where American spectators watched the battle and cheered on the vastly outnumbered Patriots.

Kingston from Fort Henry, etching by James Gray, 1828. A similar view would have greeted the incarcerated Patriots if they had been able to see through the thick stone walls of Fort Henry.

Green Ponds, Van Diemen's Land, lithograph P. Blanchard, 1841?. Green Ponds was the site of the third probation station where the Patriots worked in convict road gangs.

St Mary's Church, Green Ponds, architectural drawing. Patriot mechanics were employed in the construction of this church while they were stationed at Green Ponds.

A contemporary painting of the Upper Canadian town of Prescott from the New York town of Ogdensburg reveals how close the two places were.

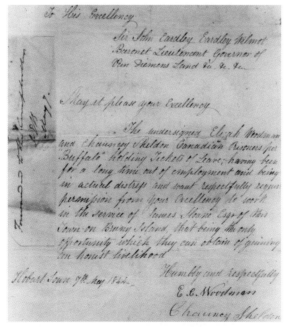

Extract from a letter of Elijah Woodman. These final words were dictated to someone on board Young Eagle as Elijah Woodman was dying. The captain undertook Woodman's last wish to the letter, salvaging the letters and journals from the shipwrecked boat and returning them to Woodman's widow, Lydia.

Petition from Woodman and Sheldon. Elijah Woodman and Chauncey Sheldon were the oldest of the Patriots and found great difficulty getting work once they had been given their 'tickets'. Woodman nearly died of starvation.

The Eagle and the Lion. The triumphant American eagle has the demoralised British lion caught in its claws in this Patriot symbol, which was reproduced on documents of the Patriot Army. In reality, the situation was exactly reversed.

Convict uniform and caps. This distinctive particoloured clothing was what the Patriots called 'magpie'.

The Windmill at Prescott, photograph by Elinor Morrisby.
This contemporary photograph of the site of the Battle of the Windmill,
now a museum, shows how close it is to the United States.

Treadwheel, lithograph, 1840, from Voyage autour du monde de l'Astrolabe et de la Zélée . . . 1837, 38, 39 et 40, Paris, 1843. *The Hobart Town treadmill was an excruciating punishment experienced by Joseph Stewart and Linus Miller* en route *to Port Arthur.*

and Miller recorded the principal features of their gaoler's countenance for the benefit of their American readership. Thus they retrospectively subjected the highest official of Van Diemen's Land to the same humiliating ordeal to which the Patriots themselves had been forced to submit. The similarity between their descriptions of Franklin and those routinely entered in the Convict Department description registers is striking—so much so, that with the simple addition of a few tabs and carriage returns, the accounts of Heustis and Miller can be converted into tabular forms almost identical to those filled out by the clerks.

Sir John Franklin Described

Feature	Miller	Heustis
Complexion	dark	dark
Forehead	low and standing back like an idiot's	low
Eyes	hazel, very large and dull	dull hazel eyes
Nose	enormous	large and prominent
Mouth	very wide	large and prominent
Chin	prominent	large and prominent
Remarks	an imbecile old man; a paragon of good nature; with an excellent opinion of himself, and little wit to uphold it [266]	impossible to discern any indications of superior intellect [100]

Yet, for all of their attempts to lampoon Franklin—to imprison him within their narratives in the same way as their features had been recorded for posterity in the records of the Convict Department—the Patriots' accounts merely serve as a reminder of their own powerlessness, ranked up in a miserable prison yard, cap in hand, at the feet of Franklin's horse. In reality Franklin was no 'old granny', as Miller claimed (297). Franklin and the British regulars standing to attention, bayonets fixed, had the Patriots squarely in their power. For all their republican spirit and retrospective bravado, the Patriots were reduced to what Thomas Laqueur has called 'objects of administration' who could be dispatched to work, victualled, punished or rewarded—all with the scratch of a goose-quill pen.[10]

Ironically Franklin, too, was a victim of the system, which the Patriots dimly understood, if only in retrospect. The governor was continually undermined by internal factions—including the nephew-in-law of his predecessor—and almost universally despised by the colonial administration for being in the thrall of his clever wife, Lady Jane. Samuel Snow caught a whiff of this in his narrative, seeing the great man as enfeebled by decrepitude, though he was only in his mid-fifties:

he was a very old man, and is known the world over, as being a noted English navigator. He had been employed by the English government in several exploring expeditions, and voyages of discovery. His imbecillity, 'that last infirmity of noble minds,' now gave opportunity to the designing members of his cabinet, to govern the affairs of the colony in a manner which suited their caprice. [11–12]

In contrast to his predecessor George Arthur, Franklin had little control over the development of the apparatus of convict management in Van Diemen's Land. It was against his wishes that he had to preside over a massive change in the organisation of Arthur's elaborate 'assignment system' which was largely dictated by London bureaucrats who had never been to the antipodes. Franklin and his principal officials tried a little trimming around the edges of the new 'probation system', but it was, for all intents and purposes, foisted upon them.[11] No wonder he dared not look his charges in the eye, for he knew only too well what awaited them.

Elijah Woodman wrote in his letters home that Franklin spoke to the men from the *Buffalo* in 'a very mild manner and also gave us good advice'.[12] Woodman's report may have been closer to the mark than those of his compatriots. For all the Patriots' retrospective demonising of Franklin, the beleaguered governor did try his ineffectual best for them. The prisoners on the *Canton* and the *Buffalo* were among the first to experience the horrors of probationary labour, and although Franklin tried to shield the Patriots from its worst effects, they were quickly caught up in the grinding gears of a system which proved from its outset to be a disaster.[13]

9

The Land of Nod

THE LAND OF NOD lay east of Eden. It was where Cain was cast into exile, condemned to wander the earth for the crime of fratricide. Fate had banished the Patriots from the Eden of the American Republic and forced them to travel eastwards, following the rising sun, until they had reached the farthest shore. The Land of Nod was a fitting description for their new destination, especially as, in their eyes, they had been condemned unjustly to penal servitude. By contrast every other inhabitant of Van Diemen's Land, from the most wretched prisoner to the governor himself, was marked with the sign of God which distinguished the sons of Cain from the rest of humanity.

It was the half-dead men on the *Marquis of Hastings* who were first carried east of Eden. Despite the nightmarish conditions they had experienced at sea, their early arrival in September 1839 was to prove a boon. As soon as they were fit enough, they were sent on assignment to work for settlers. As Wait recalled, Lieutenant-Governor Franklin waxed almost lyrical about the benefits of assignment and told them:

> 'you must submit to the legal control of your masters; for when put in their custody we hold them accountable for your conduct; and if you pass with good conduct your probationary periods, you will be entitled to the indulgence of a ticket of leave, with which you may choose your own masters and employment, and receive wages; but still subject to restrictions and surveillance; and close upon its heels comes the emancipation, with its *high privileges* of citizenship, and, at last, the *free pardon* from Her Majesty, *God bless her*. These are favors of great import, and worth aiming at; but they cannot be obtained without good conduct.' [262]

It was still some weeks before Franklin actually granted this great privilege of assignment. In the meantime, according to Wait, Mr Gunn had put them to work on the roads, telling them '*as a friend,* to go out with the gangs, as the work would be light, and the free air would contribute more to their health than remaining shut in the yard' (263–4). The work turned out to be:

> quarrying, breaking, and wheeling stone for McAdamizing the streets of Hobarttown [*sic*]. It was not easy employment, but still they found more bitterness attending a 'proper submission' to the tormenting annoyances of the convict overseers, who took pleasure in vexing them, for the purpose, most probably, of getting an opportunity of complaint, on account of the distinctive features of their class. [264]

After four or five weeks, James Waggoner, Norman Mallory, George Cooley and John Vernon were much relieved to be sent on assignment to different settlers in the country, leaving Samuel Chandler and Benjamin Wait at the hospital until they too were assigned to work on the property of a prominent landowner 50 miles north of Hobart. As it happened, Chandler and Wait were among the very last convicts in Van Diemen's Land to have that particular convict experience. Within three months of their arrival, the landscape of penal servitude was to change completely.

The assignment system was perfected by Lieutenant-Governor George Arthur and he defended it to the last. It was in effect a huge system of coerced labour, designed to achieve the dual objectives of fostering colonial growth and reshaping the Empire's transported criminals into dutiful servants, imbued with the Protestant work ethic, servants who knew when to tip their hats to their social betters. Technically, assignment had been put on a regular footing in Van Diemen's Land by Arthur's predecessor Lieutenant-Governor Sorell, who had introduced most of its key features. When Arthur became the governor in 1824, he had set about the huge task of reorganising the existing bureaucracy while developing a centralised record-keeping system.[1] This information-processing engine was maintained by a small army of clerks who worked under the supervision of the Superintendent of Convicts, a man named Josiah Spode. Spode was a member of the family who had pioneered the introduction of factory discipline in the Staffordshire potteries.[2] For the next sixteen years, Van Diemen's Land operated as one giant multi-site factory, controlled from a series of offices in Hobart which collated detailed information on the day-to-day behaviour of every convict.

At the heart of Arthur's system lay a partnership between public and private interests. When each transport docked in Hobart, the Superintendent of the Prisoners' Barracks, William Gunn, was charged with drawing up an allocation list that contained information on the prior employment of each prisoner. On the basis of this list, some convicts were sent to the public works to man lighters, slaughter government cattle, build carts, mend tools, and perform a plethora of other tasks required to maintain the apparatus of the convict system.[3] After the government had taken its cut, the remaining convicts were assigned to settlers to work on farms, or in shops and businesses, or as domestic servants. Settlers were required to feed, house and clothe their assigned servants, but they did not have to pay them a wage. Much was made of the duties of the settler, who in effect became an unofficial arm of government charged with policing Britain's transported felons. Because the settlers were in effect provided with a labour force free of charge, the profits which accrued from assignment were considerable.[4]

Although settlers were prohibited from beating their convicts, they were far from powerless. The authority of the master was backed up by the full force of the state. If they had reason to be disgruntled with the behaviour of their assigned charges, masters could bring their convict servants to a local magistrates' bench.[5] There they could be subjected to summary justice, and if found guilty sentenced to an array of punishments including flogging, solitary confinement and a stint on the treadwheel. The local magistrate could also recommend that the convict be dismissed from the master's service and sent to a road or chain gang. A bench of three magistrates could impose draconian punishments for more serious offences, including sentence extensions or an order to remove the convict to one of a number of hard-regime penal stations, including the notorious Port Arthur on the Tasman Peninsula. Each quarter, every magistrate in the colony was instructed to send a copy of all cases heard, together with a statement of offences awarded, to the office of the Muster Master, where they were transcribed into an enormous multi-volume offence register ordered according to each prisoner's police number, name and ship of arrival. Armed with this information, it was possible to retrieve a copy of each convict's colonial record, and in a single glance pronounce him 'good', 'bad', 'troublesome' or 'indifferent'.

For Arthur this was the crux of his grand design. He saw convict Van Diemen's Land as a moral barometer whereby the character of a prisoner determined the position that he occupied. At any moment this could be verified by reaching for his record, in the same way as a log book could be opened to check the progress of a ship. The convict would enter Arthur's 'system' at the assignment level. There he would work under relatively benign conditions unless by dint of future misconduct he should earn a demotion to one of the various levels of punishment—which, like Dante's tiered vision of hell, formed the sub-basements of the penal landscapes of Van Diemen's Land.[6]

Whatever its moral pretensions, Arthur's mechanism for 'grinding rogues honest' was driven by simple economics.[7] It did not make sense to push convicts engaged in complex tasks to the point where they dropped or, worse still, sabotaged the enterprise. Most masters knew it was in their best interests to reward their workforce; they often turned a blind eye to the depredations of their assigned servants, especially where pressing charges meant running the risk of losing the services of valued prisoners. Conversely, most of the punishment labour undertaken on the roads and in penal stations was organised around a work gang under an overseer, whose task it was to detect those who did not pull their weight. Under the constant eye of a monitor, ganged convicts were pulled up before the magistrates' bench at a far greater rate than assigned prisoners. While Arthur's design was well calculated for extracting labour from the bodies of prisoners, the levels of punishment that it inflicted bore little or no relation to the severity of crimes for which they had been transported. In effect, convicts were rewarded or beaten into submission on the basis of their ability to generate profits for private masters and the state.[8]

In the case of the Patriot prisoners sent on assignment to settlers, it is possible to piece together something of their movements. Wait was an educated man with clerical and accountancy skills, while Chandler was a wheelwright and carpenter. Their services had been requested by Commissary-General Roberts, to work on his huge rural property at Ashgrove, north of Hobart: Wait as a clerk and storekeeper and Chandler as a carpenter. According to Wait, Roberts had a great difficulty to surmount in obtaining the two Americans, as it had been ordered 'by the Gov. in council, that none of them should be allowed to remain in a seaport, or two go to one master' (268). However, by threatening to resign, Roberts got his way. The men 'were happy in being sent together to his farm', where they were well-treated and surrounded by 'some of the most beautiful mountains, sugarloaves, and other scenes, that you can possibly fancy' (268). However attractive his setting, Wait found his unpaid job to be an arduous one, as he told his wife:

> My duty is to collect, issue, and account for, all provision and clothing wanted by twenty men employed on the place—to keep a minute diary of occurrences—to muster the two thousand sheep, quarterly, with the two hundred cattle, and several horses; and at the same time to furnish a most particular description of them—naming every spot and mark and brand—to keep secure, under lock and key, and account for every particle of wool, produce, &c. raised on or coming to the farm—and render a weekly schedule to Mr. R. Then add to this, the duty of a teacher of five children, which has been part of my vocation for the last six months, and the multiplicity of cares would seem to exclude the possibility of my writing these letters. Indeed I have found it extremely difficult, for almost every moment of my time has its engagement, from four in the morning until eleven at night . . . [268–9]

If Roberts were forced to pay for these services, as well as Chandler's work as carpenter and wheelwright, he would have been up for a pretty penny. As it was, all he was required to do was feed and house his two valuable bonded servants. John Vernon's new master would have been well pleased to receive the services of a carpenter for next to nothing, and the masters of George Cooley and James Waggoner found themselves with skilled ploughmen, who were much in demand and could ask for a good wage as freemen. As a sawyer, Norman Mallory would likewise have been a desirable addition to a rural establishment in Van Diemen's Land. From their convict records, it is clear than none of their masters saw fit to bring any of these men before a magistrate. It was clear that the American prisoners, despite being transported for a capital offence, were well treated when they were in Van Diemen's Land. Other poor wretches, who may have been convicted for a minor felony, found themselves at the mercy of the system only because they were possessed of skills for which there was little colonial demand.

The opponents of transportation seized on this contradiction, which they saw as the assignment system's fatal flaw. They argued that such heavy reliance on coerced labour smacked of slavery.[9] This was a point on which the Patriot narratives were in complete agreement. All of them likened the prisoners' condition to that of slaves held against their will in a cruel and corrupt system. Robert Marsh was particularly scathing about assignment. He thought that the whole system was rotten to the core: the wealthy settlers exercised a great influence over the local magistrates, whom he described as 'petty tyrants' who, 'for a small salary, leave England for the honorable office of assisting to crush the poor prisoner to the dust' (86). He added that they were 'so hardened and eager to punish, they have been known to leave their dinner for that purpose, which I believe an Englishman was never known to do on any other occasion' (85).

Marsh was not alone in criticising the masters of convict labour for their misuse of the rules and regulations governing assignment. In the early 1830s two visiting Quakers, Backhouse and Walker, had reported that many settlers used the magistrates' bench as an unofficial hiring and firing mechanism to dispose of unskilled convicts in the expectation of receiving more useful replacements. They alleged that many magistrates colluded with such practices, sending prisoners to be flogged or to labour on the roads for what were essentially trumped-up charges.[10]

Flogging, above all else, symbolised the misuse of authority. This was seen not just as a barbaric and savage form of punishment, but as a practice that associated convict Australia with the whipping of slaves on Caribbean sugar estates. In his bitter critique of the misuse of convict labour by settlers,

Marsh accused one landowner of sending a man to be flogged accompanied by a letter, 'telling the magistrate to be in a hurry, to give the man sixty lashes, that he may return to his work without delay, and in the letter, a promise of a fat pig or goose, when he calls to make him a visit' (85).

The changes to the penal system which separated the men of the *Marquis of Hastings* from their Patriot comrades came as the result of a damning parliamentary report on penal transportation in 1837–8. On the strength of this, the British government decided to abandon transportation to New South Wales and to change Arthur's system in Van Diemen's Land, stripping it of its connotations with slavery.[11] Franklin was instructed to cease the process of assigning convict labour to settlers free of charge and to devise a new system which would ensure that convicts were punished according to the severity of the sentence that had been passed upon them, rather than according to their utility as unfree workers. It was for this reason—nothing to do with a supposed malevolence on Franklin's part— that the experience of the Patriots from the *Canton* and the *Buffalo* was so different from that of their comrades who had arrived a few months earlier.

As of January 1840, every new arrival was required to serve a period of probationary labour on the roads of Van Diemen's Land.[12] These probationers were to be segregated from convicts who had arrived under the old system and were to be managed according to a new set of rules and regulations adapted from the instructions Arthur had devised for organising punishment gangs. The period of probationary labour to be served was fixed at twelve to eighteen months for those sentenced to seven years' transportation, eighteen to twenty-four months for those sentenced to ten or fourteen years' transportation, and over two years for lifers.[13]

Each probation station was to be managed by a superintendent, assisted by a team of overseers and other junior officers, and visited on a regular basis by a magistrate who presided over any cases brought by the station's officers. A catechist was also attached to each probationary gang, charged with the duty of reporting on the moral welfare of the prisoners.[14] The system was predicated on the assumption that it would be self-regulating. Thus it was assumed that the wicked would sink to oblivion, while the good would rise out of the gangs and escape from the torments of hard labour on the roads. With this in mind, the landscape of probationary Van Diemen's Land was constructed to repeatedly impress the message that salvation from daily torment could only be obtained by abject submission and hard work.

Most probation stations were divided into three yards reserved for the first-, second- and third-class gangs. All fresh recruits were fed into the second-class gang, but future good or bad behaviour could result in physical relocation within the bounds of the station to mark the convict's rise or fall on the probationary scale of being. Further 'bad' behaviour could be punished with a sentence to the probationary chain gang stationed on the Domain in Hobart. Those who were especially 'wicked' were shipped to the Port Arthur Penal Station. The reward for good behaviour was promotion to a billeted position in the first-class yard, where the workload was lighter, accommodation was superior, and incentives of tea and sugar were provided. Continued good service entitled the prisoner to a transfer to a loan gang, where he could be hired out to a settler for a small payment. Those who continued to doff their caps and bend their backs became eligible for a ticket-of-leave, a pass which allowed the convict to seek employment for a full wage under the condition that he remain within the confines of a designated police district.

At first no one knew what to do with the four Patriots on the *Canton*. After a few days they were separately called in to see the superintendent, Mr Gunn, who told them that they would be required to serve certain periods of probation on the roads. Miller and his two companions were informed that 'we must serve two years of this horrid slavery, before any indulgence whatever would be granted us' (275). However, on Miller's objection Gunn assured them:

> this notice was only formal, and would not be enforced unless the governor, after due consideration of our cases, should feel it his duty to treat us with severity. He also added that there was little doubt that the liberty of the island would be granted us upon certain conditions, on account of our being state prisoners, and the circumstances of no orders with reference to our treatment having accompanied us from England. [275]

So the following day, when all of the English prisoners were sent out to labour on the roads, the Patriots were left to twiddle their thumbs. Their confidence was short-lived. Miller told a similar story to that recounted by Wait. Both claimed that the Patriots were *tricked* into performing unpaid work for the British government. In Miller's account he was politely summoned to see Mr Gunn, who flattered him by saying the colony needed 'such young men as yourself', urging him to give up his 'republican notions' in the interests of self-advancement. Having gained Miller's trust, he went on to say, 'I know that you Americans detest idleness, and thought you would deem it a privilege to do some trifling labor for exercise. ... The service will be perfectly voluntary on your part, and as the governor has his eye upon you, it may influence him in his decision upon your cases' (278). Miller and his companions debated Gunn's proposition and agreed, 'inasmuch as it was voluntary, to take half an hour's exercise every morning at sweeping'. This was their fatal error, Miller believed, 'for Mr. G. was only trying the yoke upon our necks to see how it would fit' (279).

When Miller reported for his 'exercise', a convict overseer handed him a broom and indicated he should sweep, to which Miller replied with contempt, ' "you must give me some instructions, as I was never bound apprentice to a *sweep.*" Here the fellow turned his back on me, and muttered the d—— Yankee *quill driver*' (279).

While he maintained the fiction of voluntary work, Miller found himself with a broom put in his hand every day, including the Sabbath. At this he rebelled, and when the threat of flogging failed to move him, the convict overseer pleaded that Miller should sweep or else he would lose favour:

> 'You will offend Mr Gunn, who is your friend, if you don't.'
>   'I shall offend my God, who is greater than Mr Gunn, if I do.'
>   'God Almighty is nothing here compared with Mr Gunn.' . . . shouted the overseer. [281]

The exchanges with this 'Depraved, debased . . . hardened wretch in whose breast every ennobling quality was forever annihilated', makes it very apparent why things might not have gone too well for Miller, who soon found himself in solitary confinement for shirking his 'voluntary' work (279–80).

The Patriots should have refused any work from the outset, Miller insisted, which 'would have saved us years of slavery' (279). It is unclear how the Patriots hit upon this explanation for being compelled to undertake hard labour, but Miller told his readers that he had it 'from unquestionable authority' that Governor Franklin expected the Americans to refuse to do the voluntary 'exercise', and would not have forced them to work '*through fear of the consequences*' (295). Miller's source for this was probably Edward Macdowell, who had been Attorney-General under Franklin and who took Miller into his law office after he got his ticket-of-leave. It does seem that the superintendent kept an eye out for Miller and his comrades, and sheltered them from the extreme brutalities of the probation system, probably under orders from Franklin.

The governor was in something of a quandary of what to do with these men. He did not want them thrown into the probation gangs, yet his instructions from the Colonial Office were that they were to be treated the same as all other felons. His response was to move Miller, Grant and Gemmell to the Brown's River Probation Station, 7 miles south of Hobart. Beemer, now a constable, was left in Hobart. Miller believed this shift was prompted purely by '*Franklin's* malice' (295). He saw the move as a terrible blow to any hope of escape, since the station was 'about three hundred feet above and three fourths of a mile distant from the Derwent [River]' (286), where visiting ships lay at anchor. It was a rudimentary penal station, consisting of 2 acres cleared in the forest. There were two huts, one for the overseer and one for the men. Miller claimed this hut barely kept out the inclement weather. Each was equipped with a large fireplace with a chimney 'which was little more than an opening through the roof' (287).

Miller claimed the Patriots worked from dawn to dark, together with forty other probationers recently arrived like themselves, felling trees and carrying spars—12 to 30 feet in length. Within days, Miller was lucky to be promoted to the job of night watchman; that relieved him of the hard work, since his sole duty was 'to see that none of the inmates got out to rob the *hen-roosts* and potato-yards of the surrounding inhabitants'. He found it was torture nonetheless, 'arising from constant contact with the depraved beings among whom our lot was cast'. As he lay on his pallet during the night, injustice burned into his brain:

> 'I am an American citizen—I am a British slave!' were thoughts which I could not banish for a moment; and, but for the sinfulness of the deed, I should have put an end to my existence rather than endure the dreadful reality. [287]

Still, all hopes of escape were not entirely extinguished. When a French whaling vessel dropped anchor in the Derwent about half a mile from shore, Miller saw the chance to escape, and proposed that he, as the station watchman, should assist Grant and Gemmell in escaping through the chimney, when the other inmates were asleep. The trio would then swim off to the whaler in the hope of a favourable reception. As nightwatchman, Miller was left outside at night, and was able to clamber onto the roof of the hut undetected, where surreptitiously he let a rope down the chimney which Gemmell tied about his waist:

> I tugged at the rope, and the great lump of flesh slowly ascended, but when about two thirds of the distance was accomplished, the rope stuck fast to my fingers. Gemmell whispered, 'It's all right; pull away.' I replied, 'It's all wrong, though, for by my hopes of liberty, I can not raise you another inch.' 'Then be d—— to you,' said he, 'it's all a flash in the pan, and there'll be h—— to pay before I get back into my nest again.' 'Grant,' whispered he, 'I say Grant where in the devil are you? can't you give me a hoist? be quick, for I shall soon roast here.' [There was a bed of red-hot coals underneath.] Grant was giggling in the corner of the fire-place, ready to split with laughter at the fun. At this moment a large turf tumbled from the top of the chimney straight into Gemmell's face, (it was all accidental, of course.) 'Let go the rope,' shouted he, loud enough to awaken all hands. I required not a second bidding, and he fell heavily into the hot-bed below. 'What in h—— is all this fuss about?' exclaimed at least twenty voices, in one breath; but Gemmell stealthily crawled away to his berth, rope and all, and was snoring at a terrible rate before they had time to make any discoveries; while Grant retreated to a dark corner to enjoy a hearty laugh at our poor friend's expense. As for myself, I scrambled down from my elevation, and with right good will roared out the watchman's cry, *'All's well!'*. [292]

There were no repercussions from this misadventure, and although Miller railed against the injustice of their treatment at Brown's River, it would seem that the regime was not particularly capricious compared to other stations. When the other seventy-eight Patriots were landed from the *Buffalo* in February 1840 and sent to the Probation Station at Sandy Bay, Miller immediately sought permission for himself and his companions to join them. Mr Gunn actually came to Brown's River Station to caution him against the move, warning that things would go much worse for those at Sandy Bay, to which Miller gave a characteristic reply:

> 'I shall esteem it a privilege to share their fate, and would rather spend my whole life in slavery with them, than two years of comparative ease among such wretches as the English prisoners.'
> . . . They were all strangers, but they were MEN. [294]

Mr Gunn did not exaggerate. Things did go much worse for the Patriots at Sandy Bay, though it was through no fault of Franklin. Despite the claims of the penal reformers who championed probation as a more equitable system than assignment, this was not the case for the Patriots. There is abundant evidence that the men from the *Canton* and the *Buffalo* would have fared much better if they had simply followed the experience of their compatriots on the *Marquis of Hastings* and had been fed into the old assignment system. The Patriots came from a colonial frontier economy, not dissimilar to Van Diemen's Land. Upstate New York was opened up relatively late; it was only in the early nineteenth century, with the building of the Erie canal, that labour and capital were attracted to the region. The local economy was heavily based on primary industry, especially timber-cutting and farming. This is reflected in the skills that the Patriots brought to Australia. On disembarkation in Hobart, 56 per cent admitted that they could handle a plough team compared to just 16 per cent of all prisoners arriving in the colony during the period of assignment. Ploughmen were in particularly high demand in a colonial labour market where rural skills were at a premium, and their services were keenly sought by landowners. A further twenty-six Patriots claimed to be 'mechanics' of one description or another—they included six blacksmiths, nine carpenters, two masons, two coopers, two millwrights, a wheelwright, a shipwright and a caulker. Such men were sought after, not just by urban and agricultural private interests, but also by the government. When each transport arrived in Hobart, the Crown made first call on the convicts on board, selecting draughts of skilled metalworkers and woodworkers, bricklayers, masons and other mechanics to fill vacancies in the various public works. Those who were left after the government had made its pick were fought over by settlers who were eager to cut their labour costs, for, as many complained, the limited number of free mechanics were able to hire out their services at exorbitant rates.[15]

There was not one single weaver among the Patriots, nor was there anybody who was described upon disembarkation in Van Diemen's Land as a common labourer. There were also few among their ranks who belonged to the legion of esoteric trades spawned by the burgeoning consumerism which had accompanied the process of industrialisation. There were many such convicts disgorged onto the shores of Australia, skilled in the arts of manufacturing such items as fishing rods, watch counter-balances, pearl buttons, optical instruments, stained paper and umbrellas. As little use could be found for these skills, such men often were used as gang fodder valued solely for their muscle power.[16]

The Patriots' occupations compared with assigned convicts in Van Diemen's Land[17]

Occupation	Patriots		Assigned Convicts	
	no.	*%*	*no.*	*%*
Unskilled urban	0	0	179	21
Skilled and semi-skilled urban	18	22	305	36
Unskilled rural	2	2	85	10
Skilled rural	45	56	135	16
Construction	14	17	68	8
Domestic	0	0	65	8
Retail	1	1	9	1
White-collar	1	1	11	1
Total	81		857	

Source: a systematic sample of one in twenty-five male convicts landed in Van Diemen's Land in the period 1817–1839, Con 18, Con 23, Con 27 and MM 33 AOT.

In many ways the Patriots were reminiscent of another group of political offenders, the followers of the mythical Captain Swing who, in their 1830 campaign against declining living standards for agricultural labourers, participated in a series of riots which swept the southern counties of England. These men were eagerly sought after by colonial masters, and few among their number were exposed to the horrors of the gangs.[18] The same was true of transported agricultural workers generally. An analysis of a sample of convicts transported during the assignment period reveals that they received on average twenty-three strokes of the lash per man over the course of their sentence, compared with seventy-four strokes for transported textile workers.[19] Instead of being driven to work, the vast majority of assigned rural convicts were supplied with 'indulgences' in order to encourage them to bend their backs for their masters. Such incentives were rarely supplied to free agricultural workers in Britain, especially in the southern counties where many rural workers eked out a miserable existence.[20] For all the indignation of being forced to work without wages, their material circumstances were surprisingly good. As the transported ploughman Richard Dillingham put it in a letter to his family 'As for tea and sugar I almost could swim in it'.[21] Unhappily for the great majority of the Patriots, their goose had been thoroughly cooked by the introduction of probation—a system that their nemesis, George Arthur, had railed against and that Franklin believed to be quite wrong-headed.[22] Rather than comparing their experience with that of the Swing Rioters, a more valid comparison would be with other political prisoners unfortunate enough to also experience probation. In the late 1830s and early 1840s, eighty Chartists, Rebecca Rioters and Bossenden Wood rebels arrived in Van Diemen's Land. While the Chartists were predominantly made up of radical artisans who campaigned for political reform, the Rebecca Rioters and Bossenden Wood rebels were rural protesters who fought against rising tithes and the destruction of independent agricultural communities. According to the data provided by Rudé, they collected an average of 3.4 colonial 'crimes' compared to 1.7 for the Swing Rioters.[23] Yet the majority of these offences were not crimes at all. Indeed, to talk of colonial crimes is to deflect the spotlight of attention away from the creaking apparatus of probation and on to the bodies of those unfortunate enough to experience this grinding species of punishment. Prisoners in the early 1840s, whether political offenders or not, were forced to run the gauntlet of ganged labour and suffer under the barking orders of an overseer in order to satisfy the pretence that this was a system which delivered its 'just measure of pain'.[24]

10

The Poor Children of Israel

FRANKLIN HAD TAKEN some care to ensure that the *Buffalo* prisoners were well looked after at Sandy Bay. The station had been selected because it offered the possibility of isolation from the public works gangs in Hobart, while keeping the Patriots within easy reach of the seat of government. By this means, he was able to ensure that they were spiritually and physically cared for in ways that were not normally extended to ganged convicts condemned to hard labour on the roads. Those who reported sick were not examined by a visiting medical officer as was the usual practice, but were brought to the Colonial Hospital in Hobart Town.[1] On Sundays, rather than being preached at in the station yard, the Patriots were rounded up and marched to Hobart. Their destination was not the chapel in the Prisoners' Barracks, but St George's, the recently completed neo-classical church at Battery Point. Possibly this move to segregate the Patriots at worship was because of a complaint from Miller about the nature of the service at the Prisoners' Barracks. He described with utter horror the pandemonium which had taken place during his first divine service at that place:

> When the clergyman made his appearance the noise subsided to a low hum of voices, amounting to a perfect jargon of oaths and curses; . . . during the whole service I did not once see him turn to his convict hearers, or address a single word of exhortation to them. . . . On looking about me, I could not discover more than twelve, among twelve hundred prisoners, who appeared to be taking any notice of the service. Some were spinning yarns, some playing at *pitch-and-toss*, some gambling with cards; several were crawling about underneath the benches, selling candy, tobacco, &c., and one fellow carried a bottle of rum, which he was serving out in small quantities to those who had an English sixpence to give for a small wine-glass full. Disputes occasionally arose which ended in a blow or a kick . . . [277]

At the elegant St George's Church they joined a regular congregation, just as if they had been assigned men accompanying their masters to church.[2]

As might be expected, Franklin also appears to have gone to some trouble to select experienced and trusted officials to look after his clutch of political prisoners.[3] The station superintendent was a man named James Skene who had served for many years in the army, rising to the rank of quartermaster-sergeant in the 63rd Regiment.[4] What better training for a man who was in charge of both maintaining discipline and managing the supply of rations and equipment. Skene did not reside in the station at Sandy Bay. He lived in a nearby cottage which had been rented by the Convict Department from David Lord, an ex-convict, who had accumulated a great deal of property and land.[5] The Patriots were placed under the daily surveillance of a ticket-of-leave overseer named Thomas Hewitt, whose job was to see that the station huts were cleaned on a regular basis and that the bedding was dried and properly folded. In addition, he inspected the works, reported any infringement of the regulations of the Convict Department to the superintendent, and supervised the allocation of rations.[6]

Despite their special treatment, the Patriots were scathing about the conditions they experienced at Sandy Bay. They were split into messes and accommodated ten or so to a hut, where they slept in two tiered berths which were divided into individual compartments just large enough for a man to lie in. Each was issued with a bed tick stuffed with grass, a woollen blanket and a cotton rug for bedding. The hut floors were made of compacted earth, and the leaky roof gave the Patriots what Wright sarcastically described as 'the benefit of rather a free circulation of air' (20). In fact, the station was exposed to the biting winds that periodically swept up the Derwent River, and when it rained, pools of water collected on the floor. Only the two huts reserved for the overseers and clerks were fitted with fireplaces. As a result, the Patriots were frequently forced to sleep in damp clothing. To make matters worse, their bedding—despite the attentions of the overseer, Hewitt—swarmed with fleas and lice.

The day that they arrived, they were mustered in the yard and ranked up, 'as if we had been cattle', Wright recalled (20), and issued with a new set of slops. Gates described the new uniform as:

> made of a grey kind of cloth, coarser and rougher even than common carpeting, and which permitted the wind to circulate through its interstices almost as freely as through a seive—a striped cotton shirt whose fabric was correspond- ingly as coarse—and a skull cap, made of stiff sole leather, closely fitting the head and projecting in four points from the four sides, which points were so made that they could be turned up or down—and a pair of thick, clumsy shoes, without socks. These, with an extra shirt for change, constituted our whole wardrobe . . . [75]

As Heustis put it: 'The fit of our clothes was a point about which very little thought was expended by those who rigged out the new suits. They sat like the coat of Daniel Lambert on Calvin Edson, or, to use a common expression, like a shirt on a bean-pole' (101). The metaphor was doubly appropriate. Lambert and Edson were 'two prodigies of nature', well known in early-nineteenth-century America. Lambert, reputed to have weighed 739 pounds when he died of a heart attack in 1809, never travelled outside his native England, although a wax model of him was exhibited in America. Edson, on the other hand, slowly declined to the dimensions of a rake after he became 'be-numbed' while lying out in the cold at the battle of Platts-burgh. By 1830 he was reputed to have weighed just 60 pounds. Ironically, while Edson had contracted his wasting disorder defending upstate New York from the invading British during the war of 1812, Lambert had worked for years as the Keeper of the Leicestershire County House of Correction. Consequently, not only would Daniel Lambert's jacket have appeared ridiculously large when placed on the shoulders of Calvin Edson, but to attempt such an act would have been to clothe the frame of a republican hero with the jacket of a British gaoler.[7]

It is no small wonder that the Patriots' clothes did not fit. Their average height was 5 feet 6 inches, fully 2 inches taller than convicts transported from the British Isles.[8] Although it is commonly held that transported convicts were drawn from a deformed stratification of criminal runts, there is in fact, no evidence that they were shorter than other working-class populations.[9] The average height of the eight Patriots who were born in Europe was 5 feet 4 inches—the same as that for the general convict population. As a rule, convict slops were issued in four different sizes, each size being marked on the inside of the garment. The smallest of these is likely to have fitted the frame of the shorter Patriots, but it is unlikely that the four men who were 6 feet or over would have found a suit of clothing to fit them. Moreover, as the Patriots were fitted out at Sandy Bay, and not at the Prisoners' Barracks clothing store, it is likely that they would have had to make do with whatever slops, regardless of size, had been dispatched to the station for their use.

Although every prisoner was entitled to a new set of clothing every six months, and a pair of shoes every four, their slops usually wore out before they were due to be replaced. According to Heustis, the shoes were particu-larly poor and often fell to pieces in less than two months, and 'then we had to go with bare feet, it being of no use to "ask for more," after the manner of Oliver Twist' (101). Once accoutred in their new attire, the Patriots looked so grotesque that they could not help bursting into a roar of laughter and, as Gates recalled, 'for once, we were right merry' (76).

Each man was also issued with a tin plate, tin cup, and an iron spoon. All utensils and every article of clothing was marked 'B.O.', standing for

Board of Ordinance, and was stamped with the broad arrow, the symbol of government property. Heustis recalled that this ubiquitous mark, which looked a little like the print of a bird's foot, was dubbed by the Patriots the 'devil's claw' (102). Each item of equipment also bore an issue number. It was one of the duties of the station clerk to record in a ledger the number of every article supplied to each convict. By this means, the administration sought to control the trafficking of government property. The blankets were specially marked with two lines of dark thread known as the rogues' yarn. Thus even a section cut from the bottom of a threadbare covering could be recognised as having been sliced from a piece of government-issue cloth.

Fully equipped, the Patriots were issued with a pint of skilly and mustered into the huts for the night. Skilly was a thin gruel made from flour, water and salt, and was their first taste of probation station fare. As Snow recalled, it 'was manufactured like patent medicines, in large quantities at a time, and measured out into pint skids for individual use' (14). Before dawn, the Patriots were aroused by the ringing of the station bell. To the shout of 'muster', they were ranked up in the stockade yard and ordered to answer 'here sir' to the call of their name. Marsh recalled that two or three did not answer, so the clerk 'repaired straightway to the huts, calling their names, and was told that they were lame or sick. "You had better come out, the Doctor will be here soon, and if you are not sick, you will be punished"' (76). So, lame as they were, the stragglers limped into the yard to be presented with their morning fare.

Breakfast proved to be somewhat more substantial than supper, if scarcely more palatable. Each man was issued with one and a half pounds of bread, in addition to the pint of flour-and-water paste. Wright complained that the bread was 'composed of oats, barley and rice, with a little wheat ground together' (21), all the fine flour having been sifted out. He declared this was bread that even a Grahamite would have starved upon—a reference to the 1830s teachings of a Newark minister, Sylvester Graham, who shunned the consumption of alcohol, tobacco and meat in favour of a diet based solely on fruit, vegetables and stale, coarse-grained bread.[10] Perhaps more properly, the bread could be described as damper, the flour being simply wet with cold water and baked in the ashes, Australian style. As Gates put it, the end product 'was as hard and gluey as could be imagined' (77).

Having consumed their skilly, the Patriots were marched out of the stockade gate accompanied by three overseers and five or six constables. They travelled nearly a mile, although, as Marsh recalled, some of the party could barely walk. When they got to the works, one of the overseers informed them that it would be good for their health, 'after being so long at sea, to exercise a little'. To Marsh and his companions' relief, however, he added, 'you need not do much to-day' (76). According to Snow, their 'employment' consisted of 'leveling DOWN hills, and levelling UP valleys, breaking stone and drawing them in hand carts to where they were wanted, for making and mending McAdamized roads' (14).

At eight o'clock in the morning they stopped for half an hour to eat a little bread before resuming work, and at midday they were returned to the station, where the sick were examined by the station surgeon. To their dismay, the doctor was entirely unsympathetic. Marsh claimed that he dismissed nearly every complaint with a cry of, 'oh nonsense, I'll give you a few pills, take two each night for a week, and you can commence work to-morrow' (78). Lunch was then served, which proved to consist of a pound of boiled mutton and half a pound of potatoes. According to Wright, the meat was fetid, 'filled with vermin—bony and stringy—and any well-fed dog would have refused to eat it' (21). As an additional 'treat' the broth in which the meat had been boiled proved little better. Heustis ventured that 'it was frequently no difficult matter to scrape off a spoonful of maggots' from a pint of this stuff. He related that on one occasion, the Patriots had discovered that their meat was so full of 'live stock' that they refused to touch it (102). It was exhibited to the station surgeon who, probably to everyone's relief (and no doubt surprise), pronounced it unfit for consumption. As no substitute was forthcoming, relief quickly turned to disappointment. That day, the Patriots went hungry.

Being short-changed of their rations was something they quickly came to expect. As Woodman subsequently wrote to his family:

> You can guess what our meat was like when it reached us, for the officers of the Station got the best meat, the clerks the second cut and the belted men (ourselves) the third. Besides this the cook and baker were robbing us every day more or less of our rations.[11]

Marsh concurred:

> The rations after being weighed out, have so many hands to pass through before they get to the prisoners, or laboring men, that they often fall short half. The clerk's, constable's, wards man, overseer's and some other favorite one's, that wait on them, have their choice of the quantity weighed out, and what is left, the poor convict has to take up with; and if he complains, is sure to be punished . . . [75]

No wonder that the Patriots were frequently reduced, as Snow confessed, 'to the necessity of picking up potatoe skins and cabbage leaves, which they would boil and eat to quiet their hunger' (14). Although it is likely that the Patriots scavenged along the foreshore for shellfish and other marine delicacies, in the same manner as Miller reported of his short stay at Brown's River Probation Station, their fare appears to have been lean.

As for sugar, tea and coffee, such articles were forbidden to probationers. According to Snow, those who had 'imbibed the habit of using tobacco' were 'compelled to make a virtue of necessity, and give it up' (14). He concluded that this was a punitive type of health cure:

> we were put upon a rigid course of DIETETICS. Were you to have seen us taking our daily rations, you would have taken us for the tenants of a hospital for the cure of dyspepsia. Our food was uniformly of the lightest kind—not in the least hard of digestion. Sir John, in the plenitude of his benevolence, wished us to expend all our energies in McAdamizing our WAYS, not in digesting English luxuries. [13]

At first, the Patriots were put to work shovelling earth into wheelbarrows, but on the third day a number of carts made their appearance. These were about 6 feet long, 4 feet wide and 2 feet deep; when filled, they carried between 15 and 18 hundredweight of broken rock. Gates described how four men were attached to each cart by means of 'leathern collars, passing over one shoulder and under the other' (87). In addition to a harness, each vehicle was equipped with cross bars against which the 'team' could push. His use of the word 'team' was, of course, a play on words—the Patriots now had to suffer the ignominy of being reduced to beasts of burden. Rigged thus, they were charged with conveying stone to the works from a nearby quarry. Though this work was considered to be harder than handling a shovel, Gates was heartily glad of the change, for his hands were so sore that he could scarcely use them. In this he was not alone. The Patriots had been long confined at sea, and 'were so enfeebled, that their hands were almost as tender as those of an infant' (87). After a few days' work with the rough heavy tools issued by the Convict Department, their hands had 'blistered and the skin peeled away, leaving in many instances a good share of the hand raw' (87). Gates remembered in particular the case of Orrin W. Smith, who 'was a single man of considerable property in the States' and 'had never been bred to manual labor—was small of stature, and naturally of a delicate constitution' (87, 88), although this seems a little unlikely, as Smith was recorded as a farmer in the papers which accompanied the *Buffalo* to Van Diemen's Land.[12] According to Gates, Smith was forced to swing a heavy pick and his 'hands blistered so that the skin peeled from the whole palm and inner surface of the fingers, and even between the fingers'. He was forced to work 'without scarcely a cessation, leaving the very flesh upon the handle of his pick'. As Gates hauled his cart past Smith, he saw the 'blood trickling from his raw hands'. The poor man glanced up and shrieked, 'Oh, my God! Gates, I can never stand this!' (87), and he sank exhausted to his knees.

Marsh also recalled that the Patriots were divided between tasks 'without any regard to size or ability to perform heavy labor' (79). Some of those who were sick asked to be relieved from drawing the stone carts. When the overseer discovered that several of them were near fainting, he asked 'who are these men that are invalids, that the Doctor sent out this morning; let them step forward, that I may know who they are' (78). Marsh and seven others stepped forward and were sent instead to crush aggregate:

> Now this was considered light work, and so it was, compared to others, but to me it was very bad work, the dirt from the stone, and constant motion with the hammer, was increasing the pain in my breast, and it was with much difficulty, that I stood it until night; when I was very tired and hungry. [79]

Marsh recalled that Tom Hewitt, their overseer, drove them particularly hard. Charged by Skene with completing the road to Hobart, Hewitt appeared to be in a constantly agitated state. He worried about the unrealistic expectations of the Principal Superintendent of Roads and about the complaints of local settlers:

> 'The principal superintendant of roads says he don't think you men will be prisoners long, and he is in a hurry to have this part of the road finished, it has been a long while doing; likewise the Governor is in a hurry to have it finished, and a good many other gentlemen are complaining of the length of time I have been to work on this piece of road. My bloody eyes, it will never do, I shall be broke of my billet. Come see what we can have done against the super comes.' [78–9]

Infused with a fear of being thrown back into the ranks, he urged the weak and exhausted Patriots on with a cry of 'Come all hands' (79). In fact Tom Hewitt's concerns appear to have been well founded. The road from Hobart to Sandy Bay was in a perilous condition, and in March 1840 two men were 'considerably' hurt when they fell down 'a precipitous bank of many feet in descent'.[13] Shortly after the Patriots left Sandy Bay, Hewitt was indeed stripped of his billet, although this appears to have had less to do with the state of the roads than with his propensity for hitting the bottle. In the following years he was charged with a string of drinking offences, culminating in an embarrassing arrest in August 1844, when he was found drunk on a racecourse dressed in women's clothing.[14]

At dusk, having finished their day's labour, the Patriots were escorted back to their cold, miserable huts. Wright recollected how one day, on returning from work 'in the midst of a perfect tempest of rain and piercing wind, and being wet to the skin, and seeing a good cheerful fire burning in the cook's room, I committed the awful outrage of warming my shivering limbs'. On being detected, he claimed that he was sentenced to receive 'seven days' solitary confinement upon one-fourth pound of bread per day and filthy water'. He underwent his punishment slammed into

> a vault without light, with an uneven floor flagged with stone, and without any room for standing erect; it was two feet wide and six in length, ventilated with irregular crevices in the wall. In some parts of the body the blood almost stops circulation while undergoing this inhuman torture; and this we received for the most trivial indiscretion, while the filth of these dens of infamy surpasses all description. . . . I thought with Doctor Franklin, I had paid a little too dear for my whistle. [22]

Although Wright was twice sentenced to solitary confinement on subsequent occasions, no record of this particular punishment appears on his conduct record.[15] According to the official returns, not one Patriot was punished with solitary confinement while stationed at Sandy Bay. Although it is possible that the official return of punishments for the probation station was never forwarded to the Convict Department, it seems more likely that, on this occasion at least, Wright's account of his sufferings is exaggerated.

It is also unlikely that, as Wright claimed, Sandy Bay was swept with storms of sleet and snow, in the summer and autumn of 1840 or that the Patriots were forced to drag their stone carts the equivalent of 30 miles in a single day, stopping to fill them on no less than thirteen occasions. Even if such a task had been physically possible, simple arithmetic suggests it could hardly have been accomplished between the hours of dawn and dusk. Assuming that they were able to haul the carts at average walking speed (and over broken ground this is a big assumption), they would have maintained a rate of about 3 miles an hour. At a conservative estimate, it would take at least half an hour for three men to load and unload each cart with 15 hundredweight of quarried stone—unless, that is, they were assisted by Daniel Lambert, who was reputed to have been able to lift 5 hundredweight with ease.[16] On the basis of a simple calculation, this would suggest a working day of twenty-three hours without accounting for breaks for morning muster, breakfast, lunch and supper—clearly impossible.

Far from rendering the Patriot accounts invalid, such exaggerations are revealing. By contemporary working-class British standards, the ration supplied to convicts was comparatively generous, yielding around 3300 calories a day. Even allowing for pilfering and ration shortfalls, this is likely to have been in excess of the daily intake of 2700 calories recommended by the World Health Organisation.[17] Such calculations are meaningless, however, without a consideration of the nature of the work undertaken. Men employed in heavy labour consume energy at the rate of ten calories a minute. Unless interspersed with frequent breaks, a working day of more than a few hours is likely to have left the Patriots exhausted.[18] Hungry, wet and inadequately clothed, they must have felt the cold and wind cut them to the bone. Thus, Wright's account may not accurately reflect what *happened*, but it should be read as an indication of what it *felt* like to work on the roads of Van Diemen's Land under constant threat of punishment. No wonder that he, like the other Patriots, often felt dejected.

Miller recalled one evening locked in their cheerless quarters after they had worked all day in the cold rain. There they sat in their damp clothes, some 'upon the forms, some in their berths, while others had covered themselves with their thin blanket and rug to court the warmth, sleep and rest which they so much needed'. All was quiet and every head was bowed low and their 'sad countenances indicated that the thoughts of the melancholy party were of bitter wrongs, or perchance of distant home and friends'. The silence was broken only by the coughs and groans of the sick. Suddenly 43-year-old Elijah Woodman leapt to his feet and 'in a tone of voice that might have been heard a mile struck up *"the hunters of Kentucky"*'. Miller recalled that the effect was instantaneous: 'As if electrified, every man sprang to the floor; sick, blind and halt, joined in the chorus; some danced, others shouted', and all, for one short moment, 'shook off the gloomy horrors of Van Dieman's Land' (299). Apart from such rare occasions, the only other relief from their labours was on Saturday afternoon, when they were given time off to wash their shirts, and on the Sabbath when they were marched to church in Hobart.

On the fifth day of hard labour, Marsh was working with Lysander Curtis and seven or eight others on what was called a 'run'. One man wheeled a full barrow until he met a prisoner coming in the opposite direction with an empty one. The two then exchanged barrows and turned about face to repeat the process running in the opposite direction. Marsh was wheeling to Curtis, who had not been well for some weeks. About mid-afternoon, Curtis told Marsh that he felt very bad. His friend advised him to speak to the overseer, but he kept on wheeling as he said 'he new [*sic*] it was of no use to ask the brute' (80). Concerned that his health was fast failing, once more Marsh urged Curtis to cease his labours, but on approaching Overseer Hewitt, his complaint was dismissed with an oath. As Curtis had been passed fit for duty by the surgeon, he was told he should either wheel his barrow 'or die by it' (80)—Hewitt not caring which. According to Gemmell, Curtis had already been sent to hospital with a 'high fever', but had been deemed to have been shamming and was returned to his station.[19] Thus it seems likely that Hewitt turned a blind eye to his charge's plight, since he himself was fearful of being punished for countermanding the orders of a superior officer. Despite the pleas of his fellow Patriots, Curtis was 'commanded to wheel on' (80) with predictable consequences. As Marsh reported:

We were all tired, myself quite unwell, having a high fever produced by the sufferings, with the pain in my breast. I could scarcely walk with the loaded barrow, but we managed so that Curtis would have but two or three paces to wheel it, however, he soon sat or rather fell on to the barrow. We took hold of him, for he could not raise himself, and laid him on the ground . . . [80]

The Patriots asked for a cart to convey their exhausted comrade back to the station. This request was also rejected by Hewitt who, according to Marsh, exclaimed, 'No, dam it, sure he won't die before quitting time' (80). Curtis lay on the ground until the gang stopped work but, by the time they returned to their huts, the surgeon had quit the station for the day and the poor fellow was forced to lie all night without medical attention. Without a fire, the hut was damp and cold; Marsh did not sleep a wink all night, although he was very tired.

In the morning Curtis was conveyed to hospital in Hobart, where according to Dresser, he died aged thirty-five on April Fool's Day 1840.[20] According to Gemmell, he died in 'great agony' the day after being conveyed to hospital, which suggests a date of death of around 23 February. Curtis left a wife, Sarah, and three children in Massachusetts.[21] Heustis recalled with great anger that, while Curtis was in hospital, the Patriots were prohibited from visiting him. Thus 'in the hour of final dissolution' he had 'no sympathizing friends around his dying bed, to minister to his wants, and offer consolation' (105). His compatriots were not even permitted to see the corpse, or to witness its interment. As a mark of respect, they cut some black silk handkerchiefs into strips and tied them round their arms. The next Sunday, as Heustis wrote, they marched to church thus adorned 'two by two, with these badges of mourning on our arms'. This gesture of solidarity for a fallen comrade was greeted with 'vile sneers' and derision, for the citizens of Hobart 'looked upon the death of a prisoner as of no more consequence than the death of a dog!' (105). Notwithstanding their distress, Gates recalled that many of the Patriots envied Curtis's fortune, 'for Death brought a reprieve for his woes, and snatched him from the iron hearted tyrants that were fattening on our toil and blood and our very heart's agony' (93). A week after the death of Curtis, William Nottage was 'cruelly mangled' in a blasting accident. According to Gates, both his thighs were broken, his arms shattered and his breast and face horribly disfigured. He was taken to hospital where he too died on 18 April (98).[22]

Several of the Patriots, Heustis included, were severely troubled with sore eyes, but despite the intense pain, they were kept at work. Heustis described how the surgeon would 'lift up our eyelids and rub in blue vitriol, which was enough to take a man's life from him' (106). He also gave him several pills but Heustis 'threw his physic to the dogs', and 'by an application of tobacco-water' effected his own cure. He recalled that:

Another man, one of the Windsor prisoners, who was tried under the name of James P. Williams, but whose real name was Nelson Recker, took the doctor's pills, was salivated, and afterwards became totally blind. He was then sent to the invalid hospital at New Norfolk, about twenty miles from Hobart Town, up the River Derwent, where he died eight or nine months afterwards.[23] [106]

As Wright put it:

Thus the vales of Van Dieman's Land are whitened by the bones of exiles from the land of Washington. There was scarcely a station where some of our number did not fade from the earth; and to look back and think of our hideous situation, where, without any attention, our brethren were sick—died and were buried, as if they had been the beasts of the field, or the fowls of the air, is horrible. [23]

Initially, the death rate among the Patriots was indeed high. In the year after they disembarked, they lost the equivalent of sixty-five men in every thousand. To put this in perspective, in the early 1830s, ganged convicts at the ultra-coercive penal station at Port Arthur died at an annual rate of forty-eight per thousand.[24] As Roland and Shannon have reported of deaths in Japanese-run prisoner-of-war camps during the Second World War, however, mortality was most common among recent arrivals weakened during transit to the camps.[25] Three of the Patriots who disembarked from the ill-fated *Marquis of Hastings* died before they could be subjected to the rigours of ganging, and if these deaths are omitted, the rate for 1840 drops to thirty-four per thousand. The following year the death rate was further reduced to twelve per thousand, a figure which is equivalent to that experienced by British troops stationed in barracks in the British Isles in the 1830s.[26] In fact, the Patriots' experience was similar to that of other convicts disembarked in Van Diemen's Land in the early 1840s. Death rates were highest in the weeks following arrival before tailing away in subsequent months.

Death rates of convicts in Van Diemen's Land, 1840–45

Time since arrival (years)	No. of convicts	No. of deaths	Annual death rate per 1000
1	1504	56	37
2	1492	12	8
3	1480	12	8
4	1469	11	7

Source: Data taken from convict transports *Mandarin*, arrived 30 June 1840; *Asia* (1) arrived 6 August 1840; *Egyptian* (2) arrived 12 December 1840; *Hindostan* (3) arrived 19 January 1841; *Lord Lyndoch*, arrived 5 February 1841; and *Lady Raffles*, arrived 17 March 1841. AOT, Con 33/1–6.

The evidence suggests that the Patriots' experience was not atypical— that they had not been singled out to undergo some especially sadistic form of punishment by Franklin's colonial administration, a point that even Elijah Woodman was prepared to concede. He noted that, although the conditions under which they toiled were much more rigid 'than we prisoners expected', this was entirely due to the laws made by a 'home government' which had been unduly influenced by the prison reform movement. As he commented dryly, the 'late law from England is more rigid than the law formerly was', and after all, the whole point of probation was that it should be applied uniformly to all prisoners without exception.[27] The Patriots may have been victims of probationary labour, but in this they were far from being alone. Throughout the 1840s there was many a poor prisoner who, in Gates's words, 'crawled to his daily work and reeled under the task, which was, if possible, more onerous, more grievous, than that wherewith Pharao tasked the poor children of Israel' (90).

It is perhaps not surprising that thought of escape was uppermost in the minds of many of the Patriots. The lure of escape was made all the more appealing in early May, when two American whalers sailed into the Derwent to refit. On the following Sunday the captain of one of these, a man named Magford from Salem, Massachusetts, visited the stockade at Sandy Bay.[28] Unfortunately, as Dresser related, all but three or four of the Patriots were at church at the time, 'So that we mised of seeing him [and of] the other Bark we cannot Lern where she is from'.[29] On 19 April they had to endure the lonely sight of Magford setting sail for Sydney on the *Augustus*, the Stars and Stripes flying proudly aloft. As Marsh recalled: 'The fact is, we were deserted by our friends in time of danger; when we most needed them, they were not to be found; we were in the lion's grasp, and there left to be devoured' (77). Others, however, refused to give up. They searched the ocean, knowing that at any point a Nantucket whaler could be just over the horizon. On 10 May Horace Cooley, Michael Morin, Jacob Paddock and William Reynolds slipped out over the stockade in the dusk of evening. After hiding out in the woods for a few days, they took a boat and put out to sea, in the hope, as Heustis expressed it, 'of falling in with an American whale-ship' (106). As Michael Morin was originally from Bordeaux in Lower Canada and probably spoke French, their chances of obtaining a free passage home were significantly increased because many French ships also worked the southern whaling grounds.[30] Two days after the *Buffalo* had reached Hobart, the French whaler *Salamander* had stopped to revictual. Three days later, two French corvettes, *Astrolabe* and *Zeelée* under the command of Commodore D'Urville, had called in on their voyage of discovery to the South Seas; and in early March, the whaler *Indian*, also from Le Havre, had called in for fresh supplies.[31]

The following Friday, the descriptions of the four men were published in the *Government Gazette*. Thus, at the same time as the four absconders scanned the horizon for a foreign sail, an army of constables was on the lookout for the red-headed Cooley, Morin the dark French-Canadian, Paddock the hazel-eyed New Yorker and the freckled Reynolds, who perhaps now regretted the star tattooed on his left arm. Their pursuers were motivated, not by thoughts of freedom, but by the £8 reward that the capture of the four Patriots would bring.[32] Unfortunately, the bottom of the absconders' boat was stove to pieces when they tried to put ashore on an uninhabited island. As Heustis relates, they managed to stay alive for a fortnight by living on rock oysters, mussels and abalone but, when Morin fell sick, they were forced to surrender to a party of constables. The four absconders were tried on 9 June 1840 before the Assistant Police Magistrate and the man with the elephantine memory, Lieutenant William Gunn. As punishment, they were ordered to serve two years' hard labour at the penal station at Port Arthur.[33] The episode, however, had served to demonstrate that the stockade at Sandy Bay was no fortress. Henceforth Franklin resolved to dispatch the Patriots to the interior of the colony, where hopes of freedom could not be succoured by the sight of the Stars and Stripes fluttering from the mast of a passing ship.

11

Scourge of the Old World

B Y THE TIME the Patriots left Sandy Bay they had been cruelly worked, but none, at least according to the official record, had been severely punished, although they had seen enough of what happened to other felons. Most dreaded of all punishments was the lash. About this barbaric form of chastisement all the Patriot narratives were eloquent. Flogging was especially associated with the evils of the assignment system, yet, as William Gates noted, at every probation station there was a set of triangles. He described these as:

> built of strong scantling; they are about ten feet square at the bottom, and secured to the ground by strong pins. From each of the four corners of this frame, posts rise to a point in the centre. Parallel, horizontal bars are fastened to these posts, for the purpose of securing the person to be flogged—who is stripped, often stark naked, and always naked to his waist, and tied upon the outside of this frame, at the feet, knees and outstretched arms, so strongly that he cannot break loose. [97]

The whole point of a flogging was to batter the convict into submission. Punishment was therefore conducted in view of the assembled gangs in order to maximise the impact of the exercise of state power. Heustis recalled how the prisoners 'were formed into a hollow square, one side of which was a guard of soldiers' (114). In the centre, surrounding the man about to be scourged, were the station superintendent, the flagellator and a surgeon who could stop the punishment at any time if he thought that the man's life was in danger. The prisoners drawn up on three sides of the square were divided into classes, each headed by its respective assistant superintendent and overseer—a measure which reflected the probation system's obsession with classification. The superintendent, having read out the warrant of the magistrate ordering the punishment and prescribing the number of lashes to be inflicted, gave the order to tie the offender to the triangles. The flagellator now removed his own jacket and let the thongs of the cat-o'-nine-tails dangle free. The cats employed in Van Diemen's Land varied from station to station, but most were constructed from nine strands of whipcord, each strand containing three knots.[1] The men selected to wield these instruments were themselves prisoners. Gates described them as 'always stout, robust men' (97). Many had previously served in the armed forces, where they would have witnessed similar floggings and were familiar with the rituals of punishment.

Flogging was designed to be an utterly humiliating invasion of the convict's body. Robert Hughes likened it to homosexual rape.[2] The surgeon at Macquarie Harbour, John Barnes, would have agreed. He thought that flogging was an 'unmanly' form of punishment designed to reduce the frame of the prisoner to a blubbering wreck.[3] Almost all who were subjected to it were battered into submission after just a few strokes. The historians Ray Evans and Bill Thorpe have likened the flagellator to a 'leviathan' who drained power from the convict with every stroke of the lash. It was, they concluded, a punishment that was impossible to resist—an emasculating ordeal.[4] Gates employed similar imagery. He recalled that he had once been forced to witness the flogging of a boy who looked no older than thirteen years of age. He 'appeared a perfect Lilliputian' by comparison with the flagellator, a man who went by the name of 'Big Sandy'. The boy, having been presented with a stage, decided to show that he was 'game'. Plucking up 'great courage [he] spoke to Sandy: "Now, Big Sandy, I want you should do good justice in your business. Just put it on, hard as you please, and I'll warrant you'll not hear this chap sing out."' The assembled convicts roared with laughter; it might have appeared for one glorious moment that the youth would triumph and the carefully choreographed act of state retribution would collapse into farce. Then the first blow was struck. It 'brought forth such a shriek and a cry of bloody murder, that the flagellator stopped at once'. It had taken just one stroke to put the state back in the driving seat. The magistrate smiled to see how quickly the boy's 'valor had oozed away' (141). The poor wretch pleaded to be spared:

> 'Good magistrate let me go, and I'll never take the bush again. Oh! good magistrate, do let me go, and I'll do anything you want me to.' His pleadings were useless; the man was commanded to proceed. Two more blows were struck, not extreme blows either, but the little fellow's cries were so pitious that Sandy again stopped. The magistrate then turned to him and with a bitter, sarcastic voice, said, 'Mark me, Sandy, do you do your faithful duty upon that boy, and if you stop again until the sentence is fulfilled, you shall be tied in his place and flogged yet more severely.' [141]

Some talked of iron men—prisoners who could take one hundred lashes and barely flinch. Heustis observed that some of the men, 'who had iron nerves, would receive an ordinary sentence without much wincing, even though their backs were badly mutilated; they had a notion that it was a mark of unmanly weakness to scream, but their countenances showed that it was difficult to refrain from it themselves' (114). This may have been so for a punishment of three dozen or so lashes but not for a hundred strokes. Heustis felt that such a punishment was 'enough to shock every feeling of humanity' (114). Gates described one prisoner as 'a strong, athletic man' (147) who was sentenced to seventy-five lashes. Before receiving his punishment he bit on a musket ball. As the cat was applied to his back it became a 'mangled piece of flesh, from which the blood had run in such quantities as to fill his shoes till they gushed over'. Each time the flagellator drew his dreadful instrument back, he would run it through his left hand to dislodge the flesh and gore. Yet, through the entire ordeal the man 'never emitted a groan or a word, or even scarcely cringed'. When the punishment ceased 'the bullet dropped from his mouth, compressed and dissevered into several fragments' (148). This prisoner could not stand, and after he was cut loose he had to be helped to the hospital. Gates reported that after five weeks' convalescing he was still 'so weak and sore that he could scarcely lift his hand to labor' (149).

Here too the state had won. For as Gates described, this remarkable prisoner who had tensed every sinew in his body in order to repel the puncturing rough-knotted whipcord, was a 'hardened man' (149). The lash may not have reduced him to a blubbering wreck but it had, nevertheless, refashioned him. He was now condemned by the state as a man consumed with hatred, a criminal beyond redemption who belonged in the lowest depth of the convict system.

As was common in other convict accounts, Heustis exaggerated the number of lashes that were inflicted. He claimed, for example, to have become acquainted with a man who had been sentenced to receive three hundred lashes for attempting to abscond:

> After he had taken 200, the doctor—who had occasionally felt of his pulse, to determine how far life would hold out—said he could not bear the other hundred then. With his back gashed and bleeding, he was thrust into a cell, where he remained two or three days, and was then taken out to receive the other hundred. He begged that the doctor would defer the punishment a few days, till his back was better, alleging that maggots had got into it. 'Yes, I see there a few,' said the doctor, as he hastily examined the wounds, 'but it will only stir them up; go on, flagellator.' [115]

It was unlikely that a convict would have been sentenced to receive three hundred lashes by the time the Patriots arrived in Van Diemen's Land.

The maximum punishment which could legally be awarded was one hundred—although occasionally, in penal stations, offences were broken down into separate charges so that two 100-stroke punishments could be awarded for what was essentially the same offence. Nevertheless, there are enough firsthand accounts to lend credence to the gist of Heustis's claim. Henry Green, who was placed on trial for bushranging in the mid-1840s, begged the judge not to send him back to Port Arthur. He had twice received 100-stroke punishments for trying to escape from the Tasman Peninsula and declared in open court that death would be preferable than to risk such a mauling again. He revealed that the last time he 'was flogged until I was dead, I may say, to the world'. Cut from the triangles and dumped in a solitary cell, he came round to find himself 'smothered in my own gore'.[5]

Nor is the gruesome touch about the maggots a concoction. Like Henry Green, flogged men were left with their lacerated backs to heal as best they could. Infestations of maggots must have happened, and would have been beneficial in keeping the wounds clean so they did not turn gangrenous. The correspondence of the Prisoners' Barracks contains a complaint from a doctor that a convict had been flogged with a scourge which had not been washed since being used several days earlier, and that the man's back had become 'a mass of the most frightful slough'. The superintendent was having none of this. His view was that the disgusting state of the prisoner's back was due entirely to 'the manner in which he has kept his back since he was flogged'.[6] Convicts had to tend to their damaged backs as best they could. Maggot infestations, we might presume, were par for the course.

James Gemmell likened the process by which a convict's arms were fastened to the triangles to crucifixion.[7] He was not the only convict to draw parallels between Christ's suffering and the plight of the poor prisoner. In the late 1820s, the missionary at Macquarie Harbour penal station, William Schofield, recounted a conversation with one of his flock, a blacksmith by the name of Thomas Warwick. Warwick revealed that religion had meant little to him until Schofield had preached a sermon on the passion of Christ. The next day he was taken out and bound to the triangles and, as each of the fifty strokes cut into his back, Schofield's description of Christ's suffering rang in his head. Slumped in a bloody mess, he resolved to join the Wesleyans.[8] As Raboteau has written of slaves, 'association with Jesus, the ultimate suffering servant, was a powerful method of resistance'.[9] For convicts, it was probably the only way of deflecting the cutting inscription of the lash as the state carved its will into the prisoner's back. It was no accident that the man who ordered the flagellator to unleash his dreadful instrument of torture at Norfolk Island was known as the 'Christ killer'.[10]

In their descriptions of their own experiences of the triangles in Van Diemen's Land, the Patriot accounts are at odds. Gemmell, the first of their number to publish a reminiscence of their sufferings, wrote that 'the triangles, ever before our eyes, was the object of our greatest horror'. He claimed that he could 'scarcely remember one American or Canadian who has not been flogged by felons, from two dozen lashes with the cat-o'-nine tails, up to six dozen'. He went on to describe how the *'freeman* of the *new* world' was stripped stark naked save for his pantaloons before being 'exposed to the lash of the *felon* of the *old.*' Here was a peculiarly Patriot reading of the ordeal of flogging: the invasion of the 'pure hearted' republican body by the hand of the British criminal, exposing the raw cut to the filth of the Empire's gaols. Gemmell recalled how 'ardently and earnestly' they prayed that 'God of their fathers in his good time and way would deliver them from this degradation, even if it were by an early death on that far distant shore!' He then provided a list of Patriots whose prayers had failed to deliver them from the curling strike of the lash.[11]

Gemmell himself had twice been 'tied to the triangles', so he claimed: once for finding fault with 'our wretched food', and once for 'hitting a blow at a felon overseer, who, in the mere wantonness of power had thrown me violently over a heap of stones'. John Swanburg, of Jefferson County, was stripped and flogged 'six or seven' times for being 'saucy'. Hiram Sharp was 'flagellated' for not touching his cap to his superintendent, and Hiram Loop 'because he grumbled or refused to work' without shoes one cold frosty morning. Stephen Wright was flogged because 'when sick the Doctor refused to exempt him' and he subsequently failed to wheel a barrow, being so weak. Orin Smith 'was flogged at the triangles because he had not loaded our hand carts heavily enough with stones'. Elijah Woodman was 'cruelly flogged' and flung into solitary cells for keeping a 'journal of the whole proceedings of the British Government, giving its cruelties and crimes in detail, with the dates and names'. He wrote his account on slips of paper 'but where he put those slips . . . the cell and the whip failed to disclose'. And last but not least, Nathan Whiting one day was tied to the triangles and 'bastinadoed, for a very trivial offence'.[12]

Gemmell's fellow Patriots, however, stoutly maintained that the lash of the Old World never cut American flesh. Gates recalled: 'We had agreed among ourselves, that if any of our number were taken up to be flogged, as we had seen some of the old hands, we would to a man resist, though death should be the result' (95). Marsh also insisted that, although 'solitary confinement on bread and water, often fell to our lot' (75), none of their party was ever beaten. Heustis agreed that 'None of the Americans were flogged; we had solemnly resolved never to submit to it. Instant death, in our minds, was far preferable to such tortures' (115).

It appears that, although Gemmell (or those who wrote the newspaper piece for him) wished to shock his readers with a long list of Patriots who had been 'bastinadoed', there is little evidence that any of these floggings actually occurred. Gemmell himself was only punished once, not twice as he claimed. While serving at Brown's River Probation Station in March 1840, he was tried for 'making skewers for his own benefit'. He was punished, however, not with a flogging, but with a sentence to three months' hard labour on the roads at Bridgewater.[13] John Swanberg was punished twice, not six or seven times as Gemmell claimed. On both occasions he was sentenced to solitary confinement.[14] Similarly, Hiram Loop was placed in solitary on three occasions, but never beaten. If their conduct records are anything to go by, Hiram Sharp, Orin Smith, Elijah Woodman and Nathan Whiting were never charged with any offence while in Van Diemen's Land, and Woodman makes no reference to any punishment in his diary or letters.[15]

Gemmell took a different route through the labyrinthine probation system from that of his fellow Patriots. He was sent first to Brown's River and, although he briefly joined the *Buffalo* prisoners at Sandy Bay, he was soon afterwards sent to a punishment station at Bridgewater—an experience his compatriots were fortunate enough to miss. It is perhaps not surprising, therefore, that his narrative, large sections of which appear to have been reported secondhand, differs from those which subsequently appeared. Yet, Gates's and Marsh's insistence that none of the Patriots were ever flogged also appears to be misplaced. While serving at Port Arthur, Michael Morin was awarded twenty-five 'stripes'. His punishment, inflicted in a penal station, is likely to have been particularly savage. Penal station cats were usually heavier than others, and it was alleged that they were soaked in seawater and dried in the sun so that they glistened with salt crystals. Other accounts claim that they were dragged through the sand between strokes.[16] Either way, the additional cutting power can be all too readily imagined. Few of Morin's fellow Patriots would have witnessed his moment of humiliation—only six of them were ever sent to Port Arthur. This small band of unfortunates included Linus Miller; he was almost certainly present when Morin was pinioned to the triangles, since the punishment took place a month after Miller arrived at the penal station. In his lengthy narrative, Miller recalled how he was forced to watch the beating of prisoners at Port Arthur. He confessed to his readers that he felt he could endure anything but a flogging. It was not so much the torture of the lash 'but the *degradation* I could not bear; and resolved that I *would not.*' His alternative in case he was sentenced to flogging was 'to perish first by my own hand' (331). However, for all his talk, Miller could not bring himself to reveal that one of his fellow Patriots had been stripped to the waist and tied to the triangles, with his legs and arms splayed wide, and then had screamed while pieces of his back were splattered on the parade ground at Port Arthur.

Of course, the Patriots were not alone in their condemnation of the barbaric practice of flogging. The beating of child labourers in factories, the flogging of soldiers and sailors and the cruel punishments meted out by slave owners had been the subject of attack both in Britain and the United States.[17] Such punishments were increasingly condemned as the product of irrational outbursts. Not only were they calculated to brutalise the flogged, but they exposed those who sanctioned them to the charge that they too were brutalised by their association with a capricious form of punishment which was as arbitrary in its imposition as it was savage in its effects.[18] It was, as middle-class folk on both sides of the Atlantic pointed out, a form of punishment associated with the aristocratic abuse of power. Like the rack and thumbscrews, it was a form of bodily torture associated with the monarchical misrule of a former age. Nor was it well suited to the extraction of labour. Many agreed with Adam Smith that the use of unfree labour, with its emphasis on brutal beatings, was inefficient compared to the virtues of the free market.[19] As has been argued over the last quarter-century by a growing number of historians, coercive systems of labour organisation may be brutal, but that does not necessarily mean they are efficient. As Stephen Nicholas has commented, to this day there 'is no greater symbol of inefficiency at work than the lash'.[20]

As the use of corporal punishment came under attack throughout the Empire, it was slowly replaced by resort to the treadmill and solitary confinement—punitive measures that had been championed by penal reformers in both Britain and the United States.[21] By the early 1840s in Van Diemen's Land, the lash was reserved for offences which were considered to be serious breaches of authority—notably absconding, refusing to work and mutinous conduct. Solitary confinement or the treadmill were the more common punishments under the probation system.

The treadmill was an immense wheel, about 30 feet in diameter and 60 feet in length. It was kept in constant motion fourteen hours of the twenty-four, by the action of thirty prisoners stepping from spoke to spoke of the wheel as it turned upon its axis (the spokes being 15 inches apart). The energy produced by the wheel was harnessed to drive machinery for grinding corn.[22] Linus Miller watched one in use at the Hobart Prisoners' Barracks. 'Every four minutes, one of the men descended from the wheel at one end, while another mounted it at the other; each man upon the wheel thus periodically shifting two feet towards the place of descent' (320). In all, each prisoner spent two hours endlessly treading on what was in effect a revolving staircase. When Miller and his fellow Patriot Joseph Stewart were at the barracks en route to Port Arthur, they were obliged to take their turn to '"tread out the corn," as it was significantly termed' (320). In a very weak condition, having been at large without food while trying to escape, they were unable to sustain the necessary labour. Somehow they gained the privilege of changing places half-way through, thus giving each other a break, otherwise they would not have been able to stand the pain of the continual motion. He thought it a hideous punishment. The only other Patriot sentenced to the treadmill was Samuel Snow, when he was at the Green Ponds Probation Station, more than a day's travelling to the north of Hobart. His narrative is strangely silent on the matter.

Nearly all the Patriots who were sentenced to punishment were ordered to spend short periods in solitary confinement. On this, curiously, the Patriot narratives have very little to say, with the exception of Wright, who after all, had the misfortune to experience solitary confinement at firsthand. The Patriot accounts dwell more on having nothing to eat but bread and water, than on the awful effects of the dark and silence. The contrast with other convict narratives is striking. John Mortlock, for example, thought that solitary was a more devastating punishment than flogging. He succinctly summed up the effects of this form of punishment—'the brain is the seat of all pain very dreadful'.[23] Gates himself commented on this difference in perception:

> I was taken before a magistrate and sentenced to seven days of solitary, on the daily allowance of a pound of 'damper' and a pint of water. This was the only solitary I received on the roads, and it seemed to me I should starve to death before I came out. By the old hands this sort of punishment is considered the hardest that can be inflicted, and they had far rather take the quota of lashes from the cat, than the week of solitary. [122–3]

For the record, there is no evidence that Gates was ever sentenced to solitary confinement while in Van Diemen's Land.

If the notion of separate treatment was popular in British middle-class circles, the citizens of the new American Republic embraced the idea with even more enthusiasm. A host of American cities constructed penitentiaries designed on the separate system. It was hoped that these 'laboratories of virtue' would soon distinguish the republican metropolis from its decaying Old World counterpart.[24] Thus compared with the horrors of the lash, solitary was a subject over which the Patriot accounts drew a veil as effective and solid as any penitentiary cell door. It was the trappings of the old system of assignment, which had been first implemented by Lieutenant-Governor Sorell and completed by his successor George Arthur, against which the Patriots railed, and not the dark cells which formed the grim cornerstone of its replacement.

12

Lovely Banks

O N 16 JUNE 1840, twenty of the Patriots were mustered in the yard at Sandy Bay and equipped for a march into the interior. A similar number departed on 17 June, and the remainder in the following week.[1] Marsh recalled that they were ordered to take their place in the line, each man equipped with 'his blanket, tin-cup and plate on his back' and with 'six constables and twelve soldiers to escort us on our way, we knew not where'. Their rations for three days consisted of 'poor mutton and bread', which they had to roll up in their blankets that were 'literally alive with fleas' (85). The Patriots had been told that they were being sent to another part of the road where, as Gates put it, 'the work was lighter and consequently easier, and where we should enjoy greater privileges' (101). Like the other Patriots, however, he knew the real reason that they were being moved was in order to place them far out of sight of visiting whalers.

Progress was slow. The roads were muddy and many of their company were unwell. On the first day of their journey they covered less than 12 miles. At dusk they were put up at a road station where there were some 150 British and Irish prisoners at work. Tired and exhausted, the Patriots huddled among them and, as Marsh wrote, 'rested as well as we could' (85). Having nothing to cook their mutton in, they borrowed a kettle from an overseer and broiled their rations round an open fire in the yard. As Marsh recalled, they spent a fitful night, as their sleep was interrupted by a visit from 'some of our old friends, called lice, which continued to increase, in spite of all our efforts, during our stay on the roads'. In the morning they were turned out by the ringing of the station bell, but before being permitted to cook breakfast, they were ranked up to watch the flogging of four British prisoners. When they were finally allowed to open their bundles of meagre provisions, they discovered that a good part of their rations had been

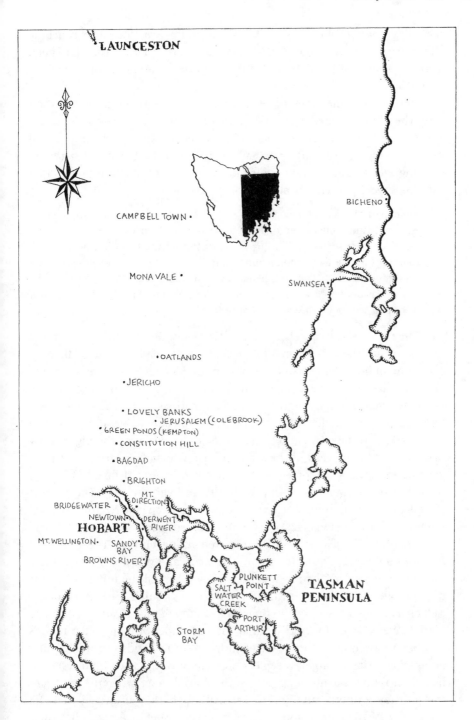

Eastern Van Diemen's Land

spirited away by light-fingered thieves. As Gates was forced to conclude after one look at 'the poor hungry fellows' whose quarters they had been forced to share, 'I could not blame them much, although it was cruelty to us' (102).

Having consumed their scanty breakfast, they were once more on their way. The march proved even more difficult than that of the previous day. The clumsy thick shoes that had been issued to them three and a half months earlier were starting to fall apart. Some even walked barefoot, carrying the remains of their boots in their hands. As Marsh recalled, their sufferings were particularly acute:

> Some part of the roads being newly laid with stone, of about the size of hens-eggs, only not quite as round, being flint stone, with edges as sharp as a knife. Our feet were sore and bleeding; tired and hungry, we got but little farther than on the first day, though continually hurried along by our drivers. If we refused to go, 'Well dam your bloody eyes, go along a little ways farther, there is a watch-house we will put you in and keep you on bread and water a few days, and see how you will like that.' [85–6]

They crossed the causeway over the Derwent River at Bridgewater and pushed on up the road, arriving that night at Bagdad, a small settlement consisting of little more than three taverns and a couple of stores clustered around a barracks and a large watch-house. This was the place where prisoners were brought from surrounding stations to be tried before the local magistrates' bench. The Patriots were mustered into the yard, and after cooking some of their depleted rations, turned in for the night. They had to sleep in the cells of the watch-house which they shared with the existing inmates, some of whom had been incarcerated for a while and were covered, in Marsh's words, 'with filth and vermin' (87). The Patriots placed all of their remaining provisions in a heap and charged Daniel Liscum with the first watch. After an hour Heustis got up to relieve Liscum, only to find him sleeping on the one remaining bundle. The rest were found in different parts of the room 'cut open, and rifled of all the articles our "fellow-boarders" had a fancy for'. They searched the other occupants of the room but all they were able to recover was a small amount of dough, hidden as Heustis described, 'in their hats, on top of their heads!' (108). The Patriots were forced to conclude that the remainder of their stolen rations had been passed out of the gaol window into the hands of some hidden accomplice. After a largely sleepless night they were raised by the station bell; their rations having gone, they were obliged to set off on the last leg of the journey without anything to eat. Although they protested that the remainder of their provisions had been stolen, Marsh recalled that their pleas fell on deaf ears. Their rations had been weighed out for three days by the storekeeper at Sandy Bay and that was the end of the matter.

At nightfall on the third day, they arrived at a place called Lovely Banks. As Miller described it, the station stood in a 'beautiful valley surrounded by high hills of a red, sandy soil' (299). He was particularly taken with she-oaks which covered the slopes and crowns of the surrounding hills. He thought that:

> These oak forests were by far the most agreeable to the eye of any thing which I saw of the kind on the island. The hills upon which they grow are generally 'sugar loaves,' from two hundred to six hundred feet high, free from under brush, and adorned only with these beautiful trees, which seldom obtain a height of more than forty feet, and diameter of one yard at the base of the trunk. Their large circular, ever-green tops however, vary from sixty to one hundred feet in circumference, and the landscape which they form, whether viewed from a distance or the base of the miniature mountains upon which they grow, can scarcely fail to excite the admiration of the beholder. [299–300]

The place may have been called Lovely Banks but, as Marsh wryly put it, 'to us it proved anything but lovely' (87).

Their new home was situated about 36 miles from Hobart. In contrast to the huts at Sandy Bay, the station here was constructed of stone. As some of the buildings were not complete, however, they were forced to share their quarters with what Gates described as between 'ten or a dozen billeted men' (104). These convict artisans had been hard at work for the preceding fortnight in an attempt to complete the station in readiness for the arrival of the Patriots. The superintendent had written to the visiting magistrate on 1 June to inform him that, although the gaol would be finished in two days, the carpenter's shop, blacksmith's shop, cells, mess shed and chapel were without roofs. The delay had been caused by the difficulty in procuring timber but, despite the state of the buildings, the superintendent thought it would be possible to accommodate about eighty men.[2]

Like many other probation stations, Lovely Banks was organised on the three-yard principle. Each yard was reserved for one of the three probationary classes. At the heart of the station was the gaol. Four sets of huts were clustered around the cell block, opening out on each side into two yards, one for the second-class men and one for the third. The yards and their associated huts were surrounded by a palisade which was interrupted only to provide access to a privy in the far corner, and by a gate which opened out onto the first-class complex. This was where the billeted men were kept to work in the carpenter's shed, blacksmith's shop and the cook and bakehouses. It was also where the hospital and the station store were located, as well as the overseer's quarters and the superintendent's office. Like so much of the landscape of the probation system, the station was organised according to a moral geography. At the core lay the gaol—the place where the wicked were condemned to lie in the dark to contemplate the error of their ways. To journey from here and through the various yards and out of the front gate was to embark on some latter-day Pilgrim's Progress. The superintendent's office, like every other building in the complex, was strategically placed. He worked right next door to the gate to the outside world, policing that step which all convicts were supposed to eagerly anticipate when they would be delivered from the grip of probationary labour and be moved on to lighter duties as a reward for deference and hard work. The only building which lay outside the stockade was the chapel—a physical embodiment of the probation station motto that relief from hard labour could only be earned by good conduct.[3]

Marsh named their new superintendent at Lovely Banks as 'Branberson'. In fact Anthony Brabezon was appointed Superintendent of the Road Department works at Lovely Banks in August following the resignation of his predecessor, Lapper, although the appointment was not confirmed until 1 September. Brabezon's principal overseer was Thomas King.[4] These two soon proved, in Gates's words, to be 'even more tyrannical than those we had just left' (104).

> They seemed to delight in having a 'down' upon some one or more of the men. The meaning of this term is, that when any of the men have done anything accidentally or otherwise, to displease the superintendent or overseer, and which is not sufficient to be taken cognizance of by a magistrate—or if a dislike be taken to the prisoner, for any cause, fancied or real—every method is taken that suggests itself, to torment and make worse their . . . situation. It is the meanest, most devilish sort of revenge that can be imagined. [105]

There were, Gates confessed, 'numberless ways by which the overseer can vent his spite on his victim'. A man could be compelled, for example, 'to do with a poor tool as much as another with a better one' (105). Or he could be forced into the worst position on the line and exposed to the full impact of the elements, or to labouring in the deepest mud. No magistrate was needed to sanction these punishments. Often it was the aim of the overseer to goad the prisoner into making a complaint or throwing down his tools in protest. Then a formal charge could be brought, and the poor prisoner was exposed to the risk of being further burdened with a stint in the cells (57–8).

Marsh was one of the prisoners victimised by King. The trouble started one warm day when several of the prisoners left their jackets and boots at the station when they went out to labour on the roads. On their return, they discovered that their possessions had disappeared from the hut where they had left them. Suspicion immediately fell on the billeted hands, and since Marsh did not want to be punished for losing his boots, he complained to the visiting magistrate. The charge was dismissed. The magistrate insisted

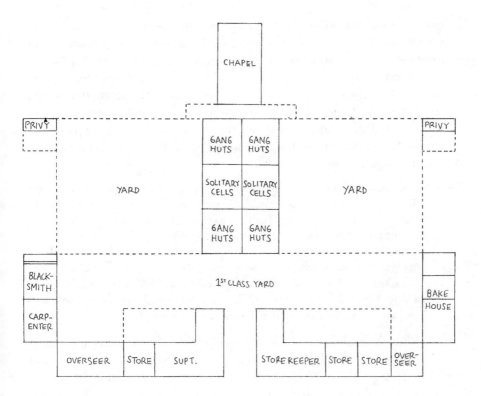

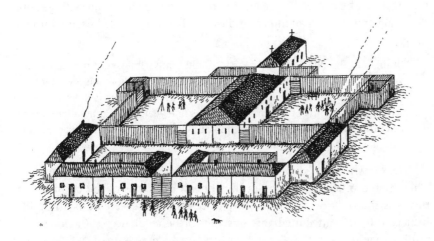

Lovely Banks Probation Station, 1840

that the doors of the huts should be locked during working hours in future, but this did not prevent King, whom Marsh had accused of being leader of the gang of thieves, from exacting his own revenge. Marsh recalled that he took 'the privilege of abusing me, in every possible manner, saying every little while, "accuse us of stealing, will you"' (89). The abuse that Marsh received from King was unrelenting. As Gates recalled, his comrades watched as Marsh daily sank under the tyranny of his detested overseer. Finally Marsh could bear it no longer and brought a complaint before the visiting magistrate:

> I told him of the overseers abuse to me, and that I could not stand it but a short time. The overseer, Tom King was called, and went on with a long list of complaints. I told the magistrate that they were all lies, and could be proven so by every man in the party; I told him the cause of the overseer's treatment to me, and that I was not the only one, who would be driven to death or the Bush, by the tyranny and villiany [sic] of our overseers; the Doctor was called and I was examined; I told him of the pain in my breast, that I had been troubled with it a long time. Said he, 'did you tell the overseer of your situation?' I told him that I had. 'That will do,' said he, giving me a plaster. [89]

After this, the surgeon and the magistrate talked together for a short time. The magistrate then turned to Marsh and told him that there was not sufficient time to put King on trial; if he wished to press the charge, the hearing would have to wait until another day. He tried to persuade Marsh to withdraw the charge before leaving to talk to King in the adjoining room. The magistrate was in a temper, and Marsh had no trouble hearing him tell King:

> 'If this suit should go on, and Marsh should bring witnesses, it must go against you; the Doctor tells me he is not able to do heavy work, and it is evident you have abused him, by causing him to work harder than he is able; you see it would send you to Port Arthur six months or a year; so you may thank me for not bringing the case to trial; put him at light work, and let me hear no more complaints of this kind.' [89]

As Marsh reported, after that he had it easier for a while although he still suffered much pain through his ill health. He was of the opinion that this was the only occasion that any of them had 'received any thing like justice' (90). He attributed this one 'act of benevolence' (90) not to the visiting magistrate, but to the station surgeon—a man named D. E. Stodart.[5] Needless to say, after a fortnight had passed, King began to manifest signs of renewed tyranny towards Marsh. One night after the gang had knocked off work and had nearly completed the march back to the station, King 'enquired for the crowbars' (90); told that they had been left at the works, he flew into a rage. The next day was a Saturday—the day that the tools were audited by the storekeeper, R. F. Hunt.[6] King halted the gang in its tracks and turned to Marsh and Wright, who was another of the Patriots he disliked, and sent them back 2 miles to collect the missing crowbars. One crowbar was small, but the other was several feet in length. On the way back the two men wrought their revenge—they managed eventually to break the small bar by lying it on the ground and smashing it across the midriff with the large one. It was nine o'clock when they arrived at the station and they were tired and hungry. Next morning they were questioned about the broken crowbar, but 'we told them it must have been broken by some one during the night', Marsh related. 'We were threatened with the cells, but as it could not be proved, we being alone, we finally received nothing but threats' (90).

When the Patriots arrived at Lovely Banks it was the first month of the antipodean winter, and they were exposed to the wind and the rain. As at Sandy Bay, they were not permitted the warmth of a fire at night, and despite the cold, they were not issued with any extra clothing. At the end of each day they were mustered into their huts with, in Marsh's words, 'no fire, no light, cold, hungry and tired—nearly every night wet to the skin, the doors locked with sentrys out side day and night' (87). Many of their number, including Gates, were by now without shoes. Although it was four months since they had been issued with their first pair, the promised supply of fresh footwear had not arrived. Gates recalled how on many mornings he had to stand barefoot in the frost, while mustered in the station yard. He resorted to binding his naked feet with old rags to protect them from the cold, but despite this expedient, darting pains shot through his limbs and he soon became lame with rheumatism. As Miller recollected, in the morning 'when the party went to their labour, BLOOD marked their footsteps in the frost' (302). Heustis claimed that one of their number, Hiram Loop, 'was shut up in a loathsome cell for several days, and fed on bread and water!' (109) for refusing to labour without shoes. This was a detail repeated in Miller's account and more loosely by Marsh, who claimed:

> Many were put in the cells for seven, eight and ten days on bread and water for very trifling offences, and in fact for no offence whatever. Two or three were put in for refusing to work without shoes in the frost and on the flint-stone road—kept in until almost starved—taken out and obliged to work, being promised shoes in a few days . . . [91]

Gemmell also insists that Hiram Loop was punished 'because he grumbled or refused to work one cold morning rather frosty, he having no shoes',[7] although in his account he claimed that Loop was flogged for the offence, rather than flung into a solitary cell.

Wright was also sentenced to three days' solitary confinement on bread and water for 'neglect of duty'.[8] He later recalled that he was punished 'for refusing to carry (in an over-worked and debilitated state,) a bar of iron, weighing one hundred pounds' (23)—possibly another version of the crowbar incident described by Marsh, although the latter was insistent that he and Wright had escaped punishment. Gemmell, however, recalled that Wright was punished 'because when sick the Doctor refused to exempt him, and the overseer ordered him to wheel a heavy loaded barrow up a plank, which he failed in doing from weakness'.[9] Gemmell also recalled that, rather than being sentenced to solitary confinement, Wright was flogged.

According to Gates's narrative, Wright, having been taken ill, asked King for permission to quit his work. Permission was refused but, probably with memories of the fate of poor Lysander Curtis uppermost in their minds, his comrades urged Wright to return to the station. When he arrived at Lovely Banks the assistant surgeon predictably declared that he was not sick, and the station superintendent 'thrust him into a cell' (107) to await a hearing before the visiting magistrate. Having returned from their labours to find that Wright was not in his hut, his comrades confronted the Superintendent, and on hearing that their compatriot had been locked in the cells, they demanded his release. To a man, they made it clear that they were prepared to break down the cell doors if their demands were not met. Brabezon conceded, confident that the magistrate would make an example of the Patriots. As Gates reported, however, the 'magistrate and doctor having come and inquired into the matter and ascertained the facts, gave the superintendent, overseer and assistant doctor, a severe reprimand, telling them at the same time, they might be indeed thankful that they were not broke of their offices' (108). After this incident Wright lay sick in the hospital for six weeks.

Other versions of the Patriots' stint at Lovely Banks survive which show their experience in a different light. In August 1840, the Patriots addressed two petitions, one to W. E. Lawrence, a member of the Legislative Council, and the other to Sir John Franklin. These make interesting reading when placed alongside the Patriots' subsequent accounts published from the safety of the United States. The petition addressed to Lawrence was authored by Linus Miller. In it he sought to remind Lawrence that while the Patriots were at Sandy Bay 'His Excellency—the Lieutenant-Governor—has visited our gang twice . . . and on both occasions, was pleased to promise us—in the strongest terms, that *"good conduct should be rewarded."*' Miller continued:

> I am happy to be able to say that the conduct of the whole Gang, has with one or two trifling exceptions, been such as to secure the approbation and esteem of those in authority over us and I know it to be the desire of any comrades

generally to conduct themselves in a becoming manner as prisoners, in whatever situation they may be placed, during the period of their exile in this colony.[10]

The second petition, signed by fifty-seven prisoners from the *Buffalo*, including Marsh, Heustis, Snow, Wright, Gates and Woodman, made a similar point:

> That your Excellencys Petitioners have sincerely endeavoured to conform in every particular to the rules laid down for their observation, and to the instructions of those in authority over them.
>
> That Your Excellencys Petitioners are happy to be able to state that their conduct generally, has hitherto been such as to meet approbation of all those in authority over them: and they are emboldened to hope from Your Excellencys high character for clemency and justice, and from the promises which it has pleased Your Excellency to hold forth to them, that—good conduct should be rewarded—.[11]

The petitions suggest that the official record is in fact correct and that, contrary to the Patriots' subsequent claims, few of their number were punished at Sandy Bay and Lovely Banks. In contrast to the line taken in their subsequent accounts, the petitions reveal the degree to which the Patriots were prepared to ingratiate themselves, in return for remission of their sentence to probationary labour. They stressed not only the extent to which they had toed the official line, but also the degree to which they were prepared to kowtow to the Queen's lackeys. To this end, they adopted the formal language of the petitioner—they asked whether His Excellency would be 'graciously pleased' to take into his 'merciful consideration' the case of 'your humble Petitioners'.[12] This was the literary equivalent of doffing cap and falling on bended knee. Revealingly, they even closed with the standard promise of future allegiance—'And as in duty bound your Petitioners will ever be'. Little evidence here of the fervent opposition to monarchical oppression so prevalent in their later accounts.

For all their ridiculing of Franklin, the petitions also reveal the extent to which they had digested his message—a message which had been preached to them from the pulpit of the station chapel every Sunday: 'that by good conduct alone can they hope to escape from Probationary punishment to which they have been respectively condemned'.[13] Notwithstanding that the Patriots bowed and scraped, Miller also made it clear that their sufferings had been great. He was quick to stress, however, that this was not the result of any unwarranted abuse of power but, as he put it, because they had 'been accustomed to enjoy all that is desirable in life' and were thus, by inference, ill-suited to hard labour. He continued: 'Many of my companions are considerably advanced in years, their health impaired by the rigours of imprisonment, and their spirits broken by sorrow and want; and unless there is soon some amelioration of our wretched condition,—must soon find a *Prisoners rest*'.[14] Thus Miller blamed their plight on the Patriots' own spiritual and physical short-comings.

Despite their grovelling pleas, both petitions were unsuccessful. As Lawrence scrawled in a note attached to Miller's letter: 'I have had an opportunity of personally pointing out to these men the impropriety of signing any Petition in a body—and if they have to petition the head of the Govt. the parties must do it individually'. He added, the men 'saw their error and said they regretted having taken such a course'.[15] The whole point of a petition was that it should bind the petitioner within a deferential chain of command. Miller, at least, understood the first principle of petitioning. The approach should be made, not to Franklin in person, but to a respectable member of the community who would forward the petitioner's pleas up the chain of command, together with his own letter of recommendation. As Snow confessed, the point was vigorously pressed upon them: 'The magistrate informed us, if we wished to offer a petition to his Excellency, we must do it individually, but the better way was not to do it at all, jointly or severally' (15). The state wished to atomise its charges, offering a hand of paternal guidance to the good and the promise of retribution to the wicked. A petition signed by the 'Political Prisoners now at Lovely Banks Road Station' was doomed to failure. It was clear now that the state would not deal with them as a political body, but as with common criminals, it would treat each case on its respective merits—punishing the wicked and rewarding the good.

If anything, the petitions served to increase the suffering of the Patriots. Faced with the tyranny of a callous and corrupt superintendent and overseer, as well as a colluding magistrate, the Patriots resolved to change tactics. No more petitions were addressed to their gaolers; they looked instead to their own countrymen. Later that month word reached Lovely Banks that there were two or three Yankee whalers riding at anchor in Hobart. It was determined, as Marsh put it, that 'Two of our party now take the Bush, for the sake of getting out of the hands of these tyrants, and if possible make some arrangement with an American Captain' (90). Having secured their means of escape, the two were to return to Lovely Banks in order to organise a mass break-out. The lot 'fell on Miller and Stewart, two men of education and intelligence', Gates reported (110).

The escape attempt was a week in the planning. During that time a stock of provisions was saved out of the Patriots' scanty rations. Prior to the escape attempt, Miller and Stewart wrote a note to Major Ainsworth, the visiting magistrate, which they left where it would be found the next morning. According to Heustis, they complained of being 'treated far worse than African slaves in any part of the world', and that they had been 'driven to take the bush, as the only chance of prolonging their lives.' As Heustis explained, however, this was merely a ruse designed 'to put the authorities on the wrong track' (109). So it was, Miller told his readers, that on the night of 29 August, after many a ' "God Bless you," many a prayer for the success of our mission' (305) that he and Stewart scrambled through a hole in the roof and slipped over the stockade. As the *Hobart Town Gazette* reported, they took with them '2 blankets, 2 tin pannicans, and 1 plate, the property of the crown'.[16] With knapsacks fashioned from the blankets on their back they 'plunged into the dark forests, and, with the Southern Cross for our guide, steered for the metropolis of the land of Nod' (305).

As they descended into one of the 'almost bottomless ravines which yawn between the hills', Miller reported that the silence was broken by his friend's shouts of 'I am *free! free! free!*' (305). Miller could not resist taking up the refrain:

> '*I am free!*' I exclaimed with indescribable transport, and the huge rocks and trees of the 'prison isle,' as if inspired with that freedom which they forever lost when Britain planted her bloody flag, that symbol of eternal slavery, upon their shores, caught the soul-stirring sounds and echoed forth 'I am *free! free! free!*' [305–6]

They travelled until early dawn, when they made their bed for the day under the cover of thick wattle scrub. At nightfall they resumed their journey, carefully avoiding all signs of habitation. As Miller recalled, 'we made the *bush* our highway, and the warm lairs of the kangaroo (as they sprang up and bounded away, measuring from twenty to thirty feet each leap,) our resting places' (306). The going was slow. At times they found the bush so thick that it would take them an hour to gain a quarter of a mile.

As dawn broke on the second day, they found themselves in open country. Seeing smoke rising from the chimneys of homesteads, they repaired to the top of a high hill covered with oak. They discovered that the crown of the hill was a mass of rocks, 'and the absence of any thing which could tempt man to frequent the place, betokened security; and without fear of being disturbed, we made our beds and were soon dreaming of native land and liberty'. In the late morning Miller was awakened, 'apparently, by a strange presentiment of coming evil' (307). Raising his head, he saw a large dog at their feet, and a few seconds later the dog's master appeared between the boulders. The man, a middle-aged gentleman, seemed as surprised as Stewart and Miller. He took one look at their grey slops and 'exclaimed, ... "I see; you are bushrangers"' (307). On inquiry, their unwelcome visitor proved to be the local district constable. On discovering their visitor's identity, Miller confessed that he would 'rather have seen the face of his Satanic Majesty' (307). Fortunately the two Patriots outnumbered their would-be captor and, after welcoming him to their 'rude habitation' (307), they invited him to sit down. A bizarre conversation followed. In Miller's account the two Patriots introduced themselves as citizens of the United States, who 'until little more than a day since' (308) had been British slaves. Preferring not to be known as bushrangers, they likened themselves to Jonathan, who with the aid of his armour bearer had delivered the people of Israel from the clutches of the Philistines.[17] On discovering that the strangers were 'the two Canadian prisoners' (308) who had absconded from Lovely Banks, the constable announced: 'Indeed! I am sorry, for it is, as you must know, my duty to apprehend you. How could you have been so foolish as to abscond?' (308). To which Miller replied:

> 'You are very kind, sir, but we can not go with you. We have taken the bush for the purpose of escaping from the island, and until we have had a fair trial, and failed, shall not surrender, unless absolutely compelled to do so.' [309]

The district constable assured them that they had no possibility of succeeding in their mission and that he was bound by oath to apprehend them. In the end it was Joseph Stewart who appealed to the constable's better nature:

> Why, it would be a crime! a crime against our suffering friends; a crime against humanity and against heaven to stop us. Would you, oh! would you send us back to the horrid slavery from which we have just escaped? No, I will not believe it. I did not know before that there was a single inhabitant of this island, this land of crime and suffering, who has a heart to feel for another's woe, but I find there is *one*, and I thank God for it. [311–12]

That appeal did the trick, at least according to Miller's account, and the constable bade them 'farewell! and may God Almighty guide you in safety to your homes' (313). On the evening of 2 September the two absconders arrived at Sandy Bay. While they had been at Sandy Bay Probation Station, Stewart had made the acquaintance of Thomas Chaffey, a 75-year-old man who had originally been transported on the *Scarborough*, and his son William who owned the Travellers Rest hotel.[18] According to Gates, Thomas Chaffey was a Freemason and his 'sympathies were first enlisted for two of our number, who were brother masons, and feeling so strong an interest for them, he also came to sympathise with us all' (111). The two absconders dared not show their face on the premises, knowing that the Travellers Rest 'was the resort of constables' (313). It was illegal for prisoners to be served liquor, and dressed in their slop uniforms they would have attracted immediate interest. So instead Miller slipped old man Chaffey a note asking him to approach one of the Yankee captains and 'if possible induce him to grant us an interview' (313). Chaffey was greatly agitated at the sight of Miller. As the harbouring of runaways was punishable by a hefty fine, detection spelt potential ruin. The two were almost instantly betrayed, according to Heustis, who observed that 'Thirty pieces of silver possess a wonderful charm in some cases' (110). No sooner had Miller made himself known to Thomas Chaffey than he found six or seven constables hard on his heels. He fled to rejoin Stewart, whom he had left at a safe distance in charge of the meagre baggage. An hour later the two were 'snugly ensconced' under a stone bridge, 3 miles below Sandy Bay, where they could mourn their fate: 'All our hopes were thus suddenly crushed; for it would be madness to think of prosecuting our designs, when, within a few hours, hundreds would be on the lookout to catch or hunt us down like wild beasts of the forest' (314).

They remained concealed under the bridge the following day, before commencing their retreat to Lovely Banks. This time they climbed up the slopes of Mount Wellington and skirted the town. There was no wind, and although 'old Wellington, whose head reached above the clouds, was clothed with snow', the day was 'intensely warm'. At length the pair became thirsty and descended into a deep gully to find water:

> The tears of old Night were still hanging upon the underbrush in the form of dew-drops, which we eagerly kissed away, and never in my life did I drink any thing which tasted half so delicious. We were nearly fainting, when to our great joy we discovered a beautiful fountain of water running from the base of a ledge of rocks, nearly one hundred feet perpendicular. After making a cup of tea and remaining at the spring two or three hours, we proceeded on our way. [315]

The luxury of tea, usually not allowed ordinary convicts, had been supplied to Stewart, who was a tailor, in return for his doing some tailoring work on the superintendent's clothes.

On 11 September, tired and dejected, they surrendered to the authorities at Bagdad. Miller admitted that 'From the time of our betrayal at Sandy Bay, we had been most wretched. All hope of escape was at an end, and the dark future was frowning upon us' (318). There they were tried by Major Ainsworth and sentenced to two years' hard labour at Port Arthur.

In some of the other Patriot accounts, the details of Miller's and Stewart's capture differ. Gates claimed that the Chaffeys proved loyal friends who succeeded in arranging a meeting with an American captain. The two were apprehended on their way back to Lovely Banks so the planned mass break-out and rush to the coast was thwarted. According to Wright, just as 'the hope of our liberty seemed brightening', two of the Patriots, Orin W. Smith and James Aitchison, betrayed Miller and Stewart to a magistrate, 'and they were taken on their return from the sea-shore, without our ever having known what they had accomplished' (24). In this instance it seems that Miller is the reliable witness of his circumstance. If he could have massaged his narrative to give a more heroic twist to his adventure, he surely would have done so. As with the story they spun of the mutiny on the *Buffalo*, neither Wright nor Gates was willing to concede that two Americans might have *consigned* themselves to two more years of hard slavery under the Queen's lackeys. Just as he had in the *Buffalo* incident, Wright was keen to find traitors. Orin Smith and John Tyrrell were the two whom Wright had named as betraying the planned mutiny. Since both Smith and Aitchison were both later promoted to positions of overseer, they could be readily made to fit the frame for this second great act of 'betrayal'.

13

Green Ponds

THE MORNING AFTER Linus Miller and Joseph Stewart were recaptured, the remaining Patriots were rounded up and force-marched back towards Hobart. Their destination proved to be the station at Green Ponds, which was closer to Hobart than Lovely Banks, and lay hard by a barracks containing a sergeant and thirteen privates.[1] Before they departed they were kitted out in particoloured slops, known as 'magpies', which were usually reserved for penal station inmates. The suits, as Heustis described them, were half black and half yellow, 'arranged so that the front of one leg was yellow and the other black ... a more striped-looking set of fellows was never seen' (111). The legs of the trousers were not stitched up the sides but were fastened with a set of buttons, to allow them to be worn by men in irons. Leg irons were riveted to the prisoner's ankle, preventing the wearing of conventional clothing. Gates recalled these clothes were looked upon by the 'government as a badge of deep disgrace'. Not only were they a badge of ignominy; the gaps between the button allowed the cold to penetrate so, Gates complained, they were an even less effective barrier against the biting cold than their 'old thread-bare' suits. To make matters worse, their new slops proved to be as ill-fitting as their old sets, since the 'suits were all of a size, or with but a slight variation, and were distributed to us as we stood in rank, without regard to their fitting our person' (112). To swap a large jacket for one of a better fit would have been to risk punishment for trafficking, as each set of numbered slops was allotted to an individual prisoner. The result, according to Gates, was that a 'short fellow' might find himself issued with 'a pair of breeches quite large enough for a child of Anak' (one of the biblical giants who inhabited the land of Canaan) and 'a roundabout [jacket] that would have done honor to "his excellency," Sir John' (112).

According to Marsh, the Patriots tried to make light of their outlandish gear. It was, he recalled, 'a comical dress, you would have laughed to have seen us; we knew it was for punishment, so we appeared to feel very proud; some would dance, others strut around very much pleased with our new suit'. He noted that their unexpected reactions had the desired effect on their gaolers, some of whom looked 'rather shamed' (91). Gates told a similar story about this grotesque get-up:

> We danced about, and shouted and sung songs as though we were in a real, perfect delirium of joy. A few cursed and swore like madmen possessed. There a short fellow, with pantaloon legs and jacket sleeves a foot too long, might be seen strutting up and down in all the pomposity of her majesty's Lieutenant-Governor ... Yonder another, perhaps aping some less renowned functionary, with equal eclat from his bevy of admirers. [113]

He confessed, however, 'we felt in our hearts more like sitting down and weeping, as did the children of Israel by the rivers of Babylon' (113).

Their new superintendent proved to be a Scotsman by the name of Robert Notman, who for years had been in charge of a road party.[2] Marsh recalled that the old hands called him a 'Tiger' (92). According to Heustis, he had 'the reputation of being the severest taskmaster in Van Dieman's Land', and it was said that on one occasion when he was superintendent at Long Meadows *'thirty-seven hundred lashes* were served out to his gang before breakfast, the men being tied to a cart to receive them' (111). Despite his reputation, however, the Patriots found Notman well-disposed towards their plight. 'He told us that the murderers, thieves and robbers who had been placed under him heretofore, could not be governed without being flogged', Snow reported, 'but he thought none the less of us, for being sent there for political offences' (16).

After the Patriots had been a short while at Green Ponds, they were 'favored with another splendid speech from Sir John Franklin', as Marsh snidely put it (96). This meeting appears to have occurred on the site of St Mary's Church, where many of the *Buffalo* prisoners were set to work.[3] When news of Franklin's imminent arrival was received, some of their number were ordered to 'set about putting things to rights about the station'. About noon, when they were at the point of breaking for their midday meal of boiled mutton and bread, a messenger arrived with the news that His Excellency was just 2 miles from the station. At that very moment, Marsh recalled, they heard the order, ' "Turn out, turn out, all hands, muster, muster;" of course, we had to leave our splendid dinner, and were soon ranked up'. Half an hour later a second messenger arrived, his horse all in a lather, to declare that the governor was close by and he would be there in a few minutes. The man, who was one of Franklin's personal bodyguards and dressed in livery, made a great show of spurring his horse round the yard two or three times. Marsh and the other Patriots were at a loss as to whether his role was 'to protect his noble person from any danger that might occur from men that have been driven by his tyranny to take the bush—or for fear the old gentleman might tumble from his horse' (96). In the end the Patriots remained standing in the yard for an hour before Franklin finally made an appearance.

At first the governor rode up and down their ranks as if reviewing a body of troops, before halting to address them from the lofty elevation of his horse. Franklin expressed his disappointment at the attempted escape of Miller and Stewart, whom he described as 'very bad men' who had been sent to Port Arthur to atone for their crime. This appears to be the first time that the Patriots had been told about the fate of their two comrades, and Marsh reported that Franklin took great delight in reporting that he had told the two absconders 'they need never look for release from punishment—they shall be punished to the extremity of the law' (97). Franklin also revealed that he was well aware of their plans to board an American whaler, and he assured them that escape was futile. He confirmed that they had been dressed in 'magpye' and sent to Green Ponds 'for punishment, and that you might be under the eye of my military'. He warned them that the detachment had been given orders to shoot them down 'like wild beasts' if they should attempt to take to the bush *en masse* (97).

Of course, dressed like canaries the Patriots would have presented an easy target for the British regulars. Marsh reported that Franklin warned them not to associate with the old hands, as these might encourage the Patriots 'to take the bush, as many of them have done' (97). The penalty for bushranging was no longer automatic execution, he told them, but secondary transportation to Port Arthur, and this was 'nearly as bad as death' (97). Here the governor spoke the truth. Seventy-five per cent of all bushrangers in Arthur's period of office had either been shot in action or had swung on the gallows tree. During Franklin's reign this appalling rate of carnage dropped to 18 per cent. The vast bulk of the remainder were condemned to labour for years in the gangs of Port Arthur and Norfolk Island—the spectre of scaffold having been replaced by the certainty of hell on earth.[4]

The governor urged them to ensure that their conduct remained favourable, as this would soon gain them a reprieve from hard labour on the roads. This message was drearily familiar to the Patriots since it would have been repeated to them every Sunday by the Rev. G. Otter, chaplain at Green Ponds. Like all catechists he was obliged to remind his charges 'that by good conduct alone can they hope to escape from Probationary punishment to which they have been respectively condemned'.[5] It was also a message which, Marsh felt, made very little sense:

> He was glad our conduct was good, yet he must punish, for fear it would be bad. This was his motto with us during our stay on the island. . . . leaving us to wonder whether bad conduct or good conduct would make any difference in the eye of a man that supposed all men sent to a penal colony, whether good or bad, must be punished. [97–8]

Marsh concluded that 'the old simpleton' thought that he had been appointed Lieutenant-Governor of Van Diemen's Land for no other purpose than to exact punishment on his charges (114).

The Patriots were now faced with a more immediate concern. One of the indulgences that the superintendent, Notman, permitted was to allow 'some of our party to be overseers of the rest of us'. Many of the other Patriots, Heustis included, were adamant that this was no blessing. He recalled that Notman made an overseer of James Aitchison and promoted Orin Smith to the rank of sub-overseer. Heustis riled against Aitchison, whom he accused of having been 'a negro-driver in the West Indies', and claimed that he had once boasted:

> that he had flogged all the men and women in his gang, being more than seventy, at one time, for a trivial offence, and that among them was a young female slave, with whom he was in the habit of improper intercourse, and by whom he had a child that he left in slavery! [111]

'Under such an overseer', Heustis lamented, 'it could only be expected that we should meet with hard usage' (112).

James Milne Aitchison was in fact a native of Scotland and—although he would never have been employed as a driver, this position being exclusively reserved for Creole slaves—it is not beyond the bounds of possibility that he had worked as an overseer. Itinerant Scots were regularly employed as overseers on Caribbean plantations, although, given their vehement opposition to slavery, such a former occupation would have been unlikely for one of the Patriots. In any case there is no evidence that Aitchison had ever been in the West Indies since he came directly to Quebec from Scotland.[6] By opting to serve the convict administration, however, Aitchison appears to have made himself, at least in some Patriot eyes, a legitimate target of abuse. As they were wont to charge the whole convict system and its administrative officials as implicated in a form of slavery, perhaps it is not surprising that Marsh would seek to tar Aitchison, the collaborator, with the same brush. It seems more likely that Aitchison was selected by Notman to serve as an overseer simply because he was a fellow Scot.

Much the same can be said for Wright's portrayal of Orin Smith, whom he looked upon as a 'double traitor'. According to Wright, not only did Smith lord it over them as a sub-overseer, but it was he who had 'played false on board the Buffalo'. Wright lamented that they had 'charitably thought that *our own countrymen* would try and alleviate our misery; but alas! we found them harder task-masters than those very convicted felons, plucked from the lowest sinks of vice in Great Britain' (24). In fact, it was John Tyrrell, and not Orin Smith, who had betrayed the would-be mutineers on the *Buffalo*. Once Smith and Aitchison were appointed to positions of authority, they appeared to have been retrospectively demonised by many of their fellow convicts. It should come as no surprise that Wright also maintained that it was these same two who had betrayed Stewart and Miller, giving to the local magistrate vital information on the route taken by the two absconders.

In the course of two or three months, Notman was replaced as superintendent of Green Ponds, although the Patriot accounts differ as to the reasons for his removal. Heustis reported that Notman left to return to Scotland. According to the official returns Robert Notman, who was once described as the 'most practical and industrious overseer of roads in the colony', left Van Diemen's Land for his native Scotland in November 1840.[7] Marsh insisted, however, that the reason for Notman's departure was that Franklin had got wind that he 'was manifesting signs of mercy'. His temporary replacement was John Pooke, who was appointed as clerk at Lovely Banks on 22 September 1840 on an annual salary of £30. Pooke was, in Heustis's opinion, a 'new hand at the business' (112). This proved to be a disadvantage, as the inexperienced Pooke left the 'direction of matters, in a great measure, to Atchison [sic], who was principal overseer, and who exercised his authority with the utmost rigor and severity'. After a short period in office, Pooke was removed, after he was caught 'selling flour that belonged to the government, and pocketing the money' (112). Pooke was superseded by Captain A. Wright, who commenced duty as superintendent on 4 December 1840 on a salary of £100.[8] Marsh reported that this man may have gone by the name of Wright, but 'to us all [he was] wrong—but the right man for the governor . . . I verily believe he lay awake nights planning and devising means to make us unhappy and miserable' (93). The Patriots seemed to have shared a universal dislike of Captain Wright. Gates thought that, 'Knowing his character, Sir John readily advanced him to the superintendency of the rebel, vagabond Yankees. He had no experience in the business, but with a fertile invention for cruelty, he worked his royal master good service' (116). Woodman thought that Captain Wright was a man possessed by an evil spirit. Snow likened him to 'an inhuman, overbearing, unprincipled, incarnate devil' who worked them incessantly and seemed hell bent on subduing their 'd——d independent Yankee spirit'. Although, as Snow added mockingly, 'If he succeeded in so doing, we have not yet learned the fact' (17).

The Patriot narratives claim that they were pushed harder at Green Ponds than at Sandy Bay or Lovely Banks. Marsh recalled that they were now driven out to work as soon as they could see in the morning, and did not stop until after dark. They returned to their station, drank their pint of skilly and were mustered into their vermin-infested huts 'tired, wet and hungry'. The impact on their health was worse than ever and he claimed that: 'Some five or six at this place, were ruined for life, and not any but can refer back to this place as one of horrible sufferings and with disgust at the petty tyrants who were over us there' (93).

Gates revealed that about 3 miles distant from Green Ponds was another probation station named Picton, where the superintendent, a man by the name of 'Sandyloe', a convict for life, also was 'noted for great cruelty' (116). There was indeed an overseer called Alexander Lowe working at Picton Station in 1841—to this day the name Alexander is often familiarised in Scotland and Ulster as Sandy.[9] Gates detested Lowe—he thought that his 'soul was completely deadened to every feeling of human nature' and that his only study in life was 'how he might add misery and woe to his fellow convicts, and give pleasure to his masters' (116). To Gates's horror this man took it upon himself to teach Captain Wright all the tricks of the trade. 'Like every petty tyrant', Gates recalled, 'he felt himself of great consequence, and of all others I ever saw, none could go beyond him for assuming dignity.' He added: 'I believe it is generally true, that the lower and more degraded the man, when raised to some petty station, the greater his tyrrany [*sic*] and the greater his would-be dignity' (117).

On his way over to tutor Captain Wright, Lowe would stop off midway at a tavern. He would arrive at Green Ponds drunk and abusive, so much so that the Patriots came to hate him worse than the Devil. In a drunken stupor, Lowe would insist on ranking them up and mustering them into their huts for the night. He insisted that whenever their names were called they should touch their caps and make a bow, 'and speak up deferentially, "Yes sir"' (117). As Gates recalled bitterly:

> This ground our feelings of independence, which were not yet dead in our bosoms, more than any thing which had yet been forced upon us. The idea of paying such homage to a felon, convicted, for aught we knew, of the most damning crimes in the dark catalogue of sin, was more than we felt disposed to submit to. Now and then a man, at first, would refuse to answer. But Sandyloe would command the clerk to call the name again, when, eyeing the man with the malignity of a demon, he would exclaim in great rage: 'Now, do you touch your cap to me, sir! and when your name is called, do you say YES SIR, or I will punish you severely.' [117–18]

Utterly powerless as they were, the Patriots were forced to yield to the drunken, petty tyrant who swayed before them.

In a regular show of intimidation, old hands who had been sentenced at Picton were brought to Green Ponds in order to be flogged. Marsh recollected that every 'few days' they were 'obliged' to witness the ordeal of a poor fellow's back being laid bare before lining up to receive their breakfast (93). The ritual of state-inflicted violence was clearly calculated to discourage all further thoughts of escape.

To make matters worse, Heustis insisted, Aitchison, with a view to promoting his own advancement, endeavoured to 'excite the men to revolt and refuse to work' (112). Heustis recollected that Aitchison took good care to keep his plans from all who knew his own character. Having 'enlisted a few men in his project', he approached Orin Smith saying: 'Now is the time for us to raise ourselves; I have talked with the men, and they have agreed to revolt; let us write to Captain Spode, divulging the plan, and we shall get promoted for it' (112). But as Heustis reported:

> Smith indignantly spurned the nefarious proposition, and immediately cautioned the men against having any thing to do with the plot. Atchison [*sic*] was ever afterwards a relentless enemy to Smith, and also to others who had used their influence to defeat his project. [112]

This story does not appear in any of the other Patriot accounts and may have been invented by Heustis, but such stratagems were not unknown in convict Van Diemen's Land. There were cases, for example, of overseers who induced convicts to abscond in order to claim the reward money.[10]

To complete their misery, the Patriots discovered that they were being shortchanged of their rations. According to Marsh, 'Wright would take for his family use all the fat and best part of our meat. We never got over half the rations allowed us by Government, which was not enough for us, working as we did' (98). As Gates pointed out, government regulation forbade the superintendent, or any officer employed about the station to keep livestock; nevertheless, 'Wright managed to hold four pigs, two dogs, and a number of fowls; and for their support, made quite heavy drafts upon our flour for the benefit of the shoats and biddies, whilst portions of the mutton passed down canine throats' (121).

This appears to have been a regular convict complaint: similar charges were brought against officers at Macquarie Harbour and Port Arthur penal stations.[11] The Patriots attempted to lay a charge against Wright but he had a ready response that the prisoners had their full tub of flour. As Gates wryly reported:

> Perhaps we did; but the deficiency of flour was counterbalanced by a superfluity of water and our 'damper' . . . came to us but half baked, and heavy as a stone. Our meat, too, was of poorer quality than any we had yet had. Less care was taken with it, so that it generally swarmed with crawling things. But such food was all we could get, and famine compelled us to eat it or die. [121]

Captain Wright and his minions were not slow to lay charges against the Patriots. As Woodman put it, 'He took every advantage of us and had as many as six of us in the cells at one time',[12] while Marsh claimed that many 'were put in the cells for eight or ten days, on bread and water, for daring to speak against the horrible treatment received' (98). According to Heustis, to miss the morning muster was to 'be doomed to seven or fourteen days' solitary confinement, in a loathsome cell, full of vermin, where he was fed on bread and water'. He alleged that while they were at Green Ponds, 'Men were often sentenced, for thirty days at a time, in these detestable dungeons' (111).

Although there is little evidence that they were sentenced to solitary six at a time, their conduct records suggest that the Patriots were punished at Green Ponds at a far greater rate than at Sandy Bay or Lovely Banks. In all, eleven charges were brought against eight of their number, resulting in sentences amounting to a total of forty-four days' solitary confinement.[13]

It seemed to Marsh that the Patriots' enemies were conspiring to drive them to 'commit some act that would be considered worthy of capital punishment, that they might have the satisfaction of seeing us plunged deeper and deeper in misery'. But, he continued:

> Seeing and knowing their intentions, we tried in all our power to disappoint them. We knew that if we took the bush, in our situation and knowing the situation of the island, we never should have lived to reach America. After being deceived and lied to so long, we thought, if it was possible, we would try to obtain our tickets and then make a trial of escape. [100]

As well as their own hardships, they were also subjected to the daily ritual of watching the prisoners from Picton flogged before the Patriots fell into line each morning to receive their pint of skilly. Sickened at the sight, they dismantled the triangles and concealed them. As Marsh revealed, when the next man was brought to be flogged the triangles could not to be found, 'so the man escaped that time, we were all threatened but no one knew anything about them' (93). The same tale was reported by Miller, although he alleged that the incident occurred at Lovely Banks and not at Green Ponds, a station in which he never served as a convict. He claimed that the triangles had been erected, not to punish men from Picton, but in order to threaten the Patriots with a beating. In Miller's version they 'gave the superintendent and overseer to understand that this was going one step beyond the boundaries of endurance, and in case any attempt was made to flog one of our party the remainder would openly rebel'. Consequently, on the first night after the triangles were set up in the muster yard they were spirited away and cast into a small lagoon 'where, doubtless, they remain at the present day' (301). Gates added a few embellishments of his own to the tale: 'We had agreed among ourselves, that if any of our number were taken up to be flogged, . . . we would to a man resist, though death should be the result' (95). The surgeon spoke to some of the men who were in the cells awaiting trial, warning them that if they persisted 'they would undoubtedly be severely flagellated' (127). That same day one of the station carpenters was ordered to repair the triangles. This got the Patriots' blood up and, according to Gates, that night:

> whilst the constables and officers were at their tea, we tore the triangle in pieces and burned it in the cook's room. The next morning another took its place, which during the day was secreted in a brush fence some distance from the station, by the baker, cook, and wardsmen, who remain behind to get the victuals and keep the station in order. Dilligent inquiries were made for the missing triangles, but as no one was seen in the acts, all remained innocent. The second morning a third one made its appearance, which was locked in the store house. [127]

In Gates's version, the news of the Patriots' manly 'determination to resist the flogging of our fellow prisoners, spread out among the settlers and caused a great excitement' (127). He recalled that many came to the station to urge the Patriots to exercise more caution before they were all tied to the triangles and flogged, to which they replied: 'Be that as it may, if those men are flogged, we shall be too, for we will *not* submit to see the punishment inflicted; come what may, we shall surely resist it' (128).

The Patriots fought back in other ways too. Since their arrest in Canada, they had become the subjects of disciplinary knowledge. Their physical features, their characters and conduct had all been meticulously described. This was an on-going process which was continued at Green Ponds by J. Oswald, writer to the visiting magistrate. He made a transcript of every bench hearing and forwarded a copy to the Muster Master for inclusion in the black books.[14] The Patriots were dissected by paperwork and shuffled from office to office, until some petty colonial official was ordered to assemble a composite picture. The whole practice was driven by the ideology of the Convict Department, which slotted them into pre-existing categories: 'generally good industrious men' who were deserving of official indulgence; or, in the case of the six who had been sent to Port Arthur for absconding, 'idle peculating offenders'.[15] At least one of the Patriots, Elijah Woodman, had attempted to redress the balance by keeping a journal of his own. This was a project that he had started while incarcerated in the Kingston gaol, but it now gave him an opportunity to record the misdealings of Captain Wright and his underlings. It may well have been this clandestine writing project, established in reaction to the bureaucratic authority of the Convict Department, that inspired the later published narratives. The immediate difficulty that they encountered was the problem of securing sufficient paper to undertake such an account, without arousing suspicion. It was not long before Captain Wright and his overseers got wind of what was afoot and ordered a search for the offending journal, fearful in Marsh's words, that 'if ever they were published, they would be exposed' (93). The Patriots were thus ranked up and had to suffer the ignominy of being searched by the 'constables, clerks, overseers, and other billeted men' (93). As Marsh had been spotted a short time previously holding a piece of paper, he was ordered to strip off his clothes. He refused to submit to such an indignity and was forcibly stripped; however, all that was found in his possession was a newspaper 'that one of the soldiers had handed me with something in it he said, respecting the Canadian prisoners' (94).

Snow reported that in Wright's attempts to uncover the secret journal he 'caused every nook and corner of our huts to be searched' (18). Snow was adamant, however, that the search proved fruitless, and as a result the detested superintendent 'probably remains ignorant to this day of our actual opinion of his contemptible meanness' (18). Marsh reported that:

> During the search there were one or two journals found, and in them his own character, with others, was partly described, but in such a manner that it could not be distinctly made out. I understood that Wright went with it to the magistrate, . . . who had a hearty laugh over it. Says he to Mr. Wright, 'there appears to be much truth in this journal, according to all accounts; if you are guilty of such little mean acts, I do not blame the men for finding fault. I shall look into it, and if true, you must expect to be punished.' [94]

There appears to be some truth in the story, since, although several diaries and letters authored by Woodman survive, no account of his time at Green Ponds can be located. According to Gates, the Patriots also embarked on a campaign of physical intimidation. Fed up with Lowe's antics, they became determined to rid themselves of the 'detested imp'. They drew lots, and it fell to Gates and Hiram Sharp to waylay the superintendent as he left the tavern on one of his regular evening trips to Green Ponds. Gates recalled that 'The carpenter made us two stout, heavy bludgeons, with which we stole out after dark, and secreted ourselves behind a large stump of the green tree' (118). It seems likely, however, that Lowe had been tipped off, for although Gates and Sharp 'watched in vain till past midnight' (118) he never made an appearance. The threat of physical intimidation achieved its effect, however, and Lowe put a halt to his evening visits.

Like much in the Patriot accounts, it is difficult to determine whether these reported acts of resistance refer to actual events. There may have been some symbolic reaction to the revolting spectre of flogging, if not as grandiose as Gates would have liked his readers to believe. If the Patriots really had dismantled the triangles, it is unlikely that the convict adminis-tration would have obliged with a mass flogging. Instead they are likely to have singled out a few ringleaders to serve as an example, and any thought of further resistance would have been extinguished by the use of troops. This is precisely how the leaders of a strike at Mersey Probation Station in the mid-1840s were dealt with. There, justice was administered by the station flagellator, while order was secured through use of British regulars who stood by, no doubt with bayonets fixed.[16]

There is an undercurrent in the Patriots' accounts, however, which does ring true. Gates reported that it was the baker, cook and wardsmen who hid the triangles. When planning the attack on the detested Lowe, it was the station carpenter who prepared the bludgeons. Some of the offences with which the Patriots were charged while at Green Ponds sug-gest that at least some of their number had been promoted to occupy such positions. For example, Beamus Woodbury was charged with 'trafficking in bread and strong suspicion of having stolen the same' on 10 December 1840, an offence for which he was subsequently sentenced to seven days' solitary confinement. Woodbury had served as a cook at the Patriot inva-sion and was wounded at the battle of the windmill when he had been shot through a door while cooking potatoes.[17] It seems likely that the offence at Green Ponds had also occurred in the cookhouse. Others too had worked in billets. For all the abuse that he levelled at Aitchison, Heustis admitted that he too was elevated to the position of sub-overseer while stationed at Green Ponds. But 'as I would not drive the men as hard as they had previously been driven, my term of service in that capacity was very short. I was "broke," and set to work again on the carts', he claims in his own defence (112).

Others among the Patriots were worked as mechanics. In May 1841 there was an angry exchange of paperwork when it was discovered that the Director of Public Works, Captain Alexander Cheyne, had employed some of the Patriots on the construction of St Mary's Anglican Church at Kempton.[18] In the course of the following correspondence it also emerged that, not only had many Patriots been at work on the Kempton church, but that while at Lovely Banks they had been employed in the construction of a bridge.[19] The returns for 1840 confirm that this was a project that was undertaken during the Patriots' stay.[20]

Despite their complaints, it is apparent that at least one in five of the Patriots had worked in billeted positions at Lovely Banks as well as at Green Ponds. This may well explain why they authored two petitions. It is clear from Miller's account that he was initially appointed station clerk at Lovely Banks, thanks to the timely intervention of the Superintendent of the Prisoners' Barracks, Gunn, who had sent the necessary instruction from

Hobart. Miller's duties included mustering the parties every morning and evening, and keeping the ration books. He was broken back down to the ranks by Brabezon, probably as punishment for instigating at least one of the round-robin petitions. Thereafter, he claimed to have been 'kept at the hardest work, and daily insulted and abused in every possible way' (300).

That Miller had worked as a clerk is revealing in other ways. Is it possible that two petitions were authored at Lovely Banks because the Patriots had actually been split into two separate classes—the filtering mechanisms of the probation system having siphoned some of them into the number one yard, while leaving the rest of their companions to toil away on the roads. The September 1840 return of convicts under sentence on the roads of Van Diemen's Land reveals that, although Lovely Banks was authorised to hold eighty convicts, there were, in fact, only fifty-six actually at work.[21] Fifty-five men signed the majority petition, suggesting that these were the Patriots who were in the second- and third-class yards. Men who signed the petition authored by Miller included the blacksmiths John Cronkhite and George Brown, stonemason and bricklayer Jehiel Martin, the wheelwright John Grant and carpenter Aaron Dresser. As an official report into the state of road parties put it, unless the barrows and other tools were kept in repair, 'the prisoners could not be kept at hard labour and the ends of prison discipline would be consequently frustrated'.[22] Without the skills of men like Grant and Dresser, the public works at Lovely Banks would have steadily ground to a halt as the tools and equipment went the same way as the men's shoes. In addition to clerks and mechanics, the station would have required the services of a number of other 'idlers'. The return of billeted men, completed in the following year, reveals that eight prisoners were employed at Lovely Banks performing such tasks. These included two watchmen, a messenger, two cooks (one for the superintendent and one for the gangs), a baker, a woodcutter and a water carrier.[23]

Just as at Lovely Banks, Green Ponds required its percentage of billeted men. In fact, this particular station had a history of being overstaffed with billeted men. According to the official regulations the appropriate ratio of billeted men to ganged men was one to ten. The actual ratio at Green Ponds in December 1837, however, had been as high as one to four.[24] In part this was due to the size of the gang—larger gangs yielded economies of scale. It was a simple fact of life that the smaller the gang, the larger the proportion of the population that would have to be employed in the various billets, if the gang was to be maintained as an operational unit. A small gang of about eighty, as the Patriots were, still required its complement of cooks, watchmen, overseers, clerks, messengers, etc. It was also clear that the number of supervisory roles depended on the nature of the work that was being undertaken. If forty convicts were set to work at one task, then only one overseer was required. In December 1837, five overseers were employed at Green Ponds—one to mind the eight prisoners excavating rock, another to watch the eighteen men who were crushing aggregate for the road surface, one to supervise thirty-three prisoners who were excavating and wheeling earth, another to those screening gravel, and one to oversee the erection of huts at Picton. Other groups of prisoners at Green Ponds worked in detached parties splitting rails, erecting fences, making bricks, mending tools, clothes and shoes, and preparing rations.[25] Since the Patriots numbered fewer than eighty men, it is likely that the ratio of billeted men to ganged men was even higher among their ranks. It appears that many of their number shared in the little privileges that came with promotion to a billet: including better clothing, housing and food.

As Woodbury appears to have found out to his cost, promotion provided access to black market opportunities. At most probation stations, the superintendent and overseers were able to employ the billeted men for their own private use, thereby lining their own pockets. It was the general practice to reward the mechanics and cooks, Gates maintained, 'so that the matter is hushed from the ears of those who would take cognizance of such transactions' (130). Captain Wright, however, proved to be as mean-spirited as he was cold-hearted. According to Gates:

> He kept the billeted men busy a good share of the time for his own benefit. In this manner he furnished himself with bedsteads, chairs, tables, birdcages, &c. Farmers would pay him a fair price for chairs or harrow teeth, with something of a sop to the overseer. Wright would then go to the smith, take government iron, and order him to make the article, saying they were for a settler, who would give him a few shillings for the job. But it was so managed that the few shillings found their way into the superintendent's pocket, whilst the pence only were visible to the billeted man. [130]

Far from being poor oppressed convicts on the roads of Van Diemen's Land, the Patriots had found themselves in a position where their skills were in demand. As Gates reveals, he was able to slip away to work in local harvest gangs for which he was rewarded with supplies of tea, sugar and tobacco. Gates was not the only Patriot who played this game to his advantage.

One of the disastrous effects of the introduction of probation was that it interrupted the flow of assigned convict labour allocated for the use of settlers. The effects of this were not felt overnight. Only after the current stock of assigned convicts started to dwindle as a result of the awarding of tickets-of-leave and pardons and the expiring of sentences, did the private sector labour supply start to tighten up. As the minimum period of probation was set at two years, settlers knew that it would not be until 1842 that the first wave of convict labour would be released from the roads to the loan gangs, to be hired out at cheap rates. In the meantime wages rose as, for the first time since the post-Napoleonic War influx of convicts, free workers did not have to compete with thousands of unfree workers.

At first, settlers sought to combat the problem by agitating for increased assisted migration. In the columns of the newspapers they argued that it was of critical importance for the maintenance of colonial progress that 'Labourers, and Operative Mechanics' be imported into the colony 'in order to obviate the evils, which it is supposed will accrue from the cessation of the assignment system'. The settlers demanded 'labour to speed the plough' (although perhaps cheap labour would have been a more apt description) and predicted that unless this was forthcoming, Van Diemen's Land's 'fertile fields' would be converted into a 'waste'. They urged that 'There are hundreds,—nay, even thousands of hard-working, labouring men,—of honest, industrious, and most reputable habits, anxious, and most willing to migrate to these Colonies'. They pointed out, however, that even if the government were to act immediately, it would take months for the first wave of assisted migrants to reach the antipodes. The settlers therefore called for an immediate reintroduction of assignment in order to avoid 'the total stagnation of agriculture and commerce'.[26]

Although both the colonial and home governments doubled their efforts to increase the rate of migration, there was no relaxation of the rules of probation. As the colonial labour market tightened in 1841, employers increasingly turned their eyes to the pools of labour corraled within the walls of the probation stations which littered the landscape of the rural mid-lands of Van Diemen's Land. Settlers offered lucrative rewards in an attempt to inveigle probationers away from the public works, and while they were stationed at Green Ponds, the Patriots found that bread and mutton were thrown their way by passing settlers. Captain Wright appears to have made some attempt to hold the line, preventing his charges from deserting *en masse* on Saturday afternoons to work on local farms, but they got away whenever his back was turned.

Now that the Patriots' labour was in demand, they were in a much stronger bargaining position. They could haggle with Captain Wright for a larger cut of the black market take as their labour skills were increasingly purchased by settlers desperate for the services of blacksmiths, carpenters, chair makers, sawyers, gunsmiths and ploughmen. Furthermore, the deeper that Captain Wright became embroiled in this quagmire of illicit dealings, the more vulnerable he became. Heustis describes an occasion when Wright sent two of the Patriots, Solomon Reynolds and Thomas Baker, out into the woods to cut timber:

After the timber was cut, Wright took it for government use, charging the usual price, and transferring the money to his own pocket. Reynolds and Baker sold the tools they had used, and told Wright they had been stolen. The superintendent disbelieved the story, but dared not say anything to the magistrate about the affair, as it would lead to the exposure of his own peculation. He found the Yankees were a little too shrewd for his purposes. [112]

Such practices, however, were not solely the preserve of sharp-witted Yankees. The sawyers at the Deloraine Probation Station were able to take similar advantage of their superintendent, when he too clandestinely attempted to obtain a quantity of blackwood for a house that he was building.[27] Exposed to blackmail, the position of some superintendents became increasingly precarious. The Patriots eventually tired of negotiating with Captain Wright and turned him in to the visiting magistrate. 'Within a few days he was arraigned and the billeted men brought forward as witnesses', Gates reported. 'The result was, that the charges were proved—Wright broke of his office and deprived of the privilege of ever holding another under the government' (131). In fact, the fallout was more widespread than Gates implied. According to the Colonial Secretary's files, both Wright and Lowe were dismissed when the extent of their black economy dealings were uncovered by Visiting Magistrate Erskine.

Apparently, Captain Wright had employed one of the station watchmen as a writer in his office, although he had been allocated a storeman to perform this duty. This breach of official regulations was discovered after Wright attempted to cover up the theft of a shirt from the store. The charges against Lowe were more serious. He apparently had failed to report one of his sub-overseers for 'using boxing gloves on the station, having cut up Government clothing to make them'. The inference of course was that Lowe had connived at the organisation of a prize fight. As such events were invariably an occasion for the placing of bets, Lowe was, almost certainly, also in breach of the Convict Department regulations which forbade gambling. Three other prisoners offered evidence that the same sub-overseer had received 'money and clothes for procuring "billets"'—again implying that a system of payments for promotion had been connived at by Lowe and Wright. Finally it was alleged that Lowe had brought a woman 'upon the station at night' whom he represented to be his wife—although no one could determine whether she actually was or not.[28] The fallout did not stop there. After news leaked out that the Patriots had been employed building the local Anglican church rather than McAdamising their ways on the roads of Van Diemen's Land, Captain Alexander Cheyne, the Director of Public Works, was called to account, and in the event he too lost his job.

In effect, Gates and his compatriots had managed in one way or another to remove a whole swathe of the penal command by doing little more than flex their industrial muscle. Perhaps it is not surprising that the decision was made to relocate them once more. The official reason for the move was that their work on the road had progressed to the point where they were 'so near to the party from Picton' as to render it impossible to stop contact between the two groups of prisoners.[29] It is unclear, however, whether the move was to prevent the Picton men contaminating the Patriots or *vice versa*. In May 1842 the *Buffalo* men were once more instructed to pack up their meagre possessions and were packed off to the station at Bridgewater.

14

Among the Thieves at Jerusalem

FROM 1830 TO 1836 Bridgewater had been synonymous with punishment. For six years a chain gang had laboured to construct a causeway over the River Derwent. Load after load of stone hacked out of a local quarry was wheeled to the water's edge by men in chains. As each barrow was tipped into the river, its contents had sunk into the mud. Ton after ton of rock was dumped in order to construct a roadway 1200 yards long out over the tidal flats. When the structure was finished, it was upheld as a feat of engineering—but for the poor convicts who had been sentenced to clank down the causeway with their heavy loads, it must have seemed like hell.[1] For years after its completion other gangs worked on tidal defences and repairs to the main causeway to keep it operational. In the late 1840s a bridge was finally put in place to span the deep water at the end of the causeway. An engraving of this celebrated structure appeared in the *London Illustrated News* and a scale model, made of Huon pine, was included in the Van Diemen's Land contribution to the Great Exhibition held in London's Crystal Palace in 1851. At the time that the Patriots were stationed at Bridgewater, however, the last part of the journey had to be completed by cable ferry.[2]

Here for the first time the Patriots worked alongside British convicts. There were, in all, about three hundred of them at the station, and according to Heustis, they were the 'the vilest of the vile, and it was only by the strictest watch that we prevented them from stealing our rations' (113). The superintendent at the station was a man named Mason, who had the distinction of being a nephew-in-law of Sir George Arthur. He was, Heustis thought, 'the meanest man there was in Van Diemen's Land', although he admitted that 'among so many mean characters, it would be difficult to decide which was entitled to the highest place on the scroll of infamy' (113). The Patriots were puzzled by their move to Bridgewater since Franklin had promised to separate them out from the old hands, although it came as little surprise to many that the 'Old Granny', as Gates called him (82), had broken his word. As Marsh put it, 'You can begin to discover, unless you are totally blind, how the old man is rewarding our good conduct and at the same time keeping his word' (101).

It appears, however, that the move to Bridgewater was a temporary measure. Franklin had a new plan for the Patriots—one that was designed to spare them from the worst excesses of hard labour on the roads. Fifteen days after their arrival at Bridgewater, eight of their number were split off and marched up the road to Jerusalem. In the days that followed, the remaining Patriots were divided into six lots and were cast to the four winds. Some were sent to the station at Constitution Hill, others to Mount Direction. A large contingent of about twenty-two was despatched to Brown's River, south of Hobart, where Grant, Gemmell and Miller had been posted when first landed from the *Canton*. Others were sent further afield still, to Salt Water Creek on the Tasman Peninsula and to Rocky Hills on the east coast, while Aitchison was rewarded for his loyalty with a position as a sub-overseer in the probation gang at New Town.[3]

The journey taken by the first group to leave Bridgewater proved to have something of a Biblical flavour. As Heustis later wrote, his friends passed 'through Jericho and crossed the River Jordan, and at Jerusalem they "fell among thieves." There were no Samaritans in that region, and the Levites, as of old, "passed by on the other side"' (113). In the Bible, the Levites were the tribe of the blessed who were chosen as priests.[4] The passage is borrowed from the parable of the Good Samaritan:

> A certain man went down from Jerusalem to Jericho, and fell among thieves, which stripped him of his raiment, and wounded him, and departed, leaving him half dead. And by chance there came down a certain priest that way: and when he saw him, he passed by the other side. And likewise a Levite, when he was at this place, came and looked on him, and passed by on the other side. But a certain Samaritan, as he journeyed, came where he was: and when he saw him, he had compassion on him.[5]

In the Patriot retelling, it was their bodies which were left battered and bruised by the assaults of common criminals, while it was the convict administration who, like 'the Levites, as of old' turned their backs on the sufferings of their fellow man. At the time, however, Heustis had little idea of the fate that had befallen his compatriots—each group being marched off was in complete ignorance of its final destination. This was, as Marsh pointed out, completely intentional, part and parcel of 'the way they deal with prisoners, never letting them know when or where they are bound'. The only time an officer addressed a convict was to give him an order for, he continued, 'It is considered a disgrace even to speak to a prisoner, and it is never done except to punish and keep them in subjection' (101, 102).

As things turned out, however, the little group of eight who set out on the road to Jericho with such trepidation found that their new destination was far from disagreeable. At their new station they were billeted in a hut in the first-class yard. Even Gates was forced to admit that they were favourably situated compared with the other prisoners, who 'had not so many rights in law as our southern slaves', adding, in a line designed to shock his Yankee readers, 'whilst the treatment of the negro is far superior' (140). Six of their number were put upon a wood cart detail and charged with collecting fuel for the officers, billeted men and the cook and bake-houses, but as Gates recalled, 'having only half a mile to draw, [this] was an easy task' (143). A further two were made watchmen—a duty which granted them the privilege of sleeping through the day—and Gates himself was elevated to the carpenter's shop, where he was placed at light work making replacement barrow handles. They were also pleasantly surprised to discover that at Jericho they received their full compliment of rations—such were the rewards of the billeted man.

After a short time they were moved on to a rather dilapidated station at Jerusalem, where a new set of stone buildings was being constructed. Again, any fears that the relocation would result in a deterioration of their conditions proved to be misplaced. As Gates described:

> Presently we learned the object of our removal. A large quantity of rails, posts, shingles and timber, were wanted for use, and being handier with the axe, we were selected for this purpose; myself and three others to split rails, &c., and the remainder to hew timber. [146]

It was ironic, therefore, that despite their famed frontier skills one of their number met with a serious accident at Jerusalem. Gates reports that John Thomas was cutting timber when 'his axe glanced, completely severing the foot from near the instep to the little toe' (151). Gates and John Morrisette carried him to the station hospital, where he remained for the duration of their stay. Despite this incident Gates quickly learned that there were many advantages to being employed as a mechanic, beyond tea, sugar and better rations. Ordered to cut timber in a tier 3 miles from the station, the Patriots were furnished with sufficient provisions for the day, which they had the 'privilege' of cooking for themselves. For the first time since their arrival in Van Diemen's Land they were set to work on their own account without the barking orders of an 'overseer or other minion' (149). In the absence of a monitor the detail was set the daily task of cutting and splitting twenty-five rails a day. Gates recollected that they found the work 'comparitively easy', and frequently 'we had a little leisure time to spend in rest

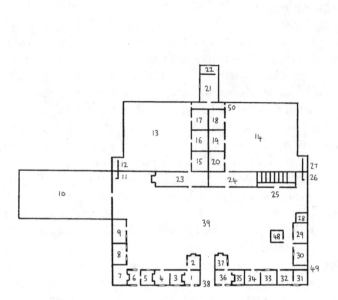

JERICHO PROBATION STATION KEY

1 SUPT. APARTMENTS	11 WATER CLOSET	21 HOSPITAL	31 OVERSEERS APARTMENT	41 CONSTABLES HUT
2 SUPT. APARTMENTS	12 WATER CLOSET	22 MEDICAL ATTENDANTS	32 OVERSEERS APARTMENT	42 SAW PIT
3 KITCHEN	13 1ST + 2ND CLASS YARD	APARTMENT	33 STORES	43 GUARD ROOM
4 OFFICE	14 3RD CLASS YARD	23 NO1. MESS ROOM	34 STORES	44 BARRACKS
5 ASSIST SUPT.APARTMENTS	15 GANG HUT	24 NO 2. MESS ROOM	35 ASSIST SUPTS +	45 SEPARATE ROOM IN
6 ASSIST SUPT. APARTMENTS	16 GANG HUT	25 CELLS	STOREKEEPERS APARTMENT	BARRACKS
7 CANADIAN HUTS	17 GANG HUT	26 WATER CLOSET	36 ASSIST SUPTS +	46 SERGEANTS APARTMENT
FORMERLY BILLETED HUT	18 GANG HUT	27 WATER CLOSET	STOREKEEPERS APARTMENT	47 SERGEANTS STORE
8 CARPENTERS SHOP	19 GANG HUT	28 OVEN	37 KITCHEN	48 WELL
9 BLACKSMITHS SHOP	20 GANG HUT	29 BAKE HOUSE	38 ENTRANCE	49 TOOL HOUSE
10 NEW BUILDING		30 COOK HOUSE	39 MAIN YARD	50 PASSAGE
			40 SAWYERS HUT	

Jericho Probation Station, 1841

or amusement, and in talking of our homes and friends, far, far away, o'er the billowy sea' (149).

Like the men at Jerusalem, the group of twenty-two Patriots which was dispatched from Bridgewater to Brown's River, including Snow and Heustis, no longer were expected to turn out to work on the roads with the ganged convicts. Instead they were employed constructing a cell block which conformed to the latest penal thinking and was designed to accommodate third-class prisoners. At night each man was to be locked up on his own, thus eliminating what the convict administration referred to as the vice of unnatural practices. In the absence of the company of others, the prisoner was left to contemplate the error of his ways. The whole layout of the new station at Brown's River resembled a huge experiment. As prisoners progressed from the third class to the second and then to the first, they were slowly introduced to the company of others. Social contact was the reward of unstinting servile labour on the roads of Van Diemen's Land, and like rats in some gigantic maze, they were encouraged by the stimulus of human contact to mould their minds and bodies to conform to Convict Department expectations.[6] As Snow recalled, it fell to the Patriots to help construct the gigantic clover-leaf apparatus which housed this engine of moral reform. Even in the process of construction, the grand design of the convict administration was everywhere in evidence. Timber was brought for the Patriots' use, not by ox teams, but on the collective shoulders of up to one hundred men who clanked along in irons. It was then handed over to teams of sawyers before being processed for use by the mechanics. Each log was thus passed through the hands of prisoners who occupied the successive levels of probation before it was fashioned into lintels, battens and rafters for the station which would incarcerate them.

The Patriots who were sent to Brown's River were not selected at random. At least ten of their number were carpenters and five were skilled metal workers. Like their compatriots at Jerusalem, they were allowed quarters of their own and so they were spared the indignity of messing with what Heustis described as the 'lowest sinks of iniquity in England' (116). Skene, the superintendent, was the same man who had charge of them at Sandy Bay and was thus well-known to the Patriots. They asked him for permission to construct a hut for their own use, and to their great joy he agreed. They worked on the building on Saturday afternoons, cutting their own timber and carrying it to the station, but, as Heustis reported, when at last it was completed and they were congratulating themselves, 'a company of soldiers came down from Hobart Town, and the magistrate gave them our hut for their barracks, without saying a word to us about it. Thus much we got for our extra toils' (116).

The magistrate in question was a man called Captain Jones, who proved to be a complete stickler for the rules. Heustis described how the Patriots also worked in their own time to construct a kitchen for one of the assistant superintendents, for which they were given some sheep's heads. No sooner had they consumed this 'great luxury' for their Sunday dinner when Captain Jones hauled them into his office, threatening to sentence them to an 'additional year's probation on the road, for receiving the present!' (116). The assistant superintendent fared worse. Like Wright and Lowe at Green Ponds, he was dismissed from his post. Heustis thought that Captain Jones

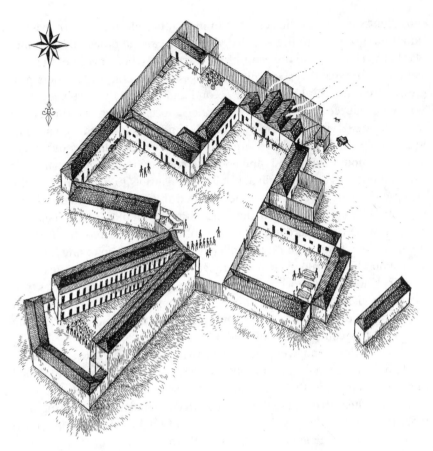

Brown's River Probation Station, 1841

was 'a hard-hearted and tyrannical man' (116). He recalled how one Sunday morning while they were bathing in the river, 'we caught a few crayfish, a species of lobster, which we cooked for dinner. Jones heard of it, and told us if we ever did it again he would punish us severely' (116). Snow recalled that 'we were told to eat nothing that Providence should offer us, unless it was first sanctioned by the British government' (19). It was as though the Crown was an authority which had set itself up above creation. As Heustis bitterly recalled, Jones left his worst for last: 'Only two or three days before we were to receive our tickets, this infamous magistrate ordered all the hair to be cut off our heads as close as possible, notwithstanding the superintendent remonstrated against it' (116). Thus, even when they were given their tickets-of-leave and allowed to dress in non-regulation clothing, their short-cropped hair marked them out as transported felons, as effectively as would any set of slops stamped with the mark of the Board of Ordinance.

The party that appears to have fared the worst was the one sent to the station at Salt Water Creek on the Tasman Peninsula. They were nine in this group and they were the last to depart from Bridgewater. At first they were escorted to the Prisoners' Barracks in Hobart, where they remained for a month before being loaded on a government schooner. Stowed away in the hold, they discovered that the vessel normally carried a cargo of coal. Marsh described how they were forced to crouch between the blackened deck beams in a space just 4 feet 8 inches high which, once the hatches were closed, was shrouded in darkness. There was no place to sit in the crowded hold which, in any event, was awash with bilge water. Once at sea the vessel started rolling and tumbling, with predictable consequences. Marsh recalled how some sang out, '"Oh God! I am dying, get off my head."—some sea sick, same crying "water for God's sake some water, I shall die." but none of the calls were responded to, except by curses and imprecations, saying, "if we did not keep quiet, every man would be taken out and flogged"' (114).

When the schooner had reached its destination, several of its pitiful cargo proved too weak to disembark without assistance from the others. The vessel had anchored just off shore from the coalmines at Plunkett Point, and the prisoners were unceremoniously disembarked into a waiting scow. The boat into which Marsh was tipped set out, not for the mines, but in the direction of another station across the bay. It was now July and they had been landed in the rain and wet, starved and chilled to the bone. Nevertheless, as he recalled:

> You would have laughed to have seen us, for as bad as it was, we had to laugh at each other to think of our transformation from white slaves into black; for the coal dust with perspiration, had so changed our complexion, we hardly knew each other. The teeth and white of the eye resembled a darkey, but the general features, lips, nose, forehead, &c., indicated the white man. But in our situation, it made very little difference which we were. [115]

The station at Salt Water Creek was still being constructed and the surrounding land cleared in readiness for the planting of crops. Most of the prisoners were employed either grubbing out trees, quarrying stone or constructing a bridge across the tidal creek from which the place derived its name.[7] Marsh was sent to labour in the water-carrying gang, charged with conveying half-cask barrels strapped to wheelbarrows a mile and a half to a point where the water in the creek was no longer brackish. Although at other stations water carriers appear on the list of billeted men, Marsh thought that this species of labour was particularly hard.[8] After falling sick, he was placed in an invalid party and employed stripping bark off trees to roof the huts. From there he graduated to a detail which was ordered to carry light timber. As he noted, Salt Water Creek had a reputation as a hard-regime station, and it is by no means clear why some of the Patriots were singled out to be sent there. If Marsh's account is anything to go by, they certainly seem to have been treated more severely than their compatriots distributed to other stations. There is no evidence, however, that he was subjected to front-line ganged labour. It seems that it was the pains in his chest as much as anything which contributed to his ordeal. As their own accounts testify, the convict administration took a comparatively hard line with invalids.[9] It seems that Marsh and his fellow Patriots were placed on the water-carrying detail to shield them from ganged labour, in exactly the same way that the Patriots at Jericho had been ordered to collect firewood. Whatever the physical effects on Marsh, the official intention appears to have been to provide his broken frame with some relief from the ordeal of hacking out stumps or hauling stone carts.

Franklin's decision to split up the Patriots and distribute them among several stations appears to have been motivated by a desire to spare them from further hard labour, without actually removing them from probation. This could not be achieved by keeping them in one group—as long as they remained together the bulk of the Patriots would have been exposed to the rigours of ganged management. It was not true that Franklin had broken his promise to keep the Patriots apart from common thieves. As is clear from the surviving probation station plans, the intention was to maintain the policy of separating them from other prisoners by accommodating them in their own huts and by working them in small groups at specific tasks. Nevertheless, this was the first time that most of them had actually seen how other prisoners were treated at close quarters. The experience appears to have shocked them. Heustis, Gates and Marsh all provided graphic descriptions of floggings that they witnessed at Brown's River, Jerusalem and Salt Water Creek, although they were equally unanimous in their condemnation of the lowly habits and demeanour of ordinary prisoners.

During one of the few occasions at Salt Water Creek when he condescended to talk to other convicts, Marsh received one piece of unexpected news. Port Arthur Penal Station lay only 15 miles from where they were quartered, and it was not unusual to meet detachments of Port Arthur men in the course of their daily work. From one such group they learned that for three or four weeks, Miller and Stewart 'had it very hard', but that they had now secured billets as servants to officers and, if anything, their treatment was better than that meted out to Marsh and the small party of Patriots at Salt Water Creek.[10] This account is borne out by Miller's testimony.

After they had surrendered at Brighton, Miller and Stewart were handcuffed and marched into town in charge of a constable. There they were placed in the treadwheel yard. Although the daily grind of stepping from slat to slat on an endlessly rotating wheel proved physically demanding, the trials that they were subjected to at night proved far worse. As prisoners under sentence for Port Arthur, they were locked into a sleeping ward by themselves. To their horror they discovered that their quarters were 'literally alive with vermin of every description'. Sleep, Miller later recollected 'was out of the question, until one became so perfectly exhausted as to be able to slumber upon a bed of *thorns*' (320). As the days passed, the number of inmates in the cell increased as more prisoners condemned to penal servitude at Port Arthur arrived in the Prisoners' Barracks. It was now not just the fleas and lice that threatened to invade their bodies, although Miller could not bring himself to spell out the new physical danger 'enacted by these wretched men, during the hours of darkness'. Instead he described their nocturnal pursuits as 'of the most revolting and diabolical character; too dark to be written—too dreadful to be thought of!' (320).

Finally they were taken out of the Prisoners' Barracks and, together with forty-four other prisoners, placed in the hold of the brig *Isabella* and dispatched by sea to Port Arthur. Like Marsh's trip to Salt Water Creek, the voyage was a living hell. Double-ironed and handcuffed in pairs, the prisoners clung to each other, but as the ship pitched and rolled they were thrown on top of one another. Miller described how the wrenching of their irons upon their limbs produced 'the most excruciating pains and torture', as the weight of the uppermost men crushed 'those beneath, half to death' (325). Other shipboard noises were:

> The most horrid oaths and imprecations mingled with the cries and groans of the poor wretches. Nearly all were sea-sick, and the deck was literally a pool of nauseous matter, produced by vomiting. Every man was wet to the skin with it, and the stench was intolerable. The only air which we breathed was admitted through a hatchway about three feet square, and those most remote from this opening were nearly suffocated. [326]

The prisoners in the hold screamed for water but, as Miller recalled, 'the monsters who had charge of us would only hand down a tin pannakin full, (less than a pint,) at stated intervals'. By the time they had arrived at their destination the *Isabella*'s wretched cargo was 'in a state of misery which language cannot describe' (326).

Like all fresh arrivals, Miller and Stewart were turned into the Port Arthur gangs to work for a time at hard labour while their conduct was assessed. As the commandant, Captain Charles O'Hara Booth, spelt out to them—the good would be rewarded with lighter work, and the wicked would sink to the oblivion of the chain gang where, weighed down with punishment irons, they would toil in constant pain and misery. The spectre of constant punishment seemed oddly out of place with their new surroundings. The settlement was built on the western side of a 'beautiful and spacious bay', which Miller described as 'containing sufficient anchorage ground for a large fleet to ride in safety upon its smooth surface' (326). Nature, he thought, had done her part in rendering Port Arthur 'one of the most pleasant and romantic places in that quarter of the globe' (326–7).

He described how the settlement resembled a picturesque village, with its clutter of stores and officers' quarters clustered around the castellated turrets of the military barracks which helped to give the place a kind of Gothic splendour. To the right was the prisoners' barracks, encased, like the probation station at Lovely Banks, by what Miller described as a 'wooden barricade' (327). At the head of the bay was a sandstone church with a steeple which towered over the whole settlement. The path up the hill to the church had been delineated by 'a beautiful alley' (327) of trees planted, no doubt, to mark the route by which salvation lay. Moving still further to his right, past a scattering of blacksmith's and carpenter's shops, Miller's eyes came to rest on the dockyards, where the timber frames of the barque *Lady Franklin* lay on the slips. The whole scene was the antithesis of an American prison with its radiating arms and grey façade, but, as Miller put it, the effect was an illusion, for man had converted this beautiful bay 'into a home of woe, sin and shame', and the dreadful scenes enacted there despoiled nature of all her loveliness and stamped 'gloominess, despair and death, upon every object' (327).

At first Miller and Stewart were employed carrying planks from the sawpits to the lumber yard. As hard as they found this task, it was nothing compared with the labour of moving larger pieces of timber—a punishment for which Port Arthur was notorious. A gang of prisoners under the charge of an overseer would be ordered to lift huge logs onto their collective shoulders and then stumble under the massive weight towards their destination. Seen from afar the gang resembled some huge insect shuffling across the landscape, and for this reason the timber-carrying detail was known as the Port Arthur centipede. The journalist William Ross described how appropriate this punishment was for condemned felons. It was, he thought, as though the weight of their crimes bore down upon them and they were forced to rise up in unison or be crushed.[11] This was penal reformation through hard labour with a vengeance, but as Miller and Stewart were to find, it was not a punishment that exerted itself on the frame of every prisoner with equal force.

Miller's feet were already lacerated. Forced to walk in crude shoes, with no socks, over rocky ground, his feet had blistered and were now raw, and although he had torn strips from his shirt with which to bind his feet,

every step was excruciatingly painful. Once placed in the centipede, however, his task took on the proportions of the labours of Hercules. As the
overseer shouted for every man to straighten his back, and Miller and
Stewart drew themselves up to their full height, they were left with the
great weight of the log bearing directly through their shoulders, pressing
through their entire frame and ramming their raw feet into the ground.
They were easily the tallest men in the gang, at 6 feet and 5 feet $7\frac{1}{2}$ respectively.[12] Thus the two Patriots were forced to carry an undue proportion of
the sins of the British convicts, who were protected from the full force of
the great weight by the insults of industrialism which had stunted their
childhood growth.[13]

Miller, whose jacket had by now been stained red with congealed
blood, complained about the unequal load with which he was burdened. To
his surprise, the superintendent removed him to another detail where the
work was lighter. Some of the administrative officers at Port Arthur were
sympathetic to the plight of Miller and Stewart and, as Marsh put it, 'manifested a disposition to treat them better' (91). Thus, despite Franklin's
promise to send the two Patriot absconders to the depths of hell to labour
without hope of relief from the physical torments of the carrying gang, they
were promoted to positions where their scholarly skills could be put to
better use—Stewart as a signalman and Miller as a clerk to the Commissariat
Officer, Thomas Lempriere. According to Miller's account, Franklin had
promised in a fit of rage to teach the 'young stripling law student, full of
Yankee conceit and impertinence a lesson', by breaking his 'low republican
independence' (340). During a visit to Port Arthur he had singled out the
two Patriots and:

> Turning to the 1300 convicts present, the refuse and scum of mankind, the
> dregs of Van Dieman's Land, and stretching forth his hand toward them, he
> concluded as follows: 'Now, *my good men*, I caution you all to *shun* this man.
> Don't let him lead you *astray*. Don't let him get up a rebellion here, which he
> is sure to do, if you listen to him. BEWARE OF HIM! *shun* him as you would a
> *viper!!*' [340]

As it turned out, however, neither Miller nor Stewart had to rub
shoulders in the carrying gang with the 'refuse and scum of mankind' (340)
for long. Indeed, Miller had a particularly easy time of it, ending up being
employed as a tutor to Thomas Lempriere's children, and being treated,
while he held the position, as pretty much one of the family. As Snow later
recalled with some irony, despite being sent to Port Arthur for the vile
'crime' of absconding, 'they were finally better off than some of us that
remained' on the roads (16).

Thus it was that by July 1841, less than a year and a half after the arrival of the *Buffalo*, most of the Patriots had been relieved from the daily traumas of punishment labour. In this respect the conditions under which they served differed markedly from the plight of the hundreds of British and Irish prisoners who had been fed into the probation system in the first months of its operation. The point can be illustrated by resort to a simple comparison. During the time that Gates and his fellow Patriots were billeted in the first-class yard at Jerusalem, the bulk of the ganged convicts at the station were men who had been disembarked from the transport *Duncan*. A glance at the conduct records of these prisoners is sufficient to confirm the extent to which the Patriots had been shielded from the full weight of probation. In their first two years on the roads of Van Diemen's Land, the *Duncan* convicts racked up over eleven strokes of the lash per man, and each spent over nine days in solitary confinement and sixty-five days in leg irons.[14] Not one single Patriot was punished to this extent, and yet this was the average experience for the *Duncan* convicts. For the record, the Patriots clocked up less than one stroke per man and spent, on average, one day in solitary confinement, and nobody was placed in irons. Placed alongside the punishment meted out to British and Irish prisoners, the Patriots' torments pale into insignificance. To make matters worse, the bulk of the punishments handed down by the visiting magistrate at Jerusalem were for routine petty offences of the likes of 'smoking in the ranks during morning muster' or 'misconduct in having a blanket in his possession not his own and the number of which had been cut out'.[15]

How did the Patriots respond to the plight of the battered and bruised ganged convicts crowded into the second- and third-class yards? They complained that Franklin had broken his promise not to work them with common thieves. Like Miller at Port Arthur, they railed against the British establishment for its wickedness in forcing them, the virtuous citizens of the new republic, to rub shoulders with a criminal residuum—the dregs of the British Empire. They might as well have stood on the steps of the temple and thanked God that they were not like these common thieves.[16] The truth was that the journey that Gates and his fellow Patriots had been forced to take was not *from* Jerusalem to Jericho, the historical route of the Good Samaritan, but *to* Jerusalem via Jericho. This, as it turns out, is no mere point of geography. At Jerusalem, Brown's River, Salt Water Creek and Port Arthur, it was the common thieves who were fleeced by the lash and the cells, while the Patriots, like the Levites, walked on the other side of the street.

15

Sir John's Indulgence

In March 1841, Lieutenant-Governor Franklin finally received a response from the Secretary of State for Colonies, Lord John Russell, bestowing the discretionary power he had sought to grant indulgences to the Patriot convicts. By way of explaining the delay in his response, Russell wrote, 'I thought it right to consult the Governor-General of Canada on the subject'. Since Lord Sydenham did not object, Russell advised, 'you will, therefore, be at liberty, after the expiration of the two years, to confer on these men the advantage of Tickets-of-Leave, should you consider them to merit it by their conduct in the interval'.[1] For the Patriots this so-called indulgence scarcely seemed a great boon. As Daniel Heustis saw it, to be allowed to work for himself and keep the proceeds of his labour was not a huge indulgence if he were also kept under very strict regulations and 'not permitted to go even from one house to another, or into the woods, without a pass, signed by his employer, or by a magistrate' (117). If caught without a pass or in the wrong place, he was liable to be returned to hard labour on the gangs. Heustis was prepared to admit that the Patriots were lucky, since their sentences had been for life and convicts with that sentence had to work eight years with good behaviour before they were entitled to a ticket. Along with most of the Patriots, he attributed his luck to Benjamin Wait's wife and her tireless campaigning, on both sides of the Atlantic, for their release:

> Doubtless we are much indebted to her for our partial emancipation; and the story of her devoted and heroic services, embalmed in all our hearts, shall be handed down to other generations, as a bright example of conjugal fidelity and active philanthropy, worthy of an immortality of honor. [118]

Although Maria Wait did her best to secure pardons for the Patriots, in reality her efforts had little to do with the decision to give the Patriots tickets-of-leave. Governor Franklin had always been uneasy about putting the political prisoners into the probation gangs and exposing them to the company of hardened felons. He disliked the new probation system and did his best to protest against its introduction.[2] His preference would have been to provide relatively comfortable assignment for men like the Patriots, as he did for the men on the *Marquis of Hastings*. Two years in the gangs, he believed, was more than enough.

The six surviving men from the *Marquis of Hastings*, who had been lucky enough to escape the probation system, were the first to enjoy the effect of Franklin's new powers. On 4 August 1841 they were granted tickets-of-leave that gave them freedom of movement across the island and the capacity to work for wages. As Benjamin Wait explained in a letter to Maria, while this did not emancipate him from the constant surveillance and arbitrary punishments of the prison code, it did mean he was free to make some money, which could assist him in getting home on what he called '*French leave*' (270).

Both Wait and his friend Samuel Chandler had used their relatively easy assignment time to plan an escape on a ship out of Hobart, which was an important port for the American whaling fleet in the Pacific. Whaling was big business in Van Diemen's Land and the Americans were by far the most aggressive in pursuit of the whales. Woodman described the thriving industry with awe and pride: 'I do believe that our Americans fish more and procure more oil than all the rest of the world', he wrote in a letter home. 'The Indian and Pacific Oceans are teeming with their ships'. Woodman claimed to have seen eight American whaling ships in the port of Hobart at one time.[3]

Most of the masters of these ships were sympathetic to the Patriots' plight and disposed to help them escape. As Wait was aware, it was precisely for that reason that these ships were under close surveillance. Often a constable with a posse would come aboard to search for escapees and would 'remain until the anchor is tripped, and the sails shook out, when the papers shall be given to the master, and the vessel to the pilot, who will see her boyond [sic] the heads' (356). Notwithstanding the threat of being caught, Chandler procured a 'pass' which allowed him to take ten days' absence from his employ at Ashgrove and go to Hobart, where he made contact with the several American whalers. He found that the ship *Julian* had a fellow Freemason as captain and he was willing to take them both, regardless of the risk. Chandler made arrangements to be taken aboard around Christmas, when he and Wait could manage to take a fortnight's absence from their employment without arousing concern.

At first Wait would not be persuaded to go, preferring to trust the efforts of his wife Maria to secure a pardon. It was only when the older man insisted he would take the risk alone that Wait relented. At the time the men were working on different estates: Chandler had remained at Ashgrove, while Wait had gone to work as accountant and tutor on William Kermode's large property, Mona Vale. In order to allay suspicion, Wait arranged for Chandler to be employed as a carpenter on a schoolhouse at Mona Vale, and both men arranged a pass for Hobart for the festive season. In Hobart they managed to hire a small whaleboat on the pretext that they were going on a fishing expedition. Because of their anxiety about their purpose being discovered, they left Hobart early and had to wait, cold and nervous, at the wide mouth of the Derwent River for several days. Wait recalled the 'danger, destitution, and extreme anxiety' (355) of being tossed about in their small boat in Storm Bay until the whaler was sighted. Chandler, leaping to his feet, gave the Freemason's signal for distress, yet he received no response. He tried several times before the whaler returned a signal to indicate it was indeed the correct ship. The rendezvous was accomplished without attracting the attention of the constabulary.[4] It was over a month later that a notice appeared in the *Government Gazette*, issued by the Chief Police Magistrate, offering the reward of a conditional pardon:

WHEREAS the two Convicts holding Tickets-of-Leave whose names and descriptions are hereafter inserted did, on or about the 22nd day of December last, abscond from the District of Oatlands, and are now illegally at large: This is to give notice, that I am authorised by His Excellency the Lieutenant-Governor to offer the reward of a recommendation to Her Majesty's mercy for a Conditional Pardon to any person who shall apprehend these Convicts, or either of them, or give such information as shall be the means of either of them being lodged in safe custody.

Samuel Chandler, per Marquis of Hastings, tried at Upper Canada, 14th July, 1838, life, trade wheelwright, height 5 feet 7, age 48 in 1839, complexion fair, head long, hair brown, whiskers red, visage oval, forehead medium, eyebrows brown, eyes hazel, nose medium, mouth medium, chin medium, native place Connecticut, remarks—scar on fore-finger left hand, mole on right cheek.

Benjamin Wait, per Marquis of Hastings, trade warehouseman, height 5 feet $4\frac{1}{2}$, age 26 in 1839, complexion fair, head round, hair brown, whiskers black, visage oval, forehead high, eyebrows brown, eyes hazel, nose medium, mouth medium, chin medium, native place Upper Canada, remarks—two scars on left hand.[5]

The enticement of a conditional pardon well might have attracted a horde of eager informers, except that Wait and Chandler were well away by the time the notice appeared. They enjoyed a comfortable trip home, Wait reported, and some six months after their escape they reached the 'gladsome shores of free America' (355). Even before Wait and Chandler arrived

at Rhode Island, James Gemmell had reached New York, having managed
to escape from Hobart in the same fashion. He immediately set about pub-
licising the plight of his fellow Patriots who remained the hapless victims of
'the terrors of that far distant prison-house'.[6] An article from Gemmell
eloquent on the gruesome horrors of Van Diemen's Land first appeared in
the *Plebeian* newspaper in New York City in June 1842, and was reprinted
in the Watertown *Jeffersonian* the following month. The piece could not
have been written by Gemmell, who was barely literate; it bore the imprint
of the Canadian rebel leader, William Lyon Mackenzie, who had arranged
its publication.[7] Either Mackenzie or another Patriot campaigner may have
been the author of another letter published in the *New York New Era* as well
as the *Ohio Statesman,* with much of the stylistic flourish and tales of flogging,
purporting to be from a transported Patriot named Mitchell Monroe. No
such person was ever transported from Canada to Van Diemen's Land and
this name was neither known as an alias, nor was it the name of any Patriot
arrested following the various raids into Canada.[8]

It was inevitable that the escapes of Wait, Chandler and Gemmell would
impact on the remaining Patriots. In February 1842, when tickets were
given to the men of the *Buffalo*—excluding those absconders confined at
Port Arthur—they found their conditions were different. The same gazette
which had carried the reward for Wait and Chandler also carried this notice:

> In consequence of a Dispatch from the Right Honourable the Secretary of
> State, the Lieutenant-Governor has sanctioned the issue of Tickets-of-Leave to
> the undermentioned Canadian prisoners, who arrived per Buffalo, but on the
> express condition that they shall reside in the following Districts only:–
>
> Fingal.   Bothwell.
> Campbell Town.   Hamilton.
> Oatlands.   Swan Port.
>
> His Excellency has also directed that they shall not be allowed to leave their
> respective Districts without the sanction of the Chief Police Magistrate being
> first obtained.

In each case these districts were several days' travelling from the ports
of Hobart and Launceston and, with the exception of Swanport, far distant
from the coastline.[9] It was a source of great bitterness to them that Franklin
had reneged on the promise he had made at Green Ponds that their tickets-
of-leave would give them freedom of the whole island. As always, Franklin
was seen as the culprit, rather than their own compatriots, especially by the
fractious Robert Marsh, who declared Her Majesty's representative a liar:

> I know him to be one, because he promised we should have our tickets at the
> expiration of two years, and that it should be for the privilege of the whole
> island, except Hobart Town and Launceston. Does he reward us for good

conduct? no, but continues to punish us. . . . did not he say he hoped when he got the letter from England concerning us, that it would be favorable and when he gets the letter, was it not in his power to show us some more favor, than he was showing?—it was. Is not Sir John Franklin, Lieutenant-Governor of the island of Van Dieman's Land, commander in chief of her Majesty's forces therein, &c., a big man and a big liar? I positively declare that he has been nothing to us but a liar, a tyrant . . . [125–6]

Even mild Samuel Snow was disgusted by Franklin's about-face, especially after he discovered the promised ticket was 'a MAGNA CHARTA on a very small scale; and that we held our liberty by a very precarious tenure; for, upon the slightest provocation, the almighty little country magistrate would wrest it from us' (19). It became very apparent that ticket-of-leave men were still a despised class of person and subject to gross exploitation by free settlers. When Gates and his companions received their tickets, they were advised 'to demean ourselves in all respects according to law—to appear contented, and be industrious' (154), an injunction Gates took to be deeply offensive to American honour. Even more offensive were the brusque rejections the men encountered as they wandered across the island searching for work, without adequate clothing, shelter or food.

When the Patriots first arrived in Van Diemen's Land, the island was enjoying an economic boom that had boosted the sale of land and created a demand for labour. Since free immigration had all but ceased and the new probation system meant that convicts would no longer be automatically assigned as an unpaid workforce for the settlers, there had been a general panic that a labour shortage was imminent. As a result, the colonial government committed itself to a costly large-scale immigration program that had begun to make itself felt just as the colony plunged into a five-year depression. In 1842, two and half thousand assisted immigrants poured into the colony also looking for work, just at the time when the first of the probation convicts were coming into a labour market beset with ruinously low prices for wheat and wool. Employers could take their pick, and they quickly discovered 'the moral taint' of convict labour once it ceased to be a free indulgence and became a service with a price attached. They saw little advantage in employing convict labour when free labourers were plentiful and cheap.[10] As a largely rural workforce, by inclination and by virtue of being confined to the interior districts, the Patriots were forced to compete for work in the hardest-hit sector of the seriously depressed Van Diemen's Land economy.

Aitchison was lucky that he was employed as the overseer of the probation gang at Victoria Valley, which, he told his friend Elijah Woodman, gave him a reasonable salary at '25S [shillings] a month with rations, Tea Sugar and Tobacco'.[11] For the rest of the Patriots, seeking employment proved a most discouraging task, as Daniel Heustis explained:

At best, he is barely able to earn a living. The best of English laborers could be hired for *twenty dollars a year!* The Yankees would not work for less than an English shilling a day, or about seventy-five dollars a year. Even these low wages were very much reduced before we left the colony. Many employers keep their laborers so meanly, that they expend a considerable part of their wages in buying additional food, and the remainder would scarcely suffice to procure very indifferent clothing. [118]

Heustis and his group arrived from their probation station in ragged convict issue clothing. Having procured their 'tickets' they went to the Hobart Prisoners' Barracks to find the clothes which had been taken from them on their arrival. They found what remained had been covered up with casks and rubbish, and on removing this impediment discovered 'the rats had ruined what two-legged thieves had left' (118). They had nothing but the prison issue they had worn for six months, 'little better than their weight in rags' (118). They were not given any rations, as Heustis reports, despite the fact that they were required to travel nearly a hundred miles into the countryside without any money or means of transport other than their poorly shod feet. Remembering the previous kindness of the Super-intendent of the Prisoners' Barracks, Mr Gunn, Heustis appealed to him for help to get provisions for the long journey. Gunn explained the rules: as ticket-of-leave men, the Patriots were 'off the hands of government', and he 'had nothing more to do in finding us provisions' (118). Nonetheless, Gunn did manage to provide each man with a small chunk of bread and meat, on his own account. Each man took his bread and meat under his arm, and marched off, according to Heustis, 'as independent as hogs on the ice' (118). The group looked a rare sight, 'like a flock of half-picked Bob-a-lincums, chattering with pleasure like so many magpies' (26), according to Stephen Wright. 'All the people looked on us as so many scape-gallows, and vagabonds. Some laughed at us and a comical figure we cut . . . all rags and tatters—pale and wan. In uniform, no militia could hold a candle to us. Misery likes company, and we had enough of both' (27).

Robert Marsh and those other Patriots at Salt Water Creek Probation Station had to wait another six weeks before they were able to get to Hobart to receive their tickets-of-leave. After a rough trip on a vastly overcrowded schooner they arrived at the Hobart Prisoners' Barracks in tatters and covered in vomit. They found there was no room available for them to sleep at the barracks and they were not permitted any rations, despite having eaten nothing for two days on the trip to Hobart. For nearly two more days, confusion reigned. While the men had their names called several times, they were neither fed nor given their tickets-of-leave, prompting Marsh to observe that Franklin's mode of granting indulgence would surely kill them. Finally they were issued with tickets and rations for two days, sufficient, it was felt, to last the trip to their destination 55 miles to the north. They set out with heavy hearts to walk the distance, not knowing whether they would find anyone to employ them or even permit them to work for their food.

Within half a day they had encountered four constables, each of whom demanded the Patriots show proof of their status before allowing them to continue. By nightfall they found temporary lodging in a shepherd's hut. The following morning some of the exhausted men overslept and woke complaining that the morning bell had not rung. Marsh recounted that, when they were informed, jokingly, that the bell had rung and the gang already gone to work, 'they sprang up, apparently in a complete state of bewilderment' (132). This was the first night for two years that these men had been allowed a good night's sleep without being obliged to turn out at the ring of the station bell. It took a bit of getting used to.

Trudging onward that day, some with bare feet bleeding from the sharp flint stones, the party was stopped many times and obliged to show 'our little inestimable treasure', as Marsh sardonically called the ticket-of-leave (130). On the second night no shelter could be found, so the group kindled a fire in the bush. Having roasted and eaten their remaining meat, they prepared to bed down for the night when they were rudely interrupted by a constable, who insisted 'it was contrary to orders to have a fire kindled in the bush' since the men might be mistaken for bushrangers and punished. Marsh patiently explained that they were ticket-of-leave men *en route* to their district and that surely they would not be punished for sleeping in the bush, since they could get no other place to sleep. The constable's reply was adamant: 'it is against the law, you must find some other place' (132).

Marsh laid out their situation for the constable: they were required to cover a distance of 55 miles in two days, yet were not able to travel more than 15 miles a day, and had no money to pay for a night's lodging. If they were not allowed sleep in the bush, with or without fire, what were they to do? '. . . have we not got a ticket of leave, which the Governor said was next thing to freedom?', Marsh asked with heavy irony. '. . . are we not almost free?' (133). Another of the Patriots took up this refrain, saying, 'almost free to be nowhere, and still bound under the penalty of severe punishment if we are not at a certain place at a certain time' (133). In the face of these gibes, the constable, who was quite probably a ticket-of-leave man himself, relented and directed them to sleep in a vacant hut nearby.

In the morning, the delight in being able to sleep without being woken at dawn by the bell was undermined by the knowledge that their rations were finished and they were only half-way to their district. At the settlement of Oatlands they tried to find work at a settler's farm, but were cruelly repulsed. Marsh recalled the settler's contemptuous remark that 'there are so many beggars in this country, it will not do to listen to all'. They travelled on, enduring the pangs of hunger, 'not knowing what to do to obtain a little something to keep from starving' (136). Having been 'denied a crumb from the gentleman's table' (137), they finally found a convict shepherd willing to share his meagre ration, which prompted Marsh to ask himself 'whether the real gentleman and lady were not the most often to be found amongst the poor and despised of our race'. Warming to his subject, he opined that 'If there were not so many grasping after wealth and power . . . there would not be so many prisoners or slaves' (138).

For the great majority of the Patriots, the contemptuous rejection described by Marsh was a familiar tale. There were some gentlemen however, who were prepared to offer assistance. Wright found work with the Chief Magistrate of his district, Mr Barrow, whom he described as living 'in the style of an English nobleman' (27). Notwithstanding all his lordly affectations, Barrow treated Wright with great courtesy, gave him access to his library and advanced him money. Gates also had little complaint to make about his employer, Mr Tabbart, whose 2560-acre property at Rushy Lagoon had been given as a free land grant. Gates was most partial to Tabbart's four handsome daughters, but to his disgust he found they considered themselves far superior to the likes of him. With evident hurt pride he wrote that these women 'entertain high notions of honor, shunning the person of him who is a convict with almost as much dread as the cold Brahmin of India would that of the despised Sudras' (157).

Another gentleman well-disposed to the Patriots was William Kermode, a leading settler who had been appointed to the Legislative Council in 1842. He was originally from the Isle of Man and had been a seaman in his youth, making several voyages to India before arriving in Tasmania in 1819. Five years later, after several more voyages to England, he was given a grant of 1000 acres on the Salt Plains near Campbell Town.[12] He added to this land with the purchase of an adjoining property of 2000 acres, which he named Mona Vale, after the Roman name for the Isle of Man. Kermode was among the most progressive of early settlers in Van Diemen's Land and his property at Mona Vale was a showcase, with a substantial stone house and an outstanding merino stud. By 1840, he had built dams on the two streams of the Salt Plains to provide a permanent water supply for animals and irrigation for crops. The sale of his fine merino wool, which was well known in the London market by its brand, the Three Legs of Man, made him very wealthy, as had convict labour. According to the census of 1843, the total population on the estate was seventy, of which only sixteen were free.[13] During the time of Lieutenant-Governor Arthur, Kermode had been engaged in bitter quarrels with the governor and his friends, and he had been heavily fined for harbouring two runaway convicts who had been found fencing for him with forged passes and tickets-of-leave. Kermode regarded the fine as an act of personal spite by Governor Arthur and was therefore inclined to look with favour on those who had also suffered at Arthur's hands.

This may have been why Kermode was keen to offer employment to as many of the Patriots as needed it, despite the fact that Wait and Chandler had escaped while in his employ. According to Heustis, Kermode 'had heard favorable reports concerning us, which made him desirous of securing our services' (119). By the time Heustis had arrived at his property, Kermode had already employed five or six of the Patriots and was keen to take on more on a crop-share basis to work his property that straddled the districts of Oatlands and Campbell Town. As Snow explains, the proposal was 'to take a farm of three hundred acres, of good land, to sow to wheat and oats', while Kermode would 'furnish teams to do the work, and provide provisions for us at a fair price' (19). This seemed a very fair offer to Snow, whereas Marsh's radical views did not incline him to look with favour on the offer from such a rich man. Marsh insisted Kermode had gained his wealth in the African slave trade and used his ill-gotten gains to acquire his massive estate—vastly inflated by Marsh to 30 000 acres—as a free land grant. Marsh would have been aware that, until 1831 in Van Diemen's Land, much of the best pastoral land had been granted freehold to settlers with money or patronage, and he went to pains to attribute the very worst character and motives to men who enjoyed this unfair privilege. Kermode's offer of friendship was no more than a pretence according to Marsh, but like his twenty-seven compatriots, Marsh had little choice but to take Kermode's offer. Four or five others, Heustis included, found employment nearby at Rothbury, on another fine property of some 3500 acres belonging to Mr Sutherland. Their job was grubbing out trees, Heustis explains, 'that is, digging them up by the roots, for the purpose of clearing the land' (120).

For one of the group the rigours of this employment, after two years of hard labour, was too great a physical strain. On 24 March 1842, while labouring on Sutherland's property, Alson Owen, a young man of twenty-seven, suffered a series of violent epileptic fits. His companions immediately sent for a doctor who came and bled him, but Owen died within thirty hours, during which time 'his whole system was shaken by the most violent convulsions', according to Heustis (120), who sat on the bed and held Owen in his arms all night.

After Owen's death the local gentry rallied to provide assistance. Mrs Sutherland made a gift of linen to lay out the body, while Kermode gave the wood for the coffin and then sent a man with a horse and wagon to carry the Patriots on his property to the funeral. Owen was buried in the Sutherland's own family graveyard with a service read by another of the neighbours. It was a rare occasion when the Patriots were treated with genuine respect. 'Though there was no parade or ostentation', Heustis wrote, 'I never attended a funeral where greater solemnity or more heart-felt sorrow seemed to prevail' (120).

The men employed by Kermode set about their new job with great enthusiasm and diligence, sowing 500 acres of wheat and oats. Kermode furnished the men with cheap clothing, beds and provisions, at agreed prices for which he would be repaid in grain, at the market price. There was a house on the farm, in which they lived in comparative comfort, taking turns at cooking and washing. To do the ploughing they hired sixteen oxen, and they got horses for the harrowing. Snow reported that they began harvesting on 10 December:

> We were engaged ten and a half weeks in cutting and putting into shocks our three hundred acres of grain, during which time we had but one slight shower of rain. We drew it to a threshing machine, in the vicinity, which was impelled by water power, and had it threshed and cleaned; and on measurement we found that for the labor we had expended in cultivating the FACE of 'mother earth,' during the summer, she had yielded us an income of three thousand bushels of wheat, and a little over three thousand bushels of oats. [19–20]

Unhappily, as Snow was to learn, this did not yield the good fortune for which they had hoped because 'while our wheat and oats had been GROWING UP, prices had been GROWING DOWN HILL' (20). They could get only half of what they had paid for the seed in the first place, and this, together with what they got for the stock, left them with about £10 each. As their tickets-of-leave prevented them from being fed or clothed at government expense, they found that mere sustenance was sufficient 'to rid ourselves of the whole of our cash capital' (20). True to form, Marsh understood the whole deal to have been a swindle by Kermode, who 'benefitted greatly by having his rough land left in a situation to be easily tilled thereafter' (141).

Even before the harvest began, half the men had decided to seek alternative work and with Kermode's consent left to find employment elsewhere. Heustis reported that the day before they left, all the Patriots in the neighbourhood gathered to celebrate the Fourth of July. This was a poignant occasion when they took time out to remember 'our dear native land, where liberty hath her dwelling-place, and where British tyrants are not allowed to pollute the soil with their odious system of government' (121).

Heustis set himself up in Campbell Town making winnowing machines, a skill he then taught several of his comrades. When his companions proved more expert than himself, he turned his hand to other pursuits with fellow Patriot Elon Fellows, 'who could make any thing, from a German flute down to a penny whistle' (121). Fellows proposed they make cradles for the cutting of wheat, since only hand sickles were used in Van Diemen's Land. When they had constructed some cradles they approached another rich farmer, Mr Benton, who had a large estate on the South Esk River, to see if he wanted his grain cradled:

> We told Mr. Benton we were experienced cradlers, because an Englishman always thinks a man must needs be a bungler, unless he has served an apprenticeship of seven years at his business, let it be ever so simple.
>
> Mr. Benton had between two and three hundred acres of grain, and he and several others went down to see us commence. Unaccustomed as we were to the work, the presence of so many spectators—including our employer, whose good opinion we were anxious to secure, at the outset—was somewhat embarrassing. When we first struck in, as a matter of course, our skill was not exhibited to much advantage. I at once complained of the cradles, and insisted that the fingers were not right, and that we must go and alter them. Off we went, and took good care not to go back until Benton and his friends had left the field. We then began anew, and in a very short time got 'the hang' of the cradles, and could lay the grain as handsomely as the very best of cradlers. [122]

Benton was well satisfied with the job; he agreed to have all his wheat cradled and to pay the Americans an extra pound for their labour. Not so impressed were the other reapers, who threatened vengeance against these labour-saving machines. Each night the cradles had to be locked away 'to keep them out of the hands of those who would have been glad to destroy them'. By cradling, Heustis and Fellows earned 'the first and only money we accumulated in the colony, and we expended nearly the whole of it in the purchase of clothes, of which we were in very great need' (122).

For the most part, the Patriots found that, no matter what backbreaking jobs they tried, be it share-farming, sinking fence posts or cutting shingles by hand, they never made enough money to pay for more than their board and food. Sometimes they were cheated of their wages, and on one occasion they were robbed of what little they had by runaway convicts known as bushrangers. All the while they were harried by the local constabulary for the most minor offences. They might find themselves put in solitary for failing to attend church on Sunday, although the Church of England service was unacceptable to many of them and they found the clergy morally repugnant. According to Wright, the local cleric was so drunk 'he could hardly stand upright, while hiccupping forth the prayers'. The reverend's wife, Wright added, 'had been caught in adultery' (27). More than a dozen of the Patriots were brought before the magistrate on charges of being out after hours or being drunk—including Wright himself—and they received sentences which ranged from a week in solitary confinement to eight weeks on a labour gang. At least three men had their tickets revoked and were returned to hard labour.[14]

It must have seemed to them that the indulgence Sir John Franklin had promised was nothing more than a sorry joke.

16

Hopes Again Blasted

To the Patriots, the presence of American sailors in Van Diemen's Land was a tantalising reminder of the possibility of escape. For many, however, the lure of escape proved less potent than their fear of reprisal should they be caught. Heustis found himself in an agonising dilemma when his brother arrived at Hobart on the whale-ship *William Hamilton*. The captain had been at school with Heustis and sent word with his brother that:

> if I were aboard his ship, he would put me where the constables of Van Dieman's Land would never find me. . . . I knew it would be worse than useless for me to attempt to escape with Captain Cole, as I was very closely watched. Indeed, as soon as it was known, at Hobart Town, that I had a brother on board the William Hamilton, a messenger was despatched to Campbelltown [*sic*], to admonish the police officers to keep an eye on me. [123]

With a heavy heart, Heustis rejected the offer of escape, reasoning that he would not have too long to wait before receiving a pardon.

For William Gates the dilemma was even more excruciating. While he had been the overseer of Mr Tabbart, Gates had been given the job of taking three drays loaded with fine merino sheep to the port of Hobart. He had dutifully reported to the police in the town and received a pass to allow him to stay in Hobart to conduct business. Walking about the town he fell into company with 'an American tar "half seas over"' (164). Once this sailor established that Gates was also an American citizen, he wanted to do all in his power to help him return to the bosom of the great republic:

> His vessel left in a few days, and beside, there were two others there. He would take me on board at once and secrete me. But I was afraid—I dared not do it then. I knew there was a strict watch kept over me, for I felt pretty well assured that I was marked at the police, and constables were continually dogging me. I told the good natured fellow that I would not then, but would think of it more.

That evening he met me again with several of his comrades, who urged me harder than ever to go with them. It was a hard struggle with me: I had hopes—strong hopes—of getting my liberty from government before many months, and I knew that if I attempted an escape and should be unsuccessful, my hope of liberty would be forever fled, if my life did not pay the forfeit. [164–5]

The next day, with money from the wool sale in his pocket, Gates found the impulse to return home almost irresistible. The sailors met him again and importuned him to go with them, saying that they 'could put me where the British would never find me' (165). He was in torment of conflicting emotions. He had $5000 in his pocket, which he felt 'would partially remunerate me for my time and suffering, and to take which seemed to be no very heinous sin' (166). But conscience got the better of him, given that Tabbart had placed so much confidence in his integrity and he felt he had no right to betray this trust:

> Had the money in my pocket belonged to the Government, I could have taken it without compunctions. I had ever been taught that honesty was the best policy, and thus far I had endeavored to live to the principle. Though in escaping I should have done no wrong, but acted perfectly right, my better judgement told me that the taking of the money was doing wrong to an individual who had himself treated me with comparative kindness. [166–7]

Gates endured a terrible trip back to Tabbart's farm, tortured by the opportunity he had let slip. For weeks after he could barely sleep for the thought of what he had forgone: 'at times I was half ready to curse myself for not attempting it', he confessed. 'The longing for home, sweet home, was doubly increased' (167). Indeed, anguished dreams of home gave many of the Patriots sleepless nights. As their period of servitude extended, the lure of home became almost too great to bear. They had no communication from their families, leading many to despair. As Elijah Woodman complained to his parents in 1843, it had been two years since he heard 'a solitary word', and his fear was that his wife and children had not written because 'something has taken place and they think I cannot stand the shock'.[1] On the other hand the Patriots did get some news from America via the local newspapers. Early in 1843, they had been in high spirits after hearing that the Governor-General of Canada had 'ordered a general amnesty releasing all prisoners concerned in the rebellion'.[2] The Patriots were even more excited by the news that a member of the US House of Representatives, Caleb Cushing, had made a formal request that President John Tyler intervene with the British government to secure the release of the American prisoners. They would not have been so pleased had they known that, while he did accede to Cushing's request, President Tyler was of the opinion that the release of the prisoners should be requested as a 'boon' rather than a matter of right.[3]

The Patriots had long held that they had been pawns in the tense diplomatic tussle between Great Britain and the United States over the disputed border between Maine and New Brunswick. Newspapers reported that negotiations between the US Secretary of State Daniel Webster and British special negotiator Lord Ashburton had finally resulted in a treaty ratified in October 1842. As part of the negotiation process, Webster had formally written to Ashburton asking him to recommend a free pardon for the American prisoners in Van Diemen's Land.[4] When he read about this in the *Hobart Town Courier*, Woodman wrote that he and his compatriots felt 'it might in some manner alleviate our present condition if not effect our liberty'. With bright expectation he added, 'you will soon see us in America if our lives are spared and we are well. The little party here with me will have money enough to take us to any part of the United States.'[5] A few months later, the Patriots' hopes were buoyed yet again by the news that an American consul, Elisha Hathaway, had been appointed in Hobart.

About this time, Marsh received a letter from his father—the only letter, Marsh said, he was permitted to receive—that told him that he and his compatriots might expect a pardon very soon as a result of the general amnesty to those involved in the rebellion in Upper Canada. 'Certainly this act of clemency will be extended to you soon, if your conduct will warrant it,' his father wrote, adding judiciously, 'behave yourselves like men, and I am almost sure a pardon will soon be granted you' (143). John Tyrrell also received a letter from his well-placed uncle in Canada which suggested that Tyrell had 'strong reason to hope that I might be set at liberty . . . not only myself but my fellow sufferers'.[6] By Independence Day, 4 July 1843, Woodman's high spirits had evaporated. Reflecting on the Patriots' effort to bring the daylight of republicanism to the darkness of monarchy, he felt they had been most unfairly punished with no hope of respite. 'There was a time', he wrote to his parents, 'when we thought the correspondence from Congress would take effect but are now in doubts of any speedy measure to obtain our liberty'. It seemed to him most unjust that the British government had 'dealt so partial to others that are in Canada', while for the Americans they had 'poured out upon us indignation and wrath, tribulation and anguish'.[7]

Equally dispirited, Tyrrell wrote to Mr Gunn to remind him that 'the time appointed by Her Majesty for our liberation has past [*sic*] and yet nothing has been done. I am anxious to know whether we might reasonably hope for anything.'[8] In reply, Gunn indicated he had no formal advice about their release; however, 'it is the belief of the government that something will be done for you'.[9] In September came the news that Tyrrell had indeed received a free pardon following intervention by his influential relative in Upper Canada.

For the Americans, the only positive news came in July 1843 when the headlines of the *Colonial Times* newspaper placards shouted 'Glorious News! Sir John Franklin's Recall'. According to the gleeful editorial, it was no longer necessary to speak respectfully of Franklin since he had lost the respect of the British government. Although the Patriots had actually been the beneficiaries of Franklin's reformist impulse, they always took vicarious pleasure in the vitriolic attacks on Franklin in the colonial newspapers, which would openly refer to 'the imbicile reign of the Polar explorer'.[10] If they had understood that the architect of the campaign to discredit Franklin was John Montagu, a close confidant and nephew-in-law of Sir George Arthur, their enthusiasm might have been more subdued. Montagu had been dismissed from his post as Colonial Secretary in January 1842, and Franklin was mortified when the new Secretary of State for the Colonies, Lord Stanley, refused to support his action in dismissing Montagu, sending instead a stinging dispatch of censure expressing his 'unqualified dis-approval'.[11] Franklin's humiliation was complete when Stanley appointed a replacement governor before any official announcement about recall had been communicated to him. Sir John Eardley-Wilmot was hardly an illustrious replacement. Even older than Franklin, he had been described by Lord Stanley as a 'muddle-headed blockhead'.[12] He arrived to take up his appointment in August 1843, three days before the formal notice of Franklin's recall.

When the new governor attended the cattle fair at Campbell Town at the end of 1843, William Kermode undertook to intercede on behalf of the Patriots in the Campbell Town and Oatlands districts. According to Heustis, the governor gave an encouraging response:

> 'the Governor said, if he had been in Sir John Franklin's place, when we arrived, he should not have received us, as the documents, on the authority of which Captain Wood had brought us there, conferred no power on the Governor to detain us on the Island' ... Such being the admitted state of the case, it would seem to have been Governor Wilmot's duty to let the captives go free. If there was originally no legal precept for holding us in bondage, the fact that we had been wrongfully and illegally deprived of our liberty for several years could certainly confer no power to continue the wrong. However, as matters then stood, he said he could do nothing but use his influence with the home government, which he would cheerfully do. [125]

Marsh, who had already sent the new governor 'a memorial of some length, setting forth our grievances', concurred that Eardley-Wilmot 'appeared astonished that Franklin should even take it upon himself to receive us in the colony at all, without a sentence' (164). According to Marsh, Eardley-Wilmot openly expressed the opinion that if he had been governor 'he would not have received us on such grounds' (164). It is hard to know whether Wilmot would have expressed such an opinion, although this view does have some weight. Eardley-Wilmot certainly knew his law, since he had studied law and had published an abridgement of Blackstone's authoritative work on the law. Given that the warrants for those on the *Buffalo* were written out by the governor of Upper Canada who could not confer the authority to detain his prisoners elsewhere, Wilmot may have expressed concern about Franklin's action. The implied criticism of his predecessor would not have been considered out of order, as Franklin was in such open disgrace.

Linus Miller's narrative gives credence to the recollections of Heustis and Marsh. Miller recounted that when he received his ticket-of-leave from Port Arthur in November 1843, he immediately paid the new governor a visit. He claimed to have been kindly received by Eardley-Wilmot, who told him he 'was sorry the Canadians had been so ill-treated, . . . and had sent a despatch . . . reccommending that all of our *pardons* be immediately granted' (350). It seems highly likely that Heustis's recollection was coloured by what he was later told of this visit by Miller. He was also influenced by Miller's account of his discussion with the lawyer Edward Macdowell, who had been the Attorney-General of Van Diemen's Land in Franklin's administration.

Macdowell took an interest in Miller and lent him law books. Macdowell told the young law clerk that, having seen all the papers that accompanied the Patriots, there was 'not a scratch of a pen to authorise the Governor to receive you upon this Island, much less treat you as convicts' (350). It was Macdowell's opinion that, according to the laws of Van Diemen's Land, the Patriots had a right 'to land as free-men, and to leave the same day if you chose to do so. Every person who has held you in custody here, is liable to an action for false imprisonment!' (350). Macdowell drew up a petition asking for an immediate pardon for Miller, and informed Eardley-Wilmot that legal proceedings for wrongful imprisonment would be instituted if the pardon were not granted. There appears to be no surviving record of this correspondence, which Miller says 'greatly alarmed' (351) the governor, but if Eardley-Wilmot had received such a communication it would doubtless have influenced the response he gave to Kermode. Whatever the governor did say, it certainly gave the Patriots heart that they were now in the hands of a more merciful tyrant than Franklin.

By January 1844, another Canadian Patriot, John Grant, was also pardoned, while Tyrrell left for Canada aboard a whaler. The remaining Patriots waited for news of their own pardons, but they heard only ominous silence. Woodman sent a letter by an American whaler in which he spoke of the Patriots' anxiety about 'a lack of energy on the part of our friends in Canada'. While he remained confident that 'the citizens of the United States have done all in their power for our liberation', so much time had passed since the Patriots read of the American diplomatic overtures to Her Majesty's government that they now 'despaired of receiving any good news from that source'. Woodman's letter was a pleading reminder that 'our friends in America will not forget us but still agitate for our redemption from this miserable state'.[13]

Communication from John Roebuck, their staunch radical friend in England, explained that Lord Stanley would not extend the amnesty to them, and that he had stated their pardons would only come as a result of petitions on their behalf addressed to the Queen. Responding to a suggestion from the governor to this effect, Kermode, on behalf of sixty-one Americans, had drawn up a petition in March 1844 which was signed by about fifty of the most influential men in the colony. Eardley-Wilmot sent the petition to London immediately.[14] Grateful though they were, the Patriots were far from sanguine about the success of any interventions made to the British government on their behalf.

The French-Canadian prisoners in Sydney had been pardoned in March following petitions from their supporters in Lower Canada, and an association had been formed to raise money for their passage home. Lord Stanley himself had even advanced the considerable sum of £400 from the Treasury to assist their return to Lower Canada.[15] As yet, nothing had come for the Americans in Van Diemen's Land. They were all astonished, Woodman told his family, to see that those transported from Lower Canada had been pardoned, as had the leaders of the rebellion in Upper Canada, yet 'we poor fellows are not so much spoken of nor the least move made in Canada for our release'.[16]

In his despairing letters, Woodman continually urged his family to stimulate some action in the United States for their release. He even went so far as to suggest that an American ship could be sent to Van Diemen's Land with a cargo of tobacco but with the real purpose of facilitating a mass escape.[17] He was not alone in pursuing this dangerous line of thought. As 1844 wore on, the idea took hold that the Patriots might be able to escape *en masse* from a remote part of the eastern coast of the island.

With this purpose in mind, two Patriots with tickets for Swanport, Garrett Hicks and Riley Whitney, had taken a farm about 5 miles from the coast. Obtaining passes to visit them was no great problem, according to Heustis, as 'there were very few officers, from the Governor downwards, who could not be bribed, if the poor prisoner had the means' (127). By means of giving a 'tip' to the authorities in Campbell Town, Heustis and fellow Patriot James Pierce got passes for Hobart, for the purpose of negotiating with an American ship's captain willing to take twenty of them from Waub's Boat Harbour, a remote spot on the east coast, now the coastal town of Bicheno.

Making the arrangements for the escape was not easy, for the men were scattered across the island. The timing was critical, as Marsh was well aware:

> there must be no mistake in the time, because some who would not be able to get their tickets changed, would be obliged to take Paddy's leave; and would be liable to be taken up on the way. Some would have fifty, some sixty, some eighty, and some an hundred miles to travel through the woods, over mountains and through swamps and perhaps miss of finding the designated place, and after wandering about perhaps three or four days, tired and hungry, obliged to surrender and perhaps glad to fall into the hands of any one. [145]

The men arrived at their friends' farm during April, mighty hungry and well pleased to find Hicks and Whitney had cultivated a fine crop of potatoes and turnips, as well as having slaughtered many kangaroo. The potatoes had been cultivated for the trip home and the kangaroo hides had been dried with a view to tanning for leather. While they waited for the ship, they dug the potatoes and carried them on their backs in sacks made of kangaroo skin 5 miles through the dense coastal heath to the beach. They were well-prepared for trouble. 'We had managed to procure four guns and had them concealed', Marsh wrote; '. . . should the vessel come in we was determined to fight our way on board if necessary' (148). After they had hidden the potatoes in the sand, they went to work chopping about eight cords of wood.

And still they waited. For five days after the appointed time, the men kept watch and kept a fire burning continuously on the rocky point at the end of the bay. Twice they had been excited by the appearance of sails rounding the point at a great distance, but with no sign of the Stars and Stripes. As Marsh told it, they 'were almost on the point of giving up, and I believe one or two had left as a sail was discovered rounding the point at a great distance' (148). Watching closely as the ship tacked against the wind, the waiting Patriots became convinced that the ship was 'endeavoring to make land not far from us' (148).

The problem was that it was blowing a near gale and unsafe to come close to shore. A small boat was lowered which bought the captain into the beach. Watching the flimsy craft battle the huge breakers, Heustis felt his heart lift. Deliverance was finally at hand. In his imagination 'we were already grasping the hands of our friends, in our dear native land!' (127). The peril of the wild sea was of no concern in that moment of joyful antici-pation. Once the captain had struggled ashore, he explained that it would be useless to attempt to get anything on board until the wind had abated. He 'had often thought of our situation', Marsh reported, and was 'fearful in waiting we would all be liable to be taken prisoners and severely punished'

(149). Given the gale force winds and wild sea, the captain explained as he departed, he would put to sea, and if the wind abated that night, he would take them aboard.

As his flimsy craft negotiated its way through the foaming maelstrom, the men on the beach noticed what appeared to be an armed schooner rounding the point. It turned out to be a government man-o'-war on the lookout for potential escapees. 'Thus were our hopes again blasted!' wrote Heustis (127). For the next few days the warship stayed in the bay, while further out to sea the American ship occasionally hove in sight, 'but the presence of the armed vessel prevented us from communicating with the noble-hearted captain' (127). Eventually the captain gave up the game and sailed away.

Very soon three constables from Swanport appeared at the farm with summonses for the Patriots to appear before the police magistrate, charged with attempting to abscond. Their luck held better on this occasion. The witnesses against them told contradictory stories, while the Patriots stuck firmly to a common defence that they were merely hunting and fishing. 'After exhausting all his cunning, in unavailing endeavors to get some sort of a confession out of us,' Heustis wrote, 'the magistrate . . . could not prove it' (128). The police magistrate was not quite done with them, though. As Marsh explained, he made a ruling that in future they could never leave their respective districts and should be mustered every Saturday night. Failure to obey this rule would mean that they 'should be immediately reported as absconders, or bush rangers, and punished accordingly' (152). Marsh accepted the grim news that he was to be confined to Bothwell with his usual sardonic fatalism, but he took some pleasure in the fate of that fine crop of potatoes, still buried in the sand. Given that the potato crop had failed in other parts of the world, Marsh enjoyed the thought that their excellent crop might be 'destined to be preserved to renew that valuable root at some future period' (153).

Curiously there is no mention of an appearance in the magistrates' court on the convict records of those men mentioned in the narratives of Marsh and Heustis. This may be because the case against them was dismissed. It is unlikely that they would have concocted this elaborate story of attempted escape. Although it is possible that Heustis copied this story from the narrative of Marsh, as he sometimes did, it must be said that despite his political rhetoric, Marsh was a trustworthy narrator of events. Furthermore, there is a good deal of variation in the narratives of the two men, though the events are the same. There can be no doubt that they went to Waub's Boat Harbour, as the description of the terrain given in both accounts was accurate. Unlike some of the heroics reported in the Patriot narratives, this one has the ring of truth about it.

After returning to Campbell Town, Heustis took a job fencing, together with Elizur Stevens and Michael Fraer. 'We made about three miles of brush fence,' he wrote; 'we worked hard, early and late, boarded ourselves, and lived cheap, for the sake of saving a little, and after all *never got a cent for our work*' (128). The employer who cheated them finally got his come-uppance when he was hanged for murder some time later. Heustis tried fencing again, this time with Hiram Loop and Chauncey Mathers. The three of them 'strained every nerve' (128) to construct a heavy log fence, and this time were paid for their back-breaking labour. Their wages could never be enough to permit them to save any money. All they had left, after paying for their board, 'was just enough to get each of us a pair of pantaloons, and provide us with travelling money till we could find other employment' (128–9).

Nevertheless, Heustis and his companions fared better than those who had been sent to Bothwell: Robert Marsh, James Fero, David House, Orlin Blodget and Leonard Delano. Marsh reported that the trip to Bothwell was about 100 miles 'through the bush swamps, and over mountains' (152), and on the way the group managed to feed themselves by snaring kangaroo to roast over a fire. They also made a kind of bread called damper:

> We managed to bake our flour by brushing the dirt from a rock, wet the flour with cold water, knead it into dough, make it into a thin cake, make a place in the embers where we had a concealed fire through the night, let it remain there till we thought it was done, then take it out and brush the ashes from it as much as possible. It would not be very light, and rather small for a number of men tired and hungry: yet, as small as it was, it was a great deal better than nothing, and I can assure you: in such times, there is no bad taste to it. [154]

By the time they had gone only a short way, Marsh fell ill, 'suffering much from pain in the breast . . . a pain in my side, which made it very difficult for me to bear up' (153). During the trip it rained heavily and Marsh contracted a high fever, which meant he was unable to continue. He was nursed by a convict shepherd who allowed the group to stay at his hut for two weeks while Marsh recovered. Realising that they could never make it back to Bothwell, some of the group undertook to visit the police and get their tickets-of-leave changed for the less remote district of Brighton, since they had heard that 'the magistrate there would be more likely to get us the privilege of going to Hobart Town' (166). Brighton was also in the vicinity of Green Ponds Probation Station, where the Patriots had some expectations that they might find work. They remembered that it was here that local landholders had been so kind to them, offering inducements for the Americans to work for them when they got their tickets-of-leave. Unhappily, times had changed dramatically. Those same landholders, who had been so desperate for labour in the boom year of 1840 that they had petitioned the colonial government to implement an assisted immigration program, were now faced with depressed agricultural prices and a glut of free labour. When Marsh and his companions arrived at Brighton and set about looking for employment, they had no success.

After four weeks at Brighton without any work, the Patriots approached a man they had known at Green Ponds, and who had recently purchased a large estate from gentlemen returning to England. This farmer had no work to offer, but he did allow them to live in the big house of the estate in order to protect it against thieves. The Patriots were not exactly gentlemen, Marsh allows: they were only camping in a mansion 'with no furniture, except our blankets, tin cups, frying pan and an old tin kettle' (168). However much they might imagine themselves as gentlemen, they understood it was a 'great condescension, on the part of the gentlemen in allowing us to even stop inside the mansion . . . after all our castle building, we were nobody— nothing but poor prisoners, or slaves' (170).

The owner finally offered to pay them a shilling a day to remove a large quantity of manure but insisted they would have to buy their rations from him. This amounted to slave labour, Marsh calculated, 'for he knew that the shilling would not purchase of himself, more poor mutton and flour than we should require while performing the labor' (171). Nevertheless, the men took the work, 'for we could do no better' (172). Times were desperate indeed.

If Marsh or any other Patriot was tempted to take the escape route of Asa Priest on the *Buffalo*, and opt for death over a life of bitter servitude at the end of the world, there is little hint of it. Choosing death as a way to escape was not common among the convict population, but it was not unknown, especially at the harsh penal stations of Macquarie Harbour and Port Arthur. As a rule, convicts were too scared of eternal damnation to commit suicide but could resort to murder as an escape route, as they would always have the opportunity to repent before they were 'launched into eternity' on the gallows.[18] Although the Patriots may have thought about suicide, as Linus Miller admits to having done in his dark moments at Port Arthur, this kind of escape had implications far too terrible, as Marsh's narrative reveals.

While at Brighton, Marsh and his companions took it upon themselves to find out the fate of their friend James Williams, who had been taken away from Green Ponds suffering from sore eyes and later was said to have died. Marsh and Fero went to the hospital to make inquiries but could find no one willing to give any account of what had happened to Williams or the manner of his death. As they were leaving, they passed four men carrying a rough coffin and followed them, out of curiosity. Nearly a mile from the hospital they came to an enclosed field that they took to be a makeshift burial ground. The men carrying the coffin set it down beside a ready-dug hole full of water, as Marsh recounted in horror:

> after considerable loud and rough talk and measuring, the box was elevated, and at the word 'drop' they sung out, 'there you are, my hearties, whoever you are it's more than we know,' the water, as the box fell, flying as high as their heads; after a man's jumping on one end to make it a little level, it was soon covered up merely level with the surface; as they came out, I asked one of them who it was they had just buried; 'O,' says he, 'it's more than I know, but it's no one in particular, but a part of three or four prisoners.' [165–6]

When Marsh asked these men if they knew of Williams and his fate, the convict orderlies told him that Williams had died after suffering greatly. His dead body was treated shamefully, 'his flesh, what little was remaining, lies somewhere in that yard, . . . his bones are in the hands of some of the young students; maybe in England before this time' (166). This whole scene could be a piece of macabre invention on Marsh's part but it certainly points to a critical anxiety. Nothing more could be calculated to reveal the absolute barbarity of the convict system than the practice of turning the bodies of dead felons over for dissection by surgeons and medical students. A similar story, with the same macabre overtones, is told by Heustis concerning the body of Alexander McLeod, who died soon after landing from the *Marquis of Hastings*. Heustis claims to have the story from Benjamin Wait, who was working with Samuel Chandler as a hospital orderly:

> They found the body on a table, cut in many pieces, with the entrails lying beside it. They gathered the pieces together and put them in a coffin of rough boards, and behold, it was poor McLeod, whom they all knew and respected. The scene was revolting, but there was no alternative. They carried him away and laid him in a stranger's grave, among felons, with no mark to distinguish the spot from the thousands of mounds around him. [103]

In both cases the gruesome scenario does seem far-fetched. Contrary to the Patriots' belief, it was not common practice to give over the bodies of dead convicts for dissection. However, it was known to be done in the case of some executed murderers, added as part of the sentence, an especially degrading ritual that would emphasise the weight of the penalty.[19] This was still in practice in Van Diemen's Land the 1840s when a number of criminals were sentenced to death and dissection. Certainly those who had worked in the hospital, such as Wright and Wait, knew of this practice because the Colonial Surgeon had a handful of medical students who took part in dissection at the hospital. In fact, during the previous decade, there was a dispute between the Colonial Surgeon and another prominent surgeon about access to the bodies handed over by law.[20] As a correspondent to the

Courier pointed out in 1842, the sentence of dissection was not to be encouraged since it instilled in the lower orders in the colony a terror of the Colonial Hospital and the surgeons who might have been named in the sentence.[21] It is likely that during the time of the Patriots, there would have been fewer bodies ordered for dissection by law, and the surgeons may have opted for more informal access to bodies in the hospital, just helping themselves to the bodies of persons with no family to claim them, or bribing undertakers and orderlies to supply them with bodies.[22] Some years later, a prominent honorary surgeon at the Colonial Hospital was able to mutilate the body of William Lanne, said to be the last Aboriginal male, as well as the body of a white schoolteacher in the Colonial Hospital, which does suggest that surgeons had a tradition of dissecting and mutilating bodies in the ways the Patriots described.[23]

One thing is sure, the practice of dissection was seized upon by the Patriots as the ultimate invasion of their bodies by the hated imperial system which had stripped and shorn them; meticulously described and categorised them; tried in every way to reduce them to a thing.[24] No matter how gravely ill he had been, in life James Williams was a singular individual whom the orderlies described as 'a fine young man' (166), who impressed the hospital convicts with his talk of home. 'America must be a fine country, according to his tell', Marsh's informant volunteered. 'I wish I was there' (166), yet in death Williams had been reduced to flayed flesh, in a grave not even distinguishable from the sodden field around it. By being thrown into the earth, with bits and pieces of other nameless felons, Williams would literally disintegrate into the despised dregs of Empire from which the Patriots had always been so careful to distinguish themselves.

This cautionary tale was told by Marsh to show that the degradation that the imperial system could not manage to inflict on the Patriots in life was accomplished in death. In this tale the Patriots' manly resistance to the cut of the lash had been negated by their being utterly unmanned by the cut of the surgeon's knife. Their great fear of dying in servitude was that the distinctiveness they asserted in life would be nullified in death, and they would be reduced to nothing more than pieces of the 'lumpen residium', like sweepings from the butcher's floor.[25]

For about six months at Brighton, Marsh and his friends played at being gentlemen in the fine house, during which time they survived as best they could, eking out their meagre existence and always on the brink of starvation. One day in late October 1844 they were accosted yet again by a constable. For the first time in five years they found the encounter to their advantage. 'There is some of you Canadians, in the morning's *Gazette*,' the constable told them, 'for a free pardon' (174).

17

'I could not blame the Rangers'

O NE OF THE ELEMENTS that contributed to the level of official harassment that the Patriots experienced in 1843 was the spectre of armed gangs of convict bolters who had taken to the bush. In principle, the Patriots were not ill-disposed to these desperadoes, known as bushrangers. 'I could not blame the Rangers so much for trying to gain their freedom', wrote Gates (183). Wright sheeted the blame home to the governorship of George Arthur, as did Snow, who believed that these men had been driven to desperation 'after suffering all the forms of punishment which the inventive genius of Sir George could contrive' (20). It was with more than a hint of admiration that Heustis described the bushrangers as 'high-spirited and resolute men' who had been 'driven to this mode of life by the severity of their treatment' (124). Given that Heustis and his companions at Campbell Town had been robbed of all their bedding, clothing and provisions by bushrangers, this magnanimous assessment was somewhat at odds with his later observation that bushrangers 'embrace every opportunity to plunder those who come within their reach, and commit murder whenever the success of their schemes cannot otherwise be secured' (124). Snow, on the other hand, insisted that as a general rule bushrangers 'pay special attention to the rich settlers only' (22). The *modus operandi* he described thus:

> In the evening, when they have made a choice of an individual on whom to bestow a special call, they sally forth with guns loaded with double charges— rush into the farm-house; and if there is no particular demonstration of resist-ance on the part of the inmates, one of the Rangers proceeds to secure the farmer and his household, by tying their hands behind them and putting them all into one room together, where an armed guard is placed over them. Then the house is thoroughly searched for money, watches, clothing, guns, ammunition, provisions, and other valuables and necessaries; and though, from the urgency of their business, their calls are necessarily SHORT, still they make a clean

sweep. If they find more of this world's goods than they can handily carry off, they compel one of the occupants of the house to assist in conveying it into the bush, when he is allowed to return in safety. When they decamp from the premises, they leave their prisoners to unloose themselves according to the best of their ability. . . . It is seldom, or never, that they kill a man, unless war is declared at the door by the party feeling himself aggrieved. At such times they stand for the rights granted to persons in all civilized countries, of fighting in self defence. [21]

In 1843, there were many bushranging gangs at large on the island. One newspaper reported that seven gangs, ranging between two and fifteen men, were operating in the north of the island.[1] Best-known of several bushranger gangs in the south were a trio of absconders from Port Arthur: Martin Cash, Lawrence Kavanagh and George Jones. The flamboyant style of Martin Cash lent a air of romance to this particular set of desperadoes and Snow was especially inclined to sing their praises as 'gallant intrepid and generous' fellows, informing his readers that they 'were never known to offer an incivility to a female, or rob a ticket-of-leave man or any other prisoner' (22). Wealthy farmers and passengers on mail coaches were their particular target, according to Snow, although 'nothing delighted them more than to rob the Magistrate's house' (23). Snow gleefully reproduced a notice Martin Cash had once placed in a Hobart newspaper:

> The undersigned respectfully solicits the attendance of the Lieut. Governor, his Private Secretary, Chief Police Magistrate and other officers, at Park Hill on a certain day, at eight o'clock P.M., to take supper. There will be a band of police constables in attendance, that no harm may result.
>
> Your humble servant when taken,
> (Signed,)   MARTIN CASH. [23]

This admiration for bushrangers was not some republican fancy on the Patriots' part. In Van Diemen's Land, the bushrangers enjoyed considerable support among the convict and emancipist population. As a local newspaper complained, even emancipated convicts displayed 'a degree of public sympathy with the robbers, quite inconsistent with the Public safety'.[2] It was to be expected. A place of punishment calculated to demean and emasculate was sure to stimulate the celebration of acts of masculine daring outside the boundaries of law, while a society stripped to the essentials of the powerful and the powerless, the gaoler and the gaoled, was fertile ground for a tradition where the oppressed could take revenge upon the strong. A traveller in the Australian penal colonies at the same time as the Patriots took notice of the great popularity of bushrangers, who were celebrated like Robin Hood or Rob Roy in Britain, and were praised 'for their generosity, their invariable respect and tenderness for women and children'.[3]

While the Patriots themselves were in no way inclined to join with the bushrangers—they understood that to take to the bush with guns meant death or a lifetime at a dreadful penal station—their narratives all record a kind of wistful yearning for the bushranger life; for what Gates saw as 'a determination to live or die in their wild freedom' (169). In this, the Patriots were typical of most of the convicts who celebrated and admired the bush-rangers, and were prepared to offer some forms of protection, but were not prepared to exchange their own chance of a legitimately gained freedom for a dream of liberty seized by force. For all the high esteem bushrangers enjoyed in the convict population, recruitment was sporadic and often met with blank refusal. The *Hobart Town Gazette* reported a telling incident in 1825, when a group of bushrangers stopped on the Bagdad road to talk to a convict construction gang: 'they called on the men . . . and asked them one by one to join them, but all unanimously refused'.[4] Too much was put at risk in a bid for 'wild freedom'. Convicts understood that the bushrangers were always caught. The key to the convict population's relationship with the bushrangers can be found in their own slang for the man who refused to bend, an 'out and outer'.[5] Such men had their value. As Alan Atkinson has remarked: 'when any single convict stood up for shared principle it was as if he declared (looking about him), "I *rebel*—therefore we *exist*" '.[6] For the Patriots, like many in the penal system, the spectre of the bushranger provided an affirmation of their own fervent aspirations to reverse the power relationships that so demeaned them.

As ticket-of-leave men were called out frequently to hunt bushrangers, it was inevitable that the Patriots would find themselves impelled into a posse to hunt for Cash, Kavanagh and Jones after they had held up and robbed a mail coach. The job did have some inducements, as Snow explained: 'any convict who shall take them, can have the reward, a free pardon, and a passage to England' (21). Even so, few would willingly offer their services. Gates was especially disgruntled at the prospect of his call-up, despite the offer a large reward, because 'a ticket-of-leave man is compelled to do this duty when it is demanded of him, and yet he receives no pay, unless he succeeds in capturing the ranger' (169). He believed his employer had recommended him out of spite, because Gates decided to quit to get a higher wage elsewhere. 'I would go only upon compulsion', he was careful to explain, 'for it was business I did not like' (183). While Gates was successful in persuading the magistrate that he should not be impressed into a posse, this was scant relief since he was compelled to become a special constable, a job which he regarded with utter contempt, as a sort of 'degraded being, scorned and condemned by the freemen and hated and despised by the lower orders' (170).[7]

After a few weeks, when the hunt for Cash and his companions had proved fruitless and the police returned to their usual duty, Gates was free to seek more appropriate work as overseer on the large estate of the local magistrate, Mr Kimberly. He got on very well with his new employer, even though the daughters were 'as proud as Lucifer and feared the sight and presence of one of low degree as much as they would the plague' (174). Kimberly himself was 'half and two thirds drunk a greater part of the time' (177). According to Gates, Kimberly was a particular target of Cash and his rogue companions, because he was a magistrate, and because a constable who resided a part of the time with Kimberly had been an informer against them. Gates recounted how one stormy night, just as Kimberly had returned drunk from a three-day binge, the bushrangers attacked Kimberly's estate looking for the constable. Surprising the assigned convicts in their huts, the bushrangers tied them up and marched them toward the house, demanding to know where the constable slept:

> Jones stepped to the window and commanded him to rise, when he fired—his ball passing through the open door of the bedroom and lodging in the mantle of the fire place, close by the cook's head, who but a minute before had risen and was standing by the fire. At the same moment the kitchen door was flung open, and the muzzles of two guns presented, backed by the command to stir not, lest death should be the result. Our hands were then secured behind us. The cook, butler, gardener, &c., were also secured, and the whole—the men from the huts as well as those from the house—marched into the parlor; all in their shirts save Kimberly and myself, who were full dressed, when we were put under guard of Caverner [sic]. [178]

Once it had been established that the constable informer was not resident in the house, the bushrangers turned their attention to plunder. Gates reports that Cash was annoyed to find there was no money in the house and sent his men to rummage in the rooms where they chanced upon Mr Kimberly's haughty daughters, 'whom they secured as they had the men, and ushered them into the parlor in their undress'. Gates had enough chivalry to be pained by 'the anguish of their mortification', yet he could not escape 'a sort of satisfaction in seeing their pride so completely humbled' (179). Cash and Jones discovered little in their hunt but a gold watch and 'a very nice new suit of clothes, worth some £16 or £18', which Jones took for himself, discarding the threadbare suit he wore. The watch was of interest to Cash until he discovered it was the property of the eldest daughter, a gift from her fiancé. Cash returned the watch to her, saying that 'he scorned to take the things of a woman' (179). They filled a sack with tea, sugar, flour, ham, and more, which they compelled the gardener, 'a stout, athletic man, but who had only a day or two before broken one of his great toes' to carry for them. He hobbled off into the bush with his captors. Jones, who lingered behind, untied Gates's hands and ordered the company to 'remain perfectly quiet for two hours, during which time he should remain outside to see that his injunctions were observed, and that his comrades had sufficient time to make safe their retreat' (180). During the two hours, Gates listened unmoved to the supplication and entreaties of the daughters to untie them, 'though to have spoken to me in any other situation would have been considered by them such a deep disgrace that no water could wash it out' (180). Not until the second hour had struck did he untie them all and send word to the police at Oatlands. The following day the gardener returned, 'looking more woebegone than if he had just passed through six months' road service' (181).

For all his hair-raising encounter with these desperadoes whose eventual capture he reported with some satisfaction, Gates's account of this armed home invasion has a good deal of romantic colouring, reminiscent of the folk tales of Robin Hood, Dick Turpin and Jack Sheppard. His tale of the bushranger who would not take a token of love from a woman was every bit the equal of the chivalrous hero of Martin Cash's own narrative, ghost-written in the tradition of the chapbooks and broadsides attributed to famous English highwaymen.[8] In his narrative, Cash described the trio blasting their way into Kimberly's residence as part of a series of home invasions of prominent colonial officials in the area:

> We demanded admittance in the name of the Queen, and as they did not appear to pay proper respect to her Majesty, Kavenagh [*sic*] immediately shot the lock off the door and we made our *entree*, each taking a different direction, being obliged to introduce ourselves in the absence of a master of ceremonies.[9]

At their entry, Cash glimpsed one man fleeing through the window. He was affronted to later discover this was none other than the constable who had been placed in the house for protection, and whom Cash castigates as a coward with no manly sense of moral responsibility. Significantly, the proud daughters of Gates's narrative, humbled by being herded into the parlour in their underclothes, were also treated differently in Cash's account:

> Jones came to a door which resisted his efforts, and while applying the muzzle of his gun to the lock with a view to blowing it open. I happened to catch the sound of a female voice inside and instantly called on him to desist . . . Having opened the door Jones was about to enter, but I told him to remain outside till the ladies were in readiness to leave. I then requested them to dress as speedily as possible, and they all three shortly afterwards made their appearance in the passage.[10]

It is quite likely that Gates's account is closer to the mark. Over the course of the history of bushranging in Van Diemen's Land, a common theme was the way in which the master's authority was damaged at the hands of armed absconders. Sometimes their methods were crude, for example, ordering masters to strip in front of their station hands. On other occasions they were more sophisticated, as when Sir Richard Dry's house at Quamby's Brook was attacked and the bushrangers seized Dry's nephew. In a complete reversal of dominant power relations, the bushrangers inquired of the assembled assigned servants as to their captive's character. For a brief moment, the unfortunate nephew's fate hung in the hands of the estate's unfree workers. The latter pronounced him a 'good man' and he was released, the convicts having exercised a prerogative of judgement that was usually the preserve of the master class.[11] This variant of the kangaroo court not only cut deep into the ruling ideology, but left the assigned convicts free from the conventional source of master retaliation, the magistrates' bench. An incident from the raid of Cash, Kavanagh and Jones on the property of Captain McKay was another fine example. Having confined all who worked on the property inside the house with Kavanagh keeping guard, several of the convict workers indicated they wanted some tobacco, with which Cash was happy to oblige:

> by-and-by they were making clouds in every direction. Captain McKay, being a great martinet, at once protested against the men smoking in his parlour, observing that such a thing had never occurred since the building was erected, upon which Kavanagh called, 'Order,' threatening to deal summarily with him if he dared to issue any commands while we were in the house, and, turning to the men, observed that he should shoot the first man who desisted from smoking in our presence.[12]

Perhaps the humiliation of Kimberly's daughters was of the same order. Although Cash could still display civility toward them, and some degree of chivalry, the bushranger was able to strike a devastating blow to elitist pretensions of these haughty colonial misses for whom, Gates told his readers, 'wealth and distinction was the sum and substance of their idea of soul' (174). By entrusting their eventual freedom to a ticket-of-leave man who had felt the sting of their scorn, Cash was literally putting the women's dignity in the hands of Gates. Here the example of the daughters being humbled permitted the tables to be turned much more effectively than if the subject had been the drunken magistrate, Kimberly. It certainly worked a tonic for Gates's self-esteem, and no doubt had much the same effect for the other convict workers assembled in the parlour.

Despite the differences in their testimony, accounts by both Cash and Gates are calculated to elicit sympathy and admiration in the reader, rather than the condemnation and outrage which would normally be expected of an activity that so transgressed established law and individual rights. Both narratives functioned within a well-established folk tradition of the outlaw hero, where the outlaw's positive virtues of manliness and courtesy were weighted against the criminal activity in which he was engaged. In this tradition, the most important moral precept was not *thou shalt not rob*, but *thou shalt not rob or harm the oppressed and the weak*. Significantly in this tradition, it was permissible to rob women of the master class, but they could not be humiliated or mistreated, even if they were rich.[13] Thus in Cash's autobiography he could not allow himself to have acted in a fashion that was other than utterly chivalrous. Gates's narrative, on the other hand, emphasised the subversive elements in the story. For him, the necessary act of chivalry was returning the gold watch, which Cash himself does not mention. Here too, Gates's version has a ring of truth about it, since it was common for bushrangers to return items that held a sentimental value, especially where women were concerned.[14] While such behaviour can readily be seen to fit those attributes that Eric Hobsbawm assigned to the 'noble robber', such displays of civility had a far more poignant purpose.[15]

Those who managed the penal system in Van Diemen's Land were quick to resort to slurs of criminality whenever they felt that the actions of prisoners eroded or threatened the hierarchical distribution of power relationships. So the official chorus proclaimed these convict bolters to be nothing better than 'scabs of humanity'.[16] Bushrangers such as Cash were engaged in an ideological counter-attack, with displays of civility that mirrored the social mores of the power elite whose position they threatened. The bushranger's 'strong inclination to assume the *habits* of a gentleman' was a powerful and effective weapon used to great effect.[17] For the ruling elite, to be attacked by thugs was simply frightening. To be robbed by convicts effectively mimicking the manners and style of the 'big house' was ideologically devastating.[18]

There can be no doubt that the Patriots understood this subversive theatre and took great heart from it, even though bushrangers were from a class of British felons whom they generally despised. In the admiring accounts of Gates, Heustis and Snow, there were echoes of English and Irish outlaw ballads, which were already being adapted to fit antipodean experience.[19] One popular ballad may have been known to the Patriots, a celebration of the 'wild colonial boy', Jack Donahoe, a bushranger in New South Wales who was shot by police in 1830.

> 'Twas a valiant highwayman and outlaw of disdain
> Who'd scorn to live in slavery or wear a convict's chain;
> His name it was Jack Donahoe of courage and renown—
> He'd scorn to live in slavery or humble to the crown.[20]

In the hell-hole of Van Diemen's Land, Gates explained to his readers, any convict must feel 'every man's hand was against him, and he might be well pardoned for standing out in his own defence' (183). As Gates himself was one 'who had felt so much and so keenly the tyrant's power', the idea that he should join the posse to hunt down those who had stood up in their own defence 'was something that my spirit revolted at' (183, 184). He was much relieved, therefore, to be overlooked when the call went out for ticket-of-leave men to hunt down a pair of bushrangers named Jeffs and Conway. Whether they liked it or not, forty of his fellow Patriots were called out, no matter what sympathy they might hold for their quarry. According to Wright, the governor insisted that 'all the prisoners, having tickets of leave, to go in pursuit', and those who refused to obey the order 'were sent in irons to Port Arthur' (32). Wright found it prudent not to resist the order.

The men were divided into search parties of six to eight, with a constable at the head of each. They were all sworn as special constables and given guns, according to Heustis, 'a musket and five rounds of ammunition, which was all the government dared to allow us, lest we should use the means thus placed in our hands to regain our own liberty' (124). Although hunting bushrangers was a continual chore for the police, they were especially keen to catch Jeffs and Conway, who had killed one of their own. On this matter, Snow's narrative was a good deal less sympathetic toward Jeffs than it was toward Cash. He supplied a graphic description of the murder of the constable:

> The constable, whose name was Ward, rushed in upon them, seized one and threw him upon the floor, and was strangling him, when the other, at the urgent cries of his friend, stepped up and ordered Ward to let up his comrade, or he would shoot him. To this Ward replied, he would never release his hold till he was secure, or as long as he had breath. The Ranger then placed the muzzle of his gun to Ward's head, and blew his brains out.—They then fled, and left Ward on the floor, a horrible spectacle to behold. [22]

Snow himself was not among the forty Americans called up. For those who were pressed into service, such as Heustis, it was a thoroughly disagreeable exercise. He was away from home when called out, and before he had a chance to change his clothes he found himself 'out *seventy-three days*, during which time I never had my clothes or boots off. We slept in the woods, in robes made of opossum skins'. Constantly scouring the hills and forests, Heustis's posse occasionally found evidence of the bushrangers, 'but it never happened to be my good or bad luck to meet them' (124–5).

The luck was all with the party that included Aaron Dresser and Stephen Wright. They too endured an unpleasant time in incessant rain, Wright detailed, but their luck turned when the party decided to seek shelter in a remote shepherd's hut:

> When within about twenty rods of the hut, we saw two men, armed to the teeth, coming out of the door, and from the description, we knew them to be the brigands. When near them, our constable cried 'halt;' but they seemed to have just discovered us, and giving a wild look around them, they ran to the

woods. We were ordered to follow them, and to fire if they did not halt. They found that we gained ground, and each taking a tree, took steady aim at us from behind it; but not one of their pieces would go off, as they had been out the last two days in steady rain. One was armed with a double-barrel gun and four pistols; the other with a rifle, and the same number of small arms. After finding that resistance was useless, they surrendered in a very gentlemanly style. [32]

The two bushrangers seemed to understand that their time was up. 'They had been without food for two days, and had left their cavern that morning in search of it' (33). After a visit to their well-concealed cave hide-out, Wright concluded that, had they not needed food, they would never have been caught. Wright was hugely impressed with the gallantry of the younger man, Jeffs, and his description conjures the archetypal romantic hero: a gypsy, whose 'face was of a melancholy cast, and his form the perfection of manliness' (33). He would be called 'devilish handsome', Wright thought, with 'dark eyes, long eye-lashes; and in his dress, was as neat and trim as a French dandy' (32, 33). True to the form of the outlaw hero, Jeffs announced to his captors that 'death was a fate he preferred to the life of a convict' (33).

At Jeffs' trial, so Wright reported, the bushranger 'made a very remarkable defense; and died, as he had lived, a fearless dare-devil' (33). Here was another common element in the folk tradition, one that required the outlaw to give a good account of himself and die bravely. In fact, Wright could not know how Jeffs died, since the two bushrangers were executed after Wright had left Van Diemen's Land. It was left to Gates to provide the heroic gloss for Jeffs' execution. According to his account, Jeffs' final request was for a clean white shirt in which to be hanged, saying 'I cannot bear to die in this dirty convict's shirt' (185). Gates was among the large crowd that witnessed the execution: he watched Jeffs mount the scaffold 'with a calm countenance and a firm step' and heard him address the assembled throng 'at considerable length in an eloquent and touching manner'. As Gates portrayed him, Jeffs died 'game' in the manner of the famous highwayman Dick Turpin, widely celebrated in songs which were as popular in the United States as in the British colonies.[21] How very sad, Gates reflected after the handsome Jeffs had swung into the air, that a man 'so well endowed to have done the world good service, should come to such an untimely and ignoble end' (185).

In a way, the career of Jeffs and Conway did the Patriots a service. As a result of their capture of the bushrangers, Dresser and Wright were both given free pardons and had their passage to England paid by the British Crown. 'From the time of their capture, we considered ourselves freemen;'

Wright recalled; 'our fondest hopes were realized, and in spirit I had already visited friends and home' (33). The two Patriots were required to wait a few weeks 'until we had been sworn before one of the judges of the Court of Queen's Bench, and our persons fully identified' (33). They were further required to give assurance that they would never to attempt to enter Canada again. It was readily given. When Wright was asked by the Superintendent of Convicts if he would 'again interfere with the British Government in Canada', he very earnestly replied, 'not until the Canadians were worthier of liberty than they are at present' (33).

On 22 June 1843, Wright and Dresser received a free pardon, £25 apiece and a free passage to England. There the US ambassador, Edward Everett, paid their fare back to New York. On arrival they began agitating for the release of the remaining Patriots. In an emotive letter to the *New York Tribune* on 17 February 1844 they recounted the horrors of Van Diemen's Land. 'To be obliged to drag out an existence in such a convict colony and among such a population, is, itself a punishment severe beyond our powers to describe', they concluded.[22] The letter had the desired effect of exerting pressure on the US government to intervene on behalf of the Patriots, and once again Ambassador Everett was directed to ask the British authorities about a pardon for the rest of the American Patriots.

A week or so after the pardons for Wright and Dresser were published in the *Hobart Town Gazette*, several of the Patriots found themselves called out to scour the scrub yet again for Cash, Kavanagh and Jones. Gates again managed to avoid being called up, but Heustis found himself roaming the bush for another seven weeks, with no success. In March 1844, others of the Patriots were called out to hunt another band of rangers. On this occasion, according to Gates, Beamis Woodbury 'had so much of the American spirit that he peremptorily told them he should not lift his hand to fight for them, though they did compel him to go so much against his will' (185). When the posse actually came upon the bushrangers, Woodbury refused to fire when ordered and they escaped unharmed. The disappointed constable, according to Gates, 'therefore vented his spite upon Woodbury, who was brought before a magistrate, his ticket-of-leave broken, and himself remanded again to the roads for a year' (185). Gates does not exaggerate. Woodbury's conduct record shows that he was made a special constable in March 1844 and that on 28 March he was charged with misconduct for 'acting in a cowardly manner on the occasion of his falling in with nine armed bushrangers'. He was deprived of his ticket-of-leave and returned to work on a road gang near Oatlands.[23] Woodbury was still doing hard labour with a road gang eight months later when notice of his free pardon was published in the *Hobart Town Gazette*.

18

Free Pardon

THE PROCESS BY WHICH free pardons were finally granted to the Patriots in Van Diemen's Land was at best chaotic and at worst dastardly.

Late in 1843, having concluded a treaty to resolve the United States' border dispute with Britain, the Ambassador to St James, Edward Everett, arranged an appointment with Lord Stanley to pressure the British authorities to pardon the Patriots. Everett later informed Daniel Heustis that he was personally committed to secure pardons for the Americans, because they 'were mostly young men who had been led by false representation . . . to suppose that the movement in 1838 resembled the revolutionary war in the United States'. Everett also claimed to have formed 'a very unfavourable opinion of Van Diemen's Land as a school of moral improvement'.[1] In response, Lord Stanley took the view that he should not grant an amnesty to the prisoners in Van Diemen's Land. He informed Ambassador Everett, as well as the Patriots' advocate, John Roebuck, that he would look favourably upon petitions on behalf of individual Patriots. Roebuck communicated this to the Patriots in Van Diemen's Land, and as a consequence, a petition by William Kermode and others was sent in April 1844 on behalf of sixty-one Americans.

The usual process of pardoning convicts in Van Diemen's Land involved the sending of a petition by an influential person—possibly a well-connected free settler such as Kermode, or the officer in charge of a penal station—to the Comptroller-General of Convicts, who would make a recommendation on the basis of the prisoner's meticulously documented convict record. This recommendation, together with the petition, would go to the Colonial Secretary, who in turn would advise the Lieutenant-Governor. The petition, plus the recommendation from the Superintendent of Convicts, would then be dispatched to the Colonial Office for the attention of the Secretary of State for the Colonies, who would refer the matter to the Home

Secretary. The consultation with the Home Office was no more than a courtesy, although it had been known for the Home Secretary to object to granting a free pardon to a political prisoner charged with high treason.[2] In due course, the Secretary of State for the Colonies would advise the Prime Minister that the Queen could exercise her royal prerogative and sign a free pardon.

Following a direction from the US President in January 1844, Ambassador Everett undertook to shortcircuit this cumbersome process by applying directly to the Prime Minister, Lord Aberdeen, for free pardons for individual American citizens whose petitions were sent to him by the US Department of State. By May 1844, Everett had applied for twenty-eight free pardons, which were promptly granted. To expedite the American pardons, Ambassador Everett also requested that the newly appointed American consul in Hobart, Elisha Hathaway, help in petitioning for those outstanding, and by July 1844 he had secured pardons for thirty-eight. Petitions for the eight remaining British citizens from Canada, supported by a recommendation by the Governor-in-Council of Upper Canada, were sent to Lord Stanley in 1843. Ambassador Everett was confident 'that every application made in favour of an American was granted as soon as it could pass through forms of office'.[3] In Canada also, there were high expectations that petitions for the eight remaining Patriots who were British subjects would see them released.

These confident expectations were not well placed. It could take up to nine months for communication from London to reach Van Diemen's Land, so the Patriots who had been granted pardons still had a long wait before they might be released from servitude. To complicate matters, Lieutenant-Governor Eardley-Wilmot took the view that he should exercise his own discretion in giving out the pardons in stages, and withholding any pardons for convicts who had bucked the system. As a consequence, not all were given their pardons at the time the pardon warrants were received in the colony. In the case of the British subjects, several of their pardon warrants never even reached Van Diemen's Land to be gazetted by the governor. Three of the Patriots were still waiting for their pardons five years later.[4]

Twenty-eight pardons were dispatched from London in May 1844.[5] They were gazetted in Van Diemen's Land on 27 November. Marsh was very prompt in presenting himself to the Colonial Secretary's office to collect his bit of paper, although he was far from being appreciative that, after being illegally compelled to become a British slave, he could now be said to be a free man. In his sardonic fashion, Marsh asked the bemused clerk whether it was customary to give a prisoner a pardon when he had never received a sentence. After a terse exchange with the chief clerk, Marsh thought it wise to desist in his provocation, 'knowing by the manner they had dealt with us, that they could take the pardon from me and prefer any charge against me they pleased' (176). Flinging over his shoulder the threat that 'the time will come when England will pay dearly for her rascality towards us', he beat a hasty retreat, holding tightly to his passport to freedom.

It took Daniel Heustis somewhat longer to discover that his name had also been gazetted. On New Year's Day 1845 he presented himself at the Colonial Secretary's office to receive the all important paper:

VAN DIEMAN'S LAND.
To all to whom these presents shall come.

I, Sir John Eardley Eardley Wilmot, Baronet, Lieutenant-Governor of the Island of Van Dieman's Land, and its Dependencies, send greeting:—
Whereas, by Her Majesty's royal warrant, under the sign manual, bearing date at Buckingham Palace, the third day of June, one thousand eight hundred and forty-four countersigned by one of Her Majesty's Secretaries of State, and addressed to the Lieutenant-Governor of the Island of Van Dieman's Land for the time being, Her Majesty, the Queen, was pleased, in consideration of some circumstances humbly represented to her, to extend her grace and mercy unto Daniel D. Heustis, who was tried at a court-martial in Upper Canada, and sentenced to death, which sentence was commuted to transportation for life, and to grant him her free pardon for his said crime; now know ye, that I, the said Sir John Eardley Eardley Wilmot, Baronet, Lieutenant-Governor of the Island of Van Dieman's Land, and its Dependencies, have received Her Majesty's warrant, and do hereby certify and declare that the said Daniel D. Heustis hath and ought to enjoy, Her Majesty's free pardon for the said crime whereof he was convicted as aforesaid. And I do hereby discharge the said Daniel D. Heustis from all custody in respect to his said sentence and transportation.
In testimony whereof I have hereunto set my hand, and caused the seal of the Island of Van Dieman's Land to be hereunto affixed.
Dated at Hobart Town, this second day of December, in the year of our Lord one thousand eight hundred and forty-four.
J. EARDLEY-WILMOT.
By His Excellency's command,
J. E. BICHENO, Colonial Secretary.

Another ten pardons were sent during June and July and these were gazetted on 6 December. In all, thirty-five Patriots were pardoned in 1844. Explaining a discrepancy in the number of warrants sent from England and those published in the *Hobart Town Gazette*, Eardley-Wilmot told Lord Stanley that he had kept back the pardons of Joseph Stewart, Linus Miller and Jacob Paddock, who were guilty of absconding, 'as an example and warning to others'.[6] Of course the process by which the pardons were granted was a complete mystery to the Patriots, who were unaware that the governor could exercise his discretion in this way. It was a source of puzzlement to the Patriots that only some of their number had been pardoned, especially those whose names had been on the petition forwarded the previous April. When Marsh tried to find out why some had been pardoned and others not, he was told that the mysterious processes of Her Majesty's government were 'none of your business' (176). The Patriots could not know that the petition sent from Van Diemen's Land on their behalf had missed out on an essential step in the process. There was no recommendation from the new Comptroller-General of Convicts as to the conduct record of each individual named in the petition. This was probably because the petition had been sent when this powerful position had just been created, and as a result the whole convict administration was in turmoil.[7] In September 1844 Lord Stanley had written to admonish Eardley-Wilmot about the petition. Noting that some of the men named had already been pardoned, he told Eardley-Wilmot that he was disinclined to do anything about the rest, since 'you have furnished me with no Report on their conduct'. No further consideration would be given to the petition, he said, 'until I shall have received such a Report from you'.[8] This letter did not even reach Hobart until July 1845, fifteen months after the petition had been sent.

While the freed Patriots were distressed to find that many of their friends were not the beneficiaries of Her Majesty's indulgence, nothing could dispel their joy at receiving this precious piece of parchment. They left the Colonial Secretary's office with a light heart, just as Samuel Snow did, knowing 'that we were at liberty to leave this country, to which none of us had formed attachments that would cause pain in dissolving' (25).

Snow was not entirely correct that none of the Americans had formed attachments in Van Diemen's Land. Two of those pardoned, Moses Dutcher and Robert Collins, did have connections which would keep them in Van Diemen's Land for the rest of their lives. Dutcher had married the previous year, and Collins would marry two years later. James Aitchison, as a rootless British citizen, was less than anxious to return to Canada and was open to the possibilities the Australian colonies presented for new settlers. The rest were simply itching to go home. Marsh undertook to collect them as they straggled into Hobart to sign for their pardons, and to keep them together until an American ship arrived. 'Accordingly we rented a house and kept bachelors' hall', he explained (176). It was a very frugal business, since few had any money, but their luck turned on 15 January, when an American whaler *Steiglitz*, from Sag Harbor, New York, docked in Hobart with 1200 casks of sperm whale oil.

The ship had a damaged rudder and Captain Youngs brought the ship into Hobart for repair. During his time in port, Youngs had trouble with his crew. After a few days' shore leave, seven of his men refused to re-board the ship and warrants had to be issued for their arrest. At the first attempt to put to sea, fourteen of the crew refused duty, forcing Captain Youngs to bring the ship back to Hobart and dismiss the mutinous crewmen.[9] Here was a godsend for the American Patriots, who immediately opened a negotiation with the short-handed captain. Youngs agreed to take all who wanted to leave, but only as far as Hawaii. This was a very generous gesture, even though the men entered into bond to pay thirty dollars when they arrived back in the United States. Few were sailors and Youngs could have easily hired experienced hands for the trip. As the *Steiglitz* sailed down the Derwent River on the morning of the 29 January, she carried 'a jovial company of twenty-seven', according to Heustis:

> How different were my feelings, as I paced the deck, from what they were when I ascended the same stream, in the prison-ship Buffalo, five years before! Then, dark forebodings racked my imagination. Now, instead of gloomy despair, mirth and joy beamed in every face, and liberty's bright banner, the glorious stars and stripes, flaunted in triumph over my head ... What was wealth to me? I was free! With scarcely a penny in my pocket, I felt as rich as Croesus! British tyranny had fastened no stain upon my reputation, and already visions of home, and brighter days, were flitting before me, and I was buoyant with hope! [131–2]

When Linus Miller, who was employed as a clerk in the law office of Mr Macdowell, discovered that his own name had not been on the gazetted list of pardons, as expected, he renewed his threat to sue for damages. At an interview with the governor in February 1845, Miller was characteristically forthright, telling the governor that he had already suffered 'years of horrible slavery' and since the Canadian and British governments had seen fit to give him a pardon, it was 'both unjust and cruel in the extreme to withhold it' (354). To Eardley-Wilmot's stern rejoinder that Miller and several others had had their pardons withheld for violations of the system, Miller exploded in indignation that they were being further punished for being 'American, in spirit and in heart, for not meekly wearing the yoke and kissing the burden upon my shoulders; for daring to evince the spirit and feelings of a man in the presence of my tyrants' (354). Miller got his pardon the next day, but the other two Patriot absconders, Stewart and Paddock, had their pardons withheld indefinitely.

Pleased though he was to be pardoned, Linus Miller was far from grateful, declaring: 'we had been, *de jure, free* men for years and that the abominable slavery we had endured was not only a wanton violation of the laws of justice and humanity, but even of Van Diemen's Land' (352). Assisted by his mentor Macdowell, he immediately set about instigating a suit against the governor for wrongful imprisonment. The Scottish Patriot, James Aitchison, had the same idea. In June, Macdowell, on behalf of Aitchison, issued a writ for trespass against the Superintendent of the Prisoners' Barracks, Mr Gunn. This lawsuit was to be heard in the Supreme Court later that year.

In July 1845, a further eleven pardons were gazetted, including that of William Gates. He was not aware of the glad tidings when he ran into William Kermode, who was a member of the Legislative Council that had just approved the pardons. At first Gates feared Kermode was merely tantalising him and would not believe he was pardoned until he saw the actual words of his name printed in the paper:

> It seemed as though my heart would burst through my bosom, or choke up my throat, it leaped so wildly; and my whole frame seemed so suddenly to expand, and to such a degree, that I incontinently put out my hands to pull down my trowsers legs, that I imagined had shrunk above my knees; whilst my coat sleeves in like manner were left near the elbows, vainly endeavouring to cover the arms below; and my vest was nigh to bursting its buttons, so tight had it come to be about my body. It actually seemed that my body would burst its garments asunder, and leave me standing there before the man of office in a state of nudity. I know not how else I acted. I was in a delirium of joy and felt entirely like a new man. [189]

Riley Whitney was another name on the list. Gates had the notion that he and Whitney should immediately quit the island and go to the Australian mainland, where employment prospects were better. Passing through Oatlands on their way to Hobart to collect their pardons, Gates claimed that they came upon an execution of a woman charged with murdering her child. A little later, they were witnesses to the execution of two women, this one especially gruesome. When the trap-door opened and the women swung free, Gates was revolted to see that one continued to struggle until the hangman 'jumped upward, grasped the feet of the criminal, which he pulled downward with his whole force, swinging himself clear of the ground for the space of a minute or more' (192). With Van Diemen's Land thus 'horribly stamped upon the memory' (192), Gates and Whitney signed for their pardons and departed for Melbourne on the very same day.

As he took a last look at the accursed place which had so broken his health that the doctors thought he would not last more than a few months, Gates reflected his experiences were like 'a terrible dream'. His first encounter in Hobart Town had been the sight of men hanging on a scaffold and almost his last was 'the more disgusting sight of women on those same gibbetts' (192). Certainly these executions provided Gates with an effective framing device, but he was overstating his case for political effect, as he so often did. Just as he had shifted the date of the executions at the time of his arrival, so Gates also exaggerated the number of women hanged to coincide with his exit. No woman was hanged in Oatlands in 1845, nor were two women hanged in Hobart. However, it is very possible that Gates witnessed the execution of one woman, Eliza Benwell, who was hanged for aiding and abetting the murder of a maidservant, Jane Saunders. Eliza was another maid at the same residence and she had protested her innocence to the very end. She was hanged with a man also convicted of the murder, William Taylor, on 16 September 1845, just about the time that Gates and Whitney were preparing to depart. Interestingly, her body was ordered for dissection by the surgeons. The newspaper account of Eliza Benwell's execution makes no mention of any struggle with death, although there was ambiguity in the comment that 'her appearance on the fatal scaffold indicated none of the weakness which from her sex many expected'. Perhaps that was a polite way of suggesting that her neck did not snap with the first jerk of the rope.[10]

Elijah Woodman was one of eight more Patriots who were pardoned in July 1845. At the time his name was gazetted, he was very ill and troubled by infected eyes that made him all but blind. His scant diary entries detail a desperate existence. For days he had been unable to leave his bed and had gone for forty-eight hours without food. He feared going out because 'I am so ragged I am not fit to be seen my clothes being pawned for food'.[11] He was entirely dependent on the goodwill of his friends and had appealed to the Freemasons to save him from starvation. Yet even in his appalling state, Woodman sat down to thank 'the wise disposer of events' as soon as he returned to his meagre lodgings with his pardon.

After enduring years of awful silence, Woodman had suddenly begun to receive mail from home. Through the intervention of Roebuck, he discovered that his letters, and those of others, had been held up for over two years. On this day he was not disposed to complain about this deliberate cruelty. His life was painfully hard, yet he was confident that he could get a passage home, just as three of his fellow patriots had done on the whaler *Eliza Ann* that had left in June. He had secured for himself a return berth on a whaler that had left Boston for Hobart the previous February, but it had been lost at sea. Now he would have to wait till December because whaling traffic to Hobart had ceased. 'Be assured', he wrote, 'I will do my utmost to be with you as soon as possible . . . no Crowned Head shall ever overshadow this child again'.[12] His only cause for gloom was that eighteen of the Patriots still had not received a pardon.

In August 1845, it became apparent that as yet nothing had been done to furnish a report on the conduct of the sixty-one Patriots named in Kermode's petition, as requested by Lord Stanley. Subsequent correspondence on the matter indicated that the petition had been lost and that no one knew which men were named in the petition. The Colonial Secretary sought help from Hathaway, the US consul, who replied with a list of the names of seventeen Americans yet to receive their pardons. Hathaway's letter was duly filed away in the Colonial Secretary's correspondence files, but there is no evidence that as a result of this letter, a report on any of these men was forwarded to Lord Stanley, or that Hathaway's list of names of those whose pardons were outstanding was referred to again.[13]

The only Patriot name not included in Hathaway's list was that of Jacob Beemer, the egregious villain of the Short Hills. By informing on and stealing from his fellow Patriots, Beemer had put himself beyond the pale. However, he did have friends in Canada and in August 1844 a pardon for him had been sent to Eardley-Wilmot, who declined to gazette it. By 1845 Beemer's convict conduct record was a litany of serious charges; at the time the pardon was received, he was still serving various sentences of hard labour in convict gangs. Eardley-Wilmot seems to have shared the opinion attributed to his predecessor that 'the most charitable thing to do with Beemer would be to hang him'.[14]

Meanwhile, by the end of 1844, the US House of Representatives Committee on Foreign Affairs had become agitated that so few of the Patriot prisoners had been released. In January 1845 it resolved that the President instruct Ambassador Everett to interpose on behalf of the American prisoners.[15] In the meantime, Linus Miller had progressed his idea of a suit against the British government to a point where he now felt able to take action in the English courts. He was dubious about the prospects of the action taken by Aitchison in the Supreme Court of Van Diemen's Land, believing that 'a disposition was early manifested by the judges to defeat it' (368). On 25 September 1845, Miller left for London, armed with a letter from Hathaway to Ambassador Everett asking for help in Miller's action for damages against the British government on behalf of those who had been 'illegally held in bondage' (368).

This move was not an example of wishful thinking: Miller had a compelling legal case. Though he was probably not aware of it, the Law Officers of the Crown and the Colonial Office had expressed great concern between July 1838 and May 1839 about the legality of the Act under which he was sentenced, and at the time they expressed the fear that the Crown would be exposed to writs for wrongful imprisonment.[16] He never did get the chance to test the legality of his transportation. *En route* to England Miller's ship encountered an American passenger ship destined for Philadelphia. The lure of home was too great. He cast his role as republican hero to the winds, negotiated a deal for his passage with the American captain, and headed for home.

One need only compare Miller's picture of himself in his narrative with the actual record of his legal encounters to understand why he was so quick to negotiate a passage to Philadelphia rather than to go to England to pursue a case for illegal imprisonment. Rhetoric aside, he had no faith in his capacity to win legal argument in a court of law, as opposed to the pages of a book, any more than he did when he chose to plead insanity at his trial in Niagara in 1838. He had already been through the British legal system, from top to bottom, and failed, with resulting mortification and misery. He probably could not face the prospect of going through it again, even though his lawsuit would hugely benefit his American comrades, especially those who still remained in penal servitude when he departed from Van Diemen's Land. At some level Miller knew he was abandoning these less fortunate comrades. Their 'forlorn condition' (368) preyed on his mind as he sailed away. 'I paced the deck for some time', he wrote at the end of his narrative, 'my breast heaving with uncontrollable emotions and tears gushing from my eyes, in spite of my efforts to restrain them' (368–9). To his credit, when he arrived back in the United States he did write a letter to a New York newspaper to plead for intervention on behalf of those Americans still in Van Diemen's Land, but he took no further part in processes to secure their freedom.[17]

At the end of 1845, only three more Americans had been pardoned: Henry Shew, Hiram Loop and Norman Mallory. For the other men listed in the American consul's letter, the silence about their pardons was intolerable. Totally bemused as to why he was still not a free man, Calvin Mathers sent an angry letter to Hathaway:

> As a citizen of the United States of North America I would Request of you as Consul for that Government to demand from the proper authorities in Vandemans land the reason that I am now or have been hear a prisoner of the Crown of England. I would further request that you would make a demand of a copy of all papers which I have been or am now held a prisoner in this colony and transmit a copy of the same to the Congress of the United States at the earliest opportunity.[18]

Likewise Jacob Paddock, still waiting to receive the pardon he had been granted eighteen months before, petitioned yet again for his freedom.[19] George Cooley, the young man who had arrived on the *Marquis of Hastings* in 1839, was in such despair of gaining freedom that he secreted himself aboard a whaler on 19 January 1846. He was found by a constable and sentenced to another year of hard labour.[20]

In December 1845, the remaining Patriots were downcast to hear that James Aitchison's lawsuit for trespass had been thrown out by the Supreme Court, without being heard, on the technical grounds that too much time had elapsed. This was a severe blow. The community of Patriots left in Van Diemen's Land had dwindled to twenty-six, of whom over half were still in servitude. Of these, Elijah Woodman was the most distressed, suffering from dangerously poor health and greatly dispirited by his failure to secure a berth to America. He had been taken in by Joseph Stewart and Robert Collins, who did their best to care for him, and he had been granted an annuity of £5 a week from the Freemasons which kept him alive. He was at his lowest ebb in February when he found a captain prepared to take him back to America on the ship, *Young Eagle*. Sick and penniless, with nothing but a sheet of paper to leave as his memorial to seven years in Van Diemen's Land, Woodman penned an unrepentant letter to those who had befriended him in his exile. His only regret, 'after all the tyranny and oppression that has been illegally dealt out and exercised over me which has broken me down and impaired my constitution' was the loss of his compatriots:

> When I look back in my minds eye and see all the blood and tears that have been shed, the cries of the widows and orphans . . . who have been deprived of their nearest and dearest ties of nature that bind them together it is heartrending. From what did this originate? I will tell you it all emanated from that sink of iniquity the Colonial Secretary's Office, Downing St, where there never came any good.[21]

When the *Young Eagle* departed 'that cursed land of Van Deman' on 3 March 1847, Woodman's friend Henry Shew was also aboard as the ship's carpenter. It was Shew who was able to complete the daily entries in Woodman's diary when he became too ill to write, and it was Shew who made the coffin for Woodman's burial at sea on 15 June. When Shew himself finally returned to his home in New Jersey in February 1848, he found that his wife had given him up for dead and married another.[22]

In his last letter before boarding the *Young Eagle*, Woodman remarked that Aitchison had gone to the mainland of Australia and he doubted that he would ever return to America. Aitchison was following in the footsteps of several others who had decided the Australian colonies were more promising than the Canada they had left. Certainly the new settlement at Port Phillip (later Victoria) was more to Gates's liking. He declared it to be 'one of the best countries for a poor man, as far as money-getting, there is on the globe' (209). He especially liked it because 'there are less convicts mixed in, and these are for the most part confined to the towns on the seaboard' (209). He and Whitney stayed contentedly in Port Phillip for over a year, working for a succession of settlers, yet they never lost the yen for home, and in 1847 they headed north to the port of Sydney in search of American ships. As soon as they arrived in Sydney they found a New Bedford whaler, the *Kingston*, which had been at sea for four years and had managed to take only 1440 barrels of oil. With such a small cargo, the apprehensive captain decided to sell up and send his ship home by other hands. Gates and Whitney were taken on as passengers to New Bedford for a hundred dollars apiece.

En route to New Bedford the *Kingston* passed close to the coast of Van Diemen's Land, and Gates was disturbed to see that the place he thought so detestable was indeed very beautiful:

> Thus it often is, that our associations make hideous what otherwise might be very pleasant. But *there* indeed the tyrants had deformed the loveliness of nature, and made the sylvan wilderness a pandemonium of misery. How then could a fair exterior look beautiful to him who knew of the vile abominations that lay hid within? [217]

The *Kingston* set a direct course from Van Diemen's Land to New Bedford and made landfall on 31 May 1848. Gates could once again tread 'the soil of glorious New England' (224). Not long after, he found himself once again in the bosom of his astonished family.

Back in England the wheels of government turned slowly for the sixteen men who remained unpardoned in Van Diemen's Land. In July 1846, the new Secretary of State for the Colonies, Lord Grey, finding himself under pressure from the US government, wrote again to Eardley-Wilmot, calling his attention to the conduct report on the American prisoners requested by Lord Stanley nearly two years before. While he acknowledged that the majority of those in the petition had been pardoned, Grey found himself 'totally without information concerning the remainder'. He reiterated the request made by Lord Stanley 'that you would report to me, by the earliest practicable opportunity what opinion you entertain of their conduct ... [and] the behaviour of any Canadian Prisoners remaining in exile in Van Diemens Land, who were not included in the Petition'.[23]

By the time this letter was received in Van Diemen's Land, Eardley-Wilmot was mortally ill. His successor, Sir Thomas Denison, who became the governor in January 1847, knew nothing of the matter. Nevertheless, a report was sent by the Comptroller-General of Convicts on 9 February. The report referred to the conduct of several prisoners, including Alson Owen who was dead, as well as Benjamin Wait and Samuel Chandler who had escaped the island five years earlier. Absent from the report was any mention of William Reynolds, George Cooley, Horace Cooley and Patrick White, even though each of these men was still in servitude and had been listed in the American consul's letter.[24] When Her Majesty's government responded to this report, it was noted that pardons had already been issued for Joseph Stewart, Jacob Paddock and Jacob Beemer, so it was presumed these men had been pardoned already. When the pardon documents were received in January 1848 their names were not appended.[25] Pardons were gazetted for only eight of the sixteen. Beemer, who was by now married, wasted no time in drawing attention to the absence of his name, and managed to secure a pardon in April, as did Paddock.[26]

Although the British government believed that the pardons gazetted in 1848 covered all the remaining Patriot prisoners, unknown to them six men still remained in servitude. The most vulnerable was Horace Cooley, who was consistently left out of any indulgences made to the Patriots because he had been sentenced for burglary in a criminal court and had not been tried on the same charge as the other Americans. Whereas all the others were given a ticket-of-leave after two years, Horace Cooley had to serve out a term of more than four years in the gangs. Also his pardon was not the same as those of his compatriots. In April 1849 he was given a conditional pardon which still confined him to the Australian colonies. Ironically, in recommending a pardon, the Comptroller-General of Convicts remarked of Cooley that he had served nine-and-a-half years of a sentence for 'a minor offence' and had no bad conduct against him, implying that he should have been pardoned long since.[27] In fact, Horace Cooley had been issued a full and free pardon in March 1844 following representations in Canada, but it had never reached Van Diemen's Land. The Irish Patriot, Patrick White, was another who had fallen through the cracks in the system. He was recommended for a pardon by the Comptroller-General in 1848, but it was not until February 1850 that he was granted a conditional pardon only.[28] Neither Horace Cooley nor White seems to have left the island. Cooley married in 1850 and White also may have married and remained in Van Diemen's Land.

Joseph Stewart had been granted a pardon early in 1844, but it was never gazetted, while William Reynolds was just ignored, perhaps because a young man using the same name had been pardoned in England. Stewart and Reynolds made good their escape from Van Diemen's Land some time in February 1850, probably on board an American whaler. Also left off the list was George Cooley. Illiterate and without family at home to intercede for him, Cooley was simply forgotten. He had not a mark against him on his convict conduct record until he had tried to escape on a whaling ship in 1846, obviously desperate that he was not going to get a pardon. He was sentenced to another year of hard labour in a Hobart road gang. In May 1849, understanding that he was in Van Diemen's Land for the term of his natural life, Cooley applied to marry a fellow convict; but no marriage took place, and his intended later married another man. After that disappointment, Cooley's clean record shows a marked change. In June 1850, he was caught out after hours, which cost him four days in an appalling solitary cell and the loss of his imminent pardon.[29] Late in 1851 he finally received a conditional pardon, which did not permit him to leave the Australian colonies. In 1853, he quit Van Diemen's Land for Victoria. George Cooley was last heard of when he was arrested by the police at Avoca in Victoria on 29 October 1856, charged with embezzling money belonging to his employer.[30] It is not known what then became of him.

Most capricious of all was the treatment of John Berry, who had gone to work as a shepherd in the remote northwest of the island in 1842. He was pardoned in October 1844, but was never told that he had been discharged from servitude. Even when he sought permission to marry on 7 February 1854, no one thought to tell him that he was no longer a convict.[31] When he came into Hobart in 1857, the authorities were very surprised to find that he was still in the country. After seventeen years in the island colony he did not suffer from torn loyalties. He caught the first American ship that would take him home. He worked his passage on a South Seas whaler, finally arriving at his home in Brockville, Upper Canada, in June 1860, twenty-two years after he had left to join the Patriots at the windmill.

Afterword

FOURTEEN OF THE Patriot exiles died as a result of their transportation to Van Diemen's Land. The great majority of those who survived, nearly 70 per cent, returned to North America. Only the first and the last to leave their antipodean place of banishment, John Tyrrell and John Berry, went back to their homes in Canada. At least ten men elected to stay in the Australian colonies, although more may have done so, as there are fifteen Patriots who cannot be traced in the official records.

It does not appear that any of them, even the firebrand Robert Marsh, was ever tempted into political action again. Certainly, they had no further interest in the liberation of their Canadian neighbours. Most would bitterly agree with Stephen Wright, that a people who could not help themselves were not worthy of the glory of a republican government. In any case, Canada had changed dramatically in their absence. As a result of Lord Durham's controversial report that had sparked uproar in the British parliament, Upper and Lower Canada had been united under one governor in 1842 and a measure of self-government implemented. By 1848 self-government was finally entrenched in Canada with the election of a reform majority in parliament and the accession to power of the reform ministry of Robert Baldwin. One of the early actions of Baldwin was to pass a bill pardoning William Lyon Mackenzie, the father of the 1837 rebellion and scourge of the Canadian Tories. Disillusioned with the United States, Mackenzie returned to Canada in 1850 to find a transformed society where new men were in control of its affairs, where the ideas of reform he had promoted to such denunciation were now part of the machinery of government, and where fellow reformers, once driven from the country, now occupied posts of high responsibility. There was no longer any reason for him to rally men across the border to help break the chains that bound his fellow Canadians to the Crown.

In the border states of the United States, restless and radical young men had other matters to consume their violent energies by the 1850s. Men who might once have joined the Patriot Hunters now turned their eyes towards the violent internecine struggle over slavery in the territory of Kansas. Had they been twenty years younger, the anti-slavery Patriots might well have been among the grim young men riding into the night with John Brown and his sons to strike the first spark of what was to become a terrible civil war. It was not until that long and bloody war was finally over that Americans in the border states turned their attention once more to the British rule in Canada. This time invasion was plotted by another secret organisation in New York.

The Fenian Brotherhood was established in 1857 by a group of veterans from the 1848 Rising in Ireland to train and recruit soldiers to drive the British out of Ireland. The Brotherhood's ambition was initially focused on the liberation of Ireland, but a militant Fenian faction advocated extending the war of liberation to British North America with the objective of seizing major cities and transportation centres in Canada, and then negotiating with the British to exchange Canada for Ireland's independence. More realistic members of the Fenian Brotherhood concentrated on the option of using a surprise attack on Canada to force the British Empire to reinforce Canada with large detachments of regular troops, and so create a favourable climate for an armed uprising in Ireland.

By April 1866, thousands of volunteers, many of them former Union and Confederate soldiers, had been organised into secret Fenian regiments along the border, replicating the Hunters' Lodges in many ways. Like the Hunters, the Fenian hierarchy had established a centralised command structure and a clandestine system of communications. They had a serious stockpile of weapons and ammunition, as well as skilled manpower, with the Civil War veterans on hand to drill and impart their experience to raw recruits. As in the late 1830s, the Fenian communications were not so clandestine that the Canadian authorities were unaware of their intentions. War plans were well-known and openly discussed in Irish-American communities and British informers easily infiltrated the Fenian ranks. Correspondence from the British Embassy in Washington notified authorities in Canada of virtually every Fenian move. As early as March 1866, 10 000 Canadian militia were placed under arms and stationed on the border as a precaution against an anticipated attack.

On the night of 31 May 1866, eight hundred armed Fenians crossed the Niagara River at Buffalo, repeating the folly of the Patriots over a quarter of a century before. Their incursion was more successful than the Short Hills fiasco, but it failed ultimately in the objective to seize the Welland Canal and paralyse shipping between Lakes Erie and Ontario. The Fenians easily managed to occupy Fort Erie, and cut telegraph lines and the railroads at Buffalo and Lake Huron. On 2 June they drove back Canadian forces at Ridgeway, with the loss of ten dead and thirty-eight wounded, before retreating to Fort Erie, where they beat off another Canadian militia force. When the US authorities cut their reinforcements, the Fenians retreated back into New York State near Buffalo, where all were captured. Just as President Van Buren had done twenty-eight years earlier, President Andrew Johnson dashed the Fenians' hopes on 5 June, when he declared that the Neutrality Laws would be upheld. Even so, another 1000 Fenians crossed the Canadian border into Quebec, but they were quickly forced to retreat when the US authorities seized their supplies.[1]

After this rash of hostilities ended, Fenians who had been imprisoned by the United States were quietly released. Those who had been captured in Canada found themselves in much the same pickle as the Patriots. In order to deal with the Fenian invaders, the Canadian parliament revived the long dormant Lawless Aggressions Act that had caused such trouble when applied to the Patriots. This act had not been disallowed by the Crown in 1839 and had been revised and strengthened in 1840.[2] Between June and August 1866, it was further amended and applied retroactively to enable subjects and foreigners alike to be tried as regular criminals. The legislation was henceforth known as the Fenian Act.[3] Unlike the Patriot raiders, who were almost all American citizens, the Fenians were largely Irish who had recently immigrated to the United States, and so most were tried as British citizens unless they could show proof of their American citizenship. Twenty-two were convicted and sentenced to death, which was commuted to life imprisonment following intervention from President Johnson. None was sent to a penal colony.

The Patriots were the last prisoners in Canada to suffer that fate. An attempt by Governor Arthur to transport two more rebels, Livingstone Palmer and Hirum Munn, who had been belatedly tried for treason in 1840, proved fruitless. Although Arthur had exacted a promise from Lord John Russell that these two would also be transported, Russell had consistently refused to send a ship to take them to the hulks.[4] In the case of the Patriots, transportation was used as a political tool for the repression of dissent in the Canadian colonies, and to curtail the cavalier activity of the Hunters' Lodges along the US border that had so profoundly threatened Anglo-American relations. The Fenian raiders represented no such threat, neither to Canadian political stability nor to relations with the United States.

Early in 1865, Prime Minister Lord Palmerston announced that penal transportation to Australia would come to an end within three years. In this matter he proved as good as his word. The last convict ship landed at Fremantle in Western Australia on 10 January 1868. Even so, the British government managed to make political use of the system until the end. Most prominent among the cargo of felons on that final ship were fifty-seven Fenian prisoners from Ireland whom the British government had determined to remove as far away from Ireland as possible, this side of the hangman's noose.[5] These Irish rebels included the writer and editor John Boyle O'Reilly, who managed to escape on an American whaling ship the following year and then helped master-mind the daring rescue of the last of his transported compatriots in April 1875.[6]

The Fenian prisoners were sent to the raw colony of Western Australia because Van Diemen's Land would no longer take them, transportation to the island colony having stopped in 1852. Even by the time the Patriots were signing for their pardons, agitation against the convict system had risen to a clamour, especially among the colony's moral guardians, who were concerned about a virtual epidemic of unnatural vice. In July 1846, twenty-five clergymen sent a petition to the Secretary of State for the Colonies, Lord Grey, begging for an end to a system they insisted was no more than an incubator of homosexuality, reiterating Linus Miller's observation that 'hundreds of abominable crimes against nature ... are daily committed at this *Sodom*, as it is significantly and properly termed' (347). Charles La Trobe, the man briefly appointed to replace Eardley-Wilmot in 1847, pronounced the probation system 'a vicious ... fatal experiment' and advised Lord Grey that the sooner it was ended the better.[7] Within two years it was not simply probation, but the entire system of transportation under concerted attack by the Anti-transportation League which had been formed by the colony's most prominent settlers.

The Crown had invested vast sums equipping the island colony for the reception of the Empire's criminal flotsam and political troublemakers, and Lord Grey was very reluctant to put a stop to penal transportation to Van Diemen's Land. It was his successor, Sir John Parkinson, who finally called the halt. Only the dreaded penal station at Port Arthur continued as the responsibility of Her Majesty's government, used to house the very last of the old lags still in penal servitude, as well as indigent and mentally ill ex-convicts.[8] Marcus Clarke, who had immortalised Port Arthur in his epic novel *For the Term of his Natural Life,* visited the penal station in the early 1870s and reported on 'the jetsam' of the transportation system who still remained about the place, making a feeble pretence of gardening and other light duties.[9] In 1877, the key turned in the lock for the last time and the bricks of the massive penitentiary, many of them under-fired and puddled with sea water, began to crumble into the dust.

In 1840, when Linus Miller first approached Port Arthur from the sea, he was struck by the natural beauty of the setting, on the edge of a spacious bay and surrounded by lovely, wooded hills. 'Nature has done her part in rendering it one of the most pleasant and romantic places in that quarter of the globe', he wrote, 'but *man* has converted it into a home of woe, sin and shame. The dreadful scenes enacted here despoil nature of all her loveliness, and stamp gloominess, despair and death, upon every object' (326). Miller would have taken much satisfaction had he known that half-a-century later, nature reclaimed Port Arthur and purged the pollution of the penal system. After the site was abandoned, a series of bushfires roared through Port Arthur on three separate occasions, the last and most destructive in December 1897, which all but obliterated the penitentiary and its sub-sidiary structures.[10] Within days of that last fire, tourists were arriving to wander through the fire-gutted ruin, which appeared rather romantic against the sylvan backdrop. The ruin of Port Arthur has persisted into the twenty-first century as one of Australia's major tourist icons.[11] Now every year, thousands follow in the footsteps of Linus Miller up the avenue of oak trees to the ruined Gothic church. From there they look down over the 'dark picture of Van Diemen's Land' and wonder if they have learned any wisdom.

Biographies of the Patriot Exiles

compiled by Elinor Morrisby

Code

MH *Marquis of Hastings*
C *Canton*
B HMS *Buffalo*
N tried at Niagara
K tried at Kingston
L tried at London, Ontario
SH invasion at Short Hills

P invasion at Prescott
W invasion at Windsor
BR Probation Station, Brown's River
SB Probation Station, Sandy Bay
LB Probation Station, Lovely Banks
GP Probation Station, Green Ponds

Aitchison/Aitcheson, James Milne (915) B W L SB LB GP
A native of Peebles, Scotland, who emigrated to Upper Canada in 1834, Aitchison was aged thirty, 5 feet 6 inches tall and the son of a wealthy Edinburgh brewer. At his trial he claimed that he came over to Windsor to inquire about a letter at the post office and was forced to march with the Patriots, but made his escape as soon as possible. He was taken prisoner the same day. Aitchison was the nephew of the Reverend William Proudfoot, and his relatives in Upper Canada made every effort to procure a free pardon for him but his character was considered 'not otherwise respectable', his political crime having been 'aggravated by the isolation of his allegiance and his disregard for those actions which connected him with Upper Canada'.

In Van Diemen's Land he was an overseer at Green Ponds, at Lovely Banks, and at Bridgewater, where a bridge was being constructed over the Derwent River. He was at Victoria Valley as an overseer when he received a ticket-of-leave on 9 February 1842 and was working in Oatlands in January 1844. A free pardon was issued on 3 June 1844 and on 11 December 1846, Aitchison brought suit against the British government for false imprisonment. He was the only political prisoner sent to Van Diemen's Land who did this, but the case was dismissed on a technicality. In 1847, Elijah Woodman recorded that Aitchison had slipped across to mainland Australia. 'I do not think he will ever reach America,' Woodman added.

Allen, David (914) B P K SB LB GP
A native of Massachusetts and resident in Volney, New York, with his wife and their four children, Allen was aged thirty-seven, 5 feet 7 inches tall, a ploughman and member of the Baptist Church. At his trial Allen said that he embarked at Oswego on the *United States* on 10 November 1838 to go to Ogdensburg for his own business, was put on board a schooner in the St Lawrence River against his will, landed at Windmill Point and was asked to take arms, which he refused.

In Van Diemen's Land he received a ticket-of-leave on 9 February 1842 but was charged with misconduct, drunkenness and rioting after hours on 8 August 1842 and subsequently fined five shillings. On 23 August, the suspicion of stealing a hammer was made against him, but this accusation was dismissed. His free pardon was gazetted on 30 July 1844. He is known to have worked in Oatlands in January 1844 and was supposed to have left Van Diemen's Land that year. In the Oswego County Census records of 1855, Allen is recorded as living in a log cabin in Volney with his wife Elizabeth and their three children. He is not listed in the 1860 Census that records his wife and five children.

Baker, Thomas (3102) B P K SB LB GP
Born in Minden, New York, and resident in Hannibal, Cayuga County, Baker was aged forty-seven, 5 feet 6½ inches tall, a farm labourer and married with seven children. He was a Methodist and had lived in Canada before the 1812 war. At his trial he said that he was told that the object was to change the government of Canada and that there would be no fighting. In the papers that accompanied the warrants from Canada, Baker was 'acknowledged to be a Drunkard; and alleged that, without any previous connection with the pseudo-patriots, he was tempted, whilst in a state of intoxication, to join in the expedition against Prescott'.

In Van Diemen's Land while a ticket-of-leave holder, he was fined ten shillings for being drunk on 19 December 1843 and received fourteen days' solitary confinement, similarly on 25 March 1844 for the same offence. His free pardon was received in Van Diemen's Land on 1 August 1845.

Barnum, Henry Verelom (3107) B W L SB LB GP
Born in Charlotteville, Long Point, Canada, a resident of Ypsilanti, Michigan, with his wife and three children, Barnum was a ploughman, aged twenty-six years and 5 feet 7 inches tall. At his trial he stated that he crossed over

from Detroit in a small boat on 3 December 1838 and landed near Windsor. When travelling toward Chatham, he heard the firing of cannon, and was subsequently arrested in the company of James Fero who had been with him the whole way.

In Van Diemen's Land he received three days' solitary confinement for feigning sickness in January 1841 at Green Ponds. In December 1841 he was working with the Mount Dromedary Party. A free pardon was signed on 27 January 1845 and on that day, he departed Van Diemen's Land on the schooner *Steiglitz*.

Beemer/Beamer, Jacob (3098) C SH N
A native of Oakland, Upper Canada, married with two children, Beemer was aged twenty-nine and described as being 5 feet 11 inches tall, with a dark complexion, long head, dark-brown hair, black whiskers, long visage, medium forehead, brown eyebrows, blue eyes, medium nose, medium mouth and long chin. He had a scar over his right eye. He was an innkeeper and carpenter and owned 300 acres in Oakland. He had been involved in the insurrection in London, Ontario, under Dr Duncombe.

When he arrived in Van Diemen's Land, the surgeon's report stated that he was 'an excellent, trustworthy, good character in every aspect' and he was almost immediately made a constable. However, the list of Beemer's offences was extensive. On 29 May 1840 while in the Prisoners' Barracks, he received twelve months' hard labour on the roads for embezzling the sum of three shillings and eight pence, the property of James Baker. As Special Messenger in the Prisoners' Barracks on 2 June 1840, he embezzled two cloth coats valued at five shillings and other articles, the whole under the value of six pounds, the property of Linus Miller and other Patriots and his sentence of twelve months' hard labour was extended by a further twelve months. It was recommended he be sent to Port Arthur, where he remained until mid-1841, during which time he was reprimanded for insolence on 29 January and suffered five days' solitary confinement for misconduct on 5 March. He was located at Mount Dromedary in December 1841 and on 4 March 1843 was placed in solitary confinement for misconduct while employed by the Public Works. On 7 April 1843, he was charged with being out after hours and received six weeks' hard labour. He worked in Bothwell from April 1843 and in July of that year was a carpenter working on the Police Buildings when he was accused of burglary and misconduct. These claims were discharged, but he was subsequently reprimanded for misconduct on 3 November 1843. He was accused of misconduct in working for private persons as a carpenter in government hours and was sentenced to hard labour for six weeks. He was assigned to Mr Reid, and on 1 October 1844 a subsequent accusation of having committed a felony was discharged.

A similar offence while in the employ of Mr Donaldson on 8 November 1844 was also discharged. On 6 January 1845, while working for Mr Fisher, Beemer was charged with misconduct in proceeding to Oatlands without permission, and he received three months' hard labour which was extended by a further six months on 30 September 1845 as a result of his having five pounds in his possession for which he had no satisfactory explanation. A free pardon was not issued until 4 November 1848. In January 1848, Beemer sought permission to marry Ann Walker and the marriage took place at St Luke's Church, Richmond, on 24 January 1848. After her death sometime between 1855 and 1860, he married Mary Kilford. He had three children from his first bigamous marriage and two from his second. In 1863, Beemer purchased land in the township of Lennon on Bruny Island.

Berry, John (3105) B P K SB LB GP
A native of Columbia County, New York, Berry was a widower aged forty-two, a farm labourer and Presbyterian, who was 5 feet $10\frac{1}{2}$ inches tall. At his trial he said he was visiting his parents in Oswego when he was promised sixteen dollars a month to assist in fortifying an island between Ogdensburg and Morristown as winter quarters for the Patriots' preparations in their attack on Canada. He boarded a steamboat at Oswego and said he wished to land at Sackets Harbor when he found out they were going to make an immediate attack.

In Van Diemen's Land, he was charged with being absent without leave on 16 November 1840 while at Lovely Banks, and at Green Ponds on 5 January 1841 he left the station without permission and returned with flour in his possession for which he could not account. For this mis-demeanour, he was given three days' solitary confinement on bread and water. From July 1841 he was located at Salt Water Creek and he was there when a ticket-of-leave was issued on 10 February 1842. He was repri-manded for exposing his person on 5 July 1842. A free pardon was received on 7 January 1845, but remained unsigned until 1857. John Berry sought permission to marry Elizabeth Donahoo on 7 February 1854, but the mar-riage, if it ever took place, was never registered. He apparently left Van Diemen's Land in 1857 and arrived in Elizabethtown, Upper Canada, in July 1860.

Blodgit/Blodgett, Orlin/Orlan/Orrin (3103) B P K SB LB GP
Born in Jefferson County, New York, a resident of Pamelia, aged twenty-three years, Blodgit was a carpenter and joiner, of no religion. At his trial he said he was promised ten dollars a month to join the Patriots, eighty dollars bounty, and 160 acres of land.

In Van Diemen's Land he was located at Brown's River when he received a ticket-of-leave on 10 February 1842. He was working in Oatlands in August of that year and a free pardon was granted on 25 October. He left on an American whaler and returned to Black River, where he died on 9 April 1873.

Bradley, John (3106) B P K SB LB GP

A native of County Antrim, Ireland, Bradley was taken to Canada in 1826 as a baby, and then to the United States in 1829. He resided in Sackets Harbor, Jefferson County, New York, was aged twenty, a hatter, 5 feet $5\frac{1}{2}$ inches tall and a Roman Catholic. At his trial he said he was standing on the wharf at Ogdensburg on 12 November 1838, was seized by three men who forced him into a skiff and took him across the river to Windmill Point, where he said 'he was all the time hid in a cellar'.

In Van Diemen's Land, while on probation at Green Ponds, he was charged with misconduct, insolence and refusing to work on 16 and 17 April 1841. He received forty-eight hours' solitary confinement for both offences, the latter on bread and water only. The Muster of December 1841 lists him as being in the Prisoners' Barracks, Hobart. A ticket-of-leave was awarded him on 10 February 1842 and as holder of this ticket, he was charged with misconduct on 15 April 1843 and was given six days' solitary confinement. On 3 November 1845, he was accused of disturbing the peace and received a sentence of fourteen days' hard labour. A free pardon was received 22 February 1848 and he married Ellen Hayes, aged nineteen, on 7 April 1856 at the Cathedral Church of St David's in Hobart Town. His occupation at that time was given as baker.

Brown, George T. Thomas G. (3101) B P K SB LB GP

A native of Evans Mill, Jefferson County, New York, Brown was aged twenty-two, 5 feet 4 inches tall, a blacksmith, of no church and never baptised. At his trial he said that a man named Wells promised to get work for him, and at Wells's request he went on board a schooner at Millen's Bay, where he learnt the object of the Patriot party.

In Van Diemen's Land he was located at Brown's River when a ticket-of-leave was issued on 10 February 1842, and he is known to have been in Bothwell on 25 March 1843. He was then located in Oatlands on 22 August 1843. A free pardon was granted on 7 December 1844. He left Van Diemen's Land on a whaler in January 1845 and reached America three years later. When the whaler landed at New Bedford, Massachusetts, the captain abandoned the crew, and Brown made his way to Theresa where he set up a blacksmith's shop. He died in 1889.

Bugby/Bugbee/Bugbie, Chauncey (3104) B P K SB LB GP
A native of Jefferson County, New York, resident in Lyme, Bugby was aged twenty-two, 5 feet 5½ inches tall, a ploughman of no religion. At his trial he said he was aboard a schooner at Millen's Bay and could not get on shore again although that was his wish.

In Van Diemen's Land he was stationed with the Mount Dromedary party when he was issued with a ticket-of-leave on 10 February 1842. He received a free pardon on 14 February 1845. He sought permission to marry Eliza Hughes in July 1846. There is no record of the marriage, but several children were registered between 1846 and 1850.

Calhoun, Hugh (2579) B PK SB LB GP
A native of County Donegal, Ireland, and resident of Salina, Onondaga County, New York, Calhoun was aged twenty-five, 5 feet 8½ inches tall, a member of the Church of England and a farm labourer. At his trial he said he was engaged by a person unknown to go to Canada to work at twelve dollars a month and was sent to Oswego; his passage was paid and he was told to take the steamboat that would carry him where he was wanted. He had a ticket from his employer who procured his passage, meals, etc., but stated he did not know his employer's name.

In Van Diemen's Land he was part of the Mount Dromedary party when a ticket-of-leave was issued on 10 February 1842. His free pardon was ultimately granted on 22 February 1848. Aged thirty-six, he married Margaret Gittens, aged twenty, in Hobart on 18 April 1853. They had three children and all births were registered in Hobart.

Chandler, Samuel (2482) MH S N
Born near Albany, Connecticut, in 1791, Chandler had resided in the Province of Upper Canada for eighteen years with his wife Elizabeth and their eleven children. He was naturalised under Canadian Naturalisation Law. He was described as being 5 feet 7 inches tall, aged forty-eight, with a fair complexion, a long head, brown hair, red whiskers, oval visage, medium forehead, brown eyebrows, hazel eyes and medium mouth and chin. He had a scar on the forefinger of his left hand and a mole on his right cheek. He was a wagon maker and wheelwright, and owned 200 acres and two village lots in St Catharines. Since 1835, he had been a Member of the Masonic Order of St George's Lodge, St Catharines. John Johnson Lefferty, a witness at his trial, stated that he had known Chandler for sixteen years; until within about two years he was always considered a most respectable inhabitant; he held real estate in the province, had built a house and voted at elections.

In Van Diemen's Land he was admitted to the Colonial Hospital, as he was sick on arrival, and was later assigned with Benjamin Wait to the property Ashgrove near Oatlands. Although he was listed in the December 1841 Muster as holding a ticket-of-leave, he absconded from his authorised place of residence and escaped with Benjamin Wait in late 1841, possibly assisted by fellow Freemasons. He left on board the American whaler *Julian*. He was reunited with his family in 1842 at Niagara Falls, after a voyage of seven months via Rio de Janeiro. He and his family moved to Jackson, Michigan, then to Maquetoka, Iowa, where he died, aged seventy-six years on 26 March 1866. He was a founder of Helion Lodge No. 36 in Iowa. Descendants of Chandler are living in Iowa.

Collins, Robert Green (2577) B P K SB LB GP
A native of Ogdensburg, St Lawrence County, New York, Collins was aged thirty-four, 5 feet 9 inches tall, a shoemaker and described as a coal merchant. At his trial he claimed he was compelled to take arms.

In Van Diemen's Land he was located with the Mount Dromedary party when a ticket-of-leave was issued on 10 February 1842. A free pardon was signed on 7 December 1844. On 17 October 1849, Collins was described as a forty-year-old shoemaker when he married Catherine Gaffrey aged thirty-two, a spinster, at the Melville St Wesleyan Chapel. Four children were baptised at St Andrew's Presbyterian Church. Collins died on 25 February 1855 and was buried in the Presbyterian burial ground, Hobart.

Cooley, George (2481) MH S N
Born in Mt Pleasant, Michigan, Cooley had lived in Upper Canada for two years. He was nineteen years old, an American farmer, labourer and ploughman, 5 feet 5 inches tall, with a dark complexion, round head, brown-black hair, oval visage, high forehead, brown eyebrows, hazel eyes, small nose, large mouth and chin, with a scar on his right cheek.

In Van Diemen's Land he was first in the Hobart Town Prisoners' Barracks, then on assignment. He received a ticket-of-leave on 4 August 1841 and is known to have been working in Oatlands in September 1843 and then in Fingal from 21 November 1843 to 6 January 1844. On 19 January 1846, he absconded and was found concealed on board the American whaler *Bail* having intended to escape. He was given a punishment of twelve months' hard labour on 23 January 1846 and his ticket-of-leave was cancelled on 10 March. He sought permission to marry Catherine McIntosh on 29 May 1849, but there is no record of the marriage. Cooley had been in the colony for eleven years and seven months when a dispatch dated 29 April 1850 gave him a conditional pardon. However, on 3 June, he was charged with being out after hours and received four days' solitary confinement. A dispatch dated 7 April 1851 from the Comptroller-General's Department notes that a free pardon had been granted. Cooley departed Van Diemen's Land in 1853 and went to Victoria, where he was charged with embezzling money from his employer in October 1856.

Cooley, Horace (2575) B
Born in Pennsylvania, Cooley and his wife resided in Michigan. He was twenty-five years old, a farm labourer, 5 feet 6 inches tall, of fair complexion with red hair, hazel eyes and a flesh mole on his upper lip. He was imprisoned in London, Ontario, in January 1838 following the invasion across Lake St Clair and was tried in Upper Canada on 26 September 1838 for burglary.

In Van Diemen's Land he attempted to escape from the Sandy Bay party with William Reynolds, Jacob Paddock and Michael Morin on 9 June 1840. He was sent to Port Arthur to hard labour for two years. It was recommended that he work separately under this sentence and his conduct be specially reported. Cooley was at Port Arthur from June 1840 until mid-1842, and he was issued with a ticket-of-leave on 24 May 1844. A conditional pardon was recommended on 6 June 1848 and granted on 12 April 1849. There is no record of his having received a free pardon. He married Mary Skinner in Hobart on 25 June 1850.

Cronkhite, John (2576) B P K SB LB GP
A native of Oswego County, New York, resident in Alexandria, Jefferson County, Cronkite was aged twenty-nine, 5 feet 9 inches tall, a blacksmith and widower with one child. At his trial he stated that he came to Millen's Bay and went on board a schooner there, but was not allowed on shore till he landed at Windmill Point.

In Van Diemen's Land he committed no offences. A ticket-of-leave was issued on 10 February 1842 and a free pardon on 27 January 1845. He left on the *Steiglitz*.

Curtis, Lysander (2578) B P K SB
Born in Vermont, and residing in Massachusetts with his wife and three children, Curtis was a shoemaker and had worked for some time in Ogdensburg. He was aged thirty-three years, 5 feet 9 inches tall. At his trial Curtis said that he had been induced to cross to the Windmill and that he was wounded in the action.

In Van Diemen's Land he fell ill while working on the roads and died in the Colonial Hospital sometime between 23 February and 1 April 1840.

Darby, Luther (1461) B P K SB LB GP
A native of Massachusetts and resident of Watertown, Jefferson County, New York, Darby was a 48-year-old widower with four children, 5 feet 8 inches tall and a ploughman of no religion.

In Van Diemen's Land he was with the Jericho party when he was issued with a ticket-of-leave on 10 February 1842. A free pardon was recorded and signed on 7 December 1844. He left Van Diemen's Land on the *Steiglitz*.

Delano/Delino, Leonard (1460) B P K SB LB GP
A native of Jefferson County, New York, and resident of Watertown, Delano was a blacksmith, aged twenty-five years, 6 feet $\frac{1}{2}$ inch tall who owned a small farm and was a member of the Episcopal Society. At his trial he said he was sworn in as a Hunter at Dexter and landed at Windmill Point on 12 November, having sent his rifle from his home before him.

In Van Diemen's Land he was stationed at Brown's River when a ticket-of-leave was issued on 10 February 1842, and was later at Campbell Town. A free pardon was signed on 10 December 1844. He left Van Diemen's Land on the *Steiglitz*.

Dresser, Aaron (1458) B P K SB LB GP
Born in Alexandria, Jefferson County, New York, Dresser was aged twenty-two years, 5 feet $10\frac{1}{2}$ inches tall, a Windsor chair maker and a Baptist. At his trial Dresser denied that he was an officer, but a paper in code taken at the same time turned out to be a commission to him as second lieutenant. He kept a daily diary while on board the *Buffalo*, which is now in the National Archives of Canada. The papers that accompanied the warrants from Canada recorded that several most respectable inhabitants of Kingston presented a petition stating that Dresser's father was a man of good character and his deep anxiety for his son was evidenced by his frequent and urgent solicitations on his behalf. A free pardon would probably have been granted for Dresser if there had not been strong reason for believing that he had an officer's commission.

In Van Diemen's Land he was with the Rochey Hill party when a ticket-of-leave was issued on 10 February 1842. On 23 June 1843, Dresser was rewarded for his part in capturing the two bushrangers, Jeffs and Conway, with a free pardon and the sum of £33 6s 8d. Dresser left Van Diemen's Land on the *Areta* on 22 July 1843 and went to England, then on to New York.

Dutcher, Moses A. (1459) B P K SB LB GP
A native of Montgomery County, New York, resident in Brownsville, Jefferson County, Dutcher was a carpenter and joiner, aged twenty-three years,

5 feet 7 inches tall, and a Methodist. At his trial he said that he came from Dexter to Ogdensburg on 13 November, crossed the river, landed about a mile from Windmill Point and spent two days going through the woods endeavouring to find his way to his uncle in Camden.

In Van Diemen's Land he was located at Brown's River Station on 30 August 1841 when charged with having tobacco in his possession. Dutcher was still with the Brown's River party when a ticket-of-leave was issued on 10 February 1842. From February to April 1842, he was at Campbell Town and from 6 June 1843 to 5 February 1844 at Swansea. A free pardon was recorded on 3 December 1844. Dutcher married Sarah Birchill/ Burchell on 27 February 1844. A daughter Sarah was born 12 September 1844. There is no record of Dutcher and his family having left Van Diemen's Land.

Fellows/Fellowes, Elon (976) B P K SB LB GP
A native of Dexter, Jefferson County, New York, Fellows was aged twenty-three, 5 feet 9 inches tall and a cooper.

In Van Diemen's Land he committed no offences and a ticket-of-leave was issued on 10 February 1842. He was located in Bothwell on 25 February 1842, and on 28 June 1843, the Lieutenant-Governor ordered that favourable consideration be given for his good conduct in the pursuit of the bushrangers Jeffs and Conway. A free pardon was signed for on 23 January 1845 and he left Van Diemen's Land on board the *Steiglitz*.

Fero, James De Witt (978) B W L SB LB GP
A native of Long Point, Upper Canada, and a resident in Ypsilanti, Michigan, Fero was aged twenty-five, 5 feet 9 inches tall and a ploughman. At his trial he stated that he crossed from Detroit to Upper Canada on 3 December 1838 in company with Henry Barnum but was not connected with the Patriots.

In Van Diemen's Land Fero was located at Salt Water Creek when he received a ticket-of-leave on 10 February 1842. From 25 August 1843 to 6 January 1844 he was in Oatlands. A free pardon was recorded and signed on 26 December 1844. He left Van Diemen's Land on board the *Steiglitz*.

Fraer, Michael (977) B P K SB LB GP
A native of Clay, Onondaga County, New York, Fraer was aged twenty-three years, 5 feet 7 inches tall and a cooper. The papers which accompanied the warrants from Canada record that 'such strong recommendations of this man have been received, that he seems to be hardly, if at all, less entitled to indulgence than those included in the class of 17'.

In Van Diemen's Land he was charged with destroying his clothing and insolence to Mr Lord, saying he wanted a trial on 11 November 1840. For these misdemeanours, he received three days' solitary confinement. On 17 March 1843, with a ticket-of-leave, he was in Campbell Town and charged with knowingly and maliciously supplying unwholesome provisions to the Ross chain gang. He was committed for trial and appeared in the Supreme Court on 7 April 1843. He was in the gaol at Oatlands on 11 April 1843 and on 28 July was in Campbell Town. At the age of twenty-seven, he married Jany Bryan, aged nineteen, in Avoca on 8 August 1843. A free pardon was issued on 7 January 1845. Fraer departed on the *Swan* on 2 May 1848.

Garrison, Emanuel (1483) B P K SB LB GP

A native of the State of Vermont, a resident of Brownsville, Jefferson County, New York, Garrison was a blacksmith, aged twenty-five years and 5 feet 9 inches tall.

In Van Diemen's Land he was stationed at Brown's River when he received his ticket-of-leave on 10 February 1842. He was in Campbell Town on 25 December 1842 and on 28 June 1843, the Lieutenant-Governor ordered that favourable consideration be given for his good conduct in the pursuit of the bushrangers Jeffs and Conway. A free pardon was signed on 19 February 1845. He left Van Diemen's Land on the *Eliza Ann* in June 1846.

Gates, William (1480) B W L SB LB GP

A native of Fairfield, New York, and a resident of Lyme, Jefferson County, Gates was aged twenty-four years, a labourer and ploughman, 5 feet 6 inches tall. The papers that accompanied the warrants from Canada record that 'Strong certificates of general good character, numerously signed, have been presented in his favour'.

In Van Diemen's Land he was at Jericho when he was given a ticket-of-leave on 10 February 1842. In April, he was located in Swansea, and he was admonished firstly for being out after hours on 26 November 1842 and secondly for misconduct while working in Campbell Town on 26 July 1844. He was in Oatlands in March 1845. A free pardon was received on 1 July 1845 and he departed Van Diemen's Land for Melbourne in September with Riley Whitney. Two years later he left Sydney bound for America, arriving in New Bedford aboard the *Kingston* on 31 May 1848.

Gemmell/Gammell, James (1474) C S N BR

Born in Kilmarnock, Ayrshire, Scotland, Gemmell had been a resident of Upper Canada for six years and was a lieutenant in the Patriot Army. He was aged twenty-three, 5 feet 8½ inches tall, of pale complexion, with a round head, dark-brown hair, red whiskers, oval visage, high forehead, dark-brown eyebrows, hazel eyes, small nose, large mouth and medium chin. He had scars on his left and right arms and left forefinger, was a gardener and Presbyterian.

In Van Diemen's Land he was first in the Hobart Town Prisoners' Barracks, then moved to Brown's River, where on 16 March 1840 he was accused of misconduct in having made skewers for his own benefit. His punishment was hard labour on the roads for three months with the Bridgewater road party. In July 1840, Gemmell was transferred to Lovely Banks, then to Green Ponds. The Director of the Probation Department on 8 November 1841 recorded that, in addition to good behaviour, alacrity, steadiness and a respectful demeanour, Gemmell volunteered to accompany officers and constables in search of five absconders and was instrumental in their capture. A ticket-of-leave was issued on 27 January 1842, but Gemmell escaped on a whaler from the colony in late 1841 and returned to America, then to Canada. Gemmell's first wife died in 1847 and subsequently he worked in Salt Lake City with the Mormons, where he was appointed Supervisor of Roads. According to his daughter, Josephine, he had five wives and twenty-two children.

Gilman/Gillman, John (1482) B P K SB LB GP
Born in Oneida County, New York, a resident in Jefferson County, Gilman was aged thirty-eight, 5 feet 8 inches tall, a labourer and ploughman and married with five children. He had neither joined any church nor been baptised. At his trial he said he volunteered freely to join the Patriot force, but understood there would be no fighting. He expected that he was rendering a service to mankind in assisting the people of Canada to obtain a free government.

In Van Diemen's Land he was issued with a ticket-of-leave on 10 February 1842 and a free pardon was signed on 7 December 1844. He left Van Diemen's Land on the *Steiglitz*.

Goodrich, Gideon A. (1484) B P K SB LB GP
A native of Massachusetts who resided in Salina, Onondaga County, New York, Goodrich was aged forty-three, 5 feet 6½ inches tall, a hatter and labourer, a widower with two children and of no church.

In Van Diemen's Land it was recorded in Goodrich's favour, in addition to good behaviour, steadiness and respectful demeanour, that he had volunteered to accompany officers and constables in search of five absconders and had been instrumental in their capture. In August 1841 he was at Constitution Hill. From September 1841 to February 1842 he was located at Swansea and was issued with a ticket-of-leave on 10 February 1842. A free pardon was signed on 5 December 1844 after some discrepancies arose regarding correct identification. He left Van Diemen's Land on the *Steiglitz*.

Grant, John (1475) C SH N BR SB LB GP
An Upper Canadian, Grant was aged thirty-four, married and a wheel-wright and wagon maker. He was described as 5 feet 4 inches tall, with a sallow complexion, round head, dark-brown hair and whiskers, oval visage, high forehead, brown eyebrows, hazel eyes, small nose, small mouth and medium chin.

In Van Diemen's Land his ticket-of-leave was issued on 27 January 1842. A free pardon was issued on 13 May 1844, but Grant did not leave Van Diemen's Land until 27 January 1845 when he departed on the whaler *Steiglitz*.

Griggs, Jerry/Jeremiah Caddy (1481) B P K SB LB GP
A native of Connecticut, resident in Salina, Onondaga County, New York, Jerry Griggs was aged twenty-four years, a labourer and ploughman, 5 feet 6 inches tall and a Methodist. At his trial he said that he was in Oswego and took a passage on the *United States* steamboat, that he was not asked for passage money but in the night was forced on board a schooner and landed at Windmill Point. The papers that accompanied the warrants from Canada record that a touching application on behalf of him and his brother Nelson was received from his aged and bereaved parents, backed by a recommendation from several persons.

In Van Diemen's Land he was issued with a ticket-of-leave on 10 February 1842 while located at Brown's River. As a holder of this ticket, he was charged with misconduct and given twenty-four hours' solitary confinement on 27 December 1842. A free pardon was recorded and signed with an 'X' on 25 January 1845. He left Van Diemen's Land on the *Steiglitz*.

Griggs, Nelson James (1485) B P K SB LB GP
Jerry Griggs's brother from Connecticut also resided in Salina, Onondaga County, New York. Nelson Griggs was aged thirty years, a labourer and ploughman, 5 feet $7\frac{1}{2}$ inches tall, married with three children. At his trial he stated that he embarked on the steamer *United States* and landed at Windmill Point, where he was induced to assist the Patriots in Canada by false representations.

In Van Diemen's Land he was issued with a ticket-of-leave on 10 February 1842. On 22 February 1842 he was assigned to Bothwell. A free pardon was signed on 20 December 1844. He left Van Diemen's Land on the *Steiglitz*.

Guttridge/Gutridge, John Seymour (1486) B W L SB LB GP
A native of Cayuga County, New York, Guttridge was aged thirty-five and a ploughman, 5 feet 4 inches tall. At his trial he stated that, believing the Canadians to be in a state of revolt, he crossed over with others to assist, but

before arriving at Windsor, ran into the woods. He said he belonged to the secret society and had been promised eight or nine dollars a month and 300 acres of land.

In Van Diemen's Land a ticket-of-leave was issued on 10 February 1842 and he received a free pardon on 10 November 1846.

Heustis, Daniel D. (2605) B P K SB LB GP
A native of Cheshire, New Hampshire, and resident in Watertown, New York, Heustis was aged twenty-seven years, a grocer and leather-goods salesman, 5 feet 10 inches tall and of no church. At his trial he stated that he paid one dollar for a passage to Ogdensburg, that he went on board a schooner in the night, was confined in the hold and refused to go on shore. The papers that accompanied the warrants from Canada noted that 'this man's station in society appears to have been rather above that of the generality of the brigands and the applications in his favour have accordingly been from persons of higher influence. But his standing in his country has been considered as furnishing an argument against, rather than in favour of, the grant of a Free Pardon, which has been solicited for him in many quarters.'

In Van Diemen's Land a ticket-of-leave was issued on 10 February 1842 and on 28 June 1843 the Lieutenant-Governor ordered that favourable consideration be given for his good conduct in the pursuit of the bushrangers Jeffs and Conway. A free pardon was recorded and signed on 8 January 1845. He left Van Diemen's Land on the *Steiglitz*. Heustis's name was not found as a resident in any of the Watertown directories, which date back to 1859 and 1860, so he probably did not return.

Hicks/Hick, Garrett (2607) B P K SB LB GP
From Alexandria, Jefferson County, New York, Hicks was a farmer aged twenty-seven years, 5 feet 10 inches tall, married with one child and belonging to no church. At his trial he denied ever having any knowledge of the Patriot party, or their designs, or having been at the mill. He said he was going to South Crosby where he had a piece of land with a crop in it.

In Van Diemen's Land a ticket-of-leave was issued on 10 February 1842 and a free pardon was received on 3 December 1844, recorded and signed with an 'X' on 9 January 1845. He left Van Diemen's Land on the *Eliza Ann* in June 1846.

House/Howth, David (2606) B P K SB LB GP
Born in Montgomery County, New York, resident in Alexandria, Jefferson County, House was aged twenty-six, 5 feet $5\frac{1}{4}$ inches tall, a labourer and ploughman, of no religion and never baptised. At his trial he said that he had been hired by a stranger to chop wood for no particular wages, and he went

as directed to Millen's Bay where this same person sent him on board the schooner. He stated that he knew nothing of the Patriot party.

In Van Diemen's Land he was located at Salt Water Creek when a ticket-of-leave was issued on 10 February 1842 and he was in Oatlands on 3 August 1843. A free pardon was recorded and signed with an 'X' on 26 December 1844. He left Van Diemen's Land on the *Steiglitz*.

Inglis, James (145) B P K SB LB GP
A native of Paisley, Scotland, resident in Adams, Jefferson County, New York, Inglis was aged thirty years, a weaver and ploughman, 5 feet 7½ inches tall. At his trial he said that he took a gun but did not fight.

In Van Diemen's Land he was working with the Salt Water Creek party when a ticket-of-leave was issued on 10 February 1842. As a holder of this ticket, he was charged with misconduct on 21 July for not going from the township when ordered and was handed a sentence of one month's hard labour with the town surveyor's gang in Hobart. His ticket-of-leave was suspended. A free pardon was granted on 31 July 1847. Inglis left Van Diemen's Land from Launceston on the *Alice* on 8 January 1852 as a steerage passenger.

Leeper, Andrew (1249) B P K SB LB GP
A native of Harrison County, Kentucky, and a resident of Lyme, Jefferson County, New York, Leeper was aged forty-two, a labourer and ploughman, 5 feet 7¼ inches tall and a member of the Church of England. He had worked in Canada, boating for two seasons. At his trial he said was promised eighty dollars bounty and ten dollars a month while on Patriot service.

In Van Diemen's Land a ticket-of-leave was issued on 10 February 1842, but Leeper died on 22 February 1842.

Leforte, Joseph (1250) B P K SB LB GP
Born in Montreal, Lower Canada, and resident in Lyme, Jefferson County, New York, Leforte was aged thirty-three, a stonemason, 5 feet 3 inches tall. At his trial he stated that three strangers paid to ferry them over and that they landed below Prescott, a little above the mill. They went off and he walked up the bank to look round; when he returned his boat was gone and he could not get away.

In Van Diemen's Land he was at Salt Water Creek when he received his ticket-of-leave on 10 February 1842. At the end of that month he was working in Campbell Town. A free pardon was received on 1 July 1845 and he left Van Diemen's Land on board the whaler *London Packet* on 15 April 1846.

Liscum/Liskum, Daniel (1247) B P K SB LB GP
A native of New York, a resident in Lyme, Jefferson County, Liscum was a
widower aged thirty-five with one child, a ploughman, 5 feet 6 inches tall
and a Methodist. At his trial he stated that he landed at the Windmill, but
had run away from the Patriot party. He added that he was promised eighty
dollars the moment he landed and 160 acres of land after the conquest of
the country.

In Van Diemen's Land a ticket-of-leave was issued on 10 February 1842.
He was working in Oatlands on 29 March 1843. A free pardon was received
on 12 October 1844 and signed with an 'X' on 17 March 1845. He left Van
Diemen's Land on the *Eliza Ann* in June 1846.

Loop, Hiram (1248) B P K SB LB GP
Born in Scruple, Onondaga County, a resident in Oswego County, New York,
with his wife and three children, Loop was aged twenty-six, 6 feet 2 inches
tall, a labourer and ploughman of no religion. At his trial he said that he
was forced to take arms and go out but surrendered without firing a shot.

In Van Diemen's Land he was charged with disobeying orders and
threatening to tackle his overseer while discharging his duty on 21 November 1840. He was given seven days' solitary confinement on bread and
water. On 4 December 1840, he was working with the Green Ponds party
and for a charge of insolence received ten days' solitary confinement. He
was accused of misconduct on 11 May 1841 while working with the probation party at Green Ponds and endured three days' solitary confinement.
A ticket-of-leave was issued on 10 February 1842. From 6 October 1842 to
5 January 1844 he was at Fingal. A free pardon was received on 9 September 1845 and he left Van Diemen's Land for Sydney on the *Longer* on 17 February 1846. He departed from Sydney on the *Two Brothers*, a whaling boat,
on 17 March 1846.

Mallory, Norman (1776) MH SH N
A native and resident of Scarborough, New York, Mallory was aged twenty-four, 5 feet 6 inches tall. He was described as having a pale complexion,
round head, reddish hair, oval visage, high forehead, brown eyebrows, blue
eyes and medium nose, mouth and chin. He had a scar on his forehead and
another on his left thumb. Mallory was a labourer and circular sawyer, a
farmer's son.

In Van Diemen's Land he committed no offences and received a free
pardon on 25 November 1845. He left the island on 9 March 1846 for mainland Australia.

Marsh, Robert (1852) B W L SB LB GP
A native of Detroit, Michigan and a resident in Niagara, New York, Marsh was aged twenty-five, 5 feet 8 inches tall, a baker and ploughman. At his trial he denied being connected with the Patriots and refused to make any further statements.

In Van Diemen's Land he was with the working party at Salt Water Creek when he received a ticket-of-leave on 10 February 1842. A free pardon was signed on 26 December 1844 and Marsh left Van Diemen's Land on the *Steigliz*.

Martin, Jehiel H./**Murton**, Jehil Hall (1847) B P K SB LB GP
Born in Grafton County, New Hampshire, and resident in Oswego, New York, Martin was aged thirty-two, 5 feet $10\frac{1}{4}$ inches tall, a stonemason and bricklayer and a Presbyterian. At his trial he said that he did not understand an immediate invasion of Canada was intended. He believed that a party was to take possession of an island in the St Lawrence River and assist in preparing the winter quarters for the party desirous of making a change in the government of Canada and that he would be paid for this.

In Van Diemen's Land he received a ticket-of-leave on 10 February 1842, and on 25 February he was known to have been working in Oatlands. A free pardon was received 1 July 1845. Martin is supposed to have gone to Sydney in September 1846.

Martin/Martins, Foster (1849) B P K SB LB GP
A native of Onondaga County, New York, resident in Antwerp, Jefferson County, Martin was aged thirty-two years, a farm labourer, 5 feet 5 inches tall, and a widower with two children. At his trial he stated that he was going from Watertown to collect about six dollars from a man who lived at the rear of Brockville. He took a passage on one of the schooners and was forced to land at the Windmill with the Patriot party.

In Van Diemen's Land he was working in Swansea when a ticket-of-leave was issued on 10 February 1842. In January 1845, Linus Miller listed him as having died in Van Diemen's Land.

Mathers, Calvin (1846) B P K SB LB GP
A native of Onondaga County, New York, a farm labourer, Calvin Mathers was aged twenty-four years, 5 feet 6 inches, belonging to no church and married with one child. At his trial he stated that he was brought to Canada against his will and left the Patriots before the battle, and that he was trying to get across the river when he was taken.

In Van Diemen's Land a ticket-of-leave was issued on 10 February 1842. On 12 April 1844, he was fined twenty pence for indecently exposing his person, and on 18 August 1845 he received fourteen days' hard labour for misconduct. A free pardon was received on 22 February 1848.

Mathers, Chauncey (1848) B P K SB LB GP
Calvin's twin brother, Chauncey Mathers was a native of Onondaga County, New York, who resided in Salina. He was aged twenty-four years, 5 feet 7¼ inches tall, a sawyer. At his trial he said that he came down the river to Sackets Harbor in search of his brother, was forced along with the Patriot party and was escaping when taken prisoner.

In Van Diemen's Land a ticket-of-leave was issued on 10 February 1842 and he was working in Campbell Town on 28 February. He received a free pardon on 22 February 1847. On 28 October 1847, he was charged with being drunk and was fined eight shillings. There is no record of his leaving Van Diemen's Land.

McLeod, Alexander (1211) MH SH N
An Upper Canadian from the town of East Gwillimbury, McLeod was aged twenty-four, a carpenter and farmer, and suspected of being a Mackenzie rebel (with James McNulty).

In Van Diemen's Land he was admitted to hospital on arrival and died on 24 July 1839.

Miller, Linus Wilson (1840) C SH SB LB
Born 1 January 1819 in Stockton, Chautanqua County, New York, Miller was aged twenty, a law student who owned no property. He was described as being 6 feet tall, having a fair complexion, round head, brown hair and whiskers, oval visage, medium forehead, brown eyebrows, hazel eyes, medium nose, mouth and chin. The report of the surgeon of the *Canton* recorded that he was a well-conducted, quiet young man.

In Van Diemen's Land, after being held in the Prisoners' Barracks in Hobart Town, Miller worked at Brown's River felling trees and as a watchman. At Lovely Banks he attempted to escape with Joseph Stewart in August 1840, which resulted in a sentence on 16 September 1840 of two years' hard labour out of chains at Port Arthur. The Muster of December 1841 lists Miller at Port Arthur, where he worked as a gardener, washerman, church clerk and school teacher for the convict settlement. A ticket-of-leave was issued on 17 November 1843 and he later became private tutor to the Lempriere family. A free pardon was recorded and signed on 8 February 1845. Miller worked for a year in a law office in Hobart. He left Van Diemen's Land on the barque *Sons of Commerce* on 25 September 1845. At Pernambuco, he transferred to the US barque *Globe* and landed at Newcastle, Delaware. In 1850, he married Ann Jeanette Curtis and settled on his old family farm near Delanti, New York, where he died in April 1880.

Moore, Andrew (1850) B P K SB LB GP
Born in Saratoga County, New York, a resident in Lyme, Jefferson County, Moore was aged twenty-six, 5 feet 8¼ inches tall, a farm labourer and Methodist. At his trial he denied taking arms and said that he was on board the steamboat and wished to leave but was prevented.

In Van Diemen's Land a ticket-of-leave was issued on 10 February 1842. On 28 June 1843, the Lieutenant-Governor ordered that favourable consideration be given for his good conduct in the pursuit of the bush-rangers Jeffs and Conway. On 14 November 1843 he was located at Fingal. A free pardon was received 1 July 1845.

Morin, Michael (1853) B W L SB
A native of Bordeaux, Lower Canada, and a resident of Lockport, New York, Morin was aged thirty-one years, a joiner, 5 feet 3 inches tall, with a dark complexion, black hair and hazel eyes.

In Van Diemen's Land, he was charged with absconding from the Sandy Bay party on 9 June 1840 with Horace Cooley, Jacob Paddock and William Reynolds and was removed to Port Arthur on 18 June 1840. He was held there to hard labour for two years and it was recommended that 'he should be worked by himself'. The abscondment notice in the *Hobart Town Gazette* dated 15 May 1840 lists Morin as being a native of France, but this is an error. He was appointed to work for the superintendent at Port Arthur and his conduct to be specially reported. On 6 November 1840, he received twenty-five stripes for misconduct. If Morin were flogged, he is the only Patriot to have received this punishment. The Muster of December 1841 lists him as being at Port Arthur. A ticket-of-leave was issued on 19 May 1843. As a ticket holder he was fined five shillings for drunkenness on 30 September 1844. He was located at Bothwell on 6 October 1843 and at Campbell Town from January to October 1844. A free pardon was received on 1 July 1845.

Morrisette, John/Jean (1851) B P K SB LB GP
A native of Lower Canada, a farm labourer, Morrisette was aged twenty-two years and 5 feet 9 inches tall. At his trial he said that he was hired in Lewisburgh by a Yankee at ten dollars a month and was placed in charge of another person (Leforte) and put on board a schooner and taken down the river; and that he did not know the design of the Patriot party.

In Van Diemen's Land he was at Jerusalem when a ticket-of-leave was issued on 10 February 1842. In June that year he was known to have worked in Oatlands. A free pardon was received on 23 July 1844 but it was never signed by Morrisette himself. Guillet asserts that Morrisette left Van Diemen's Land in 1844, but no verification of this has been found.

Mott, Benjamin (3008)
Born in Alberg, Vermont, Mott was aged forty-seven, married with five children, described as a farm labourer, 5 feet 9½ inches tall, with a fresh complexion, flat head, grey hair, grey whiskers, square visage, medium high forehead, grey eyebrows, grey eyes, long nose, medium mouth, round chin and was a member of the Church of England. He was tried at a court martial in Montreal on 1 May 1839 for his part in the invasion of Lower Canada. He was transported on the *Buffalo* and arrived in Van Diemen's Land on 12 February 1840 but did not land and went to New South Wales with the rest of the Lower Canada prisoners.

Mott returned to Van Diemen's Land on the *Waterlily* in February 1844, after having applied to be with the Americans. Mott worked for Elijah Hathaway, the American consul, and received his free pardon on 14 January 1845.

Nottage, William (502) B W L SB
A native of Halifax, Nova Scotia, a resident in Amhurst, Ohio, married with six children, Nottage was aged forty, 5 feet 5 inches tall and a ploughman. At his trial he stated that he went on board a steamboat for the purpose of being brought over to Canada and when the Patriots took possession of the boat, they asked him to take arms, which he refused. When he saw burning buildings he hid in a barn, left at daylight, stayed at a tavern and was arrested there.

In Van Diemen's Land, Nottage died on 18 April 1840 after an accident involving explosives while he was working at the Sandy Bay Probation Station.

Nulty Mc, James John (489) MH SH
An Upper Canadian, McNulty was aged thirty-one, a carpenter possibly from Niagara. He owned property along Yonge Street in Toronto and was suspected of being a Mackenzie rebel before the invasion of the Short Hills.

In Van Diemen's Land he died in the Colonial Hospital on 19 July 1839, having contracted consumption on the voyage.

Owen, Alson (264) B P K SB LB GP
A native of Palermo, Oswego County, New York, Owen was aged twenty-seven, 5 feet 7¼ inches tall, a farm labourer and an Episcopal Methodist. At his trial he said that he landed at Windmill Point, having come with his uncle David Allen from Ogdensburg, and that he knew nothing of the expedition and took arms because he was threatened.

In Van Diemen's Land he received a ticket-of-leave on 10 February 1842 and died later that year while working on the property of William Kermode.

Paddock, Jacob (1559) B P K SB LB GP
Born in Lyme, Jefferson County, New York, and resident of Salina, Onondaga County, Paddock was aged twenty, single, a farm labourer, 5 feet 4 inches tall, with a dark complexion, dark brown hair and hazel eyes. At his trial he denied taking arms and said he was pulled on board the steamboat *United States* and brought against his will. The papers that accompanied the warrants from Canada stated: 'The very bad conduct of this individual prevented him from participating in the free pardon which was granted to all the other youths'.

In Van Diemen's Land he attempted to escape from Sandy Bay with Horace Cooley, William Reynolds and Michael Morin on 9 June 1840 and was subsequently captured and removed to Port Arthur to hard labour in chains for two years. It was recommended that Paddock 'be worked by himself and his conduct at Port Arthur specially reported'. He was charged with wilfully destroying government bedding on 27 June 1840 and suffered three days' solitary confinement on bread and water. On 16 March 1842, he received the same sentence for misconduct and on 28 March 1843 was reprimanded for disorderly conduct. He received a ticket-of-leave on 19 May 1843, but on 10 December was reprimanded for spitting in church. He was sentenced to hard labour at Salt Water Creek. A free pardon was listed in a government notice on 27 November 1844 but withheld by the Lieutenant-Governor Sir John Eardley-Wilmot for six months because of further attempts by Paddock to abscond. Paddock was assigned to Launceston and on 15 September 1845 was accused of a felony and committed for trial at Launceston's Supreme Court to be heard on 8 October. A free pardon was eventually granted on 18 April 1848. Jacob Paddock left Van Diemen's Land from Launceston on 23 August 1849 as a passenger on the schooner *Red Rover* bound for Adelaide.

Pierce/Pearce, James (1558) B P K SB LB GP
Born in Oneida County, New York, and resident in Orleans, Jefferson County, Pierce was twenty-two years of age, was 6 feet 1 inch tall and a ploughman. He had never been baptised and was of no religion. At his trial he stated that he fell asleep in the hold of the *Charlotte* and was carried off in the boat.

In Van Diemen's Land a ticket-of-leave was issued on 10 February 1842 and he was located at Oatlands in March 1842. A free pardon was received on 8 July 1845. He was supposed to have left Van Diemen's Land for Sydney in September 1846.

Polly, Ira (1561) B P K SB LB GP
A native of Lyme, Jefferson County, New York, Polly was aged twenty-three years, a carpenter and joiner, 5 feet 8 inches tall.

In Van Diemen's Land he was located at Brown's River when he was issued with a ticket-of-leave on 10 February 1842. He was in Campbell Town on 25 February 1842 and on 15 September 1843 in Oatlands. A free pardon was received on 12 October 1844. Polly left Van Diemen's Land on the *Steiglitz*.

Priest, Asa (1560) B P K
Born in Massachusetts, a resident of Auburn, Cayuga County, New York, Priest was aged forty-two years, of no religion but brought up as a Quaker. At his trial he said that he came from Auburn to Oswego to obtain the price of a cow and found the debtor on board one of the Patriot schooners, but said that he fell asleep and was brought down the river and forced to land at the Windmill but denied fighting with the Patriots. On 3 December 1838, the *Rochester Daily Democrat* listed Priest as being 'wounded and confined in the new hospital'. He died on the voyage to Van Diemen's Land and was buried at sea on 19 October 1839.

Reynolds, Solomon (1415) B P K SB LB GP
Born in Washington County, New York, resident in Queensbury, Warren County, Reynolds was aged thirty-three, 5 feet 8 inches tall, a carpenter and millwright and belonging to no church. At his trial he said he came to Sackets Harbor with two other men for company, one of whom paid the expenses on the steamboat *United States*. Reynolds stated that he was then put on board a schooner, volunteered to go in a small boat from one of the schooners to Ogdensburg and was not allowed to return.

In Van Diemen's Land he was at Brown's River when he received a ticket-of-leave on 10 February 1842. As a ticket holder, he was charged with misconduct on 24 February 1843 and was given a sentence of three months' hard labour. A free pardon was received on 8 July 1845. He left Van Diemen's Land on the *Harriet* as a carpenter on 17 January 1846.

Reynolds, William (1416) B P K SB
Born in Orleans, Jefferson County, New York, and resident in Pennsylvania, Reynolds was aged nineteen, a farm labourer and saddler, described as being 5 feet 8 inches tall, with a fair complexion, brown hair and hazel eyes. His face and arms were freckled and he had a star tattooed on his left arm. At his trial he said that he left the Patriot party on Tuesday, 13 November, before the action, but gave no account of where he spent the intervening time. He said that the families of the married men were to be taken care of during their absence on Patriot service.

In Van Diemen's Land he was charged with absconding from the Sandy Bay party with Jacob Paddock, Horace Cooley and Michael Morin on 9 June 1840 and was removed to Port Arthur for hard labour for two years. It was recommended that he 'should be worked by himself'. On 26 March 1842, he was given a sentence of two months' hard labour in chains for insubordination. He worked in the Police Superintendent's Office in October 1842 but was reprimanded for misconduct on 2 January 1843; however, a ticket-of-leave was issued on 19 May 1843. This ticket was revoked *in absentia* on 6 March 1850 as he had escaped with Joseph Stewart earlier that year.

Richardson, Asa H. (1414) B P K SB LB GP
A native of Oswego County, New York, Richardson was a widower, aged twenty-four, 5 feet 7 inches tall, and a farm labourer who had owned land in Upper Canada and had one child. At his trial he said he was brought against his will and kept prisoner in the mill until the evening.

In Van Diemen's Land it was recorded in Richardson's favour, in addition to good behaviour and respectful demeanour, that he had volunteered to accompany the officers and constables in pursuit of five absconders and was instrumental in their capture. From February 1842 until August 1844, Richardson resided and worked in Campbell Town, and he was issued with a ticket-of-leave on 10 February 1842. The Lieutenant-Governor ordered on 28 June 1843 that favourable consideration be given for his good conduct in the pursuit of the bushrangers Jeffs and Conway. On 2 June 1845 as a ticket holder, he was charged with being out after hours and in a disorderly house. For this misdemeanour he received two months' hard labour in a Hobart gang. A free pardon was received on 22 February 1848.

Sharpe/Sharp, Hiram (2764) B P K SB LB GP
A native of Vermont residing in Salina, Onondaga County, New York, Sharpe was aged twenty-four years, a farm labourer, 5 feet 9 inches tall. At his trial he denied taking arms or knowing anything of the designs of the Patriot party.

In Van Diemen's Land, he was issued with a ticket-of-leave on 10 February 1842 and the Lieutenant-Governor ordered on 28 June 1843 that favourable consideration be given for his good conduct in the pursuit of the bushrangers Jeffs and Conway. A free pardon was recorded 5 August 1845 but never signed for. Sharpe possibly left Van Diemen's Land on the *Belle* in August 1846.

Sheldon, Chauncey (2776) B W L SB LB GP
A native of Vermont resident in Utica, Michigan, Sheldon was aged fifty-seven, 6 feet $\frac{1}{2}$ inch tall, a ploughman and widower with nine children. At

his trial he stated that he came over on the boat with the Patriots, having business in Canada, but that he refused to join them although he followed the Patriot party towards Windsor but heard the firing when the Patriots retreated and moved up the river.

In Van Diemen's Land he was located at Salt Water Creek when he was issued with a ticket-of-leave on 10 February 1842. A free pardon was recorded and signed on 6 December 1844. Sheldon left Van Diemen's Land on the *Steiglitz*.

Shew/Sheir, Henry (2766) B P K SB LB GP
A native of Jefferson County, New York, a resident of New Jersey, Shew was married with two children; aged twenty-three, 5 feet 6 inches tall, a pedlar and ploughman who had never been baptised and belonged to no church.

In Van Diemen's Land he was located at Jerusalem when he was issued with a ticket-of-leave on 10 February 1842. From February 1842 he worked in Oatlands and on 8 August was charged with misconduct and being out after hours, for which he was fined five shillings. On 18 December 1843, he was again fined five shillings for being drunk. Another charge of drunkenness on 22 March 1844 resulted in a punishment of fourteen days' hard labour. A free pardon was received on 9 September 1845. He left Van Diemen's Land with Elijah Woodman on the *Young Eagle* in 1847 and arrived home in New York to find his wife had remarried.

Simmons/Simmonds, Henry John/John Henry (2775) B P K SB LB GP
Born in New York State and resident in Lockport, Simmons was aged twenty-three years, 5 feet 8 inches tall and single, a blacksmith and shoeing smith. At his trial he stated that he crossed over to Canada a week before the battle of the Windmill to look for work and was arrested on a back road near the mouth of the Thames, in company with William Nottage.

In Van Diemen's Land a ticket-of-leave was issued on 10 February 1842 and in that month he was located in Oatlands. A free pardon was requested on his behalf from the United States in 1845, but Linus Miller lists Simmons as having died in January 1845.

Smith, Orin/Orren W. (2768) B P K SB LB GP
Born in Charlotte, Vermont a resident of Watertown, New York, Smith was aged twenty-six, 5 feet 6 inches tall and a farmer. At his trial he said he was induced to join in the invasion of Canada by false representations and that he prevented the effusion of blood as much as possible. The papers that accompanied the warrants from Canada record that strong recommendations were made on his behalf by several respectable individuals.

In Van Diemen's Land he was issued with a ticket-of-leave on 10 February 1842 and a free pardon was signed on 7 December 1844. Smith left Van Diemen's Land on the *Steiglitz*. He set up business in Peru, New York, and married Celecta Everest who regrettably died shortly afterwards of brain fever. There was one child, a daughter, who died in infancy. Orin Smith returned to Clayton and was postmaster there from 1867 to 1885. He subsequently retired and died on 6 January 1892.

Snow, Samuel (2770) B W L SB LB GP

A native of Massachusetts, resident in Strongsville, Ohio, Snow was aged thirty-eight years, 5 feet 7 inches tall, a ploughman and married with five children. At his trial he stated that he crossed from Detroit to Windsor with the Patriots, but when he saw the barracks on fire and heard firing, he went into the woods. The papers that accompanied the warrants from Canada record that he was strongly recommended by several respectable individuals.

In Van Diemen's Land he was charged with idleness and was given three days on the treadwheel at Green Ponds on 11 February 1841. He was at Brown's River when a ticket-of-leave was issued on 10 February 1842. He was working in Oatlands on 25 February 1842. A free pardon was signed on 5 December 1844, and Snow left Van Diemen's Land on the *Steiglitz*.

Sprague/Spragge, John (2772) B W L SB LB GP

Born in New York State and resident in Amhurst, Ohio, Sprague was aged twenty-three years, 5 feet 5¼ inches tall, a carpenter and joiner. At his trial he stated that he crossed over in the steamboat *Champlain* with the Patriots because he was intoxicated and dragged on board.

In Van Diemen's Land he was at Brown's River when he was issued with a ticket-of-leave on 10 February 1842. Later that month he worked in Campbell Town, where he died on 24 September 1845.

Stevens, Elizur/Elizar (2771) B W L SB LB GP

A native of the United States and resident in Lebanon, Madison County, Stevens was aged twenty-seven, 5 feet 9½ inches tall and a ploughman. At his trial he stated he was induced to join the Patriot invasion by a promise of 160 acres of land and eight dollars per month. The papers that accompanied the warrants from Canada noted that seven ministers of the Gospel in the United States recommended him as having borne a good character.

In Van Diemen's Land a ticket-of-leave was issued 10 February 1842, and on 28 June 1843 the Lieutenant-Governor ordered that favourable consideration be given for his good conduct in the pursuit of the bushrangers Jeffs and Conway. A free pardon was signed on 24 January 1845. Stevens left Van Diemen's Land on the *Steiglitz*.

Stewart, Joseph (2767) B P K SB LB
A native of Pennsylvania, aged twenty-five, Stewart was a clothier by trade and of no church. He was described as being 5 feet $7\frac{1}{2}$ inches tall, with a swarthy complexion, black hair and hazel eyes. At his trial he stated that he was going to Ogdensburg to see his brother, took a passage in the steamboat *United States* and was ordered on board a schooner and put on shore. He claimed he had no intention of invading Canada and denied taking arms.

In Van Diemen's Land Stewart was charged in August 1840 with absconding with Miller from the Sandy Bay Probation Station, which resulted in two years' hard labour in chains at Port Arthur. He was charged with idleness on 21 October 1840 and received three days' solitary confinement. On 29 April 1841, a charge of misconduct resulted in six weeks in chains. The Muster of December 1841 lists him still at Port Arthur. A ticket-of-leave was issued on 17 November 1843. On 1 January 1844, as a ticket holder in the position of constable, he was charged with being absent from his station without leave when the station was taken possession of by absentees, and of not having made a manly resistance to recover it from them. It was recommended that he be dismissed from the police. A letter dated 9 December 1844 refused the granting of a pardon which had been issued in London on 9 July 1844. His ticket-of-leave was revoked on 26 March 1850 because he had absconded with William Reynolds, probably on an American whaler.

Stewart/Stuart, Riley Monson (2773) B W L SB LB GP
A native of Massachusetts and resident in Avon, Ohio, Riley Stewart was aged thirty-one years, 5 feet 9 inches tall and a gunsmith.

In Van Diemen's Land he was located at Brown's River when a ticket-of-leave was issued on 10 February 1842. On 25 February 1842, he was working in Oatlands and signed for his free pardon on 1 July 1845. It is not known whether he left Van Diemen's Land.

Stockton, Thomas (2765) B P SB LB GP
A native of Rutland, Jefferson County, New York, Stockton was aged twenty-six years, a blacksmith and shoeing smith, 5 feet 6 inches tall, single and a Methodist. At his trial he claimed he came over to Prescott on his way to Montreal looking for work and he had been stopped by the people at the mill, was forced to take a gun and bayonet, but knew nothing of the proceedings.

In Van Diemen's Land he was located at Brown's River when a ticket-of-leave was issued on 10 February 1842. A free pardon was received on 1 July 1845 but he died before he was able to acknowledge it.

Swanberg/Swansburgh, John G. (Augustus) (2769) B P K SB LB GP
A native of the city of Philadelphia and resident in Alexandria, Jefferson County, New York, Swanberg was aged twenty-seven years, a farm labourer, 5 feet 4 inches tall. At his trial he said that he had crossed over on the *United States*, but knew nothing of an invasion of Canada till he was taken prisoner on 16 November.

In Van Diemen's Land he was charged with using improper language and insolence on 23 December 1840 while on probation at Green Ponds, for which he received ten days' solitary confinement on bread and water. On 18 January 1841, still at Green Ponds, he was charged with fighting and was given four days' solitary confinement on bread and water. He was located at Jerusalem in August 1841 and at Swansea in January 1842. A ticket-of-leave was issued on 10 February 1842. On 28 June 1843 on the Lieutenant-Governor's orders, favourable consideration was recorded for his good conduct in the pursuit of the bushrangers Jeffs and Conway. A free pardon was signed on 9 December 1844. Swanberg left Van Diemen's Land on the *Steiglitz*.

Sweet/Swete, Alvin (Sylvanus) Burroughs (2774) B W L SB LB GP
A native of Windfield, Herkimer County, New York, a resident of Northampton, Sweet was aged twenty-two years, 5 feet 8 inches tall, single and a joiner and painter. At his trial he stated that he crossed in the steamboat *Champlain* having taken a passage for Bear Creek, but was forced on shore near Windsor; as soon as the firing commenced he turned up the river for about six or seven miles when he was arrested.

In Van Diemen's Land a ticket-of-leave was issued on 10 February 1842, and on 25 February he was located at Oatlands. On 4 April 1843, a charge of misconduct was made against him and he received forty-eight hours' solitary confinement. On 9 May 1843 an accusation of being absent from the muster was discharged. His ticket-of-leave was suspended on 7 July 1843. On 31 July a suspicion of felony was discharged, likewise a charge of misconduct on 7 August. However, on 15 July 1844, another charge of misconduct resulted in seven days' hard labour. A free pardon was signed on 31 December 1844. Sweet left Van Diemen's Land on the *Steiglitz* and was back in Wisconsin in 1850.

Thomas, John (1227) B P K SB LB GP
Born in Vermont and a resident in the town of Madrid, St Lawrence County, New York, Thomas was aged twenty-six years, a dealer and farm labourer, 5 feet 8 inches tall, who had previously lived in Canada for some years.

In Van Diemen's Land a ticket-of-leave was issued on 10 February 1842 and a free pardon signed for on 20 January 1845. Thomas left Van Diemen's Land on the *Steiglitz*.

Thompson, Joseph (1228) B P K SB LB GP

A native of Lyme, Jefferson County, New York, Thompson was aged twenty-six, 5 feet 9 inches tall, a ship's carpenter and labourer and a member of no church.

In Van Diemen's Land he was located at Brown's River when he was issued a ticket-of-leave on 10 February 1842. At the end of that month he was working in Campbell Town. The Lieutenant-Governor ordered on 28 June 1843 that favourable consideration be given for his good conduct in the pursuit of the bushrangers Jeffs and Conway. A free pardon was received on 3 December 1844. Thompson left Van Diemen's Land on the *Steiglitz*.

Tyrrell, John Burwell (1229) B W L SB LB GP

A native of Malahide in Upper Canada, Tyrell was aged twenty-five, 5 feet 9 inches tall, a carpenter, married with two children. Tyrrell stated that his proper name was John Burwell. At his trial he said he had gone on board the *United States* to see a friend and was brought over against his will, since orders were given to shoot anyone who attempted to escape. He was forced to march with the Patriot party, but deserted as soon as he could. His uncle Mahlon Burwell was London's Tory member of the Legislative Assembly in Ontario. The papers that accompanied the warrants from Canada record that, because of his uncle's merits, the extension of an indulgence to him may have been justified, although he was not entitled to claim it.

In Van Diemen's Land he was charged with misconduct on 6 May 1841 while on probation at Salt Water Creek, and was given twenty-four hours' solitary confinement. A ticket-of-leave was issued on 10 February 1842 and as a ticket holder, he was reprimanded for misconduct on 8 August 1842. A free pardon was received on 20 September 1843 because of his family connections. He was the first Patriot to be released from Van Diemen's Land. He returned to Canada and resumed farming.

Van Camp/Vanchamp, Garret (2480) MH SH

Born in Burford, New York, Van Camp was aged twenty-eight, a ploughman and shepherd, and described as 5 feet 5½ inches tall, with a fresh complexion, long head, red hair and whiskers, a round visage, high forehead, brown eyebrows, blue eyes, medium nose, mouth and chin. He had a scar on his right arm. Van Camp had been a Duncombe rebel before the Short Hills invasion.

In Van Diemen's Land Van Camp died in the Colonial Hospital on 3 September 1839.

Vernon, John (115) MH SH
A native of Markham, Upper Canada, Vernon was aged twenty-one, a carpenter and millwright, 5 feet $8\frac{1}{2}$ inches tall, with a pale complexion, round head, brown hair, long visage, high forehead, brown eyebrows, grey eyes, medium nose and mouth and a long chin.

In Van Diemen's Land he was initially in the Prisoners' Barracks in Hobart Town, then on assignment. A ticket-of-leave was issued on 5 August 1841. On 8 August 1843 as a ticket holder, he was fined five shillings for being out after hours and drunk. A free pardon was received on 3 December 1844, but not acknowledged by Vernon until February 1846. He left Van Diemen's Land on 9 March 1846 for mainland Australia.

Waggoner, James (2597) MH SH
A native of Lewiston, New York, who had lived in Lower Canada, Waggoner was aged thirty-three, a farmer, 5 feet $6\frac{1}{2}$ inches tall, with a sallow complexion, round head, black hair and whiskers, a long visage, high forehead, brown eyebrows, hazel eyes, medium nose, mouth and chin. He had a scar on his right hand and two scars on the left.

In Van Diemen's Land he was initially in the Hobart Town Prisoners' Barracks, then on assignment. A ticket-of-leave was issued on 4 August 1841. He was charged with misconduct in raising a false report on 8 November 1842, and given a sentence of six months' hard labour and his ticket-of-leave was revoked. On 18 July 1843, he was located in Campbell Town. His ticket-of-leave was reinstated on 25 August 1843 and in September 1845 he is known to have been in Campbell Town. It was speculated that he escaped in January 1846 as a stowaway, although a free pardon was received in Van Diemen's Land on 22 February 1848.

Wait/Waite, Benjamin (2598) MH SH
A Canadian and a resident of Markham, married with one child, Wait was aged twenty-six, described as being a trade warehouseman, merchant and clerk, 5 feet $4\frac{1}{2}$ inches tall, with a fair complexion, round head, brown hair, black whiskers, oval visage, high forehead, brown eyebrows, hazel eyes, medium nose, mouth and chin. He had two scars on his left arm.

In Van Diemen's Land, Wait was initially in hospital, then on assignment at Ashgrove in Oatlands from 25 October 1839 until September 1840, where he was employed as a clerk, storekeeper, overseer and schoolteacher.

Wait was issued with a ticket-of-leave on 4 August 1841 and later absconded with Chandler on board the American whaler *Julian*. He was reunited with his family in 1842 after a voyage of seven months via Rio de Janeiro. He settled in Haldimand County, where he operated a sawmill on the Grand River near York. His wife Maria died in 1843 and Wait remarried in 1845. He settled in Grand Rapids, Michigan, where he died on 1 November 1893.

Washburn, Samuel (2657) B P K SB LB GP
A native of Warren County, New York, Washburn was aged twenty-five years, 5 feet 7 inches tall, a ploughman of no particular church, but held to the principles of the Communion Baptists. At his trial he said that he was sick all the time and did not take arms at the windmill.

In Van Diemen's Land a ticket-of-leave was issued on 10 February 1842 and on 17 April 1844, he sought permission to marry Ann Scott who had arrived on the *Nautilus*. This was approved and they married at Campbell Town in 1844. A free pardon was received on 8 July 1845.

White, Patrick (2659) B P K SB LB GP
A native of Limerick, Ireland, who came to Canada in 1831, White was aged twenty-two, a labourer and 5 feet 2 inches tall. At his trial he said he was forced among the Patriot party and made his escape as soon as he could.

In Van Diemen's Land he was charged with misconduct on 18 January 1841 and was given two days' solitary confinement. In July and August 1841, he was located at Salt Water Creek when a ticket-of-leave was issued on 10 February 1842. On 15 April 1843, as a ticket holder, he was reprimanded for misconduct, and again on 10 June 1844 for being out after hours for which he received one month's hard labour. His ticket-of-leave was suspended. On 2 September 1844, he was charged with being out after hours and was reprimanded. From July to September 1844, he is known to have been in Campbell Town. For disturbing the peace, he was fined five shillings on 3 September 1844 and deprived of his ticket-of-leave, but it was reinstated on 29 April 1845. On 13 September 1845, he was charged with a felony and was committed for trial, but on 9 October, this offence was discharged by proclamation. On 5 November 1846, he was found drunk and fined five shillings. This same offence and resulting fines occurred again on 8 and 10 February 1847, and on 16 February 1847 he received forty-eight hours' solitary confinement for being drunk. On 1 June 1847, he was fined five shillings for using obscene language, and on 12 November was admonished for misconduct. On 4 December 1848, he breached his ticket-of-leave conditions, received one month's hard labour and had to forfeit all wages due to him by his masters. On 8 November 1849, a charge of being drunk resulted in yet another fine of five shillings. He was recommended for a conditional pardon on 5 December 1848 and this was approved on 4 February 1850. From November 1849 to May 1850, he was located at Swansea. He sought permission to marry Martha Somerville, who had arrived in Van Diemen's Land on the *Nautilus* in 1844, but there is no record of this marriage.

Whiting, Nathan (2654) B P K SB LB GP
A native of Connecticut, with a wife and nine children resident in Liverpool, Onondaga County, New York, Whiting was aged forty-one, 5 feet $11\frac{1}{2}$ inches tall and a ploughman who belonged to no church. At his trial he said he was forced to land with the Patriot party and subsequently made his escape from them.

In Van Diemen's Land a ticket-of-leave was issued on 10 February 1842 and a free pardon received on 3 December 1844. Whiting left Van Diemen's Land on the *Steiglitz*.

Whitney, Riley (2655) B P K SB LB GP
A native of Vermont, resident in Leroy, Jefferson County, New York, Whitney was aged twenty-five years, farm labourer, 5 feet 3 inches tall. At his trial he denied taking arms and said that he hid in a cellar during the action and helped cook for the wounded.

In Van Diemen's Land he was charged with misconduct at Green Ponds on 6 May 1841 and was reprimanded. A ticket-of-leave was issued on 10 February 1842 and a free pardon was received on 8 July 1845. Whitney departed Van Diemen's Land in September, and two years later left with Gates on the *Kingston* from Sydney bound for New Bedford, arriving there in May 1848.

Williams, James Peter (aka Nelson Recker) (2660) B W L SB LB
A native of New York State, resident in Cleveland, Ohio, Williams was aged twenty-four, 5 feet $6\frac{1}{2}$ inches tall and a ploughman. At his trial he stated that he had been in Canada travelling about looking for an uncle.

In Van Diemen's Land he died in the Colonial Hospital on 29 April 1841.

Williams, John Chester (2662) B W L SB LB GP
Born in Vermont, Rochester, New York, Williams was a widower with one child, aged thirty-nine, 5 feet 7 inches tall, a carpenter and joiner.

In Van Diemen's Land he was reprimanded after being charged with misconduct on 6 May 1841. He was in Jerusalem when a ticket-of-leave was issued on 10 February 1842. He received a punishment of fourteen days' hard labour on 9 August 1842 for being drunk, and on 4 November while in Oatlands was admonished for being absent from muster. He was again admonished on 27 March 1843 for gambling and likewise on 8 August 1843 for misconduct. On 11 August while working in Bothwell on the Police Buildings, he was charged with being out after hours and with intoxication and was sentenced to one month's hard labour. His ticket-of-leave was subsequently suspended. On 29 July 1844, a charge of misconduct was dismissed, and on 8 August another charge of misconduct resulted in three days' solitary confinement. A free pardon was received on 1 July 1845. Williams left Van Diemen's Land on board the *Jantha* on 2 February 1846.

Wilson, Edward A. (2656) B P K SB LB GP
A native of Pompey, Onondaga County, New York, Wilson was aged twenty-seven years, a widower with one child, a cabinet-maker and described as 5 feet 9 inches tall. He belonged to no particular church. At his trial he said that he had gone with two others to Windmill Point from curiosity and the boat that conveyed them had been taken away.

In Van Diemen's Land he was issued with a ticket-of-leave on 10 February 1842 while in Campbell Town and sought permission to marry Mary Ann Sly (free) in May 1844 but there is no record of the marriage. A free pardon was signed on 10 December 1844. He left the island on the *Steiglitz*.

Woodbury, Beamis/Beamus/Bemis (2658) B P K SB LB GP
A native of Massachusetts, a resident in Auburn, Cayuga County, New York, Woodbury was aged twenty-five, 5 feet 10 inches tall and a ploughman. At his trial he said that he was at the Windmill cooking potatoes, was wounded through the door and taken prisoner.

In Van Diemen's Land, on 10 December 1840, he was charged with trafficking bread at Lovely Banks, with a strong suspicion of having stolen it, for which he received seven days' solitary confinement. A ticket-of-leave was issued on 10 December 1842, but on 28 March 1844, in the position of Special Constable, he was charged with misconduct in acting in a cowardly manner on the occasion of his falling-in with nine armed bushrangers and he was deprived of his ticket-of-leave. A free pardon was received on 10 December 1844. Woodbury left Van Diemen's Land on the *Steiglitz*.

Woodman, Elijah Croker/Elizah (2661) B W L SB LB GP
Born in Buxon, Maine, a resident of Canada, Woodman was aged forty-two and described as 5 feet 4½ inches tall. He was a farmer, carpenter, lumberman and millwright, married with seven children. At his trial Woodman stated that he had lived in Canada for about six years but never took the oath of allegiance. He claimed he went on board the *Champlain* as he heard it was going to Black River, Michigan, but was forced off when it anchored on the Canadian side.

In Van Diemen's Land Woodman had constant problems with his health. A ticket-of-leave was issued on 10 February 1842 and a free pardon was received on 8 July 1845. Woodman departed on board the *Young Eagle*, but died on 15 June 1847 *en route* to America. Soon after, the *Young Eagle* was wrecked, but luckily Woodman's diaries and letters were rescued and later returned to his family.

Wright, Stephen S. (2653) B P K SB LB GP
A native of Denmark, Lewis County, New York, Wright was aged twenty-five, a carpenter and joiner, 5 feet 7 inches tall. His father was a Methodist minister. At his trial he said that he was forced into the Patriot party, denied taking arms and said he was in a house upstairs keeping out of the way when he was wounded in the arm.

In Van Diemen's Land he was charged with neglect of duty at Lovely Banks on 5 August 1840 and received a punishment of three days' solitary confinement on bread and water. He was located at Brown's River when a ticket-of-leave was issued on 10 February 1842. He was in Bothwell on 25 February, and on 8 August as a ticket holder was charged with misconduct in being out after hours and drunkenness, for which he was fined five shillings. On 21 December 1842, a charge of being out after hours was made and he received seven days' solitary confinement. A free pardon was granted on 23 June 1843 as a result of Wright's capturing the two bushrangers Jeffs and Conway. He was also rewarded with the sum of £33 6s 8d. Wright left Van Diemen's Land on 22 July 1843 on the *Areta* bound for England and then made his way to New York.

Sources

Manuscript

Archives Office of Tasmania: Con 16, Con 18, Con 23, Con 27/8, Con 31, Con 33, Con 35, Con 52, Con 60; CSO 5/203, CSO 5/268, CSO 8/8, CSO 16/22, CSO 20/3, CSO 20/13, CSO 20/34, CSO 20/38, CSO 22/137; GO 1/48, GO 1/50, GO 1/52, GO 1/53, GO 1/54, GO 1/55, GO 1/56, GO 1/57, GO 1/58, GO 1/63, GO 1/66, GO 33/49, GO 33/53, GO 33/70; Departure Records; Marine Board Records; POL 20/9, POL 220/1; Pioneer Index of Births, Deaths and Marriages.
State Library of New South Wales: Tasmanian Papers 147.
National Archives of Canada: RG 1/E1 vol. 56, RG 5/B37 vols. 1–18, RG 5/B41 vols. 1–20, RG 7/G12 vol. 29, RG 7/G12 vol. 30, RG 7/G12 vol. 30, RG 7/G1 vol. 91, RG 7/G1 vol. 92, RG 7/G1 vol. 93, RG 7/G1 vol. 92, RG 7/G12 vol. 30.

University of Western Ontario: The Talman Collection, Woodman Papers and Fred Landon Papers.
Oswego County Historical Records.
Archives of Victoria: Police Gazette; Records of Births, Deaths and Marriages.

Newspapers

Van Diemen's Land: *Colonial Times, Hobart Town Courier, Hobart Town Gazette*.
Canada: *Kingston Chronicle, Toronto Mirror*.
United States: *Watertown Daily Times, Rochester Daily Democrat*.

Books

Guillet, Edwin C., *The Lives and Times of the Patriots: an account of the rebellion in Upper Canada, 1837–1838; and the patriot agitation in the United States, 1837–1842*, Thomas Nelson, Toronto, 1938.
Landon, Fred, *An Exile from Canada to Van Diemen's Land: being the study of Elijah Woodman transported overseas for participation in the Upper Canada troubles of 1837*, Longmans, Green and Co., Toronto, 1960.
Masonic Research Society, 'In the Shadow of the Gallows', in *Jewels of Masonic Eloquence and True Stories of Mercy and Assistance*, Masonic Research Society, Oklahoma, 1919.

Notes

Abbreviations

SRNSW	State Records of New South Wales
AO	Archives of Ontario
AOT	Archives Office of Tasmania
LOC	Library of Congress
NAC	National Archives of Canada
PRO	Public Record Office, Kew
SLNSW	State Library of New South Wales
USNA	United States National Archives
UWO	University of Western Ontario

Authors' Note

[1] See Frost and Maxwell-Stewart, eds, *Chain Letters*; Duffield 'Problematic Passages' in Duffield and Bradley, eds, *Representing Convicts*.

[2] The quote is taken from Robert Hughes's classic work, *The Fatal Shore*.

Introduction

[1] Tiffany, *The Relations of the United States to the Canadian Rebellion of 1837–1838*, p. 63.

[2] Graves, *Guns Across the River*, p. 98.

[3] Beckles, *White Servitude and Black Slavery in Barbados*, pp. 5–23; Reece, *The Origins of Irish Convict Transportation to New South Wales*, p. 5; Coldham, *Emigrants in Chains*, pp. 41–57.

[4] Defoe, *Moll Flanders*, p. 331; Grubb, 'The Statutory Regulation of Colonial Servitude', p. 60.

[5] Ekirch, *Bound For America*, pp. 26–7; Gemery, 'Markets for Migrants', pp. 39–40.

[6] See for example Brand, *The Convict Probation System*, p. 52.

[7] Nicholas and Shergold, 'Transportation as Global Migration', pp. 30–4; Sen, *Disciplining Punishment*, pp. 264–71.

[8] Bogle, *Convicts*, pp. 5–21; Atkinson, *The Europeans in Australia*, pp. 52–3; Nicholas and Shergold, 'Transportation as Global Migration', p. 30; Conway, 'The Recruitment of Criminals into the British Army, 1775–81', pp. 49–54; Chatrand and Chappell, *British Forces in the West Indies, 1793–1815*, pp. 33–5; Anderson, *Convicts in the Indian Ocean*; Craton, *Testing the Chains*, p. 206; Ekirch, 'Great Britain's Secret Convict Trade to America, 1783–4', pp. 1285–91; Reece, *The Origins of Irish Convict Transportation to New South Wales*, pp. 101–16, 150–208.

⁹ Reece, *The Origins of Irish Convict Transportation to New South Wales*, p. 3.

¹⁰ Coldham, *Emigrants in Chains*, p. 48.

¹¹ Gilmour, *Riot, Risings and Revolution*, pp. 26–9; Ekirch, *Bound For America*, p. 17; Coldham, *Emigrants in Chains*, p. 89.

¹² Craton, *Testing the Chains*, pp. 206, 211–23.

¹³ Linebaugh and Rediker, *The Many-Headed Hydra*, p. 57; Rudé, *Protest and Punishment*, pp. 37–8, 73.

¹⁴ Rudé, *Protest and Punishment*, pp. 103–12.

¹⁵ Sen, *Disciplining Punishment*, pp. 61, 265.

¹⁶ Hopkins, 'Fighting Those who came Against Their Country', pp. 49–67; Duly, 'Hottentots to Hobart and Sydney', pp. 39–50; Malherbe, 'David Stuurman', pp. 47–57; Malherbe, 'South African Bushmen to Australia?', pp. 100–24.

¹⁷ See Thompson, *The Making of the English Working Class*; Manwaring and Dobrée, *The Floating Republic*; Hutchinson, 'Glasgow Working Class Politics', pp. 98–108; Reay, 'The Context and Meaning of Popular Literacy', pp. 89–129; Hobsbawm and Rudé, *Captain Swing*; Stevenson, *Popular Disturbances in England, 1700–1870*.

¹⁸ Letter from 'Americans', *Pennsylvania Gazette*, 9 May 1751, reproduced in Coldham, *Emigrants in Chains*, p. 185.

¹⁹ Genesis 3: 14.

1 Patriot Hunters

¹ Read, *The Rebellion of 1837 in Upper Canada*, p. 5.

² Shirreff, *A Tour through North America* (1835), quoted in Landon, *An Exile From Canada*, p. 24.

³ Read, *The Rising in Western Upper Canada, 1837–8*, p. 5.

⁴ For an account of the 'type riot', see Raible, *Muddy York Mud*.

⁵ See Lindsey, *The Life and Times of William Lyon Mackenzie*; Kilbourn, *The Firebrand*.

⁶ See Boissery, *A Deep Sense of Wrong*.

⁷ See Read, *The Rising in Western Upper Canada, 1837–8*.

⁸ The statute was Vic. 1 c. 3, discussed in Greenwood and Wright, eds, *State Trials* vol. 11.

⁹ Read, *The Rebellion of 1837 in Upper Canada*, p. 21.

¹⁰ Corey, *The Crisis of 1830–1842 in Canadian American Relations*, p. 34.

¹¹ Graves, *Guns Across the River*, p. 35.

¹² Kinchen, *The Rise and Fall of the Patriot Hunters*, p. 31.

¹³ Ibid., p. 32.

¹⁴ For a fuller discussion of these developments see Kinchen, *The Rise and Fall of the Patriot Hunters*; Corey, *The Crisis of 1830–1842*.

¹⁵ Corey, *The Crisis of 1830–1842*, p. 71.

¹⁶ Kinchen, *The Rise and Fall of the Patriot Hunters*, p. 35.

¹⁷ Quoted from Hough, *A History of Jefferson County in the State of New York*, in Graves, *Guns Across the River*, p. 53.

¹⁸ Preston, *Three Years Residence in Canada*, p. 76.

¹⁹ Corey, *The Crisis of 1830–1842*, p. 76.

²⁰ Kinchen, *The Rise and Fall of the Patriot Hunters*, p. 31.

²¹ Tiffany, *The Relations of the United States to the Canadian Rebellion of 1837–1838*, p. 63.

²² See for example Davis, *The Canadian Farmer's Travels in the United States of America*.

²³ Quoted in Read, *White Prosperous and Free*, unpublished paper held by the author.

2 Theatre in the Short Hills

¹ Colin Read, personal communication with the authors.

² RG 1/E3/51 NAC.

³ For a full account of the Short Hills raid, see Cruikshank, 'A Twice-Told Tale', pp. 180–222.

⁴ Quoted in ibid., p. 186.

[5] Gemmell, *The Plebeian*, 25 June 1842.

[6] See Beer, *Sir Allan Napier MacNab*.

[7] See Kinchen, *The Rise and Fall of the Patriot Hunters*, pp. 31–2.

[8] Handwritten notes of the Special Commission at Niagara in the Alexander Hamilton Papers, NAC.

[9] *St Catharine's Journal*, 26 July 1838.

[10] Quoted in Cruikshank, 'A Twice-Told Tale', p. 185.

[11] Arthur to Durham, 26 June 1838, CO 42, vol. 448 PRO.

[12] Greenwood and Wright, *Canadian State Trials*, vol. 11.

[13] See Arthur to Glenelg, 5 May 1838, RG 7/G12 vol. 29 NAC, and the Law Officers' Opinion, 6 June 1838, RG 7/G1 vol. 85 NAC.

[14] Account of the Court of Special Commission at Niagara, Sheriff Alexander Hamilton Papers, NAC.

[15] Glenelg to Arthur, 30 May 1838, RG 7/G1 vol. 85 NAC.

[16] Arthur to Glenelg, 27 July 1839, NAC; *Correspondence Relative to the Affairs of Canada*, p. 336.

[17] Glenelg to Arthur, 22 June 1838, CO 42/453 PRO.

[18] Glenelg to Arthur, 23 June 1838, ibid.

[19] Account of the Court of Special Commission at Niagara, Sheriff Alexander Hamilton Papers NAC.

[20] All the quotes in this paragraph are taken from the official report on the Short Hills Trial, RG 1/E1 vol. 56 NAC.

[21] James Waggoner was induced to change his plea from not guilty to guilty in the expectation of a pardon.

[22] Arthur to Durham, 27 June 1838, CO 42/448 PRO.

[23] The letters of Maria Wait are included in Wait's *Letters From Van Dieman's Land Written During Four Years Imprisonment for Political Offences Committed in Upper Canada*, pp. 21–2.

[24] Law Officers to Colonial Office, 21 May 1838, CO 42/452 PRO.

[25] See Robinson to Stephen, 10 June 1839, CO 4/468 PRO.

[26] Arthur to Durham, 27 June 1838, CO 42/448 PRO.

[27] 29 August 1838, State Book L, RG 1/E vol. 56 NAC.

[28] Arthur to Glenelg, 26 October 1838, CO 42/449 PRO.

[29] Glenelg to Arthur, 23 August 1838, CO 42/454 PRO; Arthur to Glenelg, 28 September 1838, CO 42/456 PRO.

[30] Glenelg to Durham, 15 September 1838, CO 42/446 PRO.

[31] See J. B. Robinson to Arthur, 2 January 1839, Sanderson, ed., *The Arthur Papers*.

3 Mr Capper's Discretion

[1] The Act Vic. 1, ch. 3 is discussed by Greenwood and Wright in *State Trials*, vol. 11.

[2] CO 44/33 PRO.

[3] HO13/74 PRO.

[4] Papers of Andrew Stevenson, LOC.

[5] Stephens to Home Office, 16 March 1839, HO 13/75 PRO.

[6] Normanby to Arthur, 19 May 1839, CO 43/48 PRO.

[7] HO 13/75 PRO.

[8] CO 44/32 PRO.

[9] Stevenson to Van Buren, 16 May 1839, Andrew Stevenson Papers, LOC.

[10] J. B. Robinson to Arthur, 2 January 1839, Sanderson ed., *The Arthur Papers*.

[11] See Robinson correspondence, CO 42/468 PRO.

[12] Normanby to Arthur, 10 July 1839, RG 7/G1 vol. 91 NAC.

[13] HO 13/75 PRO.

[14] Law Officers to Colonial Office, 21 May 1838, CO 42/452; see also RG 7/G1 vol. 85, 21 May–26 October 1838.

[15] Stevenson to Russell, 13 July 1839, Andrew Stevenson Papers LOC.

[16] 19 July 1839, CSO 5/203/4989/100 AOT.

4 Great Hunt in the North Woods

1 Wittke, 'Ohio and the Canadian-American Crisis of 1837–38', p. 31.
2 Graves, *Guns Across the River*, pp. 66–7.
3 Ibid., p. 78.
4 Ibid., pp. 86–102.
5 Quoted from *The Ogdensburg Times and Advertiser*, ibid., p. 119.
6 Quoted in the *Oswego County Whig*, 21 November 1838.
7 See Wilson, *The Presidency of Martin Van Buren*.
8 PG 5, B1/1/22 NAC.
9 PG 5, B1/1/7 NAC.
10 PG 5, B1/1/20 NAC.
11 Ibid.
12 All the references in this paragraph come from Fox to Arthur, 31 January 1839, CO 42/458 PRO.
13 Woodman, 'Night Thoughts Sandwich Jail', December 1838, Woodman Papers UWO.
14 Essex Historical Society Papers and Address, vol. 2, p. 15.
15 See Stevenson to Van Buren, 8 and 12 December, Andrew Stevenson Papers LOC.
16 Tiffany, *The Canadian Rebellion of 1837–1838*, pp. 78–82.
17 RG 5/B/37 NAC.
18 Woodman, Gaol Diary, 19 and 20 December 1838, Woodman Papers UWO.
19 Woodman to family, 24 July 1839, ibid.
20 Woodman Gaol Diary, 26 January 1839, ibid.

5 The Caprice of the Mercenaries of Royalty

1 Arthur to Glenelg, 2 January 1839, CO 42/456 PRO.
2 Glenelg to Colborne, 18 January 1839, CO 42/468 PRO.
3 Glenelg to Arthur, 2 February 1839, CO 42/468 PRO.
4 Arthur to Colborne, 12 March 1839, CO 42/458 PRO.
5 Fox to Arthur, 31 January 1839, CO 42/456 PRO.
6 Arthur to Glenelg, 2 April 1839, CO 42/458 PRO.
7 *Kingston Chronicle*, 8 December 1838.
8 Arthur to Colborne, 12 March 1839, CO 42/458 PRO.
9 Russell to Melbourne, 2 December 1838, 33/22–3 Russell Papers PRO.
10 For a discussion of the 'Aroostook War', see Stuart, *Prologue to Manifest Destiny*.
11 Glenelg to Colborne, 25 January 1839, CO 43/48 PRO; Arthur to Glenelg, RG 7/G12, vol. 30 NAC.
12 Glenelg to Colborne, 27 March 1839, RG 7/G1/91 NAC.
13 The report was sent on to Arthur, who acknowledged it on 3 April 1839, RG 7/G1 vol. 42 NAC.
14 Russell to Normanby, 8 February 1839, HO 13/74 PRO.
15 Vail to Forsyth, Washington, 5 May 1838, Papers of 27th Congress Document no. 39, House of Representatives USNA.
16 Woodman to his brother and sister, 7 August 1839, Woodman Papers UWO.
17 Arthur to Glenelg, 21 March 1839 RG 7/G1 vol. 92 NAC.
18 Arthur to Glenelg, 9 March 1839, RG 7/G12 vol. 30 NAC.
19 Woodman, Gaol Diary, 1 April 1839, Woodman Papers UWO.

6 Bound for the Fatal Shore

1 See New, *Lord Durham*, p. 493.
2 The original list of eighty-two for transportation given to the Colonial Office includes the names of five men who did not in fact leave, CO 42/458 PRO.
3 Master of the *Buffalo*, 1 October 1839, RG 7/G1 vol. 45 NAC.

4 For the warrants of Van Diemen's Land see George Arthur to Franklin, 21 September 1839, CO 5/230/5677 AOT.
5 Woodman to his parents, 23 December 1839, Woodman Papers UWO.
6 Ducharme, *Journal of Political Exile in Australia*, p. 15.
7 Log of Mr. James Wood Master of *Buffalo*, 8 April–30 September 1839, ADM 51/3066 PRO.
8 RG 5/41/20 NAC.
9 Woodman to parents, Ship *Buffalo*, 23 December 1839, Woodman Papers UWO.
10 Ducharme, *Journal of Political Exile in Australia*; Prieur, *Notes of a Convict of 1838*.
11 *Greenock Advertiser*, vol. XL, no. 5550, 26 November 1839, p. 3, republished in the *St Catharine's Journal* in August 1840 and quoted in Landon, *An Exile from Canada to Van Diemen's Land*, p. 180.
12 This letter was signed by James M. Aitchison, Orin W. Smith, John Thomas and Daniel D. Heustis.
13 Prieur, *Notes of a Convict of 1838*.

7 Mysteries of a Penal Colony

1 Bradley and Maxwell-Stewart, 'Embodied Explorations', pp. 183–203.
2 After 1817 ships' masters were paid a bonus for each live convict landed: Bateson, *The Convict Ships*.
3 Maxwell-Stewart and Duffield, 'Skin Deep Devotions', pp. 118–35.
4 Chapman, 'The Island Panopticon', pp. 6–10.
5 Johnston, 'Building the Ideal Prison', pp. 31–45.
6 Maxwell-Stewart and Bradley, 'Behold the Man', pp. 74–5.
7 Police Number 4811 William Lauder per *Isabella* (2) arrived Van Diemen's Land, 2 May 1842, Con 33 AOT.
8 Police Number 2361 Joshua Moore per *Layton* (4) arrived Van Diemen's Land, 1 September 1841, Con 33 AOT. See also Duffield, 'Stated this Offence', pp. 119–35.
9 Con 31/32 AOT.
10 *The True Colonist*, 21 February 1840, p. 7, col. 3.
11 Colonial Secretary Correspondence 1840/4/2484 SRNSW. We are indebted to Dr Brian Petrie for alerting us to this material.
12 This letter is dated 19 July 1839, CSO 5/203/4989, p. 100 AOT.
13 CSO 5/203/4989, pp. 100, 137, 145, 182 AOT.
14 Mortlock, *Experiences of a Convict Transported for Twenty-One Years*.
15 Hughes, *The Fatal Shore*, p. 530.
16 This description is from Heustis, *Narrative of the Adventures and Sufferings of Captain Daniel D. Heustis*, p. 100.

8 Ben Franklin's Nephew

1 Franklin to Lord John Russell, 15 February 1840, CO 280/118, pp. 252–3 PRO.
2 *Hobart Town Courier*, 14 February 1840.
3 Marginal comment signed Vernon Smith, 5 June 1840, CO 280/118, pp. 252–3 PRO.
4 Lord John Russell, marginal comment, 5 June 1840, ibid.
5 *Colonial Times*, 18 February 1840, p. 7, col. 3.
6 Bateson, *The Convict Ships, 1787–1868*, pp. 362–4.
7 Maxwell-Stewart and Duffield, 'Skin Deep Devotions', pp. 120–4.
8 Bateson, *The Convict Ships, 1787–1868*, pp. 364–5.
9 Hughes, *The Fatal Shore*, pp. 485–6.
10 Laqueur, 'Bodies, Death and Pauper Funerals', quoted in Dunning, 'Convict Bodies in Van Diemen's Land', p. 135.
11 See Shaw, *Convicts and Colonies*, pp. 276–7.
12 Woodman to family, 15 January 1840, Woodman Papers UWO.
13 Brand, *The Convict Probation System*, pp. 13–25.

9 The Land of Nod

1 Eldershaw, *Guide to the Public Records of Tasmania. Section Three: Convict Department*.
2 Green, 'Spode, Josiah (1790–1858)', p. 466; McKendrick, 'Josiah Wedgwood and Factory Discipline', pp. 30–55.
3 See Con 27 Series AOT; Brand, *The Convict Probation System*, p. 5.
4 Nicholas, 'The Care and Feeding of Convicts', pp. 195–6.
5 Forsyth, *Governor Arthur's Convict System, Van Diemen's Land, 1824–1836*, pp. 89–98.
6 Maxwell-Stewart, 'Convict Workers, "Penal Labour", and Sarah Island', p. 145.
7 Hughes, *The Fatal Shore*, pp. 382–3.
8 Maxwell-Stewart, 'The Rise and Fall of John Longworth', pp. 110–14.
9 Townsend, 'A Mere Lottery', pp. 58–86.
10 *BPP*, Vol. XLII (1837–8), Copy of Despatch from Lieutenant-Governor Sir John Franklin to Lord Glenelg, Note (G), Testimonials by Messrs Backhouse and Walker, p. 25.
11 Brand, *The Convict Probation System*, pp. 9–12.
12 *BPP*, Vol. XXXVII (1845) Correspondence between the Secretary of State and the Governor of Van Diemen's Land (659) p. 14.
13 Syme, *Nine Years in Van Diemen's Land*, p. 185.
14 *BPP*, Vol. XXXV (1845) 'Regulations for the Religious and Moral Instruction of Convicts in Van Diemen's Land', Convict Department, 1 December 1843, Correspondence Between the Secretary of State and the Governor of Van Diemen's Land on the Subject of Convict Discipline, pp. 21–2.
15 Based on a systematic sample of one in twenty-five male convicts landed in Van Diemen's Land in the period 1817–1839, Con 18, Con 23, Con 27 and MM 33 AOT.
16 Brand, *The Convict Probation System*, pp. 5–7; Nicholas, 'The Convict Labour Market', pp. 111–26.
17 Maxwell-Stewart, 'Convict Workers, "Penal Labour" and Sarah Island', p. 149.
18 See for example, Kent and Townsend, *Joseph Mason*, pp. 1–24; Rudé, ' "Captain Swing" and Van Diemen's Land', pp. 13–21.
19 Based on a sample of one in twenty-five prisoners landed in Hobart 1817–39—note data was not collected for offences committed after 1839. Con 18, Con 23, Con 27 and MM 33 AOT.
20 Thompson, *The Making of the English Working Class*, pp. 233–58; Kent, 'Popular Radicalism and the Swing Riots in Central Hampshire', pp. 1–3.
21 Forster, ed., *The Dillingham Convict Letters*, p. 19; see also Hindmarsh, 'Beer and Fighting', pp. 150–6.
22 Shaw, *Convicts and Colonies*, pp. 276–7.
23 Rudé, *Protest and Punishment*, p. 251.
24 See Ignatieff, *A Just Measure of Pain*.

10 The Poor Children of Israel

1 Alexander Cheyne to Colonial Secretary, 2 April 1840, CSO 5/236/6025 AOT.
2 F. Smith to Colonial Secretary, 24 February 1840, CSO 5/233/5912 AOT.
3 Sir John Franklin to Lord John Russell, 15 February 1840, CO 280/118, pp. 252–3 PRO.
4 GO 49, p. 614 Enclosure to 4 January 1844, AOT.
5 David Lord to John Montagu Esq., Colonial Secretary, 12 May 1841, CSO 8/8 C15, pp. 5–6 AOT.
6 Report of the Board of Inquiry into the Condition of Road Parties, LSD 1/2/633 AOT.
7 Kennell, ed., *Dictionary of National Biography*, pp. 448–9.
8 Appropriation list for the *Buffalo*, Con 27/8 AOT.
9 Hughes, *The Fatal Shore*, p. 174.
10 Sokolow, *Eros and Modernization*.
11 Woodman to family, 1 September 1844, Woodman Papers UWO.
12 Tasmanian Papers, SLNSW.
13 *Colonial Times*, 10 March 1840.

[14] Thomas Hewitt, per *Isabella*, Con 31/21 AOT.

[15] 2653 Stephen Wright, per *Buffalo*, Con 31/48 AOT.

[16] Kennell, ed., *Dictionary of National Biography*, pp. 448–9.

[17] Nicholas, 'The Care and Feeding of Convicts', p. 186; Paul and Southgate, *McCane and Widdowson's The Composition of Food*.

[18] David, *Reckoning with Slavery*, pp. 265–8.

[19] *The Plebeian*, 25 June 1842.

[20] Diary of Aaron Dresser Jr, NAC.

[21] 2578 Lysander Curtis, per *Buffalo*, Con 31/8 AOT.

[22] 502 William Nottage, per *Buffalo*, Con 31/32 AOT.

[23] According to his conduct record, Williams died on 29 April 1841: 2660 James Peter Williams, per *Buffalo*, Con 31/48 AOT.

[24] Maxwell-Stewart, 'The Rise and Fall of John Longworth', pp. 104–5.

[25] Roland and Shannon, 'Patterns of Disease among World War II Prisoners of the Japanese', p. 83.

[26] Curtin, *Death by Migration*, p. 194.

[27] Woodman to Mrs Lydia Woodman, 11 March 1840, Woodman Papers UWO.

[28] Captain of the *Augustus* which arrived in Hobart on 29 March: Nicolson, *Gazetteer of Tasmanian Shipping 1803–42*, p. 161.

[29] Diary of Aaron Dresser Jr, NAC.

[30] 1853 Michael Morin, per *Buffalo*, Con 27/8 AOT.

[31] Nicolson, *Gazetteer of Tasmanian Shipping 1803–42*, entries for 12 and 17 February, 6 March 1840.

[32] *Hobart Town Gazette*, Friday, 15 May 1840, p. 475.

[33] 2575 Horace Cooley, per *Buffalo*, Con 31/8; 1853 Michael Morin, per *Buffalo*, Con 31/32; 1559 Jacob Paddock, per *Buffalo*, Con 31/36 and 1416 William Reynolds, per *Buffalo*, Con 31/36 AOT.

11 Scourge of the Old World

[1] Hughes, *The Fatal Shore*, p. 430.

[2] Ibid., p. 429.

[3] *BPP*, Vol. XII (1837–8), Testimony of John Barnes Esq.

[4] Evans and Thorpe, 'Commanding Men: Masculinities and the Convict System', pp. 17–34.

[5] *The True Colonist*, 22 March 1844.

[6] Crowther, 'Practices and Personalities at Hobart Town as Indicated by the Day Book of James Scott, M.D., R.N., Colonial Surgeon', pp. 421–30.

[7] *The Plebeian*, 25 June 1842.

[8] 61 Thomas Warwick, per *Morley* (1) NSW and *Duke of Wellington* VDL, Con 31/45 AOT; Rev. William Schofield, Journal, 24 November 1829, Mitchell Library A428 SLNSW.

[9] Raboteau, *Slave Religion*, pp. 301–2.

[10] Hazzard, *Punishment Short of Death*.

[11] *The Plebeian*, 25 June 1842.

[12] Ibid., 25 June 1842.

[13] 1474 James Gemmell, per *Canton*, Con 31/17 AOT.

[14] 2769 John Swanberg, per *Buffalo*, Con 31/41, 23 December 1840 and 18 January 1841, AOT.

[15] 1242 Hiram Loop, per *Buffalo*, Con 31/28, 21 November, 4 December 1840 and 11 March 1841; 2764 Hiram Sharpe, per *Buffalo*, Con 31/41; 1768 Orin Smith, per *Buffalo*, Con 31/41; 2661 Elijah Woodman, per *Buffalo*, Con 31/48; 2654 Nathan Whiting, per *Buffalo*, Con 31/48 AOT.

[16] Hughes, *The Fatal Shore*, pp. 403–4; Barnes, Minutes of Evidence, 12 February 1838, p. 38, *BPP*, Vol. XII (1837–8), Memoranda by Convict Davis, Mitchell Library, SLNSW.

17 Fogel and Engerman, *Time on the Cross*, pp. 146–7, 217; Nardinelli, 'Corporal Punishment and Children's Wages in Nineteenth Century Britain', pp. 283–95.

18 Hirst, *Convict Society and its Enemies*, pp. 75–6.

19 Fogel, *Without Consent or Contract*, p. 72; Temperly, 'Capitalism, Slavery and Ideology', pp. 94–118.

20 Nicholas, 'The Convict Labour Market', p. 113.

21 Johnston, 'Reforming Criminals', pp. 23–9; Foucault, *Discipline and Punish*, especially pp. 88–9; McConville, *A History of English Prison Administration*, pp. 78–88.

22 Bogle, *Convicts*, pp. 83–5.

23 Mortlock, *Experiences of a Convict*, p. 76.

24 See for example Meranze, *Laboratories of Virtue, 1760–1835*.

12 Lovely Banks

1 Town Surveyor to Colonial Secretary, 16 June 1840, CSO 5/240/6188, p. 56 AOT.

2 J. Laffer to Captain Ainsworth, 1 June 1840, CSO 5/240/6188, p. 57 AOT.

3 Proposed station for Jericho also the lower one for Lovely Banks, Tasmanian Papers, F 84 290/1140 SLNSW.

4 CSO 50/15, p. 182 AOT.

5 CSO 50/16, p. 147 AOT.

6 CSO 50/16, p. 132 AOT.

7 *The Plebeian*, 25 June 1842.

8 2653 Stephen Wright, per *Buffalo*, Con 31/48 AOT.

9 *The Plebeian*, 25 June 1842.

10 Linus Miller to W. E. Lawrence MLC, Lovely Banks Road Station, 16 August 1840, CSO 5/268/6963, p. 97 AOT.

11 The humble Petition of the undersigned Political Prisoners, now at Lovely Banks Road Station, CSO 5/268/6963, p. 95 AOT.

12 Ibid.

13 Forster to Colonial Secretary, CSO 22/59/890 AOT.

14 Linus Miller to W. E. Lawrence MLC, Lovely Banks Road Station, 16 August 1840.

15 Ibid.

16 *Hobart Town Gazette*, 4 September 1840, p. 875.

17 Samuel 1: 14–16.

18 HO/10/42 PRO; *Hobart Town Gazette*, 8 October 1841; *Hobart Town Courier*, 1 December 1842.

13 Green Ponds

1 Military Barracks for the year 1841, CSO 50/15 AOT.

2 CSO 50/14, p. 159 AOT.

3 John Montagu, Colonial Secretary, to Captain Cheyne, Director of Public Works, 19 June 1841, CSO 8/8/45 AOT.

4 Maxwell-Stewart, 'I Could Not Blame the Rangers', p. 117.

5 Forster to Colonial Secretary, CSO 22/59/890 and CSO 50/16, Civil Establishment for the year 1841, p. 141 AOT.

6 See Murison, 'Riches to Rags to Rebellion', pp. 257–75.

7 *Advertiser*, 10 January 1834; *Colonial Times*, 17 November 1840.

8 CSO 50/15, Civil Establishment for the year 1840, pp. 182–4 AOT.

9 John Montagu to [?], 6 July 1841, CSO 8/5/C313, p. 154 AOT. See also CSO 7/1—entry for Lowe, Alexander, Overseer Road Department, file 4022 AOT.

10 See for example the case of Thomas Watson and David Brown, Tasmanian Papers 131, 17 November 1835, SLNSW, and William Gates's observations of the Jericho Probation Station.

[11] See for example the statement of William Green reprinted in the *True Colonist*, 22 March 1844.

[12] Woodman letters, Woodman Papers UWO.

[13] The charges and sentences were: 1248 Hiram Loop, 4 December 1840, 'Insolence', 10 days solitary; 2658 Beamus Woodbury, 10 December 1840, 'Trafficking in bread and strong suspicion of having stolen the same', 7 days solitary; 2769 John G. Swanberg, 23 December 1840, 'Using improper language and insolence', 10 days solitary; 3105 John Berry, 5 January 1841, 'Leaving the station without permission and returning with flour in his possession for which he could not account', 3 days cells; John G. Swanberg was again charged on 18 January 1841 with 'Fighting', 4 days cells; 3107 Henry Barnum, 20 January 1841, 'Feigning Sickness', 3 days solitary; 2770 Samuel Snow, 11 February 1841, 'Idleness', 3 days treadwheel; 3106 John Bradley, 16 April 1841, 'Misconduct, insolence and refusing to work', 48 hours cells; 915 James Aitchison, 3 May 1841, 'Misconduct', case dismissed; 1248 Hiram Loop, 11 May 1841, 'Misconduct', 3 days cells.

[14] Civil Establishment for the year 1841, CSO 50/16, p. 141 AOT.

[15] Dunning, 'Convict Bodies in Van Diemen's Land', p. 136; Syme, *Nine Years in Van Diemen's Land*, p. 186.

[16] J. B. Jones to Assistant Comptroller General, 20 December 1845, Con 1/2026 AOT.

[17] Canada correspondence.

[18] MacLeod, *Green Ponds Municipality*, p. 16.

[19] Captain Cheyne, Director of Public Works, to John Montagu, Colonial Secretary, 10 June 1841, CSO 8/8/41 AOT.

[20] Return of all public works, civil roads, canals, bridges etc. for the year 1840, CSO 50/15, p. 94 AOT.

[21] Stations for the Department of Public Works showing the authorised strength under sentence and strength required on 19 September 1840, CSO 5/240/6180, p. 634–5 AOT.

[22] Ibid.

[23] Return of Billeted Men in Road Stations, 1 July 1841, CSO 8/10/395 AOT.

[24] List of Billet Men at Road Parties consisting of large numbers of Convicts, LSD 1/2/631, and Green Ponds Road Station Return of Men as Employed on 1 December 1837, CSO 5/88/1975 AOT.

[25] Ibid.

[26] *Colonial Times*, 14 April 1840.

[27] J. B. Jones to Asst Comptroller-General, 20 December 1845, Con 1/2026 AOT.

[28] John Montagu to [?], 6 July 1841, CSO 8/5/C313, p. 1546 AOT.

[29] [?] May 1841, Mr Logan, CSO 7/249/6523, p. 106 AOT.

14 Among the Thieves at Jerusalem

[1] R. O'Connor, Report on the works at Bridgewater, 28 July 1834, GO 33/21/320 AOT.

[2] Whitham, 'The Bridges, Roads and Rails of Bridgewater', pp. 57–9.

[3] Return of Billeted Men in Road Stations, 1 July 1841, CSO 8/10/395 AOT.

[4] See Numbers, 3: 39–41.

[5] Luke, 10: 30–2.

[6] Brand, 'The Convict Probation System', pp. 17–18.

[7] Ibid., p. 15.

[8] Return of Billeted Men in Road Stations, 1 July 1841, CSO 8/10/395 AOT.

[9] Earnshaw, 'The Lame, the Blind, the Mad, the Malingerers', pp. 25–39.

[10] Marsh, *Seven Years of my Life*, p. 122.

[11] Extracts from *Ellison's Almanak and Ross's Van Diemen's Land Annual*, 1837, p. 91.

[12] Allocation list for the *Buffalo*, Con 27/8 AOT; *Hobart Town Gazette*, 4 September 1840, p. 875.

[13] Nicholas and Shergold, 'Convicts as Workers', pp. 78–82.

[14] Description list for the transport *Duncan*, Con 33 AOT.

[15] Offences for 1727 Cornelius Burke, 1746 James Cooke, 1735 John Coles, all 26 June 1841, and 1753 James Drayton, 19 August 1842, Con 33 AOT.

[16] Luke, 18: 9–14.

15   Sir John's Indulgence

[1] Russell to Franklin, 20 October 1840, CO 280/118/257 AOT; also GO 1/40/151/215 AOT.

[2] Fitzpatrick, *Sir John Franklin in Tasmania, 1837–1843*, pp. 222–37.

[3] Woodman to family, 9 April 1844, Woodman Papers UWO.

[4] See biography of Chandler, 'In the Shadow of the Gallows'.

[5] *Hobart Town Gazette*, 11 February 1842, p. 140 col. 1.

[6] Gemmell, *The Plebeian*, 25 June 1842.

[7] James Gemmell to William Lyon Mackenzie, 24 January 1843, Mackenzie-Lindsey Papers, Correspondence AO.

[8] Mitchell Monroe to his brother, 3 January 1841, Mackenzie-Lindsey Papers AO. The authors are grateful to Chris Raible for this information.

[9] Government Notice No. 47, Colonial Secretary's Office, 10 February 1842; *Hobart Town Gazette*, 11 February 1842, p. 142, col. 2.

[10] See Hartwell, 'The Van Diemen's Land Government and the Depression of the Eighteen Forties', pp. 185–97.

[11] Murison, 'Riches to Rags to Rebellion', p. 269.

[12] GO 33/18/836 AOT.

[13] Cameron, 'William Kermode', *Australian Dictionary of Biography*, Vol. 2, pp. 49–50.

[14] These were Woodbury, Waggoner and White.

16   Hopes Again Blasted

[1] Woodman to family, 16 March 1843, Woodman Papers UWO.

[2] Ibid.

[3] Tyler to Webster, 27 July 1842, Tyler, *Letters and Times of the Tylers*, p. 264.

[4] Webster to Ashburton, 29 August 1842, in Webster, *Correspondence*.

[5] Woodman to family, 5 February 1843, Woodman Papers UWO.

[6] Tyrrell to Gunn, Fred Landon Papers, Box 4217 UWO.

[7] Woodman to family, 4 July 1843, Woodman Papers UWO.

[8] Tyrell to Gunn, Fred Landon Papers UWO.

[9] Gunn to Tyrrell, ibid.

[10] *Van Diemen's Land Chronicle*, 24 January 1842.

[11] Fitzpatrick, *Sir John Franklin*, pp. 336–41.

[12] Peel papers, Add. MS 40467, British Library.

[13] Woodman to family, 22 February 1844, Woodman Papers UWO.

[14] GO 33/48/94/7 AOT.

[15] Boissery, *A Deep Sense of Wrong*, p. 268.

[16] Woodman to family, 9 April 1844, Woodman Papers UWO.

[17] Ibid., 22 February 1844.

[18] Maxwell-Stewart and Duffield, 'Beyond Hells Gates', pp. 83–97.

[19] See Gatrell, *The Hanging Tree*; Richardson, *Death, Dissection and the Destitute*.

[20] Crowther, 'Practices and Personalities at Hobart Town', pp. 421–30.

[21] Davis, *The Tasmanian Gallows*, p. 42.

[22] This kind of practice in England is discussed in Richardson, *Death, Dissection and the Destitute*.

[23] Pybus, *Community of Thieves*, p. 169.

[24] This is discussed in Dunning, 'Convict Bodies in Van Diemen's Land', p. 136.

[25] The phrase is from Mayhew's monumental work, *London Labour and the London Poor*.

17 'I could not blame the Rangers'

[1] *Cornwall Chronicle*, 6 May 1843.
[2] *Launceston Advertiser*, 14 September 1843.
[3] Howitt, *Impressions of Australia Felix Etc.*, 1845, quoted in Seal, *The Outlaw Legend*, p. 120.
[4] *Hobart Town Gazette*, 31 December 1825.
[5] This is genuine 'Vandiemenian parlance' according to Lempriere, The Penal Settlements of Van Diemen's Land.
[6] Atkinson, 'Four Patterns of Convict Protest', p. 50.
[7] Over 70 per cent of police were convicts: see Petrow, 'After Arthur: Policing Van Diemen's Land, 1837–1846', pp. 176–98.
[8] See Rawlings, *Drunks, Whores and Idle Apprentices: Criminal Biographies of the Eighteenth Century*.
[9] Cash, *Martin Cash: His Personal Narrative as a Bushranger in Van Diemen's Land in 1843–4*, p. 108.
[10] Ibid., pp. 108–9.
[11] Calder, *Brady* (1873), reprinted 1979, p. 57.
[12] Cash, *Martin Cash*, p. 102.
[13] Seal, *The Outlaw Legend*.
[14] Korbell, Bushranging in Van Diemen's Land, 1824–34, pp. 5, 22, 63.
[15] Hobsbawm, *Bandits*, pp. 41–56.
[16] *Hobart Town Gazette*, 14 October 1826.
[17] Ibid., 17 September 1825.
[18] Maxwell-Stewart, ' "I could not blame the rangers": Tasmanian Bushranging, Convicts and Convict Management'. In another context see Roberts, 'Caravats and Shanavests: Whiteboyism and Faction Fighting in East Munster, 1802–11', pp. 66–73.
[19] Linebaugh, *The London Hanged*, pp. 203–5.
[20] Quoted in full in Seal, *The Outlaw Legend*, p. 122.
[21] Linebaugh, *The London Hanged*, p. 205.
[22] Reprinted in Wright, *Narrative and Recollections of Van Diemen's Land*, p. 44.
[23] 2658 Woodbury, Con 33 AOT.

18 Free Pardon

[1] Reprinted in *Narrative of the Adventures and Sufferings of Captain Daniel D. Heustis* and also as an appendix to Guillet, *The Lives and Times of the Patriots*, p. 293.
[2] The man was one of the York weavers, William Rice: see Chapman, ed., *Historical Records of Australia*, pp. 338–9.
[3] Everett to Heustis, 5 December 1845, reprinted in Heustis, *Narrative*, pp. 161–3.
[4] Patrick White, James Waggoner and Joseph Stewart.
[5] Listed in *Colonial Times*, 15 October 1844.
[6] Eardley-Wilmot to Stanley, 9 December 1844, GO 33/49/702 AOT.
[7] See Eldershaw, 'The Convict Department', pp. 114–22.
[8] Stanley to Eardley-Wilmot, 9 September 1844, GO 1/56/300/33 AOT.
[9] Scott, 'The Patriot Game: New Yorkers and the Canadian Rebellion of 1837–1838', pp. 281–96.
[10] *Hobart Town Courier*, 13 September 1845.
[11] Woodman, Hobart Town Diary, 17 July 1845, Woodman Papers UWO.
[12] Woodman to family, 24 July 1845, Woodman Papers UWO.
[13] For the correspondence on this matter, see CSO 20/2/52/110 AOT.
[14] This quote is attributed to Franklin by Canadian historian Louis Blake Duff, 12 March 1837, correspondence file AOT.
[15] United States National Archives House of Representatives, 25 January 1845, 28th Congress, second session.

[16] See Law Officers to Colonial Office, 21 May 1838, CO 42/452 PRO. On the question of lawsuits see also Maule to Stephen, 9 February 1839, RG 7/G1 vol. 91 NAC; CO 42/465 PRO; Russell to Maule, 9 May 1839, HO 13/75 PRO.

[17] Letter from Linus Miller, *New York Express*, 28 January 1846.

[18] CSO 20/20/423/218 AOT.

[19] CSO 20/24/520/60 AOT.

[20] Con 33 AOT.

[21] Memorial to friends in Hobart Town, Woodman, Hobart Town Diary, February 1847, Woodman Papers UWO.

[22] Letter from Lapthrop to Mrs Woodman, 5 March 1846, Woodman Papers UWO.

[23] Grey to Eardley-Wilmot, 4 December 1846, GO 1/62/7/410 AOT.

[24] GO 1/66/196/368 AOT.

[25] Ibid.

[26] Con 33 AOT.

[27] HO 10/61 PRO.

[28] Con 33 AOT.

[29] Earl Grey to Denison, 8 November 1850, GO 1/79/171/73 AOT.

[30] *Victorian Police Gazette*, 4 September 1856, p. 317, and 6 November 1856, p. 398.

[31] If this marriage took place, it was never registered. See Con 52/7/29 AOT.

Afterword

[1] Neidhardt, *Fenianism in North America*.

[2] Greenwood and Wright, eds, *State Trials*, Vol. 11.

[3] The authors are indebted to Professor Barry Wright of Carlton University for this information.

[4] Arthur to Russell, 25 July 1840, CO 42/471 PRO.

[5] CO18/163 PRO.

[6] Manera, 'The Fenian Escape', pp. 24–7.

[7] Hughes, *The Fatal Shore*, pp. 531–2.

[8] Brand, *Penal Peninsula*, pp. 193–200.

[9] Reported in *Argus*, 12 July 1873.

[10] Brand, *Penal Peninsula*, pp. 201–16.

[11] Young, *Making Crime Pay*, pp. 70–83.

Bibliography

Patriot Narratives

Gates, William, *Recollections of Life in Van Dieman's Land*, D. S. Crandall, Lockport 1850.

Heustis, Daniel, *A Narrative of the Adventures and Sufferings of Captain Daniel Heustis*, Redding and Co., Boston 1848.

Marsh, Robert, *Seven Years of My life, or a Narrative of Patriot Exile*, Faxon and Stevens, Buffalo 1847.

Miller, Linus, *Notes of an Exile in Van Dieman's Land*, W. McKinstry and Co., New York 1846.

Snow, Samuel, *The Exiles Return or Narrative of Samuel Snow who was Banished to Van Diemen's Land, for Participating in the Patriot War in Upper Canada in 1838*, Smead and Cowles, Cleveland 1846.

Wait, Benjamin, *Letters from Van Dieman's Land Written During Four Years Imprisonment for Political Offences Committed in Upper Canada*, A. W. Wilgus, Buffalo 1843.

Wright, Stephen, *Narrative and Recollections of Van Dieman's Land During Three Years Captivity of Stephen S. Wright*, ed. Caleb Lyon, New York 1844.

British Parliamentary Papers

BPP, Vol. XII (1837–8), Minutes of Evidence.

BPP, Vol. XXXV (1845), Correspondence Between the Secretary of State and the Governor of Van Diemen's Land on the Subject of Convict Discipline.

BPP, Vol. XXXVII (1845), Correspondence between the Secretary of State for the Colonies and the Governor of Van Diemen's Land.

BPP, Vol. XLII (1837–8), Copy of Despatch from Lieutenant-Governor Sir John Franklin to Lord Glenelg.

Manuscript Sources

Archives of Ontario

Mackenzie-Lindsey Papers.

Archives Office of Tasmania
Blue books, CSO 50.
Convict indents, Con 16.
Colonial Secretary's correspondence files, CSO 1; CSO 5; CSO 8; CSO 16; CSO 20.
Description registers, Con 18; Con 23.
Offence records for convicts arriving in the Assignment period, Con 31.
Offence records for convicts arriving in the Probation period, Con 33.
Outward bound dispatches GO 1.

British Library
Peel Papers.

Library of Congress
Andrew Stevenson Papers.
Van Buren Papers.
Daniel Webster Papers.

Mitchell Library, State Library New South Wales
Lempriere, T., The Penal Settlements of Van Diemen's Land, manuscript, 1839.
Memoranda by Convict Davis, Servant to Mr Forster, Supt. of Convicts, Norfolk Island, 1843.
Schofield, Rev. William, Journal, 24 November 1829.
Tasmanian Papers.

National Archives of Canada
Account of the Court of Special Commission at Niagara, Sheriff Alexander Hamilton Papers.
Colonial dispatches to governors of Upper Canada and Lower Canada, RG 7/G1; RG 7/G12.
Confidential dispatches to the Governor of Upper Canada, RG 7/G3.
Correspondence Governor of Upper Canada to Governor of Lower Canada, RG 7/G7.
Minute Books of the Executive Council of Upper Canada and Lower Canada, RG 1/E1.
Preliminary hearings and court at London and Kingston, Upper Canada and the Habeas Corpus Applications to the Queen's Bench, series RG 5/B37–41.
Submissions to the Executive Council of Upper Canada, RG 1/E3.
The Upper Canada Sundries RG 5/A1.

National Archives of United States
Papers of 27th Congress, Document no. 39, House of Representatives.

Public Record Office
Correspondence of the British Ambassador to Washington, FO 7/71.
Correspondence of the Secretary of State for the Colonies and the governors of Upper Canada and Lower Canada, CO 42–45; CO 47.

Log of the HMS *Buffalo*, ADM 51.
Lord John Russell Papers 33/22.
Transportation Records, HO 10; HO 11; HO 13.

Talman Collection, University of Western Ontario
Fred Landon Papers.
Woodman Papers.

Newspapers

Argus, Melbourne, Victoria.
Colonial Times, Hobart, Van Diemen's Land.
Cornwall Chronicle, Launceston, Van Diemen's Land.
Greenock Advertiser, Scotland.
Hobart Town Courier, Van Diemen's Land.
Hobart Town Gazette, Van Diemen's Land.
Kingston Chronicle, Ontario.
Launceston Advertiser, Van Diemen's Land.
New York Express, New York.
Oswego County Whig, Oswego.
Pennsylvania Gazette, Pennsylvania.
The Plebeian, New York.
Rochester Daily Democrat, Rochester.
St Catharine's Journal, Ontario.
The True Colonist, Hobart, Van Diemen's Land.
Van Diemen's Land Chronicle, Van Diemen's Land.
Victorian Police Gazette, Victoria.

Books and Articles

Anderson, Clare, *Convicts in the Indian Ocean: Transportation from South East Asia to Mauritius, 1815–35*, Macmillan, Basingstoke 2000.
Atkinson, Alan, *The Europeans in Australia*, vol. 1, Oxford University Press, Oxford 1998.
—— 'Four Patterns of Convict Protest', *Labour History*, vol. 37, 1979, pp. 28–51.
Bateson, Charles, *The Convict Ships*, Brown, Glasgow 1959.
Beckles, Hilary, *White Servitude and Black Slavery in Barbados, 1627–1715*, University of Tennessee Press, Knoxville 1999.
Beer, Donald, *Sir Allan Napier MacNab*, W. L. Griffin Ltd, Hamilton 1984.
Bogle, Michael, *Convicts*, Historic House Trust, New South Wales 1999.
Boissery, Beverly, *A Deep Sense of Wrong*, Dundurn Press, Toronto 1995.
Bradley, James and Maxwell-Stewart, Hamish, 'Embodied Explorations: Investigating Convict Descriptions', in I. Duffield and J. Bradley, eds, *Representing Convicts: New Perspectives on Convict Forced Labour Migration*, Leicester University Press, London 1997, pp. 183–203.

Brand, Ian, *The Convict Probation System: Van Diemen's Land, 1839–1854*, Blubberhead Press, Hobart 1991.

—— *Penal Peninsula: Port Arthur and its Outstations, 1827–1898*, Regal, Launceston 1989.

Buckley, Roger, *The British Army in the West Indies*, University of Florida Press, Gainesville, 1998.

Cahill, Jack, *Forgotten Patriots: Canadian Rebels on Australian Convict Shores*, Robin Brass Studio, Toronto 1998.

Calder, J., *Brady* (1873), reprinted (ed. E. Fitzsymonds), Adelaide 1979.

Cameron, J., 'William Kermode', *Australian Dictionary of Biography*, Vol. 2, *1788–1850*, Melbourne University Press, Melbourne 1967, pp. 49–50.

Cash, Martin, *Martin Cash: His Personal Narrative as a Bushranger in Van Diemen's Land in 1843–4*, J. Walch and Sons, Hobart, 8th edn, 1967.

Chapman, Peter, 'The Island Panopticon', *Historical Records of Australia*, vol. 1, no. 2, Centre for Tasmanian Historical Studies, Hobart 1990, pp. 6–10.

——ed., *Historical Records of Australia*, vol. 6, Centre for Tasmanian Historical Studies, Hobart.

Chatrand, Rene, and Chappell, Paul, *British Forces in the West Indies, 1793–1815*, Osprey, London 1986.

Coldham, Peter, *Emigrants in Chains: A Social History of Forced Emigration to the Americas, 1607–1776*, Sutton, Stroud 1992.

Conway, Stephen, 'The Recruitment of Criminals into the British Army, 1775–81', *Bulletin of the Institute of Historical Research*, vol. 58, 1958, pp. 46–58.

Corey, Albert, *The Crisis of 1830–1842 in Canadian American Relations*, Yale University Press, New Haven 1941.

Craig, Gerald, *Upper Canada: The Formative Years*, McClelland and Stewart, Toronto 1963.

Craton, Michael, *Testing the Chains: Resistance to Slavery in the British West Indies*, Cornell University Press, London 1982.

Crowther, W. E. L., 'Practices and Personalities at Hobart Town as Indicated by the Day Book of James Scott, M.D., R.N., Colonial Surgeon', *Medical Journal of Australia*, 20 March 1954, pp. 421–30.

Cruikshank, E. A., 'A Twice-Told Tale: Insurrection in the Short Hills in 1838', *Ontario Historical Society Papers and Records*, vol. VIII, 1926, pp. 180–222.

Curtin, Phillip, *Death by Migration: Europe's Encounter with the Tropical World in the Nineteenth Century*, Cambridge University Press, Cambridge 1989.

David, P., *Reckoning with Slavery: A Critical Study in Quantitative History of American Negro Slavery*, Oxford University Press, New York 1976.

Davis, Richard, *The Tasmanian Gallows*, Cat and Fiddle Press, Hobart 1974.

Davis, Robert, *The Canadian Farmer's Travels in the United States of America in which remarks are made on the arbitrary colonial policy practised in Canada and the free and equal rights and happy effects of the liberal institutions and astonishing enterprise of the United States*, Steele's Press, Buffalo 1837.

Douglas, R. A., 'The Battle of Windsor', *Ontario History*, vol. 61, 1959, pp. 137–52.

Ducharme, Leon, *Journal of Political Exile in Australia*, trans. George Mackaness, Australian Historical Monographs, Sydney 1944.

Duff, Louis, 'Samuel Chandler of St Johns', *Welland County Historical Society Papers and Records*, vol. V, 1939, pp. 115–49.

Duffield, Ian, ' "Stated this Offence": High Density Micro Narratives' in Lucy Frost and Hamish Maxwell-Stewart, eds, *Chain Letters: Narrating Convict Lives*, Melbourne University Press, Melbourne 2001, pp. 119–135.

—— 'Problematic Passages: "Jack Bushman's" Convict Narrative' in Ian Duffield and James Bradley, eds, *Representing Convicts: New Perspectives on Convict Forced Labour Migration*, Leicester University Press, London 1997.

Duly, L. C., 'Hottentots to Hobart and Sydney: The Cape Supreme Court's Use of Transportation, 1828–1838', *Australian Journal of Politics and History*, vol. 25, no. 1, 1979, pp. 39–50.

Dunning, Thomas, 'The Canadian Rebellions of 1837–38: An Episode in Northern Borderland History', *Australasian Journal of American Studies*, vol. 14, no. 2, 1995.

—— 'Convict Bodies in Van Diemen's Land: The North American Experience', *Australian Studies*, vol. 13, no. 1, 1998, pp. 135–6.

Earnshaw, Beverley, 'The Lame, the Blind, the Mad, the Malingerers: Sick and Disabled Convicts within the Colonial Community', *Journal of the Royal Historical Society*, vol. 81, part 1, 1992, pp. 25–39.

Ekirch, A. Roger, *Bound for America: The Transportation of British Convicts to the Colonies, 1718–1775*, Clarendon, Oxford 1987.

—— 'Great Britain's Secret Convict Trade to America, 1783–4', *American Historical Review*, vol. 89, no. 5, 1984, pp. 1285–91.

Eldershaw, Peter, *Guide to the Public Records of Tasmania. Section Three: Convict Department*, State Library of Tasmania, Hobart 1965.

—— 'The Convict Department', *Tasmanian Historical Research Association*, vol. 15, no. 3, 1968, pp. 114–22.

Enders, Mike, and Dupont, Benoit, eds, *Policing the Lucky Country*, Hawkins Press, Annandale 2001.

Essex Historical Society Papers and Addresses, vol. 2, Essex Historical Society, Windsor 1904.

Evans, Ray, and Thorpe, Bill, 'Commanding Men: Masculinities and the Convict System', *Journal of Australian Studies*, vol. 56, 1998, pp. 17–34.

Fitzpatrick, Kathleen, *Sir John Franklin in Tasmania, 1837–1843*, Melbourne University Press, Melbourne 1949.

Fogel, Robert, *Without Consent or Contract: The Rise and Fall of American Slavery*, Norton, London 1989.

Fogel, Robert, and Engerman, Stanley, *Time on the Cross: The Economics of American Negro Slavery*, Norton, New York 1989.

Forster, H. W., ed., *The Dillingham Convict Letters*, Harley W. Forster, Melbourne 1970.

Forsyth, W. D., *Governor Arthur's Convict System, Van Diemen's Land, 1824–1836*, Longmans, London 1935.

Foucault, Michel, *Discipline and Punish: The Birth of the Prison*, Allen Lane, London 1977.

Frost, Lucy, and Maxwell-Stewart, Hamish, eds, *Chain Letters: Narrating Convict Lives*, Melbourne University Press, Melbourne 2001.

Fry, Alfred A., *Report of the Case of the Canadian Prisoners with an Introduction to the Writ of Habeas Corpus*, Milliken, London 1839.

Fryer, Mary, *Volunteers and Redcoats, Rebels and Raiders*, Dundurn Press, Toronto 1987.

Gatrell, V., *The Hanging Tree: Execution and the English People, 1770–1868*, Oxford University Press, Oxford 1994.

Gemery, Henry, 'Markets for Migrants: English Indentured Servitude and Emigration in the Seventeenth Century' in P. C. Emmer, ed., *Colonisation and Migration: Indentured Labour before and after Slavery*, Martinus Nijhoff, Dodrecht 1986, pp. 34–46.

Gilmour, Ian, *Riot, Risings and Revolution: Governance and Violence in Eighteenth-Century England*, Pimlico, London 1982.

Graves, Donald, *Guns Across the River: The Battle of the Windmill, 1838*, Robin Brass Studio, Toronto 2001.

Green, F. C., 'Josiah Spode', *Australian Dictionary of Biography*, vol. 2, *1788–1850*, Melbourne University Press, Melbourne 1967, p. 466.

Greenwood, M., and Wright, B., eds, *Canadian State Trials*, vol. 11, Osgoode Society and University of Toronto Press, Toronto 2002.

Grubb, Farley, 'The Statutory Regulation of Colonial Servitude: An Incomplete Approach', *Explorations in Economic History*, vol. 37, 2000, pp. 42–75.

Guillet, Edwin, *The Lives and Times of the Patriots: an account of the rebellion in Upper Canada, 1837–1838; and the patriot agitation in the United States, 1837–1842*, Thomas Nelson, Toronto 1938.

Hartwell, R., 'The Van Diemen's Land Government and the Depression of the Eighteen Forties', *Historical Studies*, vol. 4, November 1950, pp. 185–97.

Hazzard, Margaret, *Punishment Short of Death: A History of the Penal Settlement at Norfolk Island*, Hyland House, Melbourne 1984.

Hindmarsh, Bruce, 'Beer and Fighting: Some Aspects of Male Convict Leisure in Van Diemen's Land', *Journal of Australian Studies*, vol. 63, 2000, pp. 150–6.

Hirst, John Bradley, *Convict Society and Its Enemies: A History of Early New South Wales*, Allen and Unwin, Sydney 1983.

Hobsbawm, Eric, *Bandits*, Penguin, Harmondsworth 1972.

Hobsbawm, Eric, and Rudé, George, *Captain Swing*, Penguin, Harmondsworth 1985.

Hopkins, Jeffery, ' "Fighting Those Who Came Against Their Country": Maori Political Transportees to Van Diemen's Land 1846–48', *Tasmanian Historical Research Association Papers and Proceedings*, vol. 44, no. 1, 1997, pp. 49–67.

Hough, Franklin, *A History of Jefferson County in the State of New York*, Joel Munsell, Albany 1854.

Huch, Ronald, and Ziegler, Paul, *Joseph Hume: The People's MP*, American Philosophical Society, Philadelphia 1985.

Hughes, Robert, *The Fatal Shore: A History of the Transportation of Convicts to Australia, 1787–1868*, Harvill, London 1986.

Hutchinson, G. C., 'Glasgow Working Class Politics' in R. A. Cage, ed., *The Working Class in Glasgow, 1750–1914*, Croom Helm, Kent 1987, pp. 98–108.

Ignatieff, Michael, *A Just Measure of Pain: The Penitentiary in the Industrial Revolution, 1750–1850*, Pantheon, New York 1978.

Johnston, Norman, 'Reforming Criminals' and 'Building the Ideal Prison', in N. Johnston, K. Finkel and J. A. Cohen, eds, *Eastern State Penitentiary: Crucible of Good Intentions*, Philadelphia Museum of Art, Philadelphia 1994, pp. 23–9, 31–45.

Jones, Howard, *The Webster Ashburton Treaty: A Study in Anglo-American Relations, 1783–1843*, University of North Carolina, Chapel Hill 1977.

Kennell, L., ed., *Dictionary of National Biography*, vol. XI, Oxford 1967–8.

Kent, David, 'Popular Radicalism and the Swing Riots in Central Hampshire', *Hampshire Papers*, no. 11, 1996, pp. 1–21.

Kent, David, and Townsend, Norma, *Joseph Mason: Assigned Convict*, Melbourne University Press, Melbourne 1996.

Kilbourn, William, *The Firebrand: William Lyon Mackenzie and the Rebellion in Upper Canada*, Clarke, Irwin, Toronto 1956.

Kinchen, Oscar, *The Rise and Fall of the Patriot Hunters*, Bookman Associates, New York 1956.

Korbell, M., Bushranging in Van Diemen's Land, 1824–34, BA Hons Thesis, University of Tasmania 1973, pp. 5–63.

Laqueur, Thomas, 'Bodies, Death and Pauper Funerals', *Representations*, 1 February 1983.

Landon, Fred, *An Exile from Canada to Van Diemen's Land: being the study of Elijah Woodman transported overseas for participation in the Upper Canada troubles of 1837*, Longmans, Green and Co., Toronto 1960.

Lindsey, Charles, *The Life and Times of William Lyon Mackenzie*, Coles Pub. Co., Toronto 1862.

Linebaugh, Peter, *The London Hanged: Crime and Civil Society in the Eighteenth Century*, Cambridge University Press, Cambridge 1992.

Linebaugh, Peter, and Rediker, Marcus, *The Many-Headed Hydra: Soldiers, Slaves, Commoners and the Hidden History of the Revolutionary Atlantic*, Beacon Press, Boston 2000.

MacLeod, T. R., *Green Ponds Municipality*, Walch and Sons, Hobart 1962.

McConville, Seán, *A History of English Prison Administration, Vol. 1: 1750–1877*, Routledge and Kegan Paul, London 1981.

McKendrick, N., 'Josiah Wedgwood and Factory Discipline', *Historical Journal*, vol. 4, 1961, pp. 30–55.

Malherbe, V. C., 'David Stuurman: "Last Chief of the Hottentots"' *African Studies*, vol. 39, 1980, pp. 47–57.

—— 'South African Bushmen to Australia? Some Soldier Convicts Investigated', *Journal of Australian Colonial History*, vol. 3, no. 1, 2001, pp. 100–24.

Manera, Brad, 'The Fenians Escape', *Wartime Magazine*, no. 16, 2001, pp. 24–7.

Manwaring, G. E., and Dobrée, Bonamy, *The Floating Republic*, Frank Cass, London 1966.

Masonic Research Society, 'In the Shadow of the Gallows', in *Jewels of Masonic Eloquence and True Stories of Mercy and Assistance*, Masonic Research Society, Oklahoma 1919.

Maxwell-Stewart, Hamish, '"I could not blame the rangers", Tasmanian Bushranging, Convicts and Convict Management', *Tasmanian Historical Research Association Papers and Proceedings*, vol. 42, no. 3, 1995, pp. 109–27.

—— 'Convict Workers, "Penal Labour", and Sarah Island: Life at Macquarie Harbour, 1822–1834' in J. Bradley and I. Duffield, eds, *Representing Convicts: New Perspectives on Convict Forced Labour Migration*, Leicester University Press, London 1997, pp. 142–62.

—— 'The Rise and Fall of John Longworth: Work and Punishment in Early Port Arthur', *Tasmanian Historical Studies*, vol. 7, 1999, pp. 96–114.

Maxwell-Stewart, Hamish, and Bradley, James, 'Behold the Man: Power, Observation and the Tattooed Convict', *Australian Studies*, vol. 12, no. 1, 1997, pp. 74–5, 118–35.

Maxwell-Stewart, Hamish, and Duffield, Ian, 'Skin Deep Devotions: Religious Tattoos and Convict Transportation to Australia', in J. Caplan, ed., *Writing on the Body: The Tattoo in European and American History*, Reaktion Press, London 2000, pp. 118–35.

—— and —— 'Beyond Hells Gates: Religion at Macquarie Harbour Penal Station', *Tasmanian Historical Studies*, vol. 15, no. 2, 1997, pp. 83–97.

Mayhew, Henry, *London Labour and the London Poor*, Griffin Bohn, London 1861.

Meranze, M., *Laboratories of Virtue: Punishment, Revolution, and Authority in Philadelphia, 1760–1835*, University of North Carolina, Chapel Hill 1996.

Mortlock, J., *Experiences of a Convict Transported for Twenty-One Years*, London 1864–5, reprint (ed. G. A. Wilkes and A. G. Mitchell), Sydney University Press, London 1965.

Murison, Barbara, 'Riches to Rags to Rebellion: James Aitcheson', *British Journal of Canadian Studies*, vol. 4, no. 2, 1989, pp. 257–75.

Nardinelli, Clarke, 'Corporal Punishment and Children's Wages in Nineteenth Century Britain', *Explorations in Economic History*, vol. 19, no. 3, 1982, pp. 283–95.

Neidhardt, W., *Fenianism in North America*, Pennsylvannia State University Press, University Park 1975.

New, Chester, *Lord Durham*, Oxford, London 1968.

Nicholas, Stephen, 'The Convict Labour Market' and 'The Care and Feeding of Convicts' in S. Nicholas, ed., *Convict Workers: Reinterpreting Australia's Past*, Cambridge University Press, Cambridge 1988, pp. 111–26, 180–98.

Nicholas, Stephen, and Shergold, Peter, 'Convicts as Workers' and 'Transportation as Global Migration', in S. Nicholas, ed., *Convict Workers: Reinterpreting Australia's Past*, Cambridge University Press, Cambridge 1988, pp. 28–39, 62–84.

Nicolson, I., *Gazetteer of Tasmanian Shipping 1803–42*, Part IV, Canberra 1985.

Oxley, Deborah, *Convict Maids: The Forced Migration of Women to Australia*, Cambridge University Press, Cambridge 1996.

Paul, A., and Southgate, D., *McCane and Widdowson's The Composition of Food*, HMSO, London 1978.

Peterson, Lois, *The Presidencies of William Henry Harrison and John Tyler*, University of Kansas Press, Lawrence 1989.

Petrow, Stefan, 'After Arthur: Policing Van Diemen's Land, 1837–1846', in Mike Enders and Benoit Dupont, eds, *Policing the Lucky Country*, Hawkins Press, Annandale 2001, pp. 176–98.

Preston, Thomas, *Three Years Residence in Canada*, Richard Bentley, London 1840.

Prieur, Francois, *Notes of a Convict of 1838*, trans. George Mackaness, Australian Historical Monographs, Sydney 1949.

Pybus, Cassandra, *Community of Thieves*, Heinemann, Melbourne 1993.

—— 'The D—Yankee Quill Driver' in Lucy Frost and Hamish Maxwell-Stewart, eds, *Chain Letters: Narrating Convict Lives*, Melbourne University Press, Melbourne 2001, pp. 15–31.

—— 'American Citizens, British Slaves: Yankee Political Prisoners in Van Diemen's Land', *Australian Studies*, vol. 16, no. 1, Summer 2001.

Raboteau, Albert J., *Slave Religion: The 'Invisible Institution' in the Antebellum South*, Oxford University Press, New York 1976.

Raible, Chris, *Muddy York Mud*, Robin Brass Studio, Toronto 1995.

Rawlings, Phillip, *Drunks, Whores and Idle Apprentices: Criminal Biographies of the Eighteenth Century*, Routledge, London 1992.

Read, Colin, *The Rebellion of 1837 in Upper Canada*, Carleton University Press, Ottawa 1985.

—— *The Rising in Western Upper Canada, 1837–8: The Duncombe Revolt and After*, University of Toronto Press, Toronto 1982.

—— 'White Prosperous and Free: Images of the United States in the Minds and Writings of the Upper Canadian rebels of 1837', unpublished paper in possession of the author.

Reay, Barry, 'The Context and Meaning of Popular Literacy: Some Evidence from Nineteenth Century Rural England', *Past and Present*, no. 131, 1991, pp. 89–129.

Reece, Bob, *The Origins of Irish Convict Transportation to New South Wales*, Polgrave, Basingstoke 2001.

Richardson, Ruth, *Death, Dissection and the Destitute*, Routledge and Kegan Paul, London 1994.

Roberts, P., 'Caravats and Shanavests: Whiteboyism and Faction Fighting in East Munster, 1802–11' in S. Clark and J. Donnelly, eds, *Irish Peasants, Violence and Political Unrest, 1780–1914*, Dublin 1983, pp. 66–73.

Roland, C., and Shannon, H., 'Patterns of Disease among World War II Prisoners of the Japanese: Hunger, Weight Loss and Deficiency Disease in Two Camps', *Journal of Medical History*, vol. 46, no. 1, 1991, p. 83.

Rudé, George, *Protest and Punishment: The Story of the Social and Political Protesters Transported to Australia, 1788–1868*, Clarendon Press, Oxford 1978.

—— '"Captain Swing" in Van Diemen's Land', *Tasmanian Historical Research Association Papers and Proceedings*, vol. 12, 1964, pp. 6–24.

Sanderson, Charles R., ed., *The Arthur Papers: being the Canadian papers mainly confidential private and demi official of Sir George Arthur KCH last lieutenant Governor of Upper Canada*, 3 vols, Toronto Public Library, Toronto 1957–59.

Scott, Stuart, 'The Patriot Game: New Yorkers and the Canadian Rebellion of 1837–1838', *New York History*, July 1987, pp. 281–96.

Seal, Graham, *The Outlaw Legend: A Cultural Tradition in Britain, America and Australia*, Cambridge University Press, Cambridge 1996.

Sen, Satadru, *Disciplining Punishment: Colonialism and Convict Society in the Andaman Islands*, Oxford University Press, Oxford 2000.

Shaw, A. G. L., *Convicts and Colonies*, Faber, London 1966.

Sokolow, J. A., *Eros and Modernization: Sylvester Graham, Health Reform, and the Origins of Victorian Sexuality in America*, Fairleigh Dickinson University Press, Rutherford 1983.

Stevenson, John, *Popular Disturbances in England, 1700–1870*, Longman, New York 1979.

Stuart, Reginald, *Prologue to Manifest Destiny: Anglo-American Relations in the 1840s*, Wilmington, Delaware 1997.

Syme, J., *Nine Years in Van Diemen's Land*, privately printed, Dundee 1845.

Temperly, Howard, 'Capitalism, Slavery and Ideology', *Past and Present*, no. 75, 1977, pp. 94–118.

Thompson, E. P., *The Making of the English Working Class*, Pelican, Harmondsworth 1981.

Tiffany, Orrin, *The Canadian Rebellion of 1837–1838*, Buffalo Historical Society, Buffalo 1905.

—— *The Relations of the United States to the Canadian Rebellion of 1837–1838*, Buffalo Historical Society, Buffalo 1905.

Townsend, Norma, 'A "Mere Lottery": The Convict System in New South Wales through the Eyes of the Molesworth Committee', *Push from the Bush*, vol. 21, 1985, pp. 58–86.

Tyler, Lyon, *Letters and Times of the Tylers*, Whittet and Shepperson, Richmond, Va. 1885.

Webster, Daniel, *Correspondence*, vol. 5, ed. Harold Moser, University of New England Press, Portland 1982.

Whitham, L., 'The Bridges, Roads and Rails of Bridgewater', *Tasmanian Historical Research Association Papers and Proceedings*, vol. 36, no. 2, 1989, pp. 57–9.

Wilson, Major L., *The Presidency of Martin Van Buren*, University of Kansas Press, Lawrence 1984.

Wittke, Carl, 'Ohio and the Canadian–American Crisis of 1837–38', *Ohio State Archeological and Historical Society Quarterly*, January 1949, pp. 21–34.

Young, David, *Making Crime Pay: The Evolution of Convict Tourism in Tasmania*, Tasmanian Historical Research Association, Hobart 1996.

Index

Patriot Army: Battle of the Windmill, 1–5, 35–9, 141; invasion of Bois Blanc, 12; invasion of Pelee Island, 12, 20; invasion of Sarnia, 15; invasion of Short Hills, 15–19; invasion at Windsor, 41–3; Navy Island, 10; organisation of, 10, 12; recruitment, 10
penal transportation: Andaman Islands, 4–5; anti-transportation, 208; Barbadoes, 4; Bermuda, 4, 25; black market, 143–4; Board of Ordinance, 98; Canada, 24–5, 207; Cape Colony, 5; Comptroller-General of Convicts, 195, 202–3; convict assignment, 84–8; convict clothing, 96–7; convict labour, 91–3; convict records, 65; death rate, 105; end of transportation, 207–8; Home Office responsibility, 25; Honduras, 4–5; hulks, 25; Cape, India, 4; induction, 65; legal issues, 25, 30–1, 46–7, 69; New South Wales, 5; New Zealand, 5; Nova Scotia, 4–5; pardons, 192–3; political prisoners, 4–6, 94; prerogative of transportation, 25; probation system, 88–9; punishment, 72, 108–15; skilled labour, 92–4; sodomy, 208; Straits of Malacca, 4; Superintendent of Convicts, 25, 48; Transportation Act 1718, 13; West Africa, 4; West Indies, 5; Western Australia, 208
Pierce, James, 175
Port Arthur, 85, 89, 107, 111, 113, 129, 133, 137, 139, 154–8, 162, 174, 179, 208–9
Prescott (Ontario), 34–6
Priest, Asa, 59, 179
Prince, Colonel John, 42–3
Prisoners' Barracks, Hobart, 65, 72, 76, 114, 153, 155, 164, 197
Probation Stations: Bridgewater, 114, 118, 146–8; Brown's River, 90–2, 114, 128, 148, 151–3, 154, 158; Constitution Hill, 148; Deloraine, 145; Green Ponds, 131–45, 162, 178–9; Jericho, 148–51, 154; Jerusalem, 148, 154, 158; Lovely Banks, 119–25; Mersey, 141; Mt Direction, 148; New Town, 148; Picton, 136–9, 143, 146, 158; Rochey Hills, 148; Salt Water Creek, 153–4, 158, 164; Sandy Bay, 76, 95–107; Victoria Valley, 163

Quebec, 9, 25–6, 53–4
Queen Victoria, 2

Reynolds, Solomon, 144
Reynolds, William (David Deal), 21, 27, 29, 30
Reynolds, William, 106–7, 202–3
Roberts, Peter, 86–7

Roebuck, John Arthur, 26–7, 31, 48, 70, 175, 192, 198
Russell, Lord John (Home Secretary and Secretary of State for the Colonies), 28–31, 47–8, 74, 159, 207

Sackets Harbor (New York), 1, 34, 59
St Lawrence River, 1–3, 35–6
St Mary's Church, 132, 141
Sharp, Hiram, 112–13, 140
Sheldon, Chauncey, 44
Shew, Henry, 200–1
ships: *Astrolabe*, 106; *Augustus*, 106; *Buffalo*, 54; *Canton*, 31; *Captain Ross*, 29, 31; *Caroline*, 29; *Champlain*, 41; *Duncan*, 158; *Eliza Ann*, 198; *Indian*, 106; *Isabella*, 155; *Julian*, 160; *Kingston*, 201–2; *Lady Franklin*, 156; *Marquis of Hastings*, 29; *Salamander*, 106; *Steiglitz*, 195; *United States*, 35; *William Hamilton*, 170; *Young Eagle*, 201; *Zelée*, 106
Six Nations, 7, 15, 19, 24
Skene, James, 96, 101, 151
Smith, Orin, 100, 112–13, 130, 134–5, 137
Snow, Samuel: arrival in Van Diemen's Land, 64; Brown's River, 150–1; *Buffalo*, 55–64; bushrangers, 182–9; convict rations, 98–100; Franklin, 81–2, 163; Green Ponds, 135–46; Hunters' Lodge, 44; ideology, 41–2; invasion at Windsor, 41–3; Lovely Banks, 119–25; Mona Vale, 167–8; mutiny, 60–2; opinion of George Arthur, 50; pardon, 46–7, 51, 195; petition, 125; Sandy Bay, 98–107; *Steiglitz*, 195–6; ticket-of-leave, 163; transportation to Van Diemen's Land, 52–4; treadmill, 114; trial, 44–5
Stanley, Lord (Secretary of State for the Colonies), 173, 175, 192, 195, 198–9, 202
Stevens, Elizur, 178
Stevenson, Andrew (US Ambassador to the Court of St James), 28–30
Stewart, Joseph, 114, 126–7, 129, 133, 135, 154–7, 194, 196, 201–3
Sutherland, James Cubbiston, 167
Swanberg, John G., 40, 112–13
Sydenham, Baron Charles Edward (Governor-General of Canada), 74, 159

Tabbart, Francis Gerard, 166, 170–1
Thomas, John, 149
Tyler, John (US President), 171–2
Tyrrell, John Burwell, 61–2, 130, 135, 172, 174, 205

United States: attitude to Patriots, 45, 171–2; Civil War, 206; dispute over northeastern